Food Science
a chemical approach

ɟ

Food Science
a chemical approach

Brian A Fox
Principal, Newport College of Further Education

Allan G Cameron
Formerly Head of Department of Applied Science
and Food Technology, Birmingham College
of Food and Domestic Arts

HODDER AND STOUGHTON
LONDON SYDNEY AUCKLAND TORONTO

British Library Cataloguing in Publication Data

Fox, Brian A.
　Food science: a chemical approach.—4th ed.
　1. Food—Composition
　I. Title　II. Cameron, Allan G.
　641.1　　　TX531

　ISBN 0 340 27863 3

First published as *A Chemical Approach to Food and Nutrition* 1961
Second edition 1970
Reprinted 1972, 1973, 1975 (with minor amendments), 1976
Third edition 1977
Reprinted 1978 (with additions), 1980, 1981
Fourth edition 1982

Typeset by Macmillan India Ltd., Bangalore.

Printed in Great Britain for
Hodder and Stoughton Educational,
a division of Hodder and Stoughton Ltd,
Mill Road, Dunton Green, Sevenoaks, Kent,
by Richard Clay (The Chaucer Press) Ltd
Bungay, Suffolk.

Preface to fourth edition

It hardly seems possible that twenty years have elapsed since two young men at the beginning of their teaching careers had the temerity to write a book on the then little known subject that we now call *Food Science*. At that time it was difficult even to find a suitable title for the book – as is shown by the rather clumsy title adopted – *A Chemical Approach to Food and Nutrition*. In the intervening twenty years *Food Science* has become respectable – its nature and usefulness have become fully appreciated and it is taught in many schools, colleges and universities.

The intention of this fourth edition, as of the first, is to provide an elementary but up-to-date account of Food Science. It combines a simple explanation of the chemical nature of food with a description of what happens to food when it is stored, processed, preserved, cooked, eaten and digested.

The first three short chapters, which are deliberately simple and descriptive, present a general account of the nature of food and enzymes, and what happens to food in the body. Chapter 4 gives a concise account of the basic chemistry needed to understand what follows. The main chemical themes of the book unfold in Chapters 5 to 11 which contain an account of the chemical nature of nutrients and of important related foods. Processes used in the manufacture and treatment of foods are discussed and changes which occur during cooking are described.

The last three chapters of the book deal with important practical applications of Food Science and for this new edition these chapters have been substantially expanded, up-dated and rewritten to take into account the many changes and advances of the last few years. A complete chapter is devoted to Cooking and Diet, both subjects of great practical importance. Indeed over recent years the whole subject of diet and its relation to health and disease have come into remarkable prominence, and this relationship is explored in some detail in this new edition.

The treatment of food preservation given in Chapter 13 is fairly extensive, for improving methods of preserving food have played a major part in the growth of supermarkets and the availability of good quality preserved foods all the year round. This chapter also includes a discussion of food spoilage and food poisoning. The recent rise in the number of food poisoning incidents in the UK serves to emphasize the importance of a proper understanding of food hygiene, and this aspect together with a discussion of the reasons for the increase in food poisoning are both discussed in this edition.

The last chapter deals with the important and controversial topic of food additives. A considerable amount of new material has been added to this chapter including reviews of the development of legislation to control the use of food additives, developments in the labelling of food and an appraisal of the balance of risk and benefit in using additives.

Although the format of the fourth edition is the same as that of the previous edition, revisions and up-dating have taken place throughout the text. In particular, units are now expressed in metric (SI) terms and values given for nutrient requirements reflect recent appraisals by the WHO and FAO and the revised sets of 'recommended daily amounts' of nutrients introduced into the UK by the DHSS (1979). Values of the nutrient content of foods are taken from the fourth edition (1978) of McCance and Widdowson's *The Composition of Foods* revised by Paul and Southgate to whom we acknowledge a considerable debt. Details of the changes made in this new edition can be better appreciated by reading *Perspectives in food science* which follows this preface.

Finally, it is hoped that this book will prove of interest and value to all who are concerned with elementary food science. In particular, it is intended for students of Food Science and Technology, Home Economics, Catering and Nutrition as well as for GCE 'A' level studies in schools and for TEC courses in Colleges of Further Education. Students of Medicine and Nursing should find it helpful as background reading.

Brian A Fox
Allan G Cameron

Perspectives in food science

The subject of Food Science and Nutrition is an engrossing one. This is partly because of the inherent interest of the subject for we are all concerned about the food that we eat and as Samuel Johnson (p. xii) phrased it 'I look upon it that he who does not mind his belly will hardly mind anything else'. Its interest lies also in the fact that our knowledge of the subject is growing, leading to an unfolding of new perspectives about what is significant, while new techniques are being developed leading to new methods of food processing and of analysing nutrients, additives and possible contaminants in food.

One new perspective that is certainly significant concerns the relation between food and disease. This has become a major preoccupation not only with scientists, nutritionists and doctors but also with the public and the popular press. For example, the evidence linking diet with coronary heart disease has led to a reappraisal of the place of fat (p. 115), fatty acids (p. 79), sugar (p. 128) and soft water (p. 229) in our diet. The lack of fibre in modern diets and its possible relation to a number of diseases (p. 172) is currently a matter of much debate and research, while the possible effects of an excessive salt intake (p. 288) are also a matter of concern.

The evidence linking particular foods or constituents of food with particular diseases is often circumstantial and great care is needed in assessing its significance. It is recognized that many diseases of our affluent society are multi-factorial in origin being related to our modern life-style of which diet is only one of a number of factors. At the present time it seems prudent to make certain changes to our diet in the interests of health but on the other hand it is unwise to seek to turn particular items of diet into the villains of the dietary scene by ascribing to them direct responsibility for particular diseases.

Over recent years the area of *Social* or *Community Nutrition* has become prominent. There is a growing understanding of the many social and other factors that affect out choice of food and our food habits (p. 255) and many attempts at defining goals for a healthy diet (p. 287) are

vii

being made. Trends in the British diet (p. 281) are now a matter of public interest, and especial attention has been paid to the diet of vulnerable groups of the community. The need for healthy diets for babies (p. 282), for elderly people (p. 284) and for the obese (p. 285) and the measures needed to achieve these are now appreciated.

The desire to achieve healthy diets for the community has led the WHO/FAO to reappraise nutritional requirements, and this has also been done by several individual countries including the UK where the DHSS have brought out a revised set of 'recommended daily amounts' of nutrients (p. 274). Studies of nutritional requirements have highlighted the importance of sunlight rather than diet as a source of vitamin D (p. 252), the need for adequate amounts of folic acid in the diet (p. 245) and a reduced need for food energy (and hence protein) (p. 273) among other things. The assessment of both protein quality and safe levels of protein intake (p. 203) have been much studied, and the high cost of animal protein has led to the development of novel protein foods (p. 204) of vegetable origin.

One other aspect of food and health deserves mention, namely, the rise in the number of food poisoning incidents (p. 326) in the UK. Such a rise emphasizes the need for an improved understanding of food hygiene (p. 325) among all who handle food. Recognition is being given to new sources of bacterial infection of food (p. 320), particularly to the organism *Bacillus cereus* (p. 324), and also to non-bacterial sources, particularly the danger associated with certain fungi that produce poisonous mycotoxins (p. 291).

The increasing importance of food processing and the production of convenience foods is accompanied by a growing dominance of super-markets in the High Street. No less than three-quarters of the food we eat has been processed in some way.

Among the different types of convenience food it is frozen foods (p. 304) that have advanced most rapidly though new techniques of heat sterilization (p. 309) show much promise for the future. The application of freezing to improved methods of catering, particularly in schools and hospitals, is gradually increasing in importance (p. 307) as is the use of cheap vegetable protein foods in convenience form (p. 204).

The development of new convenience foods has resulted in the use of an increasing amount and variety of additives and consequently much new legislation to control their use (Chapter 14). In addition Great Britain's membership of the EEC requires a long process of harmoniz-ation of our food laws with those of other member countries (p. 338). New classes of additive have been defined and their use controlled by law (p. 336). The problems of the possible toxicity of additives have continued to earn a high priority in research resulting, for example, in an evaluation of the balance between risk and benefit in using them (p. 352). The use of nitrites and nitrates (p. 297), colouring agents (p. 341), sweeteners (p. 346) and polyphosphates (p. 349) in food are but a few examples of the reappraisal of additives carried out in the UK by the FAAC (p. 337). New forms of retailing using prepacking and the pressure of consumer interests has led to much work being done on food labelling (p. 339).

Finally, recent years have seen a number of changes in the units in which food values and weights and measures are expressed. For example, the joule is finding increasing acceptance as a unit expressing the energy value of food (p. 7), while international units previously used to express vitamin content have been replaced by metric units (p. 232).

It seems that in the UK a dual system of weights and volumes, with both imperial and metric units remaining in use, will persist for the foreseeable future (p. 356), though almost all prepacked foods are now sold in metric packs. It seems that the time-honoured pint for both milk and beer will remain as reminders of the 'good old days'.

Contents

Some people have a foolish way of not minding, or of pretending not to mind, what they eat. For my part, I mind my belly very studiously and very carefully; for I look upon it that he who does not mind his belly will hardly mind anything else.

SAMUEL JOHNSON

Chapter One

Food and its functions

The basic function of food is to keep us alive and healthy, and in this book we shall consider how food does this, although we shall also need to think about many other related matters. Indeed we cannot answer such a fundamental 'How' question without first finding out the answer to some simpler 'What' questions, such as what is food, what happens to it when it is stored, processed, preserved, cooked, eaten and digested. The answers to such questions can only be found out by experiment, and many different sciences play a part in helping to provide the answers. In recent years the study of food has been accepted as a distinct discipline of its own and given the name *food science*.

It is a good deal easier to suggest the term food science than to define it and it is difficult to improve on the definition of J. R. Blanchfield that it is 'a coherent and systematic body of knowledge and understanding of the nature, composition and behaviour under various conditions, of food materials'. The basic sciences of mathematics, physics, chemistry and biology are all involved as are the newer sciences of biochemistry and microbiology. Yet food science is more than the sum of these separate disciplines, for it is a subject with its own outlook. It is, in a sense, a 'pure applied science' in that it exists not only to pursue academic knowledge, but also to promote the fulfilment of a basic human need—the need for a diet that will sustain life and health. Thus to be effective food science must be applied and this is the province of *food technology*.

The dividing line between the science and the technology of food is often blurred because the latter uses and exploits the knowledge of the former. The link between food science and food technology is well exemplified in considering how to solve what must be the foremost problem of our day; namely that of how to feed adequately the world's rapidly expanding population. The problems involved in determining what foods best meet the dietary needs of different countries, of what constitutes an adequate diet, of the nutritional merits of various new foods, of how to store and preserve food with minimum nutritional loss; these are the province of food science. But in order to use this information it must be applied—food must be grown, stored, processed, preserved and transported on a large scale, and this is the province of food technology.

Although food science embraces many sciences, a chemical approach to the subject is both a natural and an important one. In the first place, although food materials may be complex mixtures of substances, they are composed entirely of chemical compounds. Some people find it hard to accept that all food is chemical but notwithstanding this it is a scientific fact, and the foundation upon which this book is constructed. In the second place, nearly all manufactured foods include 'additives', and these substances, whether they are added to improve colour, flavour, texture or other qualities, are nothing but chemical compounds. Then again, the changes that occur in food when it is stored, processed, cooked, eaten and used by the body are chemical changes. Even the agents that bring about many of these changes both within and without the body, and which are discussed in the next chapter, are chemical substances.

Further insight into the nature and properties of food is gained by considering physical–chemical aspects. For example, many food systems are colloidal in nature and can best be considered as colloidal systems; emulsions and emulsification provide one important example. Physical conditions, such as temperature and pressure, often have pronounced effects upon food systems and the rate at which changes occur. Also changes that occur during food preparation—both on a small and large scale—are often primarily physical ones.

Having defined food science and put forward reasons for making a primarily chemical approach to the subject, we must now define what we mean by the term food. Only those substances which, when eaten and absorbed by the body, produce energy, promote the growth and repair of tissues or regulate these processes, are foods. The chemical components of food which perform these functions are called *nutrients* and it follows that no substance can be called a food unless it contains at least one nutrient. Some particularly valuable foods, such as milk, contain such a variety of nutrients that they can fulfil all the functions of food mentioned above, while others, such as glucose, are composed entirely of a single nutrient and have only a single function. The study of the various nutrients in relation to their effect upon the human body is called *nutrition*.

Types of Nutrient

Nutrients are of six types, all of which are present in the diet of healthy people. Lack of the necessary minimum amount of any nutrient leads to a state of *malnutrition*, while a general deficiency of all nutrients produces *under-nutrition* and, in extreme cases, starvation. The six types of nutrient are: *fats, carbohydrates, proteins, water, mineral elements* and *vitamins*. Apart from the nutrients already mentioned, the body also requires a continuous supply of oxygen. Oxygen is not normally regarded as a nutrient, however, because it is supplied from the air and passes into the body, not through the digestive system, but through the lungs.

Nutrients can be considered from two points of view—their functions in the body and their chemical composition. These two aspects are closely related, nutrient function being dependent upon composition, and in later chapters they will be considered in conjunction with each other, though the main emphasis will be on chemical composition.

The two basic functions of nutrients are to provide materials for growth and repair of tissues—that is to provide and maintain the basic structure of our bodies—and to supply the body with the energy required to perform external activities as well as carrying on its own internal activities. The fact that the body is able to sustain life is dependent upon its ability to maintain its own internal processes. This means that though we may eat all sorts of different foods and our bodies may engage in all sorts of external activities and even suffer injury or illness, yet the internal processes of the body absorb and neutralize the effects of these events and carry on with a constant rhythm. This is only possible because the components of our bodies are engaged in a ceaseless process of breakdown and renewal; a theme to which we shall return.

It is apparent that if the body's internal processes are to be maintained constant in spite of its ceaseless activity, and in the face of external pressures, some form of control must be exercised and, considering the complexity of the body's activities, it is evident that this control must be very precise. Thus nutrients have a third function, namely that of controlling body processes, a function which will be considered in the next chapter.

We have seen that food provides us with nutrients that perform three functions in our bodies. Though habits and patterns of eating may vary from person to person, and diets may be selected from hundreds of different foods, yet everyone needs the same six nutrients and needs them in roughly the same proportions. The relation between nutrients, their functions in the body and important foods that supply them is shown in Fig. 1.1.

Nutrients may also be considered according to their chemical composition. For example, though different oils and fats, such as olive oil and palm oil, do not have identical compositions, they are chemically

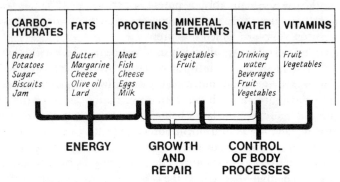

CARBO-HYDRATES	FATS	PROTEINS	MINERAL ELEMENTS	WATER	VITAMINS
Bread Potatoes Sugar Biscuits Jam	Butter Margarine Cheese Olive oil Lard	Meat Fish Cheese Eggs Milk	Vegetables Fruit	Drinking water Beverages Fruit Vegetables	Fruit Vegetables

ENERGY   GROWTH AND REPAIR   CONTROL OF BODY PROCESSES

FIG. 1.1. The nutrients—showing their functions and representative foods in which they are found

similar. In the same way different proteins (and carbohydrates) are constructed according to the same chemical pattern and are therefore conveniently grouped together. Vitamins are an exception to the method of classification according to chemical type; at the time of their discovery in food their chemical nature, which in most cases is complex, was unknown. They were grouped together because it was known that small quantities of them were essential to health. At first they were identified in terms of their effect on growth and health and distinguished by letters as vitamin A, B, C and so on; their chemical composition is now known, and it has become apparent that they are not chemically related to each other. Nevertheless it is still convenient to consider them together.

Classification of Substances as Foods

Some components of our diet, which might be assumed to be foods, prove on examination not to be whereas others, which might be thought to have no food value, contribute nutrients to our diet and are therefore properly classified as foods. The following examples illustrate this.

Salt and pepper, both of which form a part of the diet, are used as condiments, but this in itself does not qualify them to rank as foods. Salt is a food because, in addition to being a seasoning agent, it acts as a regulator of body functions, but pepper has no function except as a flavouring agent and is therefore not a food.

The mineral element iron is classified as a nutrient because it is necessary for the formation of *haemoglobin*, which is essential to life because it regulates the flow of oxygen round the body. Thus, any substance which supplies iron to the diet is a food. This leads to the curious conclusion that rusty pots should be considered as a food because they are, indubitably, a potent source of iron! It has been suggested that much of the high iron content of curry powder is derived from the iron vessels in which it is prepared.

Tea, coffee and cocoa are all widely used beverages which most people would classify as foods. The infusion obtained by adding boiling water to tea leaves has little more nutritional value, however, than the water itself. Tea and coffee are both esteemed on account of their flavour and mild stimulating action, the latter being due to the presence of *caffeine*. They are, in fact, drugs and not foods because they act through the nervous system and not the digestive system. The nutritional value of a cup of tea or coffee is almost entirely derived from the milk, sugar and water which it contains. Cocoa, on the other hand, contains the crushed cocoa bean and is, therefore, a true food because the nutrients of the bean are present in the beverage.

Alcoholic beverages contain *ethyl alcohol*. This substance is both a drug and a food because it affects the nervous system and is also broken down inside the body with the liberation of energy. Alcoholic beverages are therefore properly classed as foods.

All foods of vegetable origin contain the complex carbohydrate *cellulose*, yet even though this is a common component of diet and is a carbohydrate, it has no nutritive value because the body is unable to utilize it.

Food as a Source of Energy

Energy is required for sustaining all forms of life on the earth. The prime source of the earth's energy is the sun, without which there could be no life on this planet. The sun continually radiates energy, a fraction of which is intercepted by the earth and stored in various ways; plants and coal, for example, act as energy storehouses. Living plants convert the sun's energy into chemical energy and some plants of past ages have been converted, during many millions of years, into coal.

Plants, by the process of *photosynthesis*, convert carbon dioxide and water into carbohydrate. Photosynthesis, which is discussed at the beginning of Chapter 7, can only take place in daylight because solar energy is used in the process. A complex series of chemical changes occurs which can be represented by the following equation:

$$x CO_2 + y H_2O \xrightarrow{\text{daylight}} C_x(H_2O)_y + x O_2$$
$$\text{Carbohydrate}$$

The formation of carbohydrate is, therefore, the method used by plants to trap and store a part of the sun's energy. Sugar beet, which synthesizes carbohydrate in the form of the sugar *sucrose*, may be taken as an example:

$$12\,CO_2 + 11\,H_2O \xrightarrow{\text{daylight}} \underset{\text{Sucrose}}{C_{12}(H_2O)_{11}} + 12\,O_2$$

When sucrose is formed from carbon dioxide and water, energy is absorbed and stored within the sucrose molecule.

Animals, unlike plants, cannot store the sun's energy directly and so must gain it secondhand by using plants as food; carnivorous animals and man take this process a stage further and also use other animals as food. In this way chemical compounds which have been photosynthesized and stored in plants are eaten by man and animals and the stored energy made available. For example, the energy that is stored within the sucrose molecule when it is synthesized by sugar beet is liberated when sucrose reverts to carbon dioxide and water. This breakdown of sucrose into simpler units is brought about in the body by digestion and oxidation, but the overall reaction is simply the reverse of that represented above, namely:

$$\underset{\text{Sucrose}}{C_{12}(H_2O)_{11}} + 12\,O_2 \longrightarrow 12\,CO_2 + 11\,H_2O$$

When sucrose is converted into carbon dioxide and water in this way, the energy stored during synthesis is evolved and made available for use by the body.

Sucrose may also be converted into carbon dioxide and water by burning it in air. The chemical reaction is the same as that represented by the equation above, exactly the same quantity of heat being liberated as when the oxidation occurs in the body. The difference in the two reactions concerns the speed at which they occur, oxidation in the body taking place much more slowly than burning in air. It is for this reason that the body is sometimes referred to as a slow combustion stove and carbohydrate as a fuel. It is clear that oxidation in the body is a most important process for it enables the energy stored in carbohydrates (and fats and proteins) to be liberated and made available for use by the body.

THE ENERGY VALUE OF FOOD. In the past energy has been measured in heat units called *calories*. A calorie is the amount of heat required to raise the temperature of 1 g of water by 1° C. As this is rather a small unit, energy derived from food is usually measured in units which are one thousand times larger and known as *kilocalories*. A kilocalorie is the amount of heat required to raise the temperature of 1 kg of water by

1 ° C. Scientists normally express the energy values of food in kilocalories but unfortunately nutritionists have traditionally used the term calories (Cal) for the kilocalorie (kcal). In these circumstances we have thought it best to abide by tradition rather than logic and accordingly use the terms calorie (instead of kilocalorie) and Cal (instead of kcal).

Measurements are increasingly expressed in standard metric units known as SI (Système Internationale) units (see Table on p. 356 showing relation of non-metric to metric units). On the SI system the unit of energy is the *joule* (J) also expressed in terms of *megajoules* (MJ) and *kilojoules* (kJ):

$$1\,Cal = 4\cdot19 \times 10^3\,J = 4\cdot19\,kJ = 4\cdot19 \times 10^{-3}\,MJ$$

At present joules are replacing calories but in the remainder of this chapter (and in Table 12.8) both units are given so that students become familiar with them and their relation to each other. Elsewhere, however, joules are used. In general it is more helpful to use the term 'energy value' in place of the older 'calorie value' when referring to food and diets.

In order to compare the energy values of different foods it is simplest to determine the amount of energy produced, calculated as heat, when one gram of the substance is completely oxidized by igniting it in a small chamber filled with oxygen under pressure. The result obtained represents the heat of combustion of food which is usually expressed as Cal or kJ per gram. If the calorie value of sucrose is expressed in this way, it is found to be 3·95 Cal/g. This means that when 1 g sucrose is completely oxidized the heat produced is sufficient to raise the temperature of 1000 g of water by 3·95° C. The average values of the heats of combustion of the energy-providing nutrients are shown in Table 1.1.

Table 1.1. Average Energy Value of Nutrients (per gram)

Nutrient	Heat of combustion		Available energy value	
	Cal	kJ	Cal	kJ
Carbohydrate	4·1	17	4	17
Fat	9·4	39	9	37
Protein	5·7	24	4	17

In order to express the energy value of nutrients in terms of the energy actually made available to the body it is necessary to calculate the available energy values. Such values are always lower than heats of combustion because of losses within the body. A small loss is due to incomplete absorption; such loss is suffered by all three nutrients and, in the case of proteins, there is an additional loss because protein, unlike carbohydrate and fat, is incompletely oxidized in the body. The magnitude of this energy loss may be appreciated from Table 1.1. It should be mentioned that there is some uncertainty about the size of losses within the body, and different nutritionists use different figures; the ones quoted may be taken as being sufficiently reliable for most purposes.

It will be appreciated that the available energy values given in Table 1.1 are average values; also they are only approximate values rounded off to the nearest whole number. Nevertheless they can be used to calculate the energy value of any given diet. The available energy value of any food can be found using the average figures, provided that its chemical compositon in terms of carbohydrates, fats and proteins is known. The energy value of summer milk, for example, can be calculated from its analysis, as shown in Table 1.2.

Table 1.2. The Energy Value of Milk

Nutrient	Amount in 100 g milk	Cal/g	kJ/g	Energy/100 g milk	
				Cal	kJ
Carbohydrate	4·7 g	4	17	18·8	79·9
Fat	3·8 g	9	37	34·2	140·6
Protein	3·3 g	4	17	13·2	56·1
	Total energy provided by 100 g milk			66·2	276·6

By similar calculations the available energy value of other foods may be estimated; some average values are given in Table 1.3.

Table 1.3. The Energy Value of some Foods (per 100 g edible protein)

Food	kJ	Cal	Food	kJ	Cal
Lard, dripping	3674	894	Eggs	612	147
Butter	3012	732	Potatoes	324	76
Cheese (Cheddar)	1708	412	Haddock	321	76
Sugar	1680	394	Milk	274	65
Beef	940	226	Apples	197	46
Jam	1116	262	Tomatoes	52	12
Bread (white)	1068	251	Lettuce	36	8
Dates	1056	248	Cabbage	92	22

Table 1.3 shows that foods, such as butter and lard, which contain a high proportion of fat have the highest energy values. Carbohydrate foods, such as those containing a high proportion of sugar (jam and dates) or

starch (bread and potatoes), are less concentrated sources of energy. In spite of this, such foods supply a considerable proportion of the energy in an average British diet. Indeed cereal foods contribute no less than one-third of our total energy intake, which is a greater proportion than that supplied by any other class of foodstuff. In Eastern countries, starchy foods, often in the form of rice, supply an even greater proportion of the total energy content of the diet.

Some foods, such as cheese and eggs, contain significant amounts of both fat and protein. In such foods, fat is the main source of energy though protein, which is not primarily an energy provider, also contributes.

The Use of Energy by the Body

Earlier in this chapter the body was described as a slow combustion stove. From this it might be supposed that, after absorption by the body, all energy foods are oxidized directly and that all the energy liberated appears as heat. This is not true, however, for although much of the energy of food eventually appears as heat, the oxidation process is a carefully controlled one and takes place in a number of steps. Each step results in the release of a small amount of energy which is used in the promotion of bodily functions and may finally result in the appearance of heat. Without attempting at this stage any chemical explanation of the nature of the steps in the oxidation process, it is possible to gain a clear idea of how energy is used by the body.

The body requires energy to maintain its internal processes, and to enable it to perform external work. Even during sleep, when the body is apparently at rest, energy is needed to ensure that essential internal processes continue. For example, energy must be supplied to maintain the powerful pumping action of the heart, the continual expansion and contraction of the lungs and the temperature of the blood. It is needed to maintain the ceaseless chemical activity of the millions of body cells and the tone of muscles. Living muscle must constantly be ready to contract in response to stimuli transmitted to it by nerves. Such a degree of readiness can only be achieved if energy is continually supplied to keep the muscles in a state of tension. Muscle tension decreases during sleep but does not become zero, so that a certain amount of energy, which ultimately appears as heat, is necessary to maintain it. The total energy needed for these vital processes is called the energy of *basal metabolism*; its value is about 1600 Cal (6720 kJ) per day for an average man, though it varies according to age, sex and size.

Energy is also needed to enable the body to perform external work. Muscular activity requires a supply of energy additional to that needed to maintain muscle tone and other internal processes. The simplest physical act, such as standing up, involves the use of many muscles, and the greater the degree of physical activity in daily life the greater is the energy requirement of the muscles. It is useful, therefore, to relate the degree of muscular activity to the energy that must be supplied by the diet.

The problem of equating muscular activity with energy requirement is complicated by the fact that the body is unable to convert energy that is supplied by food completely into mechanical work. The efficiency of conversion by the body, considered as a machine, is of the order of 15–20 per cent. If the higher value is taken it means that 100 units of energy supplied by food enable the body to perform physical work, e.g. running, equivalent to twenty units. The other 80 units appear as heat and account for the fact that heat is lost from the body surface at an increased rate when physical work is done. If allowance is made for this wasted heat energy it is possible to draw up a list relating a particular form of activity with the total energy expended. This is done in Table 1.4. It will be understood that such figures are average values and can only be taken as a rough guide. Such figures enable the average energy requirements of diet to be worked out for people engaged in different types of activity. Such figures are very useful to the dietitian, for they enable him to plan a nutritionally adequate diet that will provide the required amount of energy.

Table 1.4. Types of Activity Related to Energy Expenditure

Type of activity	Example	Energy expenditure/hour	
		Cal	kJ
None	Sleeping	70	293
Sedentary	Office work	120	503
Light	House work	210	880
Medium	Cycling	360	1509
Heavy	Coal mining	480	2012

In the United Kingdom the figures used for energy requirement are those published by the Department of Health and Social Security, and reproduced in Table 12.8 on page 274. When using this table it needs to be understood that the average body weights of men and women have been taken as 65 kg and 55 kg respectively and energy expenditure has been worked out by dividing the day into three parts—in bed (8 hours), at work (8 hours) and leisure (8 hours). The recommended intake of energy given in Table 12.8 is the same as the calculated energy expenditure, no allowance being made for individual variation.

Table 12.8 refers to three occupational grades for men and two for women. Typical 'sedentary' workers include office and shop workers and most professions while 'moderately active' workers include those in light industry, postmen, bus conductors and most farm workers, and 'very active' workers include coal miners, steel workers and very active farm workers.

The recommended daily amounts of energy for babies and young children are not closely related to body weight and so ages are used instead; the weights referred to in Table 12.12 are average weights at these ages.

Chapter Two

Enzymes and life

The human body is composed of some hundred thousand million cells, each of which is complete in itself. These cells are grouped together in the body to form tissues with specialized functions. Thus some cells comprise connective tissue and bind together the various organs of the body, others are concerned with muscular and nervous tissue while others form the skeletal framework of bone that contributes strength and rigidity to the body.

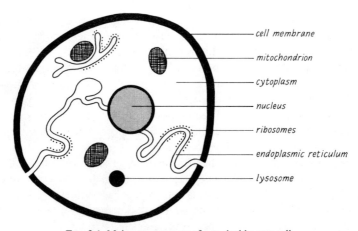

cell membrane

mitochondrion

cytoplasm

nucleus

ribosomes

endoplasmic reticulum

lysosome

FIG. 2.1. Major components of a typical human cell

An individual cell is so tiny that no ordinary microscope can reveal its internal structure. The advent of the electron microscope, however, makes it possible to investigate and reveal the cell's internal organization. The picture of the cell that emerges is one of very considerable complexity as can be appreciated from the much simplified diagrammatic representation of a typical human cell shown in Fig. 2.1. The largest component of a cell is its *nucleus*, and this is surrounded by a waterly fluid called *cytoplasm*. The cytoplasm contains a network of membrane-like material—the *endoplasmic reticulum*—which is studded with small dark bodies known as *ribosomes*. The cytoplasm also contains a number of bodies, among which are the egg-shaped *mitochondria* and the smaller *lysosomes*. We shall return to the function of these cell components at the end of the chapter.

The complex activities needed to sustain life in the human body take place within the body's cells, and we may liken the activity of a cell to that of a chemical factory in which a great variety of raw materials are processed and converted into finished products. In a single cell many different raw materials are required, though they are largely composed of only four elements: carbon, hydrogen, oxygen and nitrogen. The processing stage, which is concerned with the conversion of these simple raw materials into the very much more complex substances required to carry out the many functions of the cell, involves thousands of different reactions. Each of these reactions comprises many steps which must be carried out in a definite sequence with the result that the chemical operations of a cell are much more complicated, and need much greater integration, than those of a chemical factory.

In order to sustain life the cell's activities must be controlled and organized into a self-regulating and self-renewing pattern. But how can such control be achieved, and how is it that although almost all human cells are built according to the same basic pattern, yet they are able to perform a multitude of different functions? The answer to these questions is to be found in the existence of a group of crucially important substances called *enzymes*. Their importance can be gauged from the fact that without them there could be no life. Without them the chemical reactions of the cell would get completely out of control.

Enzymes control all the chemical changes, that is the *metabolism*, which occur in living cells. They regulate the building up or *anabolic* reactions that result in the formation of complex substances such as proteins from single building units. They also regulate the breaking-down or *catabolic* reactions that result in release of energy. The role of enzymes can perhaps be appreciated more fully, when it is realized that anabolic and catabolic processes involve very many steps, and that each step is controlled by its own enzyme. This control must be so carefully regulated that the life of the cell continues smoothly at all times, the whole metabolic process being kept carefully balanced.

The fact that different cells perform different functions is explained in terms of the enzymes that are present. Some thousand different enzymes have been recognized in the body, but in any one cell only a selection are present. Even so most cells contain about 200 different enzymes, each of which is responsible for controlling a particular step. The complement of enzymes present in a cell automatically selects and controls those reactions which are to proceed.

THE CHEMICAL NATURE OF ENZYMES. One of the earliest known sources of enzymes was yeast, which is the simplest possible type of living organism. In fact this is how the name enzyme arose, for it means literally 'in yeast'. The fermentation of grape juice by yeast and the leavening effect of yeast in making bread have been known for many centuries. However, it is now appreciated that enzymes are of much more general significance than was originally realized, and that the chemical processes occurring in all living organisms are dependent on enzymes, those of the human body no less than those of yeast.

In spite of the importance of enzymes, a long time elapsed between the discovery of the first known enzyme in yeast and the isolation of an enzyme in the pure state. For many years it was believed that they were living organisms. This idea was only shown to be false at the end of the last century when the German chemist Buchner extracted from yeast cells a cell-free liquid which had a similar enzyme activity to the original living cells. So, although enzymes are made by living cells, they themselves are not living.

The problem of extracting an enzyme in a pure state from a living source was not solved until 1926 when the American biochemist Sumner obtained the enzyme *urease* in pure crystalline form from the 'jack-bean' seed. Since that date some 150 enzymes have been obtained in a pure state, and on analysis each has proved to be a protein. As there is no evidence to the contrary, it has been assumed, as a general rule, that all enzymes are proteins.

The structure of proteins is considered in some detail in Chapter 9. Here it may be observed that in 1969 an exciting breakthrough occurred when an enzyme was synthesized for the first time. The enzyme made artificially, called *ribonuclease*, is the smallest enzyme known, but this success will stimulate research into the synthesis of larger enzymes which in turn will make it possible to discover much more about the mechanism of cell life. The properties of proteins—their ability to change their shape, their sensitivity to changes of conditions of temperature and acidity, their capacity to oppose changes of acidity that would upset the smooth working of the cell—make them peculiarly suited to control cell metabolism.

CLASSIFICATION OF ENZYMES. The substance upon which an enzyme acts is called the *substrate*, and enzymes are usually named after this substance. Thus the enzyme that acts on *urea* is called *urease* and that which acts on *maltose* is called *maltase*. It is a general rule that enzymes are named after the substrate upon which the enzyme acts and given the suffix *-ase*. In company with most general rules, however, there are notable exceptions, mainly those enzymes which were named before the rule gained general acceptance. Some of these, such as *pepsin* and *trypsin*, will be encountered in the next chapter.

Enzymes may be classified in a number of ways, but one of the most useful is to group them according to the type of reaction which they control. The five main groups of enzyme are shown in Table 2.1. Of these the first two are the most important in connection with what follows.

Hydrolases control the *hydrolysis* of the substrate, that is its reaction with water, and as we shall see in the next chapter, this type of enzyme is of paramount importance in digestion. *Oxidases* control the *oxidation* of the substrate, and this usually takes the form of removal of hydrogen as indicated in the equation shown in the table.

Table 2.1. Classification of Enzymes

Name	Reaction catalysed	General equation
Hydrolases	Hydrolysis	$AB + H_2O \longrightarrow AOH + BH$
Oxidases	Oxidation	$ABH_2 \longrightarrow AB + 2H$
Isomerases	Intramolecular rearrangement	$ABC \longrightarrow ACB$
Transferases	Transfer of a group	$AB + C \longrightarrow A + BC$
Synthetases	Addition of one molecule to another	$A + B \longrightarrow AB$

CATALYTIC ACTION OF ENZYMES. Enzymes are organic catalysts; they operate by speeding up a chemical process while appearing unchanged at the end of the reaction. In many respects their action is similar to that of the more familiar inorganic catalysts such as are often used in industry to accelerate chemical manufacturing processes. In the manufacture of margarine, vegetable oils are converted into solid fats by chemical reaction with hydrogen. In the absence of a catalyst the conversion of the oils into fats is very slow indeed but the addition of small quantities of finely divided nickel produces a remarkable increase in the rate of the reaction; moreover, the nickel catalyst may be used time after time, for it is not used up in the process.

It is remarkable that only one part of nickel is needed to catalyse the conversion of several thousand parts of oil into fat, but this achievement appears quite insignificant when compared with the startling catalytic power of enzymes. One of the enzymes concerned with the breakdown of starch during digestion is amylase produced by the pancreas. Only one part of amylase is needed to effect the conversion of four million parts of starch into the sugar maltose. Where the efficiency of man-made catalysts is measured in thousands, that of nature's catalysts is measured in millions.

It should be noted that although enzymes speed up reactions, they cannot turn impossible reactions into possible ones. Neither can they affect the equilibrium position of a reversible reaction; this means that the *amount* of product in a reaction is the same whether an enzyme is involved or not. The presence of the enzyme merely reduces the time taken to reach the equilibrium position. In a cell thousands of different reactions are possible but the function of the enzymes present is to speed up particular ones, so that some reactions proceed rapidly while others proceed at a relatively insignificant rate. In this way cell metabolism is controlled and directed so that different cells are enabled to fulfil different functions.

We must now consider how an enzyme speeds up a reaction, though we can best approach this by considering first how an ordinary non-catalytic reaction proceeds. Suppose a reaction involves the conversion of reacting substances represented by A into products represented by B. The reaction will not start until A has received a 'push' in the form of energy, often supplied in the form of heat. The reason for this can be appreciated from Fig. 2.2.

Before A can react to form B it must surmount the energy hump shown by moving along path (i), and this requires an amount of energy E_1. When A has absorbed energy E_1, known as the *activation energy*, it is in an activated state and can decompose to form B.

This process can be likened to that of transferring a ball from one side of a hill to the other. If Fig. 2.2 represents a hill, the problem is that of transferring a ball from X to Y. If the only path lies over the summit of the hill, then it is necessary to push the ball up the hill—that is to work on it by supplying energy—until it reaches the top. Once there, it will run down the other side to Y of its own accord. The ball may now be at a lower level than it was at its starting point, as is the case in Fig. 2.2. This means that an amount of energy E_3 has been released though this could not have been achieved without first pushing the ball to the top of the hill, which involved supplying it with energy E_1.

In the cells of the human body, activation energy cannot be supplied in normal ways, such as heat, because this would damage the cells. The function of enzymes is to enable the reaction to proceed at a much lower activation energy than would otherwise be possible. In terms of Fig. 2.2 we must replace the reaction path (i) over the summit of the hill by one at a lower level such as (ii) involving a lower activation energy E_2. For

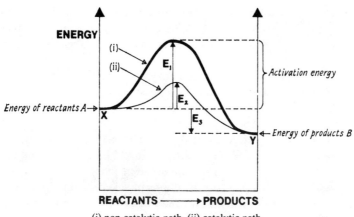

(i) non-catalytic path, (ii) catalytic path.

FIG. 2.2. Reaction paths

example, the activation energy required for the decomposition of hydrogen peroxide to hydrogen and oxygen in the absence of a catalyst is 50 kJ/mole, but in the presence of the enzyzme *catalase* this is reduced to 8 kJ/mole.

Enzymes catalyse reactions by replacing a single-step high-energy mechanism with a two- or multi-stage process, each step of which involves a low activation energy. If the enzyme catalyst is represented as C and the substrate as A we have:

$$A + C \longrightarrow AC$$
$$AC \longrightarrow B + C$$

Overall reaction: $A \longrightarrow B$

If both stages require little energy the reaction path is as represented by (ii) and the reaction will be a rapid and near spontaneous one with the catalyst C being regenerated. Thus we have a simple picture of how enzymes act as catalysts.

SELECTIVITY OF ENZYMES. Enzymes are highly selective in choosing which reaction to catalyse. It is this characteristic which enables them to preserve order in living cells, for frequently one enzyme will catalyse only one cell reaction. Thus, although many other reactions may occur in a cell, the rate at which they proceed is insignificant compared with that of the catalysed reaction.

The selective power of enzymes is sometimes compared with the action of a key in a lock: the enzyme is the lock and only certain molecules can act as the key which exactly fits it. If reaction between two

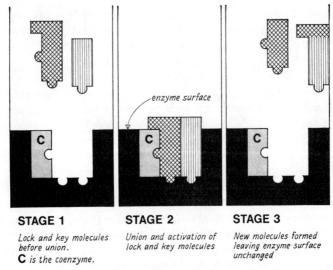

STAGE 1   **STAGE 2**   **STAGE 3**

Lock and key molecules   *Union and activation of*   *New molecules formed*
before union.   *lock and key molecules*   *leaving enzyme surface*
C *is the coenzyme.*   *unchanged*

FIG. 2.3. The lock and key theory of enzyme reaction

molecules is catalysed by an enzyme the lock can be imagined as having grooves into which the two molecules fit side by side; this leads to a brief union between the enzyme and the two molecules which are acting as keys, as is shown in stage 2 of Fig. 2.3. The key molecules are thus brought together and converted into an active state which enables them to react with each other. After reaction new molecules are formed, but as shown in stage 3 of the diagram the enzyme remains unchanged and can catalyse further reaction.

In order to achieve a good fit between lock and key molecules, an enzyme frequently needs the help of another substance called a *coenzyme*, the action of which is indicated in Fig. 2.3. Coenzymes are smaller than enzyme molecules and are not proteins. They are normally united with the enzyme, the combination being called a *conjugated protein* (see classification of proteins on p. 189), although the coenzyme may be detached from the enzyme by hydrolysis. Where the structure of coenzymes has been ascertained it has been found that they are either closely related to vitamins or are the vitamins themselves. One of the functions of the B group of vitamins seems to be to provide the body with suitable starting materials from which to make the coenzymes that it needs. The exact function of coenzymes is still only partly understood, but they certainly play an active and vital part in many reactions involving oxidizing enzymes. This is shown by the fact that if a coenzyme needed by an enzyme is absent, the enzyme can exert no catalytic effect.

In some cases it is found that metallic ions, such as magnesium, or non-metallic ions, such as chloride, are required to increase the activity of enzymes. Such substances are known as *activators*, and an example of their action will be encountered in the next chapter.

Sometimes several molecules, which are similar to each other, can approximately fit the grooves of the same lock. In such cases the enzyme does not distinguish between them and acts as a catalyst to them all. In most cases, however, enzymes show great powers of discrimination as the following examples show.

Urease is an example of an enzyme which has a completely specific catalytic action. It catalyses the hydrolysis of urea to ammonia, but it will not catalyse any other reaction. In this instance urease can be compared with a lock which has grooves that only the urea key will fit.

The three enzymes, *maltase, lactase* and *sucrase*, are present in the small intestine, and during digestion these enzymes catalyse the hydrolysis of the sugars *maltose, lactose* and *sucrose* respectively. These three enzymes have considerable specificity and in the case of lactase complete specificity, for it will catalyse the hydrolysis of lactose and of no other substance, not even a similar sugar. Maltase and sucrase, however, catalyse the hydrolysis not only of maltose and sucrose but also that of certain other similar sugars.

A further example of enzymes which show a remarkable selectivity are those which catalyse the hydrolysis of proteins. The three enzymes, *pepsin, trypsin* and *chymotrypsin*, each select certain links of protein molecules and catalyse hydrolysis only at these links. This is illustrated and discussed further on page 198.

SENSITIVITY OF ENZYMES. Enzymes are very sensitive to effects of temperature and environment. All enzyme activity is destroyed on boiling but even much lower temperatures may inactivate them. In general, plant enzymes work best at about 25° C and those in warm-blooded animals at about 37° C. An increase in temperature usually increases the rate of a chemical reaction, but in the case of an enzyme reaction it may also lead to inactivation of the enzyme. Fig. 2.4 shows the effect of temperature on the rate of catalysis. At 37° C the initial rate of reaction is rapid, but after a time the reaction rate slows down and stops, no further product being formed. This may be due to one of several causes. For instance the reaction may be complete, all the substrate having reacted, or it may be that the products of reaction have made the environment unfavourable for enzyme activity and the enzyme has been deactivated. If the temperature is raised to 70° C, the initial rate of reaction is increased. This is because the greater energy input

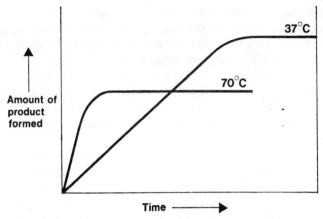

FIG. 2.4. The effect of temperature on the rate of catalysis by an enzyme

increases the energy of substrate and enzyme molecules, and these molecules more rapidly gain the activation energy needed for reaction to take place. Although the initial rate of formation of products is rapid, it soon stops because the enzyme is rapidly inactivated at the higher temperature. The net result is that less product is formed at the higher temperature than at the lower. Enzymes catalyse reaction efficiently in man, the temperature being high enough to give rapid formation of products but low enough to avoid inactivation of the enzyme.

Enzyme activity is also dependent upon the acidity or alkalinity of the medium in which the enzyme acts. Most enzymes operate most efficiently in an environment which is nearly neutral, and if the medium becomes strongly acid or alkaline the enzyme becomes completely inactivated. Some enzymes, however, can only operate in an acid or alkaline solution. For example, the enzyme pepsin is present in gastric juice and during digestion it catalyses the initial hydrolysis of proteins. It can only act in strongly acid conditions such as are produced by the hydrochloric acid in the stomach; on the other hand, the enzyme trypsin which is present in pancreatic juice requires a slightly alkaline medium before it can catalyse protein hydrolysis. When food passes from the stomach into the small intestine the hydrochloric acid is completely neutralized and the medium becomes alkaline. Under these conditions pepsin becomes inactivated and trypsin carries on the digestion of proteins.

Cell Metabolism

At the beginning of this chapter we noted that each cell in the body is a complicated structure and that its activities can be likened to those of a complex chemical factory. We have also seen that these activities are related to the enzymes contained within the cell; indeed the cell's metabolism is entirely controlled by its complement of enzymes. It has been found that the enzymes which control cell metabolism are not evenly distributed throughout the cell, but that they are dispersed among the different cell constituents in such a way that each has a clearly defined role to play in the life of the cell.

The nucleus of a cell—see Fig. 2.1—contains genes and a small number of enzymes that together control cell growth and division while the surrounding cytoplasm contains water-soluble enzymes that control a variety of anabolic and catabolic processes. The mitochondria are important because they are the power houses of the cell and contain a number of oxidases responsible for the manufacture of high energy materials used for energy production. The important job of protein synthesis in the cell is controlled by enzymes found in the endoplasmic reticulum. Finally, one of the most interesting bodies in the cell is the lysosome, also sometimes called the 'suicide bag'. Lysosomes contain a sufficient variety of hydrolases to destroy nearly all the components of the cell. Normally these 'suicide' enzymes are safely contained within the impermeable membrane that encloses the lysosome, but if the cell becomes injured or dies, the enzymes are released and the cell destroys itself.

Each cell, and each component of a cell, is surrounded by a membrane. The membrane allows only those raw materials needed by the cell to pass through it, all other substances being prevented from entering. This selection mechanism ensures that only those substances required for a particular job are available, and it also ensures that only those enzymes required to control this function are allowed through the membrane.

In later chapters we shall develop the theme of what happens to nutrients in metabolism in rather more detail, but enough has been said in this introductory survey to show that all the activities and functions of the body which constitute life are entirely dependent upon enzymes.

SUGGESTIONS FOR FURTHER READING

BARKER, G. R. *Understanding the Chemistry of the Cell*. Edward Arnold, 1968. A short clearly-written book on this complex subject.

CHEDD, G. *What is life?* BBC Publications, 1967. Contains an interesting account of enzymes, proteins and ATP.

MALCOLM, A. D. B. *Enzymes; an introduction to biological catalysis.* Methuen Educational, 1971.

MOSS, D. W. *Enzymes.* Oliver and Boyd, 1968.
A short, simple and clear introduction to the subject.

PALMER, T. *Understanding Enzymes.* Ellis Horwood, 1981.

WISEMAN, A. and GOULD, B. J. *Enzymes, their Nature and Role.* Hutchinson, 1971.

WYNN, C. H. *The Structure and Functions of Enzymes*, 2nd edition. Edward Arnold, 1979.

Chapter Three

Digestion and absorption

Its a very odd thing—
As odd as can be—
That whatever Miss T eats
Turns into Miss T.

De la Mare

It is indeed a very odd thing—an extraordinary and remarkable thing—
that no matter what we eat, the structure of the body, both flesh and
blood, changes very little. There is no obvious similarity between the
nature of the food we eat and the nature of our bodies. Yet within a few
hours of being eaten, food is transformed into flesh and blood. This
transformation is so complete that it cannot be accomplished before
food has undergone a drastic breaking-down process known as
digestion.

Digestion is both physical and chemical; the physical process involves
the breakdown of large food particles into smaller ones while the
chemical process involves the breakdown of larger molecules into
smaller ones. Foodstuffs are mainly complicated insoluble substances
that must be converted into simpler, soluble, more active ones before
they can be used by the body. Not all nutrients need digesting, however,
for there are some such as water and simple sugars (e.g. glucose) and
many vitamins and mineral salts which do not need to be broken down.
Whether or not nutrients need to be broken down by digestion they
cannot be utilized by the body until they have passed into the
bloodstream, a process which is known as *absorption*. Once in the
bloodstream nutrients are distributed to all the cells of the body where
they sustain the complex processes of metabolism.

The Role of Enzymes in Digestion

The chemical processes involved in digestion are brought about by
enzymes. The chemical breakdown of food molecules, which in the
absence of enzymes would be very slow indeed, is thereby speeded up so

that digestion is completed in a matter of hours. Thus in the space of some three or four hours a remarkable change in the nature of the food has occurred. Substances such as starch, which may contain as many as 150 000 atoms in a single molecule, have been converted into molecules containing only twenty-four atoms (simple sugars such as glucose). The breakdown of protein molecules is almost equally spectacular, for an average protein molecule is split up into about five hundred amino acid molecules during digestion. These two examples perhaps make clearer the magnitude of the chemical task performed by the enzymes of the digestive system.

Each stage of digestion involves hydrolysis and is catalysed by a hydrolysing enzyme or hydrolase (see p. 15). The hydrolysis can be represented: $AB + H_2O \longrightarrow AOH + BH$. The equation shows how water is involved in splitting up a molecule AB into two smaller molecules AOH and BH. In some instances, e.g. sucrose, a single step involving the breakdown of a molecule into two parts is sufficient to produce a small soluble molecule that can be absorbed. In other instances, e.g. proteins, a very large number of hydrolytic steps is required before breakdown is complete.

The digestive process involves a fairly small number of different enzymes which catalyse the chemical breakdown of proteins, carbohydrates and fats. The names of the hydrolases that catalyse the hydrolysis of these different nutrients are shown in Table 3.1. Unfortunately there is no general agreement about these names and different authors use different names according to fancy and fashion. The names given, however, are descriptive of the main changes brought about by hydrolases in digestion. *Peptidases* can conveniently be subdivided into *exopeptidases*, which split off amino acids from the end of protein molecules, and *endopeptidases*, which attack and split the inside of protein molecules.

Table 3.1. Hydrolases involved in Digestion

Name	Substrate	Product
Amylases	Starch	Maltose
Maltases	Maltose	Glucose
Lipases	Fats	Fatty acids and glycerol
Peptidases	Proteins	Amino acids

The selectivity or specificity of enzymes was discussed in the last chapter. It was pointed out that peptidases show considerable selectivity and only catalyse hydrolysis at certain points of a protein molecule.

Amylases, and enzymes which break down sugars, show a similar high degree of selectivity. It is therefore evident that a whole series of such enzymes is required to achieve the stepwise breakdown of proteins and carbohydrates. Lipases, on the other hand, are relatively unselective, so that only a few lipases are required to break down fats.

Stages of Digestion

The digestive system is separate from the body system proper and can be regarded very simply as a series of tube-like organs which pass through the body from the mouth at one end to the anus at the other. Food enters the system at the mouth, passes down the oesophagus into the stomach and then through the small intestine and large intestine, being gradually digested and absorbed in the process. Any that remains leaves the body at the other end of the system. In what follows the stages of digestion are described in a very simple way, to give an overall picture of the process. The chemical details will be filled in later after a discussion of the chemical nature of the nutrients concerned. The main parts of the digestive system are illustrated in Fig. 3.1 and the digestive process is summarized in Fig. 3.2.

DIGESTION IN THE MOUTH. When food is eaten, the size of the individual pieces is reduced and saliva is secreted by the salivary glands. The secretion of saliva takes place in response to various sorts of stimuli; the sight of a well-cooked meal, an appetizing smell or even the thought of a good meal may cause the salivary glands to pour forth saliva. This fluid becomes well mixed with food during mastication, lubricating it and so making it easier to swallow. Saliva is a dilute aqueous solution having a solid content of only about 1 per cent. Its main constituent is a slimy substance called *mucin* which assists lubrication. It also contains the enzyme *salivary amylase*, and various inorganic salts, the most abundant being sodium chloride which furnishes chloride ions that activate the enzyme. The initial hydrolysis of cooked starchy food is catalysed by salivary amylase in the mouth, and this catalytic action is continued as the food moves down the oesophagus and into the stomach. The enzyme soon becomes inactivated in the stomach, however, because it cannot tolerate a strongly acid environment.

Food is carried down the oesophagus by gentle muscular action called *peristalsis*. The muscles contract, producing a peristaltic wave and this moves down the oesophagus, carrying the food with it.

DIGESTION IN THE STOMACH. The stomach may be regarded as a reservoir in which food is prepared for the main stage of digestion in the

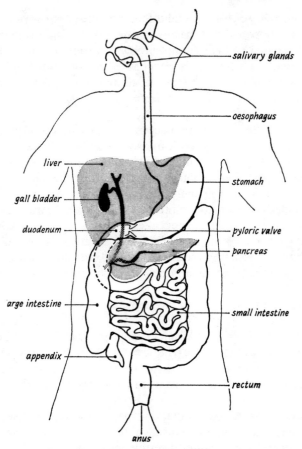

salivary glands

oesophagus

liver

stomach

gall bladder

duodenum

pyloric valve

pancreas

arge intestine

small intestine

appendix

rectum

anus

FIG. 3.1. The Digestive System

small intestine. This does not mean that no digestion takes place there, however, for cells in the lining of the stomach produce a fluid called *gastric juice*. The two essential constituents of this dilute aqueous solution are its enzymes and its acid content. The main enzyme is pepsin which is secreted as the inactive pepsinogen and which, as indicated in Chapter 2, becomes activated when it comes into contact with the hydrochloric acid which forms the acid constituent of the gastric juice.

Some twenty minutes after starting to eat a meal, vigorous muscular movements begin in the lower region of the stomach. Muscular contraction produces an inward pressure and this moves down the stomach wall as a peristaltic wave, so moving food through the stomach and causing it to become intimately mixed with the gastric juice. In this way the acidity of the semi-fluid food mixture called *chyme* increases, until the endopeptidase pepsin is able to catalyse the conversion of part of the protein into slightly simpler molecules called *peptones*. The other enzyme in the gastric juice is *rennin*, which also acts in an acid medium and brings about the coagulation or clotting of milk. The acidity of the gastric juice also causes some bacteria, which enter with the food, to be killed.

A copious flow of gastric juice is necessary during a meal and its production is stimulated both by psychological and chemical means. The former is the more important and is governed by involuntary nervous action which may be brought about by the appearance, smell and taste of food. The mere thought of food may be sufficient to stimulate gastric secretion; on the other hand, the flow of gastric juice may be inhibited by such factors as excitement, depression, anxiety and fear. Certain foodstuffs act as chemical stimulants to secretion. *Meat extractives*, for instance, which are dissolved out of meat when it is put in boiling water, are particularly potent in this respect. Soups and meat dishes in which the extractives have been preserved are therefore valuable aids to digestion in the stomach.

Peristaltic action moves the chyme into the lower region of the stomach which is separated from the upper region of the small intestine, called the duodenum, by the pyloric valve. The valve opens at intervals, so allowing small portions of chyme to leave the stomach. This process continues until no chyme remains in the stomach.

DIGESTION IN THE SMALL INTESTINE. The main stage of digestion occurs during the passage of chyme through the long, small intestine. As soon as food enters the duodenum, digestive juices pour forth. There are three sources: the liver secretes *bile* which is then stored by the gall bladder, and the pancreas secretes *pancreatic juice*—these two secretions enter the small intestine through a single duct situated a short way down the duodenum; the third secretion is produced in the lining of the small intestine and is called the *intestinal juice*. They are all produced at the same time and as they are alkaline they neutralize the acidity of the chyme. Under these conditions the enzymes of the three secretions are able to exert their catalytic influence.

The pancreatic juice contains enzymes which enable it to help in the digestion of the three main types of nutrient. The endopeptidases trypsin and chymotrypsin among others, carry on the degradation of proteins begun by pepsin in the stomach; they complete the breakdown of proteins into peptones. *Pancreatic amylase* is another enzyme present in the pancreatic juice; its capacity for catalysing the hydrolysis of large

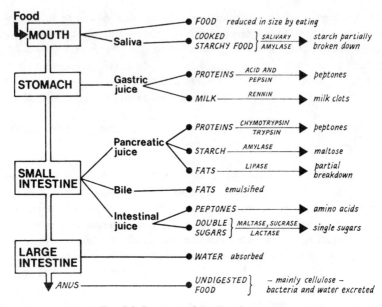

FIG. 3.2. Summary of the digestive process

amounts of starch and converting it into maltose was mentioned on page 15. Finally, *pancreatic lipase* brings about the partial hydrolysis of some fat molecules converting them into simpler substances which can be absorbed.

The bile has no enzyme action, but contains bile salts which convert fats (which are liquefied by the warmth of the stomach) into a fine emulsion of tiny oil droplets which may then be acted upon by the lipase of the pancreatic juice.

The intestinal juice contains a number of enzymes, three of which have already been mentioned, namely maltase, lactase and sucrase, which break down the double sugars maltose, lactose and sucrose respectively into simple sugars that can be absorbed. In addition to these, a group of exopeptidases, called *erepsin*, continue the breakdown of proteins begun by the endopeptidases pepsin, trypsin and chymotrypsin. The exopeptidases attack the ends of the chain-like peptone molecules until they are broken down into small units called dipeptides containing only two amino acids. Finally another group of enzymes called *dipeptidases* break down the dipeptides into free amino acids which can be absorbed.

Apart from these chemical changes, muscular activity continues, so causing the various substances to move slowly down the small intestine.

ABSORPTION IN THE SMALL INTESTINE. The digestive process is almost complete after the food material has been in the small intestine for some time. The most complicated of all nutrients, the proteins, have been converted by stages into amino acids; all carbohydrates, except cellulose, have been broken down into simple soluble sugars, while fats have been emulsified and partly split into simpler substances called *fatty acids* and *glycerol*. However, as will have been realized, the digestive system is distinct from the rest of the body, being separated from it by the walls of the digestive tube. Before nutrients can be utilized by the body they must pass through these walls and into the bloodstream, by the process of absorption.

The walls of the long small intestine are formed into folds and ridges and thus have an enormous surface area. The digested food is present in the small intestine for about three or four hours, and as it is well mixed by the peristaltic movements of the walls it comes into intimate contact with the absorbing walls of the intestine. The absorptive process is not a simple one, however, and involves both *diffusion* and *active transport*.

Diffusion takes place through the water-filled pores of the lining of the small intestine. This lining is relatively impermeable, and large molecules are unable to pass through; even small soluble molecules diffuse through only slowly. The mechanism of diffusion is explained in terms of *osmotic forces*, which depend for their existence upon a concentration gradient across the membrane. Diffusion of dissolved substances takes place so as to reduce the concentration gradient, that is from the more concentrated to the less concentrated solution, provided that the membrane is permeable to the dissolved materials. Diffusion of soluble nutrients from the small intestine to the bloodstream depends therefore on the concentration gradient and the permeability of the membrane.

Although diffusion undoubtedly plays a part in absorption it cannot be the sole mechanism involved, for the rate of absorption is greater than could be accounted for by diffusion alone. Moreover, as absorption proceeds, the concentration of nutrients in the blood increases and may eventually exceed that in the small intestine. In these circumstances, in which the direction of the concentration gradient is reversed, diffusion opposes the absorptive process. That absorption still takes place under these conditions is shown by the fact that absorption of most nutrients continues until almost none remain in the small intestine.

The mechanism whereby nutrients are absorbed *against* the concentration gradient is known as active transport. The way in which this happens is complex and a number of different mechanisms is probably involved. It is clear that active transport involves doing work against osmotic forces, and this is only possible because the energy output from body cells is available for this purpose.

The products of protein and carbohydrate digestion, namely amino acids and simple sugars, are certainly absorbed by both diffusion and active transport, but the mechanism of fat absorption is a subject of some controversy. It seems safe to say that some fat is absorbed undigested in an emulsified form and that the minute fat droplets pass directly through pores in the intestinal wall; also that some fat is absorbed in a partially hydrolysed state and some is absorbed as fatty acids and glycerol.

THE LARGE INTESTINE. About four hours after a meal has been eaten any food that has not been digested and absorbed in the small intestine passes through the ileocaecal valve into a wider and shorter tube called the large intestine. No new enzymes are produced by the body during this stage but the large intestine is a rich source of bacteria. These may attack undigested substances such as cellulose with their own enzymes and partially break them down. In addition, vitamin K and certain vitamins of the B group are synthesized, i.e. built up by the bacteria. Such bacterial action is not on a large scale but the small molecules so formed, if able to be absorbed, pass through the walls of the large intestine into the blood.

The main function of the large intestine is to remove water from the fluid mass; this process continues as the fluid passes along, so that by the time it reaches the end of the tube it is in a semi-solid form known as faeces. In a day, between 100 and 200 grams of moist faeces may be produced containing undigested food material, residues from digestive juices, large numbers of both living and dead bacteria, and water. After having been in the large intestine for about twenty hours these materials are passed out of the body.

TRANSPORT IN THE BODY. Food, after digestion and absorption, provides nutrients that are the raw materials of body metabolism. But this process is not complete without an efficient transport system capable of carrying nutrients to the cells that require them. We have already seen that nutrients, during absorption, pass into the blood and it is the constant circulation of blood through the body system that enables these nutrients to be transported to where they are needed. Blood, which is four-fifths water, contains many substances, such as nutrients and hormones, in solution. Other substances, such as the red blood corpuscles which transport oxygen are present as cells in the blood and are carried round with it in suspension. The heart pumps blood through the arteries and into successively smaller tubes, the smallest of which are capillaries. In the capillaries, nutrients and oxygen from the blood diffuse into the surrounding cells, while waste products from the cells diffuse into the blood. Blood carrying the waste material passes into a network of veins, carbon dioxide being removed by the lungs, while soluble substances are removed by the kidneys. There is also free diffusion of water between the blood and tissue fluid, which enables the fluid bathing the cells to be continually renewed.

Chapter Four

Basic chemistry

THE NATURE OF ATOMS

The atoms of an element are so small that they cannot be weighed directly. It is possible, however, to calculate the weight of a single atom; a hydrogen atom, for example, weighs 0·0000000000000000000017 g. It is very difficult to appreciate just how small this is; 0·001 g of hydrogen would be sufficient to provide every person on the earth with about two million million hydrogen atoms. It is more convenient to express atomic weights as relative weights than to use the extremely small absolute weights. Originally, the weight of a hydrogen atom was taken as the standard of comparison because hydrogen is the lightest element. On this basis the atomic weight of an element is the weight of one atom of it, compared with the weight of one atom of hydrogen.

In more recent times the carbon isotope (see page 35) of mass 12 has been selected as the standard for comparative purposes. Atomic weights calculated using C^{12} as a basis for comparison differ slightly from those calculated by comparison with hydrogen. The atomic weight of hydrogen, for example, is no longer 1·000 but 1·008. The exact atomic weight is not important for the purposes of this book, and the values given in Table 4.2 will be sufficiently accurate.

If the elements are arranged in order of increasing atomic weight then the number of an element in this series is called its atomic number. The lightest element, hydrogen, has an atomic number of 1, the lightest but one, helium, an atomic number of 2 and so on. Over one hundred elements are now known; those with an atomic number greater than ninety-two are artificial man-made elements. Few of the heavier elements are of importance in a study of food chemistry.

Atoms vary in size according to their atomic weight but their diameters are of the order of 10^{-8} cm (i.e. one hundred millionth of a centimetre). This figure is so small that it is almost impossible to get any idea of the size of an atom from it. One atom for every person in Great Britain would, if placed side by side, form a line only about 5 mm long.

Atoms are composed of smaller particles, the more important of which are listed in Table 4.1.

Table 4.1. Atomic Particles

Name	Mass	Electrical charge
Proton	1	Positive
Neutron	1	None
Electron	1/1840	Negative

The electron and proton carry equal but opposite charges; in every atom there are equal number of them, so the atom as a whole is uncharged. The mass of these particles is expressed as a number in the same way as the atomic weight of an element. Protons and neutrons, are equal in mass and are about as heavy as a hydrogen atom and 1840 times as heavy as an electron.

The protons and neutrons occur together in the centre of an atom; this centre is known as the nucleus. It has been found that the number of protons in the nucleus of an atom is the same as the atomic number of the element concerned. The electrons are distributed in space about the nucleus and are never stationary. The space they occupy is very large indeed compared to the size of the nucleus, the diameter of an atom being some ten thousand times that of its nucleus. If we imagine the nucleus as being the size of a pea the atom containing it would be a sphere about 60 metres in diameter. The electrons, of course, are even smaller than the nucleus and the surprising conclusion is that all material things, including our own bodies, are well over 99·9 per cent empty space.

The electrons in an atom occupy a series of energy shells, or concentric zones around the nucleus, all the electrons in a given shell having similar energies. The shells are designated K, L, M, N and so on, starting from the nucleus and working outwards. Electrons occupying shells nearest to the nucleus have less energy than those further away. Each shell can accommodate only a certain maximum number of electrons; the K shell can take up to 2, the L shell up to 8, the M shell up to 18 and so on.

The arrangement of electrons in shells in a hydrogen atom and a carbon atom is shown in Figure 4.1. The hydrogen atom, which is the simplest possible atom, consists of one proton in the nucleus and one electron in the K shell. Carbon, the atomic number of which is six, is only slightly more complicated. The nucleus consists of six protons and six neutrons (to make up the atomic weight of 12) and there are six extra-nuclear electrons. Two electrons occupy the K shell and the remaining four the L shell.

It must be emphasized that Fig. 4.1 is merely a simple pictorial method of showing the distribution of the electrons in an atom. The electrons do not circulate about the nucleus on fixed paths in the way that planets move in fixed orbits about the sun. At one time this was thought to be so but it is now realized that it is not possible to specify the exact paths that electrons follow in their journeys about the nucleus.

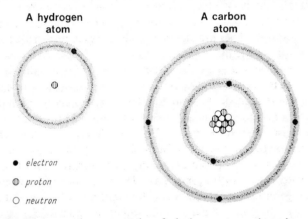

A hydrogen atom   A carbon atom

● electron

◍ proton

○ neutron

FIG. 4.1. Diagrammatic representation of a hydrogen atom and a carbon atom

It is very much an over-simplification to regard an electron as a small particle circulating on a fixed path or orbit about the nucleus. As well as its particle-like properties an electron has wave-like characteristics and this is true also of other atomic particles. We need not be unduly concerned about this here but it should be borne in mind that all pictorial representations of atoms and molecules are, to some extent, misleading because they represent protons, neutrons and electrons as *particles* and appear to show electrons patrolling about the nucleus on fixed paths. It is more accurate, but still only a mental approximation, to regard the electrons in their energy shells as occupying zones of space about the nucleus known as *orbitals*. An orbital may be said to represent a zone in which an electron is likely to be found; they are not all spherical in shape even though those shown in Fig. 4.1 are so represented.

All electrons are considered to spin and the electrons in a given energy shell occupy orbitals each of which contains either one or two electrons. Every orbital in a shell must contain one electron before any one of them can accept a second, and when this happens the two electrons occupying the same orbital have opposed spins and are said to be paired. In the case of carbon, for example, the two electrons in the K shell both occupy the same orbital, which is spherical, and have opposed spins. The L shell contains four electrons and of these two are paired in a spherical orbital and the other two occupy separate dumb-bell-shaped orbitals.

The identity of an element is determined by the number of protons in the nucleus and hence by the number of electrons in the extra-nuclear structure. Two atoms of the same element may have different numbers of neutrons in their nuclei and they are called *isotopes*. A chlorine atom, for example, can have either eighteen or twenty neutrons in its nucleus; both isotopes have seventeen protons in the nucleus and seventeen extra-nuclear electrons. They are identical in all chemical properties but differ in mass; the atomic mass of the isotope with eighteen neutrons in the nucleus is 35 and that of the other isotope 37. Naturally occurring chlorine is a mixture of the two isotopes and this is why its atomic weight is not a whole number. It approximates more closely to 35 than to 37 because ^{35}Cl is more abundant than ^{37}Cl. Isotopic forms of most other elements also exist; for example ^{18}O and ^{15}N are present in naturally occurring oxygen and nitrogen but only in very small amounts.

Isotopes can be prepared artificially by bombardment of naturally occurring isotopes with atomic particles. Some isotopes are unstable and change into more stable forms by emitting radiation and atomic particles, i.e. they are radioactive. The radiation and particles emitted by these *radioisotopes*, as they are called, are extremely harmful to living cells.

Radioisotopes are not normal constituents of foods but, since 1945, small amounts of these insidious poisons have been finding their way into the diet. This is because radioisotopes of several kinds are produced during nuclear bomb explosions; they are distributed by atomospheric air currents and find their way into the diet, and ultimately into the human body in diverse ways.

The chemical properties of isotopes of the same element are identical because they depend on the number of extra-nuclear electrons and not on the number of neutrons in the nucleus. In consequence, isotopes cannot be distinguished by chemical means; they can, however, be distinguished and their concentration measured by physical instrumental methods. Both stable isotopes and radioisotopes have been extensively used as *tracers* in biochemical studies. For example by feeding isotopically labelled nutrients to animals it is possible to determine exactly what happens to them by examining an animal's organs, tissues and excretion products instrumentally. Examples of this procedure will be found in Chapters 6 and 9 in connection with the metabolism of fats and proteins respectively.

Some data for the elements of most importance in food chemistry are given in Table 4.2. Except in the case of chlorine, only one isotope has been shown for each element, because the other isotopes occur in relatively small amounts.

Table 4.2. Data for Elements of Importance in Food Science

Name of element	Symbol	Atomic Number	Atomic Weight	Nucleus		Electrons					
				Protons	Neutrons	Total Number	Arrangement in shells				
							K	L	M	N	O
Hydrogen	H	1	1.0	1	0	1	1				
Carbon	C	6	12·0	6	6	6	2	4			
Nitrogen	N	7	14·0	7	7	7	2	5			
Oxygen	O	8	16·0	8	8	8	2	6			
Fluorine	F	9	19·0	9	10	9	2	7			
Sodium	Na	11	23·0	11	12	11	2	8	1		
Phosphorus	P	15	30·0	15	15	15	2	8	5		
Sulphur	S	16	32.0	16	16	16	2	8	6		
Chlorine	Cl	17	35·5	17	18 or 20	17	2	8	7		
Potassium	K	19	39·0	19	20	19	2	8	8	1	
Calcium	Ca	20	40·0	20	20	20	2	8	8	2	
Iron	Fe	26	56·0	26	30	26	2	8	14	2	
Iodine	I	53	127·0	53	74	53	2	8	18	18	7

THE NATURE OF MOLECULES

A molecule contains two or more atoms which are chemically combined. Several types of union are possible but all of them involve either sharing of electrons between the atoms or complete transfer of one or more electrons from one atom to another. The electrons involved are those in the outermost shell, which are referred to as valence electrons. It is known that an atom is in a particularly stable condition when its outermost shell contains eight electrons, or in the case of hydrogen, two electrons, called an octet and duplet respectively. The electron sharing or transfer, which occurs during a chemical reaction, takes place in such a way that a stable octet of electrons (or duplet in the case of hydrogen) is obtained.

Electrovalence

One method by which atoms can complete their octets or duplets during chemical combination is by electron transfer. This is called electrovalence. In sodium chloride, for example, the valence electron of the sodium atom is transferred to the chlorine atom. An electron is negatively charged, so in the process the chlorine atom acquires a negative charge and the sodium atom a positive charge. The charged

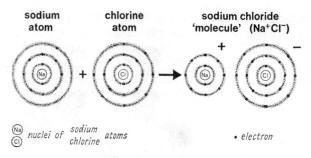

FIG. 4.2. Formation of sodium chloride

particles are called *ions*, and compounds containing them *ionic compounds*. The electron transferred from sodium to chlorine enters an energy shell previously occupied by seven electrons and completes the octet of the outermost shell of the chloride ion. Similarly the outermost shell of the sodium ion contains eight electrons. The electron transferred from the sodium atom enters an orbital in the M shell previously occupied by only one electron and the spins of the two electrons are paired.

The formation of a sodium chloride 'molecule' is illustrated diagrammatically in Fig. 4.2, but for the reasons already given it would be wrong to regard this as more than a convenient mental picture of what actually occurs.

It is interesting to note that there is no actual bond between the two ions; they are held together by electrostatic attraction. A crystal of sodium chloride contains many millions of sodium ions and an equal number of chloride ions. The ions are arranged in a three-dimensional geometrical pattern known as a space lattice as shown in Fig. 4.3a. This represents about one five million million millionth part of a 1 mm cube of sodium chloride. It shows clearly the geometry of the space lattice but suffers from the defect that the sodium and chloride ions appear to be widely separated whereas in fact they are closely packed. In Fig. 4.3b a portion of the lattice has been enlarged and is shown in a more realistic way. In the interior of a sodium chloride crystal each sodium ion is surrounded by six equidistant chloride ions and, similarly, each chloride ion is surrounded by six equidistant sodium ions.

A sodium ion is not associated with a particular chloride ion and in this sense it is wrong to think of a sodium chloride molecule. However, it is convenient and customary to speak of the sodium chloride molecule, and its formula is written $NaCl$ and not Na^+Cl^-. The lines in the diagram do not, of course, represent bonds between the ions but merely

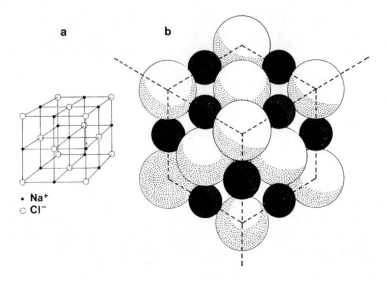

FIG. 4.3. A sodium chloride lattice

indicate the geometrical properties of the space lattice. Further, the ions appear to be widely separated whereas in fact they are quite closely packed. When sodium chloride dissolves in water this orderly space lattice breaks down and the ions become free to move; this process is described more fully in Chapter 10.

Covalence

This is the second main method by which an atom may acquire an octet (or duplet in the case of hydrogen) of electrons in its outermost shell. Covalence involves the sharing of a pair of electrons between two atoms. Usually each atom contributes one electron to the shared pair, which is known as a covalence or covalent bond. For example, in a hydrogen molecule each electron contributes one electron to the covalent bond and the molecule may be represented very roughly as shown in Fig. 4.4a. The two electrons are not stationary between the nuclei, however, as one might imagine from Fig. 4.4a but occupy a new orbital, called a *molecular orbital*, which surrounds both nuclei as shown in Fig. 4.4b.

A covalent bond may be represented by a pair of dots, crosses or circles to indicate the bond electrons. A hydrogen molecule, for example, may be represented **H:H**.

The element carbon, which is of particular importance in connection with foods, has four valence electrons and is almost invariably tetrava-

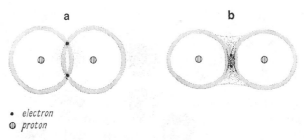

a   b

• *electron*
① *proton*

FIG. 4.4. A hydrogen molecule

lent because it requires four more electrons, from other atoms, to complete its octet. In the compound methane, for example, the molecule of which contains one carbon atom and four hydrogen atoms, the carbon and hydrogen atoms are connected by covalent bonds as shown.

H
·x
H ˣ C ˣ H
x·
H

A methane
molecule

Only the four valence electrons of the carbon atom are shown and they are represented by crosses to distinguish them from the valence electrons of the hydrogen atoms which are shown as dots.

The electrons are represented by different symbols to show their origin, but they are, of course, identical and those in the covalent bond belong to both carbon and hydrogen. As a result of this process of electron sharing, the carbon atom has eight electrons in its valence shell and the hydrogen atoms two each.

Nitrogen has five electrons in its valence shell. It needs three more to complete its octet and consequently can form three covalent bonds. Ammonia is a compound of this type.

H
x·
H ˣ N ˣ
·x   ˣ
H

An ammonia
molecule

Two of the valence electrons of the nitrogen atom are not involved in bond formation and are referred to as a *lone pair*.

The nitrogen atom in ammonia can use its lone pair to form a special type of covalence with a suitable atom or group. For instance, ammonia will combine with acids to give ammonium salts; when this happens the ammonia molecule uses its lone pair to form a bond with a hydrogen ion.

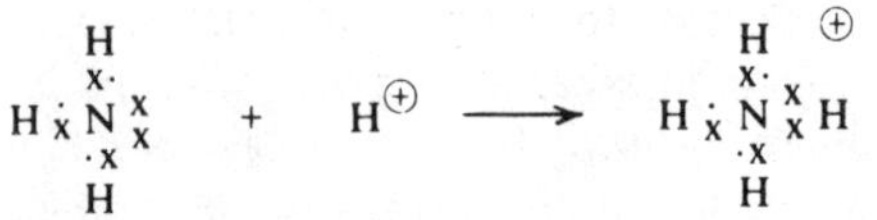

$$
\begin{array}{ccc}
\overset{\textstyle H}{\underset{\textstyle H}{\overset{\text{x·}}{H \overset{x}{\underset{\cdot x}{N}} {}^{x}_{x}}}} & + & H^{\oplus}
\end{array}
\longrightarrow
\begin{array}{c}
\overset{\textstyle H}{} \;{}^{\oplus} \\
H \overset{\text{x·}}{\underset{\cdot x}{N}} {}^{x}_{x} H \\
H
\end{array}
$$

An ammonium ion, $NH_4^{\oplus}$

Such a bond, in which both shared electrons have been provided by one of the combined atoms is called a co-ordinate bond or a co-ordinate covalence. The ammonium ion has a positive charge because it is formed by combination of a neutral molecule and a positively charged ion. The nitrogen atom still has a complete octet in its outermost shell and the hydrogen atom which originally had no electrons now shares two with the nitrogen atom and so has a stable duplet. In the ammonium ion the co-ordinate bond differs in its method of formation from the other three covalent bonds but, once formed, is identical with them.

Ammonium ions cannot exist on their own; as with all other positive ions they must be associated with an equal number of negative ions. In ammonium chloride, for example, there is a negatively charged chloride ion for every ammonium ion. The nitrogen atom in ammonium chloride is displaying a valency of five—four covalent bonds and one electrovalence.

The methods used above to represent the structure of hydrogen, methane, ammonia and the ammonium ion are rather cumbersome. With large molecules, or atoms of high atomic number, the method is most inconvenient. Because of this, when it is necessary to show the structure of a molecule it is usual to represent the shared electron pair of covalent bonds by dashes as shown below.

H–H

Hydrogen, H_2

$$H{-}\overset{\textstyle H}{\underset{\textstyle H}{C}}{-}H$$

Methane, CH_4

$$\overset{\textstyle H}{\underset{\textstyle H}{N{<}}}$$

Ammonia, NH_3

$$\left[H{-}\overset{\textstyle H}{\underset{\textstyle H}{N}}{-}H \right]^{\oplus} Cl^{\ominus}$$

Ammonium chloride, NH_4Cl

The number of valence electrons largely determines the valency of an element and also whether it forms electrovalent or covalent bonds. Sodium, for example, has only one valence electron; it cannot acquire an outer shell of eight electrons by the formation of covalent bonds because it has only one electron to share. By losing its single valence electron, in the formation of an electrovalent bond, however, the sodium atom acquires a stable octet. This is why sodium has a valency of one and forms electrovalent compounds.

A chlorine atom, on the other hand, has seven electrons in its valence shell. It needs one more electron to complete its octet. It can get this by accepting one electron from another atom and becoming an ion as in sodium chloride. Alternatively, it can form a covalent bond by sharing a pair of electrons with another atom. In methyl chloride, CH_3Cl, for example, the chlorine and carbon atoms are connected by a covalent bond.

Hydrogen Bonding

Hydrogen is univalent, as explained above, but in certain circumstances it appears to display a valency of two. In the bifluoride ion, $HF_2^{\ominus}$, for example, which occurs in potassium bifluoride, KHF_2, two fluorine atoms are linked together by a hydrogen atom. The linking of two atoms in this way by a hydrogen atom is known as *hydrogen bonding*. Only highly electronegative atoms can be so linked and in practice hydrogen bonding occurs to any extent only with the three most electronegative elements fluorine, oxygen and nitrogen. If we represent two electronegative atoms by X and Y a hydrogen bond may be represented $X-H\text{---}Y$ or $X\text{---}H-Y$ or, since the bond really extends over the three-atom system, by $X\text{---}H\text{---}Y$.

A hydrogen bond is not a true chemical bond but only a weak cohesive force arising from electrostatic attraction. Hydrogen bonds are only about one-tenth as strong as normal covalent bonds and they are easily broken. Even a slight increase in the temperature of a substance, which increases the energy of molecular vibrations and collisions, can lead to the breakdown of hydrogen bonds. Electrostatic attraction can only occur between polar molecules, that is molecules in which there are permanent fractional positive and negative charges present as a result of electron displacements. As we have seen, there are positive charges in the nuclei of all atoms, and electrons themselves, of course, are negatively charged. In a neutral molecule the number of such positive and negative charges is identical, but their electrical 'centres of gravity' do not always coincide and there may be a concentration of negative charge at one point in a molecule and positive charge at another. Such a molecule is said to be polar and may be regarded as a minute magnet. In a molecule X–Y, for example, if Y is more electronegative than X the bonding pair of electrons will not be equally shared between X and Y, but Y will have a larger share and as a result a dipole $\overset{\delta\,|\,\delta-}{X-Y}$ will exist. The nucleus of X is still adequately shielded by a screen of electrons, however, even though there has been a drift of electrons from X to Y. In a molecule of H–Y, on the other hand, formation of a dipole $\overset{\delta+\,\delta-}{H-Y}$ leaves the hydrogen nucleus (a proton) relatively exposed and unshielded and hence it is attractive to an atom of Y in another H–Y molecule or, for that matter, to any other electronegative atom able to come near enough for electrostatic attraction to occur. In this way molecules may be linked together or 'associated' and this is one of the main consequences of hydrogen bonding. Water molecules, for example, are associated into clusters by hydrogen bonds as shown below:

$$\overset{\delta+\quad\delta-}{\text{H—O}} \qquad\qquad \text{H—O}\text{---}\text{H—O} \qquad\qquad \text{H—O}\text{---}\text{H—O}\text{---}\text{H—O}$$

$$\underset{\text{A water molecule}}{\overset{|}{\text{H}}\ \delta+} \qquad\qquad \underset{\qquad\qquad\text{Two and three molecule clusters}}{\overset{|}{\text{H}}\qquad\overset{|}{\text{H}} \qquad\qquad \overset{|}{\text{H}}\qquad\overset{|}{\text{H}}\qquad\overset{|}{\text{H}}}$$

The effect of such association is to increase the apparent molecular weight and this causes an elevation in the boiling point—a phenomenon which is discussed in more detail in Chapter 10. In the absence of hydrogen bonding the boiling point of water would be about $-80°$ so it is fortunate for us that it occurs. Hydrogen bonding is by no means rare and in fact it occurs quite commonly in compounds containing O–H or N–H bonds. The molecular shape must be such, however, that the atoms concerned can approach each other quite closely or hydrogen bonding will not occur. In some cases the shape of a molecule may be influenced by the formation of hydrogen bonds. Glucose, for example, contains five O–H groups and in the solid state the molecule arranges itself in such a manner that the maximum number of hydrogen bonds is formed between adjacent molecules. Extensive hydrogen bonding also occurs in solid sucrose (cane sugar; see page 124) and this is one reason why impressive crystals are so easily formed from its solutions.

As well as acting between adjacent molecules, when they are said to be *intermolecular*, hydrogen bonds can also be formed between two parts of the same molecule and in such cases they are said to be *intramolecular*. Intramolecular hydrogen bonds may assist in holding a molecule in a particular shape. We shall see that hydrogen bonds play a part in holding the large molecules of proteins in a special shape. There may be several hundred hydrogen bonds in one large molecule and although individually they are much weaker than covalent bonds they can collectively exert a powerful influence on the properties of a compound. Hydrogen bonding is also involved in the formation of enzyme-substrate complexes. The specificity of many enzymically controlled reactions may be attributed not only to the closely related shapes of the enzyme and its substrate but also to the occurrence of hydrogen bonding between them.

Molecular Weight and Size

The weight of a molecule depends upon the number and type of atoms it contains. It can easily be calculated if the formula of the substance is known by adding together the weights of all the constituent atoms. Water, for example, has a molecular weight of 18 because its molecule contains two hydrogen atoms each weighing one unit and one oxygen atom weighing 16 units. The units of molecular weight are, of course, the same as those of atomic weight, and molecular weight may be defined as the weight of a molecule compared with the weight of one atom of hydrogen.

Molecules vary in weight from the very small, such as hydrogen with a molecular weight of two, to the relatively large. Food contains molecules of diverse size from water, with a molecular weight of 18, through the simple sugars and fats with molecular weights of a few hundred, polysaccharides with molecular weights of thousands, to giant protein molecules which have molecular weights of several millions.

Molecules, like the atoms of which they are composed, are extremely minute. Even the largest protein molecules, which contain several hundred thousand atoms are exceedingly small by normal standards. One gram of such a protein contains several thousand million times more molecules than there are people on the earth.

Differences between Inorganic and Organic Compounds

It is convenient to study the chemistry of carbon compounds separately from the chemistry of compounds of the other elements. Carbon compounds are known collectively as *organic* compounds, and those of other elements as *inorganic* compounds.

In general, inorganic compounds are electrovalent, that is they exist as ions, whereas in organic compounds the covalent bond is of major importance. Exceptions to these general rules are numerous, and many inorganic compounds containing no electrovalencies, and organic compounds containing electrovalencies, are known.

Ionic compounds usually have high melting points compared with those which are purely covalent. In a liquid there is a greater degree of relative motion between the molecules or ions than in a solid. A solid melts on heating because the increase in temperature causes a corresponding increase in molecular or ionic motion. The ions in an ionic substance are so tightly bound that such an increase in more difficult to achieve than in a covalent substance where there are no comparably strong forces acting between molecules. The lack of volatility of ionic compounds compared with covalent compounds can be explained in the same way. When a covalent liquid boils, some of the molecules escape from the liquid into the vapour phase above it; with an ionic compound there are no molecules to escape and the attraction between the ions is sufficiently strong to prevent their escape into the vapour phase, except at very high temperatures when they may enter the vapour phase as ion-pairs. This explains why, in general, organic compounds have low melting and boiling points, and inorganic compounds high melting and boiling points. Very large organic molecules, however, such as are commonly found in foods, usually have high melting and boiling points or may not melt and boil at all because their size renders them comparatively immobile.

The presence or absence of ions also determines, to a large extent, the chemical properties of a compound. The chlorine atom in methyl chloride, for example, behaves quite differently from the chloride ion in sodium chloride. In methyl chloride the chlorine atom is tightly held as part of a molecule and is not free to take part in reactions on its own account as the chloride ions in ionic compounds are. For instance, sodium chloride and similar inorganic chlorides, where the chlorine is present as an ion, react instantly with silver nitrate solution to give a precipitate of silver chloride. Compounds in which a chlorine atom is held by a covalent bond do not give such a precipitate because the chlorine is not free to react with the silver nitrate.

All the nutrients are organic in nature, with the exception of water and the mineral elements, and before the chemistry of the common foodstuffs can be profitably discussed it is necessary to have an understanding of the more important features of organic chemistry. Certain common carbon compounds are studied in inorganic chemistry; these include carbon monoxide, carbon dioxide, carbon disulphide, cyanides, carbonates and bicarbonates. All the remaining carbon compounds are studied in organic chemistry. In addition to carbon, organic compounds always contain hydrogen and frequently oxygen. Nitrogen, sulphur, phosphorus and the halogens are also found in some organic compounds. Almost any of the remaining elements may also occur but those mentioned are by far the most important.

At one time the only organic compounds known had been obtained from plants and animals, and it was thought that organic compounds were associated with some 'vital force' and would never be produced artificially by man. In 1828 the German chemist Wöhler prepared the organic compound urea, $CO(NH_2)_2$, from inorganic starting materials and hence destroyed the vital force theory. Many thousands of organic compounds have now been prepared by chemists and it is possible to start with the element carbon and build up, or synthesize as it is called, most organic compounds by a series of reactions. Except for the simplest compounds, however, this process involves many separate steps and is exceedingly tedious. In practice, when it is necessary to synthesize an organic compound, another organic compound, which is readily available, is used as a starting material.

Many of the components of foodstuffs are so complex that they have not been synthesized, but some fats, sugars and vitamins have been prepared synthetically. Except in the case of the vitamins the syntheses are of purely scientific interest and fats and sugars are not synthesized for use as foods. Some of the vitamins, however, are synthesized in large quantities and used for the enrichment of flour, margarine and other foods.

Newcomers to the study of chemistry often wonder why carbon should be sufficiently important to merit a branch of chemistry to itself while the remaining elements are treated together in inorganic chemistry. One reason has already been mentioned, namely that organic compounds occupy a special place as products of living cells. Another is that there are very many more compounds of carbon known than of all the other elements put together. Although comparatively few elements are found in the majority of organic molecules the number of atoms in a molecule is usually higher than in inorganic chemistry. Simple organic molecules are certainly known but others may contain thousands of atoms; in such large molecules there are almost endless possibilities for different arrangements of the component atoms, even though they are of only a few different kinds. For example, hundreds of compounds containing only carbon and hydrogen are known and an unlimited number can theoretically exist. A further reason for the multiplicity of organic compounds, of which more will be said later, is the fact that in organic chemistry a single molecular formula may represent many different compounds.

HYDROCARBONS

Compounds containing only hydrogen and carbon are known as hydrocarbons. They are not nutrients and do not occur in food. However, a knowledge of the chemistry of the hydrocarbons is essential if the chemistry of the nutrients, which are more complex, is to be appreciated.

Alkanes

The simplest hydrocarbons are called *alkanes* or *paraffins*. Many of these are known, from the gas methane which contains one carbon atom, to compounds with sixty or so carbon atoms in the molecule. The formulae and names of the simpler alkanes are given below:

CH_4	Methane	C_5H_{12}	Pentane
C_2H_6	Ethane	C_6H_{14}	Hexane
C_3H_8	Propane	C_7H_{16}	Heptane
C_4H_{10}	Butane		

The group or family of hydrocarbons is known as a *homologous series*. The molecular formula of each member differs from that of its neighbours by CH_2 and they may all be represented by the general formula C_nH_{2n+2}. Such series are common in organic chemistry. The members of a homologous series are known as *homologues* and they all have similar chemical properties. Once it is known to which series a compound belongs it is possible to predict its chemical properties fairly accurately; conversely, if the chemical properties of an organic compound are known it is possible to say to which series it belongs. A method suitable for preparing one member of a series may often be used, with appropriate starting materials, for preparing any other member of the same homologous series. Such methods are called general methods of preparation.

The physical properties of the members of a homologous series vary gradually and more or less uniformly from one member to the next. In the alkane series, for example, the members of low molecular weight, up to pentane, are gases; those of higher molecular weight from pentane to $C_{17}H_{36}$ are liquids, the boiling points of which increase as the molecular weight increases. Above $C_{17}H_{36}$ the alkanes are solids and the melting point increases as the molecular weight increases.

The alkanes are purely covalent compounds and methane, ethane and propane may be written as shown below. Each line represents a covalent bond as explained on page 38. These so-called *graphic formulae* are obviously cumbersome and it is more convenient to write CH_3CH_3 for ethane and $CH_3CH_2CH_3$ for propane.

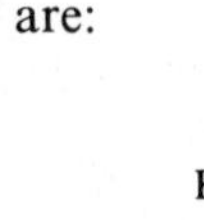

$$
\begin{array}{ccc}
\begin{array}{c}
H \\
| \\
H{-}C{-}H \\
| \\
H \\
\text{Methane}
\end{array}
&
\begin{array}{c}
H \quad H \\
| \quad\, | \\
H{-}C{-}C{-}H \\
| \quad\, | \\
H \quad H \\
\text{Ethane}
\end{array}
&
\begin{array}{c}
H \quad H \quad H \\
| \quad\, | \quad\, | \\
H{-}C{-}C{-}C{-}H \\
| \quad\, | \quad\, | \\
H \quad H \quad H \\
\text{Propane}
\end{array}
\end{array}
$$

Two quite distinct hydrocarbons have the molecular formula C_4H_{10}. They are:

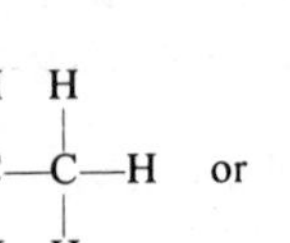

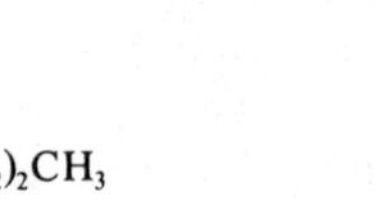

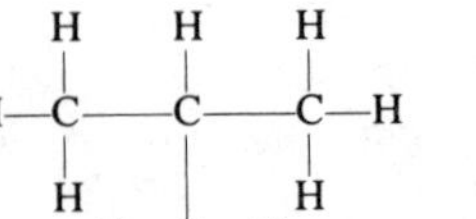

$$
\begin{array}{c}
H \quad H \quad H \quad H \\
| \quad\, | \quad\, | \quad\, | \\
H{-}C{-}C{-}C{-}C{-}H \\
| \quad\, | \quad\, | \quad\, | \\
H \quad H \quad H \quad H
\end{array}
\quad \text{or} \quad CH_3(CH_2)_2CH_3
$$

n-Butane

$$
\begin{array}{c}
H \quad\quad H \quad\quad H \\
| \quad\quad\; | \quad\quad\; | \\
H{-}C{-}\!\!-\!\!-C{-}\!\!-\!\!-C{-}H \\
| \quad\quad\; | \quad\quad\; | \\
H \quad\quad\; | \quad\quad\; H \\
\quad\quad H{-}C{-}H \\
\quad\quad\quad\; | \\
\quad\quad\quad\; H
\end{array}
\quad \text{or} \quad (CH_3)_2CHCH_3
$$

Isobutane

When two different compounds have the same molecular formula they are called *isomers*, and the phenomenon is known as *isomerism*. There are many types of isomerism; the example above is conveniently named *chain isomerism* because the two compounds have a different arrangement of the carbon chain. The prefix *normal* (often abbreviated to n) indicates that the carbon chain is unbranched, whereas the prefix *iso* indicates that the grouping $(CH_3)_2C-$ occurs in the molecule.

There are three isomeric pentanes each with the formula C_5H_{12}.

or $CH_3(CH_2)_3CH_3$

n-Pentane

or $(CH_3)_2CHCH_2CH_3$

Isopentane

or $(CH_3)_4C$

Neopentane

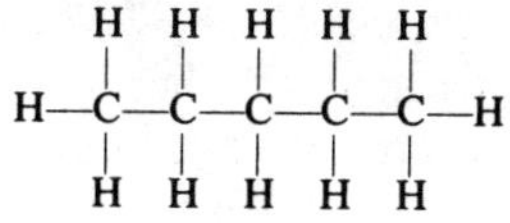

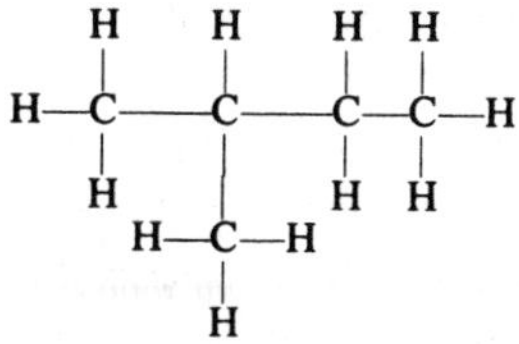

As the number of carbon atoms increases, the number of isomers with different structures becomes very large. There are eighteen possible isomers of this sort with molecular formula C_8H_{18} and 366 319 with the formula $C_{20}H_{42}$.

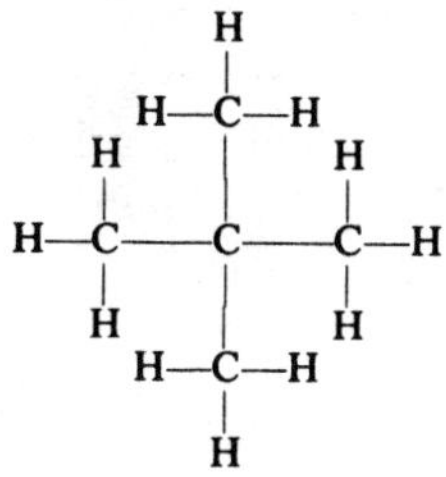

Petroleum oil, which is pumped from the ground in many parts of the world, consists essentially of alkanes. They burn in oxygen or air, like most organic compounds, with the evolution of a great deal of heat. With an unlimited supply of air all the carbon in the compound is converted to carbon dioxide and all the hydrogen to water. Ethane, for example, reacts as follows:

$$2C_2H_6 + 7O_2 \longrightarrow 4CO_2 + 6H_2O$$

One or more of the hydrogen atoms in the molecule of an alkane can be replaced by other atoms or groups. For example, methane can react with chlorine to give *methyl chloride*, CH_3Cl.

$$CH_4 + Cl_2 \longrightarrow CH_3Cl + HCl$$

In a similar manner ethane gives *ethyl chloride*, C_2H_5Cl, propane gives *propyl chloride*, C_3H_7Cl, and so on. The groups CH_3-, C_2H_5- and C_3H_7- named *methyl, ethyl* and *propyl* respectively, are known collectively as *alkyl groups* and have the general formula C_nH_{2n+1}. Compounds containing alkyl groups are obtained by the reactions of other paraffins with chlorine. Reactions of this type in which hydrogen atoms are replaced by other atoms or groups are called *substitution reactions*.

The alkyl chlorides can all be prepared by similar methods and have similar chemical properties and gradually varying physical properties. They can be represented by a general formula $C_nH_{2n+1}Cl$, and the molecular formula of each member differs from that of its neighbours by CH_2. Clearly they constitute a new homologous series and this shows the way in which different homologous series can be quite closely related to each other.

More than one of the hydrogen atoms in a hydrocarbon molecule can be replaced by chlorine if enough chlorine is used. *Methylene chloride*, CH_2Cl_2, *chloroform* $CHCl_3$ and *carbon tetrachloride* CCl_4, can all be obtained from methane in this way. In practice a mixture of substitution products is obtained when methane reacts with chlorine.

Alkenes

In another homologous series of hydrocarbons, the numbers of which are known as *alkenes* or *olefins*, at least two of the carbon atoms are connected by what is known as a *double bond*. Four electrons are involved in the formation of a double bond—two from each of the carbon atoms concerned. Because there are four electrons in the double bond of an alkene there are less electrons available for forming bonds with hydrogen. Consequently alkenes always contain less hydrogen than the corresponding paraffins, and they are said to be *unsaturated* hydrocarbons. *Ethylene*, for example, which is the simplest alkene, has the formula C_2H_4 and can be represented thus:

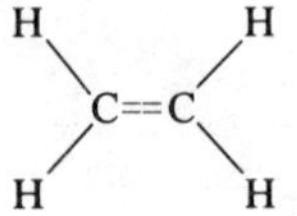

Ethylene

The names and formulae of the simpler alkenes are given below:

C_2H_4	Ethylene	or ethene	C_5H_{10}	Amylene	or pentene
C_3H_6	Propylene	or propene	C_6H_{12}	Hexylene	or hexene
C_4H_8	Butylene	or butene	C_7H_{14}	Heptylene	or heptene

Inspection of the above formulae will show that the general formula for the alkene series is C_nH_{2n}. Alternative names have been given for each hydrocarbon: the first is the name originally given to the compounds and the second the modern name. For the simple alkenes the older names are still widely used.

In the olefin series the possibilities of isomerism are greater than in the paraffin series. In addition to variation in the arrangement of the carbon atoms, the double bond may be in one of several positions. For example, there are three isomeric butenes of formula C_4H_8 compared with only two isomeric butanes of formula C_4H_{10}.

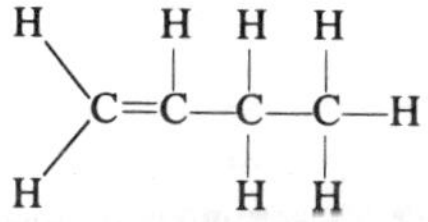

or $CH_2{=}CHCH_2CH_3$

1 Butene

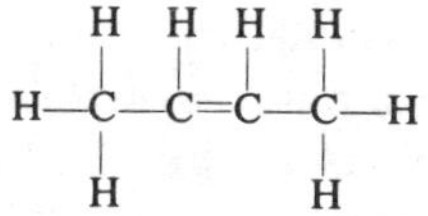

or $CH_3CH{=}CHCH_3$

2-Butene

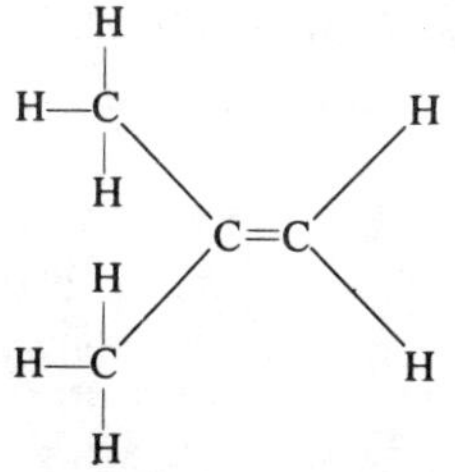

or $(CH_3)_2C{=}CH_2$

Isobutene

It must not be supposed that the double bond in an alkene molecule is a sign of great strength and stability. A double bond between two carbon atoms does not signify that they are united twice as strongly as those connected by a single bond. On the contrary, alkenes are much more reactive than alkanes and when they react the double bond is usually converted into a single bond. Halogens, for example, react with alkenes in the following way:

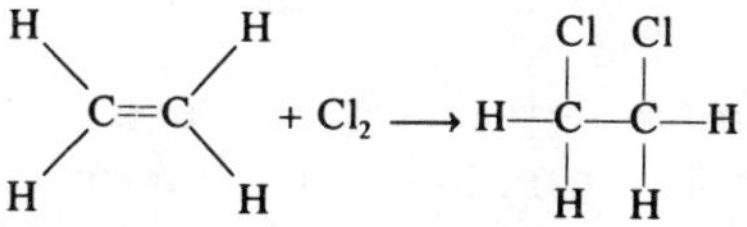

Ethylene dichloride

This is a reaction of quite a different type from the substitution reactions discussed in connection with the alkanes. It is called an *addition reaction*. By the addition of a molecule of hydrogen an ethylene molecule is converted into a molecule of ethane. A catalyst is necessary before hydrogen will add to an olefinic double bond at a reasonable speed and it has been found that finely divided nickel is an excellent catalyst for this reaction:

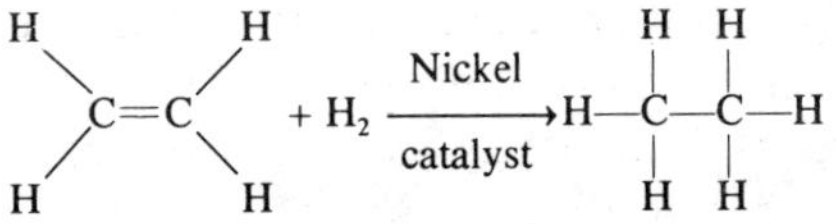

$$
\begin{array}{c}
\text{H} \\ \diagdown \\ \diagup \\ \text{H}
\end{array}
\text{C}=\text{C}
\begin{array}{c}
\diagup \text{H} \\ \\ \diagdown \text{H}
\end{array}
+ \text{H}_2
\xrightarrow[\text{catalyst}]{\text{Nickel}}
\text{H}-\overset{\displaystyle \text{H}}{\underset{\displaystyle \text{H}}{\text{C}}}-\overset{\displaystyle \text{H}}{\underset{\displaystyle \text{H}}{\text{C}}}-\text{H}
$$

An olefinic double bond in any molecule may be saturated with hydrogen in this way. The process known as *hydrogenation*, is used for converting oils into fats as is described in Chapter 6.

Cyclic Hydrocarbons

In the molecules of alkanes and alkenes the carbon atoms are connected together in chains; such compounds are said to be *aliphatic*. This is not the only way in which carbon atoms may be connected, however, and in many compounds, known as cyclic compounds, they are arranged in rings. In the hydrocarbon cyclohexane, C_6H_{12}, for example, the six carbon atoms are arranged in the form of a hexagon. In *benzene*, C_6H_6, the six carbon atoms are connected alternately by single and double bonds to form a ring. When a ring of this type, known as a benzene ring, occurs in a molecule the substance is said to be *aromatic*. Benzene is the first member of a homologous series of hydrocarbons; the structures of benzene and two of its homologues, *toulene* and *ethylbenzene*, are shown below:

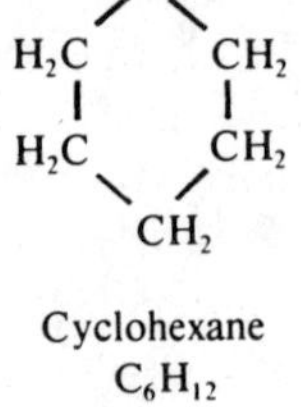

| Cyclohexane C_6H_{12} | Benzene C_6H_6 | Toluene $C_6H_5CH_3$ | Ethylbenzene $C_6H_5C_2H_5$ |

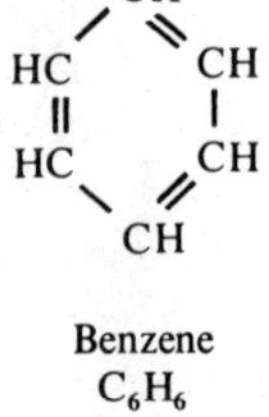

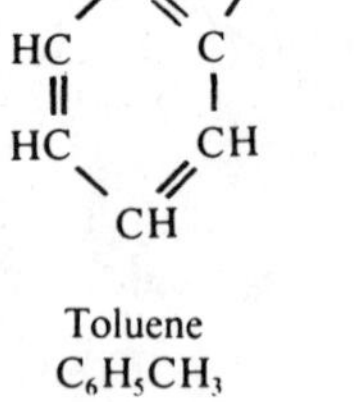

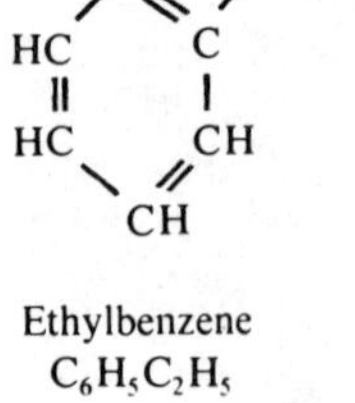

Cyclic compounds are very important in organic chemistry, and as they have to be drawn so many times it is convenient and customary to omit the carbon and hydrogen atoms. If this is done, the examples just given may be written:

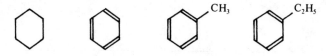

The double bonds in a benzene ring do not behave in the same way as olefinic double bonds. They are by no means as reactive, and benzene rings undergo substitution reactions rather than addition reactions in spite of the presence of three double bonds. With chlorine, for example, in the presence of iron filings as a catalyst, an *aryl halide* called chlorobenzene is obtained:

$$\text{benzene} \quad + \quad Cl_2 \quad \xrightarrow[\text{filings}]{\text{Iron}} \quad \text{chlorobenzene} \quad + \quad HCl$$

Many ring systems are known which contain elements other than carbon. When such a ring occurs in a molecule the compound is said to be *heterocyclic*. Heterocyclic ring systems occur widely in natural products and form part of the molecule of several vitamins. Some simple examples of heterocyclic compounds are given below:

Pyridine	Pyrazine	Pyrimidine	Thiophen	Purine

OTHER HOMOLOGOUS SERIES

It has already been shown that if a hydrogen atom in the molecule of a paraffin is replaced by a halogen atom an alkyl halide, which is a member of a different homologous series, is obtained. Many other homologous series are known which may be regarded as being derived from the hydrocarbons by replacement of one or more hydrogen atoms by other groups known as *functional groups*. The relationship is a purely formal one, however, and it is not always possible to replace directly a hydrogen atom in a hydrocarbon by another atom or group. The nature of the functional group determines, to a large extent, the chemical properties of a compound. The more important classes of organic compound are included in Table 4.3.

THE GEOMETRY OF ORGANIC MOLECULES

It is convenient to write the structural formulae of organic compounds as though the four covalent bonds from a carbon atom lie in one plane.

Table 4.3. Important Classes of Organic Compounds

Class of compound	Name and nature of functional group	Example
Alkyl halide	Halogen atom $-F$, $-Cl$, $-Br$ or $-I$	CH_3Cl Methyl chloride
Aryl halide	Halogen atom attached to a benzene ring $-F$, $-Cl$, $-Br$ or $-I$	C_6H_5Cl Chlorobenzene
Alcohol	Hydroxyl group $-OH$	CH_3OH Methyl alcohol
Phenol	Phenolic hydroxyl group. Always attached to a benzene ring $-OH$	C_6H_5OH Phenol
Aldehyde	Aldehyde group $-C{\overset{\displaystyle H}{\underset{\displaystyle O}{}}}$	CH_3CHO Acetaldehyde C_6H_5CHO Benzaldehyde
Ketone	Carbonyl group $\diagdown C{=}O$	CH_3COCH_3 Acetone $C_6H_5COCH_3$ Acetophenone
Acid	Carboxyl group $-C{\overset{\displaystyle O}{\underset{\displaystyle OH}{}}}$	CH_3COOH Acetic Acid C_6H_5COOH Benzoic Acid
Amine	Amino group $-N{\overset{\displaystyle H}{\underset{\displaystyle H}{}}}$	CH_3NH_2 Methylamine $C_6H_5NH_2$ Aniline
Amide	Amide group $-C{\overset{\displaystyle \parallel}{\underset{\displaystyle O}{}}}-N{\overset{\displaystyle H}{\underset{\displaystyle H}{}}}$	CH_3CONH_2 Acetamide $C_6H_5CONH_2$ Benzamide

In fact, however, they are distributed symmetrically in space. If a carbon atom is supposed to be at the centre of a regular tetrahedron (i.e. a pyramid, all the faces of which are equilateral triangles), its valence bonds will be directed towards the corners of the tetrahedron, as shown in Fig. 4.5.

For reasons which will be clear later, the tetrahedron should not be drawn as in Fig. 4.5b but with a horizontal edge at the front, and a vertical edge at the back as shown in Fig. 4.5c. There is always a carbon atom at the centre of the tetrahedron and this, and its four valencies, may be omitted without danger of ambiguity. Two of the hydrogen atoms

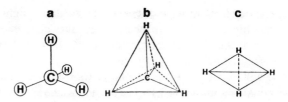

FIG. 4.5. Tetrahedral model and diagrams of a methane molecule

(those connected by the horizontal line) should be imagined as being in front of the plane of the paper and the other two behind.

Calculation shows that in methane the angle between a C–H bond and any of its partners is 109° 28′. When the four groups attached to a carbon atom are not identical, as for example in methyl chloride CH_3Cl, the arrangement of the bonds is still tetrahedral but the angles between them are not all equal. In such cases the tetrahedron is not quite a regular tetrahedron, but the departure from regularity is quite small and may, for most purposes, be ignored.

If a carbon atom is connected to four different atoms or groups the molecule as a whole is usually asymmetric, that is, it cannot be cut by an imaginary plane into two mirror-image halves. Such a carbon atom is referred to as an asymmetric carbon atom, though in fact it is the molecule containing it which is asymmetric and not the carbon atom itself. As a result of this asymmetry any compound which can be represented Cabde exists in two isomeric forms as shown in Fig. 4.6.

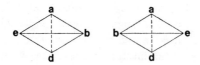

FIG. 4.6. Isomeric forms of Cabde

These may appear to be identical, but if an attempt is made to superimpose them, that is to place one on top of the other, it becomes clear that they are different. They are in fact mirror-images and bear the same relationship to each other as, for example, a right hand to a left hand. Such mirror-image pairs are quite common in organic chemistry. The isomers have identical physical and chemical properties, but they differ in their effect upon polarized light; for this reason they are often referred to as *optical isomers* and are said to be optically active.

The wave motions in light normally occur in an infinite number of planes. In polarized light, which is obtained when ordinary light is passed through certain minerals, the wave motion only takes place in one plane, which is known as the plane of polarization. If a beam of polarized light is passed in turn through equally concentrated solutions of two optical isomers, one will rotate the plane of polarization to the right and the other by an equal amount to the left. The isomer, which rotates the plane of polarization to the right, is said to be *dextrorotatory* (indicated by a (+) before the name of the compound) and the other *laevorotatory* (likewise indicated by a (−) before the name).

The molecule of *lactic acid* $CH_3CHOHCOOH$ contains an asymmetric carbon atom and in consequence it exists in two forms. (+)-Lactic acid is found is muscle and (−)-lactic acid can be obtained by fermenting cane sugar with certain bacilli. These two optical isomers may be represented as shown in Fig. 4.7.

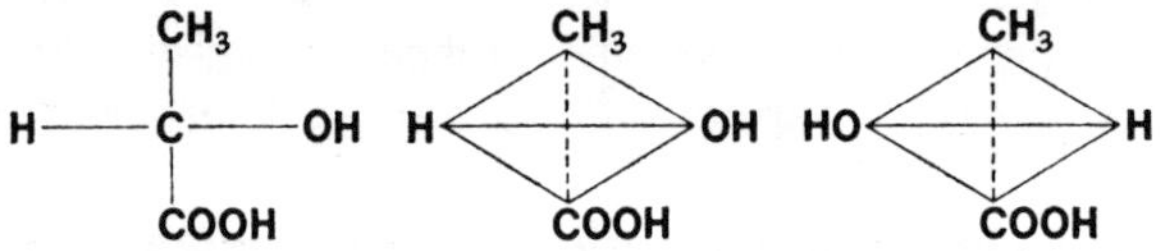

FIG. 4.7. Lactic acid. (+) and (−) forms of lactic acid

It should be noted that both forms of lactic acid contain the same atoms or groups connected together in the same way. They differ in the disposition of the valency bonds, or configuration as it is called, at the asymmetric carbon atom. Optical isomerism is an example of isomerism in space or *stereoisomerism*.

Although optical isomers have identical physical and chemical properties the body has the capacity for distinguishing between some pairs of isomers with certainty. (−)-Nicotine, for example, which is present in tobacco, is about three times as poisonous as the dextrorotatory isomer which is also known. Again, the efficacy of vitamin C in preventing scurvy is not shown by its optical isomer. These differences in physiological properties, of which many examples are known, arise from the fact that many of the constituents of the cells of the body are themselves optically active.

PROJECTION FORMULAE. The difference in configuration between optical isomers is clearly seen when tetrahedral diagrams such as those used above are employed. With constant repetition the drawing of these tetrahedra becomes tedious, however, especially in the case of molecules containing several asymmetric carbon atoms; it is customary to draw instead the projections of the tetrahedra as shown in Fig. 4.8.

Projection formulae of this type are of use only if they are projections of a tetrahedron in a standard position. By convention the tetrahedron is arranged with a horizontal edge in front and a vertical edge at the rear. This may seem a trivial point but it is, in fact, of paramount importance and without this convention projection formulae would be meaningless. Before one could decide by examining a tracing of a hand whether it represented a right or left hand, it would be necessary to know whether the tracing had been done with the palm or the back of the hand

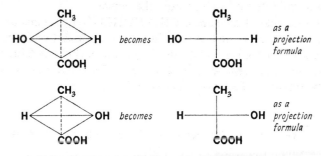

FIG. 4.8. Relationship of projection formulae to tetrahedral diagrams

uppermost. So it is with projection formulae. The position of the tetrahedron is vital; hence the need for the convention. Groups connected by a horizontal line in a projection formula are those which, in a tetrahedral diagram, must be imagined to lie in front of the plane of the paper. Those groups joined by a vertical line in a projection formula are those which, in a tetrahedral representation, must be imagined to lie behind the plane of the paper.

INADEQUACY OF STRUCTURAL FORMULAE. The customary way of writing the graphic formula of an aliphatic compound appears to indicate that the carbon atoms are connected in long straight chains. For example, the graphic formula for n-heptane is:

$$
\begin{array}{ccccccc}
\text{H} & \text{H} & \text{H} & \text{H} & \text{H} & \text{H} & \text{H} \\
| & | & | & | & | & | & | \\
\text{H—C—C—C—C—C—C—C—H} \\
| & | & | & | & | & | & | \\
\text{H} & \text{H} & \text{H} & \text{H} & \text{H} & \text{H} & \text{H}
\end{array}
$$

n-Heptane

Because of the tetrahedral disposition of the four valencies of a carbon atom the angle between any two bonds is 109° 28′ (or something near to this in cases where the four groups attached to the carbon atom are not identical). In consequence a chain of carbon atoms cannot possibly form a straight line but adopts zigzag or spiral arrangements such as those shown in Fig. 4.9.

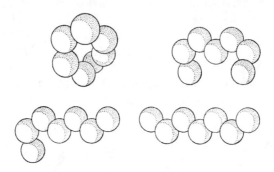

FIG. 4.9. Possible spatial arrangements of the carbon atoms in n-heptane

Theoretically there is no limit to the number of 'shapes', or *conformations* as they are called, that a molecule may adopt by twisting about the C−C bonds. In practice, however, some conformations are more stable than others and these are usually the preferred shapes. Long chain molecules usually adopt an extended zigzag conformation. Sometimes hydrogen bonding between different parts of a molecule assists in forming and maintaining a particular conformation and we shall see in Chapter 9 that the long thread-like molecules of proteins are held in a spiral or helical shape by intramolecular hydrogen bonds.

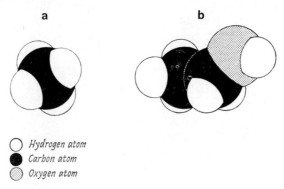

○ Hydrogen atom
● Carbon atom
◎ Oxygen atom

FIG. 4.10. Molecules of (a) methane and (b) ethyl alcohol drawn to scale

Another disadvantage of the customary graphic formulae is the fact that the atoms appear to be widely separated from each other. Nothing could be further from the truth; the nuclei of two atoms united by a covalent bond are much nearer together than the nuclei of non-bonded atoms can ever be.

SUGGESTIONS FOR FURTHER READING

BROWN, G. I. *A New Guide to Modern Valency Theory*, 3rd edition. Longmans, 1978.

HOLUM, J. R. *Elements of General and Biological Chemistry: an Introduction to the Molecular Basis of Life*, 4th edition. Wiley, USA, 1975.

PAULING, L. and HAYWARD, R. *The Architecture of Molecules*. Freeman, USA, Paperback 1970.
A beautiful pictorial record of molecular structure.

ROSSER, W. E. and WILLIAMS, D. I. *Modern Organic Chemistry for 'A' level*. Collins, 1974.

SACKHEIM, G. I. *Introduction to Chemistry for Biology Students*. Pitman. 1966.
A simple programmed text covering atomic and molecular structure.

WHITE, E. H. *Chemical Background for the Biological Science*, 2nd edition. Prentice Hall, USA, 1970.

WOOD, C. W., HOLLIDAY, A. K. and BEER, R. J. S. *Organic Chemistry: an Introductory Text*, 3rd edition. Butterworths, 1968.

Chapter Five

Alcohols and acids

In an alcohol, one of the hydrogen atoms of a hydrocarbon molecule has been replaced by a hydroxyl group. The hydroxyl group consists of an oxygen atom combined with a hydrogen atom and the group is connected to a carbon atom by the remaining oxygen valence.

The simplest alcohol is methyl alcohol which may be regarded as derived from methane (though in practice it is not possible to convert methane to methyl alcohol easily). The relationship may be understood by examining the graphic formulae below:

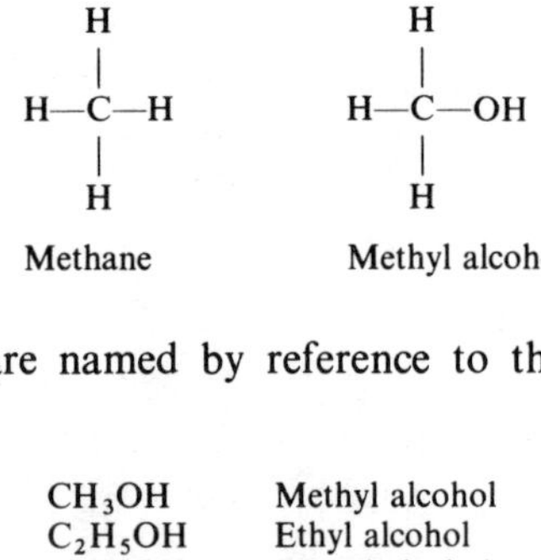

$$
\begin{array}{cc}
\text{H} & \text{H} \\
| & | \\
\text{H---C---H} & \text{H---C---OH} \\
| & | \\
\text{H} & \text{H} \\
\text{Methane} & \text{Methyl alcohol}
\end{array}
$$

Simple alcohols are named by reference to the alkyl group they contain:

CH_3OH	Methyl alcohol
C_2H_5OH	Ethyl alcohol
C_3H_7OH	Propyl alcohol
C_4H_9OH	Butyl alcohol
$C_5H_{11}OH$	Amyl alcohol

Isomerism is possible in the case of propyl alcohol and alcohols of higher molecular weight. There are, for example, two propyl alcohols:

$CH_3CH_2CH_2OH$	n-Propyl alcohol
$(CH_3)_2CHOH$	Isopropyl alcohol

Isopropyl alcohol is called a secondary alcohol because the carbon atom to which the hydroxyl group is attached is connected to two other carbon atoms. Secondary alcohols differ in some chemical properties from primary alcohols.

With butyl alcohol, four isomers are possible:

$CH_3CH_2CH_2CH_2OH$	n-Butyl alcohol
$(CH_3)_2CHCH_2OH$	Isobutyl alcohol
$CH_3CH_2CHOHCH_3$	Secondary butyl alcohol
$(CH_3)_3COH$	Tertiary butyl alcohol

Tertiary butyl alcohol is so called because the carbon atom to which the hydroxyl group is attached is connected to three other carbon atoms. In the case of amyl alcohol, eight isomers are possible, but of these only the following three are of interest to us:

$CH_3CH_2CH_2CH_2CH_2OH$	n-Amyl alcohol
$(CH_3)_2CHCH_2CH_2OH$	Isoamyl alcohol
$CH_3CH_2CH(CH_3)CH_2OH$	'Active' amyl alcohol

Active amyl alcohol is so called because its molecule contains an asymmetric carbon atom and so the compound is optically active.

Alcohols such as the above, which contain only one hydroxyl group, are called monohydric alcohols. Those with two hydroxyl groups are called dihydric alcohols and so on.

Ethyl Alcohol

All alcoholic beverages contain ethyl alcohol, and for this reason it is often merely referred to as alcohol. Like methyl alcohol it is a colourless liquid, and it boils at 78° C to give a vapour which when ignited burns with a hot blue flame which is just visible. The reaction is represented by the equation:

$$C_2H_5OH + 3O_2 \longrightarrow 2CO_2 + 3H_2O$$

Ethyl alcohol reacts with *acetic acid* to form a fragrant compound called *ethyl acetate*, which has a fruity smell:

$$C_2H_5OH + CH_3COOH \rightleftharpoons CH_3COOC_2H_5 + H_2O$$
$$\text{Acetic acid} \qquad \text{Ethyl acetate}$$

Compounds of this type, formed by reaction of an alcohol and an acid, are known as *esters*, and are important in the manufacture of alcoholic beverages.

MANUFACTURE OF ETHYL ALCOHOL. One of the ways in which alcohol is made is by a process called *fermentation*. The preparation of alcoholic beverages containing ethyl alcohol has been carried on for thousands of years and in more recent times pure ethyl alcohol for use by the chemical industry has been manufactured in very large quantities by this method. Other methods of production are also known and nowadays over half the ethyl alcohol produced in this country is made from ethylene. For alcoholic drinks, however, the fermentation process is still used exclusively and we shall confine ourselves to a study of this method.

The starting material in the fermentation process is a naturally occurring substance containing a high proportion of carbohydrate. For the production of pure alcohol in Britain a material called *molasses* is used; this is a syrup, rich in sugar, obtained as a by-product during sugar refining. In other parts of the world alternative cheap sources of carbohydrate are used, such as potatoes, grain or rice. The carbohydrate in these cases is starch, which is a high molecular weight compound most simply represented by the formula $(C_6H_{10}O_5)_n$, where n is a large whole number. In molasses, on the other hand, the main carbohydrate is the sugar sucrose which has the formula $C_{12}H_{22}O_{11}$.

The conversion of starch into alcohol occurs in three main stages which are considered below.

In the first stage, the complex starch molecule is hydrolysed by the enzyme *diastase* to the relatively simple sugar maltose, $C_{12}H_{22}O_{11}$, and dextrins which are intermediate stages in the conversion of starch to maltose. The importance of enzymes as catalysts has already been emphasized in Chapter 2; it will now be seen that they have a major part to play in fermentation. Diastase, a mixture of α- and β-amylases (see page 140) occurs in malt, which is the name given to germinating or sprouting barley. Malt is obtained by steeping barley in water and then removing it from the water and allowing it to stand in warm air for a few days, before it is very slowly and gently dried. During the germination period amylases and also some peptidases are produced and these at once begin their work of hydrolysing the carbohydrate and protein present in the barley. Their action ceases, however, when the malt is dried.

When ground malt is mixed with a mash of starchy materials in water at 50–60° C and allowed to stand for about an hour the diastase hydrolyses the starch to maltose and dextrins:

$$2(C_6H_{10}O_5)_n + nH_2O \xrightarrow{\text{diastase}} nC_{12}H_{22}O_{11}$$
$$\text{Starch} \qquad\qquad\qquad\qquad\quad \text{Maltose}$$

In the second stage the C_{12} sugar maltose is broken down to the C_6 sugar glucose. In this case the hydrolysis is catalysed by the enzyme *maltase* that is present in yeast which is added:

$$C_{12}H_{22}O_{11} + H_2O \xrightarrow{\text{maltase}} 2C_6H_{12}O_6$$
$$\text{Maltose} \qquad\qquad\qquad\quad \text{Glucose}$$

After the yeast has been added the process continues for several days, the temperature being kept at about 30–35° C.

In the third stage, *zymase* (which is the name given to a collection of at least fourteen enzymes), also present in yeast, is responsible for the fermentation of glucose into alcohol. Fermentation means *boiling* and the name arose because during the reaction the liquid is agitated by bubbles of carbon dioxide, which produce a frothing or boiling appearance.

$$C_6H_{12}O_6 \xrightarrow{\text{zymase}} 2C_2H_5OH + 2CO_2$$
Glucose

This equation merely represents the start and the finish of the reaction, which is a complex one involving many stages. The result is a solution of alcohol in water, the alcohol amounting to less than 16 per cent of the whole.

It should be noted that only the last of these stages is a true fermentation, as it is only here that a gas is produced. The first two stages are examples of enzymatic hydrolysis although for convenience the whole process is usually referred to as *alcoholic fermentation*.

If the starting material in alcohol manufacture is molasses instead of a starchy material, then the initial hydrolysis stage is not necessary. The main component of molasses is sucrose and this is hydrolysed by the enzyme *sucrase*, also present in yeast, into the two sugars, glucose and fructose. The equations in this case are the same as before, because sucrose has the same molecular formula as maltose, and fructose the same as glucose:

$$C_{12}H_{22}O_{11} + H_2O \xrightarrow{\text{sucrase}} C_6H_{12}O_6 + C_6H_{12}O_6$$
Sucrose   Glucose   Fructose

$$C_6H_{12}O_6 \xrightarrow{\text{zymase}} 2C_2H_5OH + 2CO_2$$
Glucose or
Fructose

For the production of alcoholic drinks the starting material used depends upon the product required. For instance, whisky is made from malt or grain and wine from grape juice. But whatever the starting point the chemical changes involved are those described above.

Fusel Oil

Fusel oil contains a mixture of propyl, butyl and amyl alcohols. All these alcohols exist in various isomeric forms and the actual isomers present in fusel oil depend upon how the mixture has been produced.

Isoamyl alcohol and active amyl alcohol are usually the main constituents together with smaller amounts of normal and isopropyl alcohol
and normal and isobutyl alcohol.

The alcohols in fusel oil are produced by the action of yeast on amino
acids present in fermenting material. Fusel oil has a revolting taste and is
more toxic than ethyl alcohol, although in very small quantities it
contributes to the normal flavour of whisky and other grain spirits.

Glycerol

Glycerol is a trihydric alcohol, that is, it contains three hydroxyl
groups; $CH_2OHCHOHCH_2OH$. It is the only trihydric alcohol of
importance and is also known as glycerine. It is a colourless, sweetish
liquid, as is indicated by its names which are derived from a Greek word
(glucus) meaning sweet. The sugar glucose is so called for the same
reason. It has similar chemical properties to the monohydric alcohols,
and is produced in small quantities together with ethyl alcohol in the
alcoholic fermentation process. For this reason small quantities of
glycerol are always to be found in undistilled alcoholic drinks, to which it
contributes a degree of sweetness. Unlike fusel oil it has no harmful
effects on the body. As will be seen in Chapter 6 it plays an important
part in the composition of oils and fats.

Effects of Alcohol on the Body

Alcohol must be regarded as a foodstuff because in the body it can be
broken down to provide energy. In fact it is a more concentrated source
of energy than either carbohydrate or protein, and has an available
energy value of 29·4 kJ/g. It is also a drug and affects the central nervous
system. These two effects must be considered together when assessing the
desirability of alcohol as a source of energy. The nature of the effects of
alcohol on the body, varying from mild stimulation when a small amount
is consumed to loss of co-ordination and even death when a large
quantity is taken, is indicated in Fig. 5.1.

Unlike most foods, alcohol can be absorbed by the body without prior
digestion; thus it provides a source of quickly available energy and it may
be used for this purpose in emergencies. Alcohol is almost completely
absorbed during its passage through the body, mainly in the small
intestine but also through the walls of the stomach. Absorption may take
anything from one half to two hours depending on the concentration of
alcohol in the beverage consumed, the amount taken and the nature and
amount of food eaten with it or immediately beforehand. An average
time for absorption is about an hour.

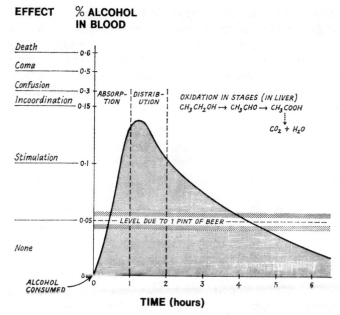

FIG. 5.1. The metabolism of alcohol showing the relation between the level of alcohol in blood and its effect on the body (after von Wartburg)

The fate of alcohol in the body is summarized in Fig. 5.1. After absorption the alcohol is distributed through the body in the bloodstream and thereafter it is broken down in a series of oxidative steps with liberation of energy. The breakdown process is controlled by a series of enzymes, each step being controlled by its own enzymes. Initial oxidation of alcohol to acetaldehyde is mainly controlled by *alcohol dehydrogenase* and, as its name indicates, this step involves removal of hydrogen; it is followed by further oxidation to acetic acid, the most important enzyme involved in this step being *aldehyde dehydrogenase.* These initial breakdown steps occur in the liver, and the acetic acid produced then becomes part of the general body pool of this substance and is further oxidized, in a complex process, to carbon dioxide and water. Alcohol is oxidized in the body rather slowly and only about seven grams can be oxidized in an hour; this means that alcohol is removed from the blood at a slow rate and that it can only make a small overall contribution to energy needs.

Alcoholic Beverages

Alcoholic beverages are prized on account of their flavour and their stimulating effect and hardly at all as a source of energy; nevertheless it is worth noting that the energy value of wine is about equal to that of milk. There are three main classes of alcoholic beverages: wines, beers and spirits. They are all made by enzymatic fermentation of carbohydrate material, though it is the raw material used and the treatment given to the liquor after fermentation that chiefly determines the character of the drink produced. The main types of alcoholic drink and their energy values are shown in Table 5.1.

Table 5.1. Alcoholic Beverages

Type	Example	Alcohol content (g/100 ml)	Energy value (kJ/100 ml)
BEERS	Bitter	3	127
	Mild	3	105
CIDERS	Dry	4	147
	Sweet	4	168
WINES			
White	Graves	9	294
Red	Chianti	9	275
Fortified	Sweet sherry	16	567
SPIRITS	Whisky	31	914
LIQUEURS	Benedictine	39	1134

The manufacture of all alcoholic drinks involves a fermentation stage, and the essentials of this have already been described on page 59. The raw materials used differ according to the type of drink being made; thus wine is made from grapes—or occasionally from other fruits—whisky is made from malt or grain, rum is made from molasses, beer is made from malt and cider is made from apples. Natural wines, beers and ciders are all drunk without further treatment as fermented liquors; they thus have a low alcohol content and energy value. Fortified wines, such as port and sherry, are made by adding extra alcohol to certain natural wines, thus giving them a higher energy value and better keeping qualities.

Spirits differ from wines in having been distilled after fermentation; brandy is made by distilling wine, rum by distilling fermented molasses and so on. The special characteristics of these drinks may be associated with a particular ingredient used in the fermentation stage, as with 'Scotch' which is said to owe much to peat fires used in drying the malt. More usually character is imparted by addition of flavouring agents after distillation is complete, as with gin to which juniper berries and other flavouring ingredients are added before a second distillation. Spirits also gain character by being matured for several years before they are drunk. Slow chemical changes occur during this time; some ethyl alcohol is oxidized to acetaldehyde, other alcohols are oxidized to corresponding aldehydes, sweet fruity-smelling esters are formed and these changes impart a mellowness of flavour and fragrance of bouquet to the product.

Liqueurs are made by steeping herbs in strong spirits for a week or two and subsequently distilling. The richly flavoured distillate contains essential oils and other flavouring matters from the plants, and to this is added sugar and colouring matter.

Many of the famous liqueurs originated in monasteries and the methods and materials used in preparing them are kept secret. An aura of romance surrounds even those liqueurs with no monastic associations. The recipe of the renowned Scots liqueur Drambuie, literally 'the drink that satisfies', is said to have been given to an ancestor of the present manufacturer by Prince Charles Edward in 1746. The Prince is said to have divulged the secret recipe as a token of gratitude for the help he received in escaping from the Scots mainland to the island of Skye. It is made from Scotch whisky, Scottish herbs and honey (presumably from Scottish bees!).

ACIDS

Acids are easy to recognize because of their familiar properties; they have a sour taste, they change the colour of some natural dyes (e.g. blue litmus turns red), they attack many metals and they react with bases to form salts. They are electrolytes which in solution form free ions; for example, though hydrogen chloride gas does not show typical acidic properties, hydrogen chloride in water behaves as a typical acid. In the gaseous state hydrogen chloride is a polar covalent molecule, but in water the following reaction occurs:

$$HCl \rightleftharpoons H^+ + Cl^-$$

This reaction can only occur in the presence of another substance, in this case water, which can combine with the hydrogen ions (protons) produced by the HCl. The complete reaction is therefore more accurately represented by the equation:

$$H_2O + HCl \rightleftharpoons H_3O^+ + Cl^-$$
(base) (acid)

In water hydrogen chloride—better known as hydrochloric acid—can act as an acid because it is able to ionize to produce protons. We can appreciate this better if we represent the reaction of the HCl with water as a two-stage process:

$$HCl \rightleftharpoons H^+ + Cl^-$$
$$H^+ + H_2O \rightleftharpoons H_3O^+$$

Overall reaction: $HCl + H_2O \rightleftharpoons H_3O^+ + Cl^-$

Thus we can summarise the situation by saying that HCl is acidic when it can furnish protons, and that water facilitates this because it can accept protons and form H_3O^+, a *hydronium* ion. Many substances act like water in being able to accept protons and they are known as *bases*.

It is important to realize that neither of the stages in the above two-stage reaction can occur alone. In other words a substance can only act as an acid in the presence of a base, because the reaction involves a *transfer* of a proton from an acid to a base. The acidic function of other typical inorganic acids such as sulphuric acid and nitric acid can be represented in a similar way:

$$H_2SO_4 + H_2O \rightleftharpoons H_3O^+ + HSO_4^-$$
$$\text{(acid)} \quad \text{(base)}$$

$$HNO_3 + H_2O \rightleftharpoons H_3O^+ + NO_3^-$$
$$\text{(acid)} \quad \text{(base)}$$

This theory of the nature of acids and bases may be less familiar than that which defines an acid as a substance that produces hydrogen ions and a base as a substance that produces hydroxyl ions. Nevertheless it has a number of advantages compared to the older theory. For example, it is a much more general theory and explains how substances, such as ammonia, which cannot furnish hydroxyl ions can act as bases. It also emphasises the interdependence of acids and bases.

It will be noted from the reactions shown above than an acid in water gives H_3O^+ ions, whereas on earlier theories it was supposed that an acid gave free protons. It can be shown experimentally that free protons do not exist in aqueous solution; they always combine with water to form H_3O^+. Thus the newer theory is in better accord with the known facts; it does not postulate the existence of free protons but only their transfer from acid to base. In what follows we shall use the symbol H^+ both for convenience and to follow convention, but it should be remembered that in aqueous solution the proton as such is not present and H^+ may be taken to represent H_3O^+.

ACIDITY AND pH. Pure water is said to be *neutral*; this does not mean that no ionization occurs, but that ionization produces equal numbers of hydrogen ions (in the form of H_3O^+) and hydroxyl ions:

$$H_2O \rightleftharpoons H^+ + OH^-$$

The extent of ionization is very small and it may be expressed quantitatively:

$$[H^+] = [OH^-] = 10^{-7}$$

or

$$[H^+].[OH^-] = 10^{-14}$$

where the square brackets denote concentration expressed in *molarity* (M), that is gram molecules or gram ions per litre.

Acidity may be expressed in terms of hydrogen ion concentration, a solution being described as acidic if its hydrogen ion concentration is *greater* than 10^{-7}. (It follows that basicity may also be expressed in terms of hydrogen ion concentration, a solution being described as basic if its hydrogen ion concentration is *less* than 10^{-7}.) The range of concentrations to be expressed in this way is so large, however, that acidity is more conveniently expressed in terms of pH, which can be defined as the negative logarithm of the hydrogen ion concentration:

$$pH = -\log[H^+].$$

By using a logarithmic scale the concentration range is compressed by a power of ten. Thus a pH change of one corresponds to a tenfold change in the hydrogen ion concentration, and a pH change of two corresponds to a hundredfold change in the hydrogen ion concentration.

Acids, such as typical inorganic acids, which are completely ionized in solution are called *strong* acids and the hydrogen ion concentration, and hence pH, may be calculated directly from their molarity. For example 0·1 M HCl is completely ionized, hence:

$$[H^+] = 10^{-1} \qquad pH = -\log 10^{-1} = 1$$

On this basis a pH scale may be drawn up and values of hydrogen ion concentration and corresponding pH values on such a scale are shown in Fig. 5.2. It will be noted that the pH scale goes from 0 to 14 so allowing acidity and basicity to be expressed in terms of 14 units rather than 10^{14}; that is a hundred million million! It will also be observed that the neutral point on the scale is at pH 7 and pHs lower than this indicate acid solutions, and pHs higher than this indicate basic solutions.

pH is measured in a variety of ways varying from the very simple method of using an indicator solution (or paper) whose colour varies with pH, to more sophisticated instrumental methods. The details of pH measurement are beyond the scope of this book but in what follows

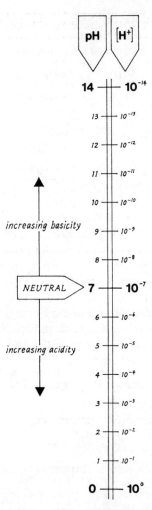

FIG. 5.2. The pH scale

considerable use will be made of the results of such measurements. The pHs of a variety of foods are given in Table 5.2. The figures quoted are average values and there may be variations of as much as one pH unit depending, for example, upon the conditions in which the food has been grown, its maturity and variety and the treatment it has been given during the growing period.

BUFFER SYSTEMS. A buffer system is one that resists change of pH when small amounts of acid or alkali are added to it and such a system is

Table 5.2. pH Values of Some Popular Foods

Food	pH	Food	pH
Lime juice	2·3	Banana	4·6
Lemon juice	2·4	Carrots	5·2
Pickles	2·7	Baked beans	5·3
Apples	3·0	Potatoes	5·5
Rhubarb	3·1	Spinach	5·4
Grapefruit	3·2	Corned beef	5·9
Cherries	3·4	Tuna	5·9
Plums	3·4	Peas	6·0
Sauerkraut	3·5	Sardines	6·0
Orange juice	3·7	Evaporated milk	6·0
Peaches	3·7	Pork luncheon meat	6·1
Pineapples	3·7	Chicken	6·2
Pears	4·2	Butter	6·2
Tomato juice	4·2	Salmon	6·4
Tomatoes	4·3		

formed by a mixture of a weak acid and its salt (or a mixture of a weak base and its salt). A weak acid differs from a strong one in that, except at extreme dilutions, it is only partially ionized in solution. At any given concentration, therefore, there is equilibrium between undissociated acid and its ions. A typical example is acetic acid, CH_3COOH or more simply HAc, which partially ionizes in water:

$$HAc + H_2O \quad H_3O^+ + Ac^-$$

(acid) (base)

or using the simpler, more conventional way of representing this;

$$HAc \rightleftharpoons H^+ + Ac^-$$

The position of equilibrium for such a system is given by the dissociation constant Ka defined as:

$$Ka = \frac{[H^+].[Ac^-]}{[HAc]} = 1·7 \times 10^{-5}$$

From this value it can be calculated that 0·1 M acetic acid is only dissociated to the extent of 1 per cent, and has a pH of about 3.

Acetic acid on its own has no buffering action, but if one of its salts, such as sodium acetate, $CH_3COO^-Na^+$ or Na^+Ac^-, is added to it a buffer system is established. Sodium acetate is completely ionised at all dilutions and therefore provides a large reservoir of acetate ions. If acid is added to such a system, the acetic acid equilibrium moves from right to left to re-establish the value of Ka:

$$HAc \leftharpoondown H^+ + Ac^-$$

Such a change is made possible by the reservoir of acetate ions which are available to combine with and hence remove the added acid. If a small amount of base is added to such a system the pH remains unchanged because the base is neutralized by the acetic acid. For example, if hydroxyl ions are added we have:

$$OH^- + HAc \rightleftharpoons H_2O + Ac^-$$

The control of pH by buffers is important both in living organisms and in the processing of foods, and several examples of the use of buffer systems will be found in what follows. One of the most important buffer systems in the human body is blood. The pH of blood is close to seven and if this pH value changes by as little as $0\cdot2$ pH units severe consequences, and even death, may result. The buffering action of blood is due to the presence of the weak acid, carbonic acid, and its salt, sodium bicarbonate.

Carboxylic Acids

A carboxylic acid contains a carboxyl group $-COOH$. This group is so called because it is a combination of a $>C=O$ or *carb*onyl group and a hyd*roxyl* group. A typical example of a carboxylic acid is *acetic acid*, CH_3COOH. Carboxylic acids are weak acids and have small dissociation constants as can be seen from Table 5.3. They occur widely in nature, particularly in fruit and vegetables, and many are used as preservatives.

Table 5.3. Dissociation Constants and pH values of Acids at 25°C

Acid	Dissociation constant		pH (0·1 N solution)
Hydrochloric		—	1·0
Acetic		$1\cdot8 \times 10^{-5}$	2·9
Benzoic		$6\cdot5 \times 10^{-5}$	2·6
Citric*	(1)	$8\cdot4 \times 10^{-4}$	
	(2)	$1\cdot8 \times 10^{-5}$	
	(3)	$4\cdot0 \times 10^{-6}$	2·2
Malic*	(1)	$3\cdot9 \times 10^{-4}$	
	(2)	$7\cdot8 \times 10^{-6}$	2·2
Propionic		$1\cdot3 \times 10^{-5}$	3·0
Tartaric*	(1)	$1\cdot0 \times 10^{-3}$	
	(2)	$4\cdot6 \times 10^{-5}$	2·2

* For di- and tri-carboxylic acids there is a dissociation constant for the ionization of each carboxyl group.

Acetic acid is a member of a homologous series of carboxylic acids known as *fatty acids* because some of the higher members of the series occur combined with glycerol in fats. Each member of the series contains an alkyl group joined to a carboxyl group. Those of interest in food chemistry are listed below:

CH_3COOH	Acetic acid	$C_9H_{19}COOH$	Capric acid
C_2H_5COOH	Propionic acid	$C_{11}H_{23}COOH$	Lauric acid
C_3H_7COOH	Butyric acid	$C_{13}H_{27}COOH$	Myristic acid
$C_5H_{11}COOH$	Caproic acid	$C_{15}H_{31}COOH$	Palmitic acid
$C_7H_{15}COOH$	Caprylic acid	$C_{17}H_{35}COOH$	Stearic acid

All the above acids, from *butyric acid* onwards, may be obtained from natural oils and fats by hydrolysis, and it may be observed here that they all contain an even number of carbon atoms. The lower members of the series are liquids at normal temperatures and will mix with water in all proportions. As the molecular weights of the acids increase, the melting points rise and the solubility in water decreases. Butyric acid, for example, which is found in sour milk and combined with glycerol in butter (from which it gets its name), is a liquid with an unpleasant rancid smell and is miscible with water in all proportions. *Stearic acid*, however, is a white wax-like solid and is not soluble in water.

Another change associated with increasing molecular weight is a decrease in acidity. Acetic and butyric acids are stronger acids than palmitic and stearic; nevertheless, the higher members of the series are still weakly acidic, and form salts. Whereas the sodium salts of acetic and butyric acid are readily soluble in water, those of palmitic and stearic acid are only slightly soluble and are known as *soaps*.

ACETIC ACID was the first acidic substance known to man. It is produced during the manufacture of wine if the fermented must is exposed to the air for any length of time. In the presence of an enzyme the oxygen in the air oxidizes the ethyl alcohol present in the wine to acetic acid. The same reaction occurs in the laboratory if ethyl alcohol is oxidized with a solution of potassium permanganate. The reaction takes place in two stages. In the first stage hydrogen is removed from alcohol producing an *aldehyde* which is an *al*cohol *dehyd*rogenated. This is then rapidly oxidized to acetic acid.

| Ethyl alcohol | Acetaldehyde | Acetic acid |

As can be seen from the structure of acetaldehyde given above, aldehydes contain a $-CHO$ group. Acetaldehyde is a colourless liquid, with a low boiling point (21° C) and a pungent odour. As was mentioned previously it is produced from ethyl alcohol during the maturing of distilled spirits.

Acetic acid is a colourless liquid with a sharp penetrating odour and is miscible with water in all proportions. Below $17°$ C it forms a solid crystalline mass known as *glacial acetic acid*.

VINEGAR. Essentially, vinegar is a dilute solution of acetic acid in water. It is produced by the bacterial oxidation of alcohol, the bacteria being members of the *Acetobacter* group, which secrete an enzyme capable of assisting the oxidation. A species that is commonly used is *Acetobacter aceti*.

$$CH_3CH_2OH + O_2 \xrightarrow[\text{Acetobacter}]{\text{enzyme in}} CH_3COOH + H_2O$$

Different sources of alcohol are used in different parts of the world, resulting in different types of vinegar. The factors governing the choice of the starting material are availability and cheapness. In France the abundance of cheap wine results in *wine vinegar* being the main variety, while in this country *malt vinegar* is mainly used. In the United States *cider vinegar* is produced in large quantities.

Malt vinegar, as its name implies, is made by fermentation of malt liquor and this stage is followed by bacterial oxidation. The product contains 4–6 per cent acetic acid as well as small quantities of esters, dextrin and various sugars. It is dark brown in colour and if the natural colour is rather light caramel may be added to darken it. When malt vinegar is distilled under reduced pressure a colourless product containing water, acetic acid and other volatile components of the original vinegars is produced. This liquid is diluted with water until its acetic acid content is similar to that of malt vinegar when it is known as *distilled vinegar*. It is used mainly for pickling purposes, particularly where the product to be preserved is light in colour as with vegetables like white onions.

UNSATURATED ACIDS. The fatty acids mentioned so far have all been of the type known as saturated, so called because their carbon atoms are linked together by single bonds. Acids obtained by hydrolysing oils and fats contain, however, a proportion of unsaturated fatty acids, the molecules of which contain one or more double bonds. Unsaturated acids have lower melting points than saturated acids containing the same number of carbon atoms, and the softness of a fat increases with the proportion of combined unsaturated acids which it contains. The simplest and most widely occurring of these acids is *oleic acid* which contains eighteen carbon atoms with one double bond in the centre of the carbon chain. Its name derives from the fact that it is the principal acid obtained when olive oil is hydrolysed. It is also the main acid obtained when human fat is hydrolysed.

It is a curious fact that the majority of unsaturated acids obtained from oils and fats contain eighteen carbon atoms. Whereas some, such as oleic acid, contain one double bond, others such as *linoleic acid* and *linolenic acid* which both occur in linseed oil contain two or more double bonds and are said to be *polyunsaturated*.

The differences in structure between the most important of the acids containing eighteen carbon atoms are shown below:

Stearic acid	$CH_3(CH_2)_{16}COOH$
Oleic acid	$CH_3(CH_2)_7CH = CH(CH_2)_7COOH$
Linoleic acid	$CH_3(CH_2)_4CH = CHCH_2CH = CH(CH_2)_7COOH$
Linolenic acid	$CH_3CH_2CH = CHCH_2CH = CHCH_2CH = CH(CH_2)_7COOH$

Some polyunsaturated fatty acids (PUFA) are known as *essential fatty acids* because they are required by the body in small quantities but cannot be made within the body. Hence they must be supplied by the diet (see p. 79). Linoleic acid (two double bonds), linolenic acid (three double bonds) together with *arachidonic acid* (four double bonds) are all called essential fatty acids, though strictly speaking only linoleic is a dietary essential because both linolenic and arachidonic acids can be made from it within the body.

The place of fatty acids in the diet is considered on page 79.

DICARBOXYLIC ACIDS. Acids containing two carboxyl groups are called *dicarboxylic acids*, the simplest of these being *oxalic acid*, which consists simply of two carboxyl groups joined together: HOOC–COOH. Traces of this acid are found in most fruits and vegetables and it occurs in spinach, rhubarb and beet tops to the extent of about 10 per cent of the total solid matter, mainly in the form of calcium oxalate.

Spinach is often recommended as having exceptional nutritional value on account of the large amount of calcium, iron and vitamin A that it contains. Table 5.4 gives a comparison of the nutrient content of spinach and cabbage, though the vitamin A content of cabbage is variable, because most vitamin A is found in outer leaves, most of which are removed before cooking. Spinach has a larger calcium content than any other vegetable normally eaten. Yet this figure is misleading, because the calcium of spinach is not available for use by the body. This is because the calcium is in the form of calcium oxalate which is insoluble and so is not absorbed by the body. Wherever calcium is found in food combined with oxalic acid it cannot be used by the body. In a similar way much of the iron in spinach is useless as far as the body is concerned. For this reason alone oxalic acid would be an undesirable constituent of the diet, because it would combine with any calcium and iron that were present and render them unavailable. Apart from this, oxalic acid and its soluble sodium and potassium salts are poisonous if present in significant amounts.

Table 5.4. Comparison of Spinach and Cabbage

	Dietary fibre	Calcium mg/100 g	Iron mg/100 g	Retinol equivalent
Boiled spinach	6 g/100 g	595	4·0	1000 μg/100 g
Boiled spring cabbage	2 g/100 g	30	0·4	50 μg/100 g

FUMARIC ACID is an unsaturated dicarboxylic acid with the formula HOOCCH=CHCOOH. It has a pleasant fruit acid flavour and though it has a low solubility it is produced commercially as a mixture of the acid and a wetting agent and in this form it is readily soluble.

HYDROXY ACIDS. The simplest hydroxy acid is hydroxyacetic acid in which one of the hydrogen atoms of the methyl group of acetic acid has been replaced by a hydroxyl group. This acid is also called *glycollic acid*: $HOCH_2COOH$. It is found in the juice of unripe grapes. As it contains both a hydroxyl and a carboxyl group it behaves both as an acid and an alcohol.

The most important hydroxy acid is hydroxypropionic acid or *lactic acid*. This acid is responsible for the sour taste that develops in stored milk. Souring is an enzyme reaction in which the sugar contained in milk, lactose, is converted into lactic acid.

$$C_{12}H_{22}O_{11} + H_2O \xrightarrow[\text{lactic bacilli}]{} 4CH_3CHOHCOOH$$

Lactose   Lactic acid

Lactic acid from sour milk contains equal amounts of the dextro and laevorotatory isomers and because of this it is not optically active. Under natural conditions other enzymes present in the sour milk ferment some of the lactic acid into butyric acid, which imparts to the milk its characteristic rancid smell.

$$2CH_3CHOHCOOH \xrightarrow[\text{butyric bacilli}]{} CH_3CH_2CH_2COOH + 2CO_2 + 2H_2$$

Butyric acid

The same chemical changes also take place in the preparation of fermented milks like yoghourt, and in the production of butter and cheese.

Lactic acid is produced in the body during the breakdown of carbohydrate and is excreted in the urine at the rate of about a tenth of a gram per day.

MALIC ACID and CITRIC ACID are two of the commonest acids found in fruits. Both these acids contain a hydroxyl group and more than one carboxyl group. A third, but less widely occurring fruit acid, contains two carboxyl and two hydroxyl groups and is called *tartaric acid.*

$$\text{CHOHCOOH} \qquad \text{CH}_2\text{COOH} \qquad \text{CHOHCOOH}$$
$$\text{CH}_2\text{COOH} \qquad \text{COHCOOH} \qquad \text{CHOHCOOH}$$
$$\text{CH}_2\text{COOH}$$

Malic acid   Citric acid   Tartaric acid

These acids usually occur in fruit in the form of their potassium salts, but also as free acids, and are responsible for the acid flavour of fresh fruit. Citric acid is the principal acid of citrus fruit and also occurs in pineapples, tomatoes and most summer fruits. Malic acid is optically active and the laevorotatory isomer is found in rhubarb, unripe apples, plums and grapes. Tartaric acid is also optically active and occurs in grapes as the dextrorotatory isomer.

All three acids are produced on a commercial scale and find wide application in food manufacture. Citric and malic acids have very similar properties; they are very soluble in water and have similar dissociation constants—1 per cent solutions have a pH of 2·3. They have similar flavour characteristics and impart a characteristic tart acid flavour to products to which they are added. In addition they cost about the same. Thus they find similar applications in food products and are extensively used in fruit beverages, preserves and boiled sweets. Tartaric acid has a less sharp flavour than citric or malic acids and is added to fruit beverages and preserves. The acid, or more commonly one of its salts, is used in baking powder.

The nutritional value of fruit acids depends upon whether they are absorbed and oxidized in the body. Most of the tartaric acid of grapes, for instance, is not absorbed and so has no effect on the body system. Citric acid, on the other hand, is largely absorbed. It might be supposed therefore that citrus fruits containing citric acid or its potassium salt would act as acid foods, but in practice the opposite is the case. Citrates are oxidized in the body to carbon dioxide and the corresponding bicarbonate salt. Thus potassium citrate is converted into potassium bicarbonate and this salt makes the urine alkaline and assists in buffering the blood and maintaining its pH at just above seven. Citric acid is also formed in the body, and is excreted in the urine at the rate of up to a gram per day.

The Action of Acids as Preservatives

The action of acids as preservatives depends upon their effect on the micro-organisms—bacteria, yeasts and moulds—present in foods. The addition of acid lowers pH by increasing the hydrogen ion concentration and it is found that low pH values often inhibit growth of micro-organisms. Most bacteria grow best at around pH 7, whereas most yeasts are favoured by mildly acid conditions and grow best at pH 4–4·5. Moulds, on the other hand, can tolerate considerable variations of pH and grow in the range 2–8·5 pH, though most are favoured by an acid pH. It is evident that acids may often be used to adjust pH to a value that is toxic to the micro-organisms present in food.

The effectiveness of an acid in lowering pH depends upon its strength, that is the degree to which it is ionized, and its concentration, that is the amount present in a given volume (often expressed as molarity). Thus a strong acid is more effective in lowering pH than the same concentration of a weak one; the relationship between acid strength, as measured by the dissociation constant, and pH is shown in Table 5.3. Thus typical inorganic acids, such as hydrochloric acid, are fully ionized in solution and give a higher hydrogen concentration and lower pH than a similar concentration of a weak acid, such as acetic acid. In spite of this it is found that, for a given hydrogen ion concentration, weak organic acids are more toxic than strong inorganic ones. This suggests that un-dissociated organic acid molecules exert a toxic effect and contribute to the total preservative action of the acid.

Acids which are either naturally present in foods or are produced during fermentation may be freely added to foods to preserve them. *Acetic acid, vinegar, ascorbic acid, citric acid, malic acid, tartaric acid* and *phosphoric acid* all come into this category. Other acids may only be used if they are included in the list of 'permitted preservatives'. *Sulphurous acid, propionic acid, benzoic acid, sorbic acid* and *p-hydroxy benzoic acid esters* are permitted preservatives but may be added only to specified foods and in restricted amounts. Table 5.5 gives examples of their use, and of the various forms in which the preservative may be used.

SULPHUR DIOXIDE, which in solution yields sulphurous acid, has gained a certain respectability as a preservative because it has been used for a very long time. The addition of sulphur dioxide to fermenting grape juice, for example, has been practised for at least five hundred years. Sulphurous acid, H_2SO_3, is a weak acid and it is most effective as a

Table 5.5. The Use of Acids which are 'Permitted Preservatives'

Acid	Other permitted forms	Examples of specified foods	Maximum amount permitted in ppm
Propionic	Na, K, Ca salt	Flour confectionery	1000
		Bread	3000*
Sulphurous	SO_2, Na, K, Ca salt	Fruit juices	350
		Jam	100
Benzoic	Na, Ca, K salt	Fruit juices	800
		Liquid coffee extract	450
p-Hydroxy	Na salt	Pickles	250
benzoic acid esters		Tomato purée	800
Sorbic	Na, K, Ca salt	Cheese	1000
		Flour confectionery	1000

* Calculated on the weight of flour.

preservative if it is added to solutions of low pH; in these conditions it is present largely as the undissociated acid. Thus it is used as a preservative in acid foods such as dried fruit, fruit pulp, fruit juices, jam, alcoholic beverages (wine, beer and cider), soft drinks and pickles.

Sulphurous acid inhibits the growth of bacteria, moulds and yeasts in food and it is therefore an effective preservative; it is used in a wider range of foods than any other permitted preservative. It also has additional advantages; it is a reducing agent and helps to conserve nutrients, such as ascorbic acid, which are easily oxidized and it is a bleaching agent and prevents the development of brown colour by enzyme action in fruits and vegetables. Unfortunately sulphur dioxide suffers from certain disadvantages. For instance, it has a strong taste, and some people can taste and smell as little as 50 ppm. This is not important, however, if the food is to be cooked before being eaten, for heat drives off most of the sulphur dioxide. Fruit used in jam manufacture may contain 3000 ppm of sulphur dioxide, but during boiling most of the sulphur dioxide is expelled and the jam produced must contain not more than 100 ppm. A further disadvantage of sulphur dioxide is that, because of its volatility, the amount present in a food may diminish over a period if the container is repeatedly opened. Moreover, the efficiency of sulphur dioxide as a preservative is reduced by certain components in food, the most important of which are vitamin B_1(thiamine) and sugars. Thiamine is rapidly destroyed by sulphur dioxide, so that it is not a desirable preservative for foods which contain significant amounts of this vitamin; pork sausages which contain sulphites as preservative, contain much less thiamine than was originally present in the pork.

BENZOIC ACID or its sodium or potassium salts are found to be relatively ineffective as preservatives at pH values greater than 5, but their preservative action increases as the pH is lowered below 5. Benzoic acid is a weak acid as can be seen from Table 5.3; its dissociation may be represented: $C_6H_5COOH \rightleftharpoons C_6H_5COO^- + H^+$. The effect of lowering the pH of the medium is to increase the proportion of undissociated acid present. It is evident, therefore, that it is the undissociated acid that exerts the main preservative effect. Benzoic acid is found to be effective in inhibiting the growth of micro-organisms in foods of low pH, and is permitted, for example, in fruit juices, fruit squashes and other soft drinks. Weight for weight benzoic acid is only about half as effective as sulphurous acid, and correspondingly greater amounts are used as can be seen from Table 5.5.

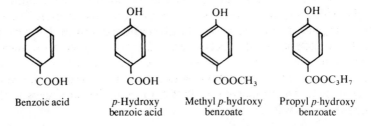

Benzoic acid   *p*-Hydroxy   Methyl *p*-hydroxy   Propyl *p*-hydroxy
                  benzoic acid   benzoate   benzoate

p-HYDROXY BENZOIC ACID has little preservative action but its *methyl, ethyl* and *propyl esters* have a similar preservative effect to benzoic acid, and these three esters are permitted as an alternative to benzoic acid in such products as beer, flavourings, fruit juices, fruit yoghourt, soft drinks, pickles and sauces. The amount of ester permitted is the same as that for benzoic acid.

PROPIONIC ACID and its sodium and calcium salts are found to be effective as preservatives at low pH, suggesting that, as with other organic acids, it is the undissociated acid which is mainly responsible for the preservative effect. In Great Britain they are permitted only in bread and flour confectionery, in which they effectively inhibit the growth of moulds. The temperatures attained during the baking of bread are sufficient to destroy all mould spores and mouldy bread results from the contamination of the loaf after it has been baked. Slow cooling of the bread favours the growth of moulds. Propionic acid and its salts also prevent the development of 'rope' which is the name given to the stringy, soggy, foul-smelling condition produced by the growth of bacteria in the interior of the loaf. Such bacteria are heat-resistant and, in the absence of propionic acid or one of its salts, would survive the baking process.

SORBIC ACID, $CH_3CH=CHCH=COOH$, and its sodium, potassium or calcium salts, are permitted preservatives for several foods, the most important of which are cheese and flour confectionery. Sorbic acid exerts its preservative action at low pH values as it is the undissociated acid that is the effective agent. When added to low pH foods it is effective in inhibiting the growth of yeasts and moulds. It is claimed that this action is selective and that the growth of undesirable micro-organisms is suppressed without interfering with those that are beneficial. For example, mould growth in cheese can be controlled without interfering with the micro-organisms necessary for the maturing process.

Fatty Acids in the Diet

As mentioned on page 73, the polyunsaturated fatty acids linoleic acid, linolenic acid and arachidonic acid are known as essential fatty acids and linoleic acid must be supplied in the diet. The amounts of these acids required by the body is small and they need only form 1–2 per cent of the total energy intake. Deficiency of essential fatty acids is extremely rare; interest in them is more concerned with the fact that they are polyunsaturated acids (PUFA)—and hence have a bearing on health, (see p. 115). The proportion of PUFA to saturated fatty acids in the British diet is 0·2:1.

Table 5.6. Percentage Composition of Fatty Acids in Foods

Food	Saturated	Monounsaturated	Polyunsaturated
Meat			
Beef	48	44	3
Lamb	54	37	4
Pork	36	42	17
Chicken	32	37	26
Liver	34	27	34
Oils and Fats			
Butter	62	30	3
Margarine, soft	32	40	23
Margarine, hard	39	41	15
Olive oil	11	74	10
Corn (Maize) Oil	15	29	51
Eggs	33	45	17
Milk	62	30	3

Chapter Six

Oils, fats and colloids

The three groups of naturally occurring organic compounds which are of fundamental importance in both the animal and vegetable worlds are oils and fats, carbohydrates and proteins. It will be remembered that these three groups are all essential nutrients, without which life would not be possible. As the oil and fat group is the simplest in its molecular architecture, it will be considered first.

Oils and fats belong to a larger group of naturally occurring substances called *lipids*. The lipids form a diverse group of compounds that have little in common except that they are soluble in organic solvents and insoluble in water, and that most of them are derivatives of fatty acids. Oils and fats, *waxes* and *phospholipids* are important examples of lipids that are fatty acid derivatives. *Steroids* are also classified as lipids though they are not fatty acid derivatives and are quite dissimilar in structure to the rest of the group. *Cholesterol* is an important steroid which is present in body tissues and is found in some foods, notably egg-yolk. Other steroids, which are related to cholesterol, are vitamin D and some bile acids. In the remainder of this chapter we shall be concerned with oils and fats, though we shall also encounter one member of the phospholipids, namely *lecithin*.

The distinction between an oil and a fat is simply that at normal temperatures oils are liquid and fats solid. However, this distinction is rather vague, as a 'normal' temperature cannot be accurately defined, and some oils—such as palm oil—are usually solid at the prevailing temperatures of the British climate.

Chemically, fats belong to a class of substances known as *esters*, which result from the reaction of acids with alcohols. We have already encountered them as being partly responsible for the maturing of wines, spirits and malt vinegar. Fats are esters of the trihydric alcohol *glycerol*. The three hydroxyl groups of the glycerol molecule can each combine with a fatty acid molecule and the resulting ester is called a *triglyceride*. The simplest type of triglyceride results when the three acid molecules are all of the same acid. For example, if three molecules of stearic acid react with a molecule of glycerol, the fat formed is *tristearin*:

$$
\begin{array}{ll}
\text{CH}_2\text{OH} & \text{CH}_2\text{OCOC}_{17}\text{H}_{35} \\
| & | \\
\text{CHOH} + 3\text{C}_{17}\text{H}_{35}\text{COOH} \rightleftharpoons \text{CHOCOC}_{17}\text{H}_{35} + 3\text{H}_2\text{O} \\
| & | \\
\text{CH}_2\text{OH} & \text{CH}_2\text{OCOC}_{17}\text{H}_{35}
\end{array}
$$

Glycerol   Stearic acid   Tristearin

Natural oils are almost always mixed triglycerides, each molecule containing more than one type of fatty acid. Most natural oils contain small quantities of a variety of combined fatty acids, although usually two or three predominate.

All oils and fats contain a proportion of combined unsaturated fatty acids, the degree of unsaturation being measured by the oil's *iodine value*. When iodine (in practice the more reactive iodine monochloride is used) is added to a triglyceride formed from an unsaturated fatty acid, it reacts with the double bonds in the molecule, and the degree of unsaturation may be calculated from the amount of iodine absorbed.

$$-\text{CH} = \text{CH} - + \text{I}_2 \longrightarrow -\text{CHI} - \text{CHI} -$$

One molecule of iodine is used to saturate each double bond. The result is usually expressed as the iodine value which is the number of grams of iodine needed to saturate a hundred grams of oil. Iodine values for some oils and fats are shown in Table 6.1.

Table 6.1. The Combined Fatty Acid Content of Oil and Fats

Oil or fat	% Combined fatty acids					Iodine value
	Myristic	*Palmitic*	*Stearic*	*Oleic*	*Linoleic*	
Palm	1	40	4	45	8	48–56
Palm kernel	15	8	2	16	1	14–20
Groundnut		12	5	57	23	84–102
Olive	1	6	4	80	10	80–90
Lard	1	28	8	56	5	47–67
Beef tallow	3	25	24	42	2	35–45
Whale	8	17	1	14	37	110–140
Butter fat	10	30	11	30	3	26–38

Table 6.1 shows the contribution made by some fatty acids in combination with glycerol to some important oils and fats. The total fatty acid content is taken as one hundred, the figures for the individual combined acids being average values, as oils from different places vary in composition. Some other combined acids not shown in the table occur

in these oils and fats. In particular, the triglycerides of whale oil contain some quantities of C_{20} and C_{22} polyunsaturated acids in combination with glycerol, and this accounts for the high iodine value of this oil. The triglycerides of palm kernel oil contain 50 per cent of combined lauric acid.

The physical characteristics of oils and fats are important in many food applications, such as their use in cake and pastry mixes and in mayonnaise and ice-cream. Unlike pure chemical compounds fats do not melt at a fixed temperature but over a range. In this temperature range they are *plastic*, that is they are soft and can be spread, but they do not flow. In other words their properties are intermediate between those of a solid and a liquid.

The plasticity of a fat results from its being a mixture of a number of different triglycerides, each triglyceride having its own melting point. When a large proportion of the triglycerides are below their melting point the mixture is solid and consists of a network of minute crystals surrounded by a smaller quantity of liquid triglycerides. The solid network is not rigid, however, and the crystals can slide over one another, so giving rise to the plastic character of the fat. If the temperature of the fat is raised an increasing proportion of triglycerides melt, the solid network gradually breaks down and the plasticity of the mixture increases until it becomes liquid when all the triglycerides have melted.

The melting point of fats is also affected by the fact that many triglycerides exist in several crystalline forms; that is they are *polymorphic*. Each crystalline form has its own melting point and when oils are cooled mixtures of different crystalline form, and therefore of different melting point, may be obtained depending upon how the cooling was carried out. The way in which an oil is cooled therefore affects the texture and consistency of the product formed. Such considerations are important in commercial methods of fat manufacture.

Table 6.2. World Supplies of Oils and Fats

Vegetable oils %		Animal fats %		Marine oils %	
Soya bean	17·4	Butter fat	13·8	Whale	0·3
Groundnut	11·7	Lard	14·4	Fish	3·5
Sunflower	9·8				
Cottonseed	7·1				
Coconut	7·1				
Olive	4·6				
Others	10·4				
Totals	68·1		28·2		3·8

Natural oils and fats can be classified according to their origin as animal, marine or vegetable. Of these the latter are nowadays the most important as can be appreciated from Table 6.2, which shows that world supplies of vegetable oils and fats are more than double the combined supply from animal and marine sources.

Animal Fats

The two most important animal fats are lard and butter, the latter being considered on page 108 together with other dairy products. Lard is prepared by melting pigs' fat and is about 100 per cent fat. The triglycerides of lard are composed of both saturated and unsaturated fatty acids as shown in Table 6.1. Many years ago lard was used extensively but in the 1950s it suffered a decline, being largely replaced by hydrogenated vegetable oils. Natural lard is a low-melting fat with good properties as a shortening agent, an acceptable white colour and bland flavour, but it suffers from the disadvantage that it has poor creaming properties and is therefore not a desirable fat for cake making. During the 1960s the consumption of lard increased rapidly partly due to its low cost relative to that of vegetable oil and partly to the improvements in its properties which have been achieved by processing.

The properties of lard may be improved by *interesterification* which, as the name implies, involves a rearrangement of the fatty acid units between the triglyceride ester molecules. This regrouping process results in a more random distribution of fatty acids. To understand why this should be so it is necessary to consider the arrangement of fatty acid units in the triglycerides of lard. Lard is peculiar among fats in that the saturated fatty acids, mainly palmitic, are found predominantly in the middle position of the triglyceride molecules. It is this factor which causes lard to form large coarse crystals that prevent it from creaming well.

During interesterification the fatty acid units interchange, thus reducing the proportion of triglyceride molecules with a saturated fatty acid unit in the centre position. This may be illustrated using a simple example. Consider a simple monoglyceride with a saturated fatty acid unit S in the middle position. After interesterification there will be an equilibrium mixture of the two possible forms; i.e. only half the molecules now have a saturated fatty acid unit in the centre position:

$$CH_2OHCHOSCH_2OH \rightleftharpoons CH_2OSCHOHCH_2OH.$$

Interesterification is carried out by heating lard at about $100°C$ in the presence of a catalyst such as sodium ethoxide, $NaOC_2H_5$, and it gives a product with greatly improved creaming properties that makes it suitable for incorporation in margarine and cooking fats.

Marine Oils

Whale and fish oils differ from animal and vegetable oils and fats in that their triglyceride molecules contain a much greater proportion of highly unsaturated acid units. Thus whale oil triglycerides contain about 75 per cent unsaturated acids containing from one to six double bonds, and acids with four or more double bonds account for about 20 per cent of the total acids. This large proportion of highly unsaturated fatty acids is reflected in the high iodine value which is in the range 110–140. Fish oils, such as herring oil, contain an even greater proportion of highly unsaturated fatty acid units and consequently have high iodine values, which may reach about 200.

The highly unsaturated nature of whale and fish oils makes them liable to spoilage (see p. 89) and they are therefore unsuitable for use until they have been processed. Nevertheless in the 1950s processed whale oil found considerable use in margarine and cooking fats while in more recent years processed fish oils have found increasing acceptance, particularly for use in margarine.

Vegetable Oils and Fats

Vegetables constitute the most important source of edible oils and fats. Most vegetable oils are liquid at 20°C, though there are a few notable exceptions such as palm oil, palm kernel oil and coconut oil which melt above this temperature. The relative importance of different vegetable oils can be appreciated from Table 6.2 and the fatty acid composition of several examples is shown in Table 6.1.

Soya beans are grown extensively in China and the USA and soya bean oil is now the most important edible vegetable oil accounting for about a quarter of all vegetable oil supplies. After the oil has been extracted from the bean, the residue left constitutes a valuable source of protein and as such is discussed on page 204. Soya bean oil is the major vegetable oil used in margarine manufacture and large quantities are also used in cooking fats.

Vegetable oils are normally extracted from seeds, kernels and nuts, either by mechanical pressure or by solvents. The latter method involves the use of a liquid solvent of low boiling point in which the oil is soluble. After the seed or nut has been ground, it is shaken with the solvent, the oil is extracted and a solid residue left behind. When the liquid mixture is heated, the low boiling solvent evaporates, leaving the oil. Groundnut oil for example occurs in groundnuts (popularly known as monkey-

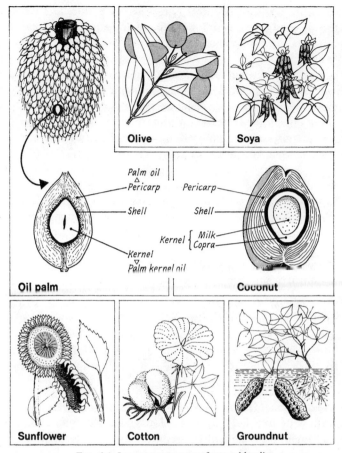

Olive

Soya

Palm oil
△
Pericarp

Pericarp

Shell

Shell

Kernel { Milk
Copra

Kernel
▽
Palm kernel oil

Oil palm

Coconut

Sunflower

Cotton

Groundnut

FIG. 6.1. Important sources of vegetable oils

nuts) to the extent of 45–50 per cent, most of which may be extracted by means of a screw-press which squeezes out the oil. In some modern methods a two-stage process is used. After an initial extraction with the press, an oil solvent is used to extract the remaining oil. The residue that is left behind is not wasted, in fact it is a valuable material owing to its high protein content, and is used as a cattle food.

Another useful source of edible oil is the oil palm tree, which is not to be confused with the more slender coconut palm. The fruit of the palm tree grows in large bunches which may contain over a thousand fruit. Each fruit is rather like a plum, having a thin orange to dark-red skin covering a fleshy interior in which is embedded a hard shell containing the kernel. Palm oil is extracted from the fleshy part of the fruit and palm kernel oil from the kernel. Both these oils are edible, and palm oil is extensively used in this country for the manufacture of margarine and cooking fats. The differences in their composition can be seen from Table 6.1.

The olive also is valuable as a source of oil, over a million tons of olive oil being produced annually. Olive oil is notable for the large proportion of unsaturated acids which it yields on hydrolysis, and also for its purity. The finest olive oil may be used without purification and is used for all manner of purposes in the Mediterranean countries, while in Great Britain it is used as a salad oil.

Refining of Crude Oils

Crude olive oil is exceptional in that it can be used for edible purposes without refining. Most vegetable oils, however, contain a number of impurities such as moisture, free fatty acids, colouring matter, resins, gums and sometimes vitamins. These impurities affect flavour, odour and clarity, and are removed during refining. The refining process is carried out in a number of stages which may be considered in turn.

1 *Degumming*. Crude oils often contain impurities in suspension which in the presence of water form gums. The impurities are removed by adding hot water to the warm oil, which is then transferred to a centrifugal separator. The separator revolves at a high speed and the gum particles, which have a higher density than the oil, are thrown to the bottom of the vessel, leaving an upper layer of clarified oil.

2 *Neutralizing*. Owing to spoilage all crude oils contain a small proportion of free fatty acid and low-grade oils may contain considerable quanities. The acids are removed by neutralizing the oil with a solution of caustic soda, which converts the fatty acid into an insoluble soap. The soap is then removed by allowing it to settle to the bottom of the neutralizing tanks. If the acid impurity is palmitic acid, for example, insoluble *sodium palmitate* is formed:

$$C_{15}H_{31}COOH + NaOH \longrightarrow C_{15}H_{31}COONa\downarrow + H_2O$$
$$\text{Palmitic acid} \qquad\qquad\qquad \text{Sodium palmitate}$$

3 *Washing and drying*. In order to remove the last traces of soap from the oil, it is washed with warm water. Two layers form and the lower water layer is run off, leaving the oil layer, which is then dried under vacuum.

In modern plants these separate stages are being replaced by a continuous automatic process in which the neutralizing stage is carried out very much more quickly in a centrifugal separator.

The oil is now clear and free from acid, but it is usually yellowish in colour and still has a distinct odour. It is, therefore, bleached and deodorized.

4 *Bleaching*. The oil is warmed and *fuller's earth* and activated carbon are added. Both these materials have a large capacity for adsorbing coloured matter. The mixture is stirred and a partial vacuum is maintained. When all the coloured matter has been adsorbed, the oil-earth mixture is passed through filter presses, from which the oil emerges as a clear colourless liquid.

5 *Deodorizing*. The oil is heated under vacuum in a tall tank and steam is injected so that the liquid mixture is violently agitated. In one method it is sprayed upwards as an umbrella-shaped fountain, so that a large surface area of liquid is continually exposed, and the volatile odiferous substances and remaining free fatty acids are stripped from the oil.

The oil is now pure and ready for use, or, as is usually the case, ready for blending. It is desirable that the oil should not come into contact with air once it has been refined, as this leads to deterioration due to oxidation. In some modern plants, therefore, the oil is stored under an inert atmosphere of nitrogen.

Hydrogenation of Oils

Pure vegetable oils play a very small part in British eating habits. Prejudice against 'liquid fats' for cooking may partly account for this, but there is the more practical reason that much of the fat required is for spreading purposes, and for this the predominantly liquid vegetable oils are unsuitable. In these circumstances it is unlikely that even refined vegetable oils would have found much favour without the discovery that oils could be hardened by *hydrogenation*. Hardening is the conversion of an oil into a fat by a chemical method.

Following this discovery, made at the beginning of the present century, there has been a rapid increase in the production of vegetable and marine oils, so much so that our eating habits have suffered a marked change. The consumption of animal fats, once such a staple feature of the diet, has decreased considerably due to increased consumption of hardened vegetable and marine oils.

Hydrogenation is simply the addition of hydrogen to the double bonds of unsaturated fatty acids combined with glycerol in an oil. During hydrogenation one molecule of hydrogen is absorbed by each double bond:

$$-CH=CH-+H_2 \rightarrow -CH_2-CH_2-$$

The most commonly occurring unsaturated fatty acids found in combination with glycerol in vegetable oils, namely oleic, linoleic and linolenic acids, contain one, two and three double bonds respectively. As they all contain eighteen carbon atoms, complete hydrogenation converts them all into stearic acid. Stearic acid has a much higher melting point ($70°$ C) than any of the other three, so the hydrogenated oil is harder than the original. The equation below illustrates the conversion of liquid triolein into solid tristearin which takes place when a molecule of triolein absorbs three molecules of hydrogen:

$$
\begin{array}{ll}
CH_2OCOC_{17}H_{33} & CH_2OCOC_{17}H_{35} \\
| & | \\
CHOCOC_{17}H_{33} + 3H_2 \longrightarrow & CHOCOC_{17}H_{35} \\
| & | \\
CH_2OCOC_{17}H_{33} & CH_2OCOC_{17}H_{35} \\
\text{Triolein} & \text{Tristearin}
\end{array}
$$

Hydrogenation only proceeds at a reasonably fast rate in the presence of a catalyst, finely divided nickel being used industrially. The nickel is usually made by reducing finely divided nickel carbonate or nickel formate. The catalyst is added in small quantities to the oil, which is contained in large closed steel vessels called converters, operating at a temperature of about $170°C$ and 4 atmospheres pressure. The oil is stirred and hydrogen gas is pumped in. The oil is heated to start the reaction, but as the reaction is exothermic, further heating is not necessary. After hydrogenation the oil is cooled and filtered to remove the nickel which can be re-used.

The way in which a catalyst affects a reaction was considered in Chapter 2 and it will be recalled that catalysts reduce the energy required for a reaction to proceed, i.e. the energy of activation; reference to Fig. 2.2 on page 17 will serve as a reminder of this. Nickel, like enzymes, catalyses a reaction by providing a surface upon which the reaction can take place, and converts a single step high energy mechanism into one involving several low energy stages.

The first stage of hydrogenation is the adsorption of reactants, in this case hydrogen and oil, on to the nickel surface. Adsorption takes place only at certain preferred parts of the surface known as *active centres* and results in the adsorbed hydrogen and oil molecules being brought close to each other. Exchange of energy between the nickel and the reacting molecules weakens the internal bonds of the latter and activates them sufficiently to provide them with the necessary energy of activation. Reaction occurs after which the hydrogenated oil molecules are desorbed, i.e. leave the nickel surface which is then available to catalyse further reaction. These stages of hydrogenation are illustrated in Fig. 6.2.

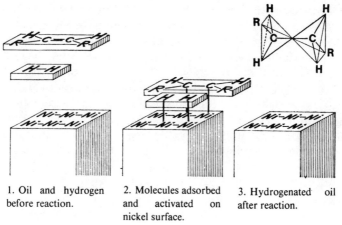

1. Oil and hydrogen before reaction.

2. Molecules adsorbed and activated on nickel surface.

3. Hydrogenated oil after reaction.

FIG. 6.2. The catalytic action of nickel in the hydrogenation of an oil

Surface catalysts, such as nickel, are easily poisoned by substances which are adsorbed in preference to the hydrogen and oil molecules. Carbon monoxide and sulphur compounds, if present in even minute quantities, poison the catalyst owing to their strong adsorption by the nickel. This means that the hydrogen gas, which is often produced from water gas (a mixture of carbon monoxide and hydrogen), must be most carefully purified before use and that the oil to be used must be carefully refined before hydrogenation.

Hydrogenation is a selective process, some triglycerides becoming saturated more rapidly than others. The most unsaturated triglycerides are partially hydrogenated before the less unsaturated ones react, so that in terms of the fatty acids combined in the triglycerides more linolenic acid is converted into linoleic in a given time than linoleic into oleic. The relative rates of reaction of oleic, linoleic and linolenic are in the ratio 1:20:40. This fact enables the hydrogenation to be controlled, and food oils are only partially saturated with hydrogen. This is important from a nutritional point of view, because some unsaturated acids are needed but cannot be produced by the body. These essential unsaturated acids must, therefore, be supplied in the diet. Also complete hydrogenation would make fats too hard and lacking in plasticity for use in food preparation. Apart from its hardening effect, hydrogenation is advantageous in that it also bleaches the oil and increases its stability.

Rancidity

Oils and fats are liable to spoilage which results in the production of unpleasant odours and flavours; such spoilage is usually described by the general term *rancidity*. Different types of oil and fat show varying degrees of resistance to spoilage; thus most vegetable oils deteriorate only slowly whereas animal fats deteriorate more rapidly and marine oils, which contain a relatively high proportion of highly unsaturated fatty acid radicals, deteriorate so rapidly that they are useless for edible purposes unless they have been refined and hydrogenated.

Spoilage may occur in many ways, but two important types of rancidity may be distinguished, namely *hydrolytic rancidity* and *oxidative rancidity*. Hydrolytic rancidity occurs as a result of hydrolysis of triglyceride molecules to glycerol and free fatty acids and it is brought about by the presence of moisture in oils. The rate of hydrolysis in the presence of water alone is negligible, but it is hastened by the presence of enzymes and micro-organisms. Oils and fats that have not been subjected to heat treatment may contain lipases which catalyse hydrolysis. They may also contain moulds, yeasts and bacteria present in the natural oil or they may become contaminated with them during processing. Such micro-organisms hasten hydrolytic breakdown.

The nature of the unpleasant flavours and odours produced by hydrolysis depends upon the fatty acid composition of the triglycerides. If the triglycerides contain fatty acid groups of low molecular weight containing 4–14 carbon atoms, hydrolysis yields free acids having characteristically unpleasant odours and flavours. For example, hydrolysis of butter yields the rancid-smelling butyric acid, while palm kernel oil yields considerable amounts of lauric and myristic acids. Oils containing combined fatty acids with more than 14 carbon atoms are not liable to hydrolytic rancidity as the free acids are flavourless and odourless.

Oxidative rancidity is the most common and important type of rancidity and it results in the production of rancid or 'tallowy' flavours. It is caused by the reaction of unsaturated oils with oxygen and its occurrence does not depend, therefore, on the presence of impurities or moisture in an oil; it can consequently affect pure and refined oils. The actual mechanism of the oxidation is complex and not completely elucidated, but the main features are known and are as follows.

The oxidation of oils takes place by means of a *chain reaction*; that is it occurs in three stages called *initiation*, *propagation* and *termination*, the propagation steps being regenerating so that the reaction is self-perpetuating. Moreover, as the activation energy of the propagation steps is low, the rate of the reaction is very fast indeed. Triglycerides containing unsaturated fatty acid radicals are susceptible to oxidation and this is because the reaction involves methylene groups adjacent to double bonds. We can represent such molecules by RH, H being a hydrogen atom of the methylene group adjacent to a double bond. The reaction sequence may be represented as follows:

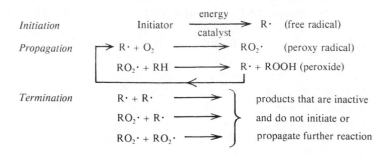

Initiation   Initiator $\xrightarrow[\text{catalyst}]{\text{energy}}$ R· (free radical)

Propagation   R· + O₂ ——————→ RO₂· (peroxy radical)

RO₂· + RH ——————→ R· + ROOH (peroxide)

Termination   R· + R· ——————→ ⎤ products that are inactive

RO₂· + R· ——————→ ⎬ and do not initiate or

RO₂· + RO₂· ——————→ ⎦ propagate further reaction

The reaction is initiated by the production of free radicals, that is groups containing an unpaired electron, the latter being represented above by a dot. The initiation step has a high energy of activation and involves the removal of a hydrogen atom from unsaturated triglyceride molecules. The energy of activation may be provided by heat or light and the initiation is catalysed by traces of metals, particularly copper.

The initiation step is relatively slow but the propagation steps are rapid and result in the formation of peroxides. For every free radical R· used up another is generated, so the reaction is self-perpetuating. The peroxides formed break down into aldehydes and ketones, which are responsible for the off-flavours of rancid fats.

The reaction may continue until all the oxygen or oil has been used up, but it may be terminated by the combination of the free radicals responsible for the propagation stage.

The control of rancidity by the use of anti-oxidants is considered in Chapter 13.

COLLOIDAL SYSTEMS

The physical nature of a solution is familiar enough and an aqueous sugar solution, for example, is known to consist of sugar molecules dispersed through water, the whole system being homogeneous. If we consider what happens when we add to water a substance consisting of very large molecules, such as a starch or a protein, we find that the system formed is *not* homogeneous but consists of two distinct parts or *phases*. The large molecules dispersed through water form one phase, known as the *disperse phase* and the water forms the other phase, known as the *continuous phase*, the complete system being described as *colloidal*.

A colloidal solution is usually called a *sol* and contains particles—consisting of single large molecules or groups of smaller molecules—that are intermediate in size between small molecules and visible particles. Such systems have properties that are intermediate between those of true solutions and suspensions of visible particles.

Table 6.3. Types of Colloidal Systems

Disperse phase	Continuous phase	Name	Examples
Solid	Liquid	Sol	Starch and proteins in water
Liquid	Liquid	Emulsion	Milk, mayonnaise
Gas	Liquid	Foam	Whipped cream, creamed fat, beaten egg-white
Gas	Solid	Solid foam	Ice-cream, bread
Liquid	Solid	Gel	Jellies, jam, starch paste
		Solid emulsion	Butter, margarine

All types of colloidal systems are similar to sols in that they contain two distinct phases and in that the disperse phase contains particles intermediate in size between small molecules and visible particles. The disperse phase may be solid, liquid or gaseous, but in every case the properties of colloidal systems depend upon the very large surface area of the disperse phase. The types of colloidal systems which are important in food are summarized in Table 6.3, and will be considered in the following pages.

Emulsions and Emulsifying Agents

When oil is added to water it forms a separate layer above the water; that is oil and water do not dissolve in each other and are said to be *immiscible*. If oil and water are shaken vigorously the two liquids become dispersed in each other and an *emulsion* is said to be formed. Such an emulsion is unstable, however, and on standing it reverts to the original two layers. Emulsions are described as being either oil-in-water (o/w) or water-in-oil (w/o) emulsions. An o/w emulsion is one in which small oil droplets form the disperse phase and are dispersed through the water (see Fig. 6.3), whereas a w/o emulsion is one in which small water droplets are dispersed through the oil.

Although food emulsions are described as being either o/w or w/o, these terms may be misleading in that the oil and water may contain other substances. Thus in addition to triglycerides the oil phase may contain other lipids and fat-soluble materials and the water phase may,

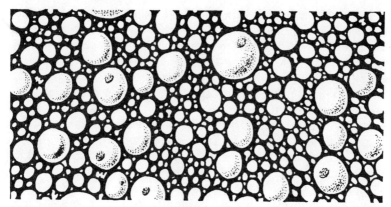

FIG. 6.3. Diagram of an oil-in-water emulsion based on a photomicrograph. The diameter of the oil droplets (light shading) is in the range 10^{-4}–10^{-6} mm

for example, be vinegar or milk. Table 6.4 gives details of some important food emulsions.

Why is it that once water drops have been dispersed in oil they come together again and form a continuous water layer? The answer is to be found in the fact that the action of dispersing water through oil in the form of drops increases the area of oil and water in contact. In order to do this, work must be done against the force of surface tension which causes a liquid to assume minimum surface area. The natural tendency is, therefore, for the water drops to coalesce, for by so doing the interfacial area is decreased and a more stable system is produced.

In order for oil and water to form a stable emulsion a third substance called an *emulsifying agent* or *emulsifier* must be present. Although the complete mechanism by which emulsifiers facilitate the formation of stable emulsions is complex, variable and incompletely understood, an outline of the main factors can be given.

Table 6.4. Examples of Food Emulsions

Example	Type	Main emulsifiers present or added
Milk, cream	o/w	Proteins (caseinogen)
Butter	w/o	Proteins (caseinogen)
Mayonnaise, salad cream	o/w	Egg yolk (lecithin), GMS, mustard
Margarine	w/o	Proteins (caseinogen), lecithin, GMS
Ice-cream	o/w	Proteins (caseinogen), GMS, plus stabilizers (gelatin, gums, alginates)

If the surface tension between oil and water, known as *interfacial tension*, is great, it is difficult for a stable emulsion to be formed. Emulsifiers lower interfacial tension by becoming adsorbed at the oil–water interface and forming a film one molecule thick round each droplet. The adsorbed film prevents the droplets from coalescing and, in some instances, may form a film which, by virtue of its mechanical strength, imparts stability. For example, protein emulsifiers are notable for the mechanical strength of the adsorption film which they produce. If an emulsifier contains charged groups the adsorption process gives rise to charged droplets which repel each other. Such droplets will not coalesce and this factor therefore promotes emulsion stability.

Emulsifying agents are substances whose molecules contain both a *hydrophilic* or 'water-loving' group and a *hydrophobic* or 'water-hating' group. The hydrophilic group is polar and is attracted to the water while the non-polar hydrophobic group, which is frequently a long chain hydrocarbon group, is attracted to the oil. Thus in a w/o emulsion the emulsifier is adsorbed in such a way that the polar 'heads' of the emulsifier molecules are in the water and the non-polar 'tails' stick out into the oil as shown in Fig. 6.4a.

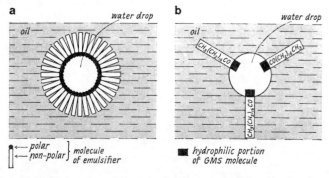

FIG. 6.4. (a) Molecules of emulsifier adsorbed at a water-oil interface forming a complete protective film round a water droplet; and (b) The adsorption of glyceryl monostearate in a w/o emulsion

The type of emulsion formed by an oil–water system depends upon a number of factors including the composition of the oil and water phases, the chemical nature of the emulsifying agent and the proportions of oil and water present. If the polar group of an emulsifier is more effectively adsorbed than the non-polar group, adsorption by the water is greater than by the oil. The extent of adsorption at a liquid surface depends upon the surface area of liquid available and increased adsorption of emulsifier by water is favoured by the oil–water interface becoming convex towards the water, thus giving on o/w emulsion.

The relative proportions of oil and water also help to determine whether an o/w or w/o emulsion is formed. If more oil than water is present the water tends to form droplets and a w/o emulsion is formed. On the other hand if more water than oil is present an o/w emulsion is favoured.

Many substances show some activity as emulsifying agents and among naturally occurring ones phospholipids, proteins and complex carbohydrates such as gums, pectins and starches are important. Natural food emulsions are often stabilized by proteins and milk, for example, is stabilized by the caseinogen and other proteins present. Artificial emulsifiers are added during the preparation of many emulsions, though in Great Britain only those on a permitted list, see page 341, may be used. Of these *glyceryl monostearate* (GMS) is the most important and will serve as an example.

GMS is a monoglyceride which is formed when one hydroxyl group of glycerol is esterified with stearic acid as shown in the following equation:

$$
\begin{array}{l}
CH_2OH \\
| \\
CHOH + CH_3(CH_2)_{16}COOH \longrightarrow \\
| \\
CH_2OH
\end{array}
\qquad
\begin{array}{l}
CH_2OH \\
| \\
CHOH \\
| \\
CH_2O-\boxed{CO(CH_2)_{16}CH_3}
\end{array}
\qquad + H_2O
$$

hydrophobic portion
of glyceryl monostearate

One part of the GMS molecule is hydrophilic because it contains hydroxyl groups and the rest of the molecule, as indicated in the formula, is hydrophobic. When GMS is added to a w/o emulsion, the hydrophilic parts of the molecules are absorbed into the surface of the water droplets and the lipophilic parts are absorbed into the surface of the oil round the drops, as illustrated in Fig. 6.4b.

Commercial GMS is not a single substance and in addition to glyceryl monostearate it contains some di- and triglycerides. It is widely used in food manufacture and is added, for example, to margarine, mayonnaise, salad dressing and ice-cream.

The phospholipid *lecithin* is an important natural emulsifier which favours o/w emulsions and which is present in egg yolk and many crude oils, particularly vegetable oils. Lecithin is extracted from vegetable oils, notably soya bean oil, and added to some manufactured products. The structure of lecithin, given below, shows that it is a triglyceride of two fatty acids and phosphoric acid:

$$
\text{Lecithin}
\begin{array}{l}
CH_2OCOR^1 \\
\mid \\
CHOCOR^2 \\
\mid \\
CH_2O \; POR^3
\end{array}
$$

R^1 and R^2 = long chain hydrophobic groups

$R^3 = CH_2CH_2\overset{+}{N}(CH_3)_3$

hydrophilic group

Sometimes *stabilizers* are added to products in addition to emulsifiers, their function being to maintain an emulsion once it has been formed. Such substances improve the stability of emulsions mainly by increasing their viscosity. As viscosity increases, the freedom of movement of the dispersed droplets of the emulsion is reduced and this lessens the chance of their coming into contact and coalescing. Stabilizers are high molecular weight compounds, usually proteins, such as gelatin, or complex carbohydrates, such as pectins, starches, alginates and gums. For example starch or flour may be added to thicken gravies, sauces and salad cream and several stabilizers, such as gelatin and gums, are added to ice-cream.

Uses of Emulsifying Agents

A number of natural foods are emulsions—milk is the prime example—and are stabilized by emulsifiers which are present as constituents of the food. Here we are concerned, however, not with natural foods but with manufactured foods to which emulsifiers are added. Emulsifiers are added to several products containing fat, such as margarine, cooking fats, salad dressings and ice-cream.

MAYONNAISE AND SALAD CREAM. Emulsifiers play an important part in making salad cream and mayonnaise, which are o/w emulsions. The term salad cream means, according to the legal definition, 'any smooth, thick stable emulsion of vegetable oil, water, egg or egg yolk and an acidifying agent with or without the addition of one or more of the following substances, namely vinegar, lemon juice, salt, spices, sugar, milk, milk products, mustard, edible starch, edible gums and other minor ingredients and permitted additives'. The minimum proportions of vegetable oil and egg yolk solids that are allowed in Great Britain are 25 per cent and 1·35 per cent respectively.

In Great Britain the legal standards for mayonnaise are the same as those for salad cream and this gives rise to the confusing situation that two products with different names can be identical. In practice, mayonnaise is normally thicker than salad cream and contains a higher proportion of both oil and egg yolk. Indeed in many countries the oil content of mayonnaise must be greater than that of salad cream. In America, for example, mayonnaise must contain at least 60 per cent oil (compared with 30 per cent for salad cream) and in certain countries as much as 80 per cent is required.

The finest oil for making salad cream is undoubtedly olive oil though, because of its high cost, other vegetable oils are normally used. Such oils must be of high purity, light colour and bland flavour and they are therefore refined, bleached and deodorized before use. As they must also be liquid, vegetable oils such as groundnut oil, soya bean oil, cottonseed oil and maize oil are employed.

Salad cream should be viscous and have a creamy consistency and this can only be achieved if the o/w emulsion is stable. In order to produce such a product emulsifying agents must be present, the chief one being lecithin contained in egg yolk. In addition, mustard and often GMS are added and these are both effective emulsifiers. The stability of the emulsion formed is increased by the addition of stabilizers which increase viscosity. Such an increase in viscosity becomes increasingly important the smaller the oil content, and is brought about by the addition of starches and gums.

ICE-CREAM. Present day ice-cream is one of the triumphs of food technology and is noteworthy as the only major food product in which air is the principal ingredient. Without air ice-cream would simply be a frozen milk ice, but with air it becomes a highly complex colloidal system. It consists of a solid foam of air cells surrounded by emulsified fat together with a network of minute ice crystals that are surrounded by watery liquid in the form of a sol.

Ice-cream is made from fat, non-fat milk solids, sugar, emulsifiers, stabilizers, flavourings and colour. A typical ice-cream might contain 12 per cent fat, 11 per cent non-fat milk solids, 15 per cent sugar and about 1 per cent minor ingredients, the rest being water. During processing air is incorporated and accounts for about half the volume of the final product; as ice-cream is sold by volume this latter point is not unimportant! In Great Britain ice-cream must contain a minimum of 5 per cent fat and $7\frac{1}{2}$ per cent non-fat milk solids and to be classified as a 'dairy' ice-cream all the fat must be milk fat. 'Non-dairy' ice-cream contains suitable vegetable fats, such as hydrogenated coconut oil.

In the manufacture of ice-cream the ingredients are mixed together, pasteurized (see p. 314) and homogenized. The latter treatment, together with the added emulsifiers, produces a stable o/w emulsion. The emulsion passes into a freezer in which the temperature is reduced sufficiently partly to freeze the mixture; at the same time air is whipped in. A solid film forms on the walls of the freezer and this is continuously scraped off and taken to a room in which the temperature is reduced further; this causes the rest of the water to freeze and the product to harden.

Fat plays an important role in determining the texture of ice-cream, and also flavour if milk fat is used. Fat converts the ice-cream mix into an o/w emulsion and when air is incorporated into the mixture it aids the formation and stabilization of a foam by forming a stable fat film round the air bubbles. The main components of the aqueous phase of the emulsion are sugar and non-fat solids. The latter are important because they contain proteins which are natural emulsifiers in ice-cream. During pasteurization the milk proteins become denatured (see p. 186) and form a solid film of considerable strength round the oil droplets. This prevents the oil droplets from coalescing and thus stabilizes the emulsion.

An important function of synthetic stabilizers added to ice-cream is to increase viscosity rather than aid emulsification. Gelatin, gums and alginates are all used and help to promote the firm texture, smooth taste and good-keeping qualities associated with modern ice-cream. These stabilizers also assist the formation of a weak network of hydrated molecules through the ice-cream and this gives a firm-textured product which is slow-melting and resistant to the formation of large ice crystals. The use of gelatin exemplifies this.

Gelatin molecules are large, have a thread-like shape and are hydrophilic. When gelatin is added to the ice-cream mix its long, thin molecules are dispersed through the emulsion, and water molecules are attracted and held at the large surface area of gelatin exposed. In this way the water molecules lose their freedom of movement, and melting, which occurs when the freedom of movement of molecules suddenly increases, is made more difficult. The gelatin molecules, by forming a three-dimensional mesh or *gel*, also give added firmness to the structure.

When an ice-cream emulsion is frozen, ice crystals are formed. If ice-cream is to give a sensation of smoothness when it melts in the mouth the size of the crystals must be very small. Because gelatin molecules are dispersed through the emulsion and because of their hydrophilic nature, they ensure that the water molecules are also dispersed. In this way the appearance of large ice crystals, which can only be formed when large numbers of water molecules come together, is prevented.

Margarine

Margarine is made from a w/o emulsion, the aqueous phase being fat-free milk and the oil phase being a blend of vegetable, animal and marine oils. The two phases are mixed together and, with the aid of suitable emulsifiers, a stable emulsion is formed. The emulsion is processed until it forms a solid product having the desired consistency.

1 The oil blend. Several different oils are blended together in preparing the oil phase. The proportions of different types of oil which are used have changed considerably in recent years, the use of animal and marine oils having increased at the expense of vegetable oils. The overall proportions of animal, vegetable and marine oils used at present are roughly in the ratio 1:2:2, lard being the predominant animal fat, soya bean and palm oils being the principal vegetable oils and anchovy and herring oils being the predominant fish oils.

It is important that the oil phase should have a bland taste and a wide plastic range; to achieve the former oils are carefully refined and to achieve the latter some are hydrogenated. It has already been pointed out that in order to have suitable plasticity both liquid and solid triglycerides must be present. In margarine the desired liquid:solid ratio is obtained by selective hydrogenation of the oils used. After hydrogenation oils are refined again as shown in Fig. 6.5 and pass to the blending tank in which they are heated until they are all liquid.

2 The aqueous blend. The skimmed milk is matured after pasteurization by adding a 'starter' in the form of lactic acid bacteria, and the ripening and souring is allowed to continue until the desired flavour is produced. Small amounts of other materials are added to the ripened milk and these have an important influence on the nature of the final product. Artificial flavouring and colouring agents, vitamins A and D and salt are all added.

3 Emulsification. The oil and aqueous phases together with emulsifying agents, such as lecithin and GMS, are now mixed together in large cylindrical tanks. These are fitted with two sets of paddles which rotate in opposite directions and mix the fluids until they form a stable emulsion, which has the appearance of a thick cream.

4 Processing the emulsion. The emulsion is now passed on to a roller which slowly revolves and which is cooled internally. When the emulsion comes into contact with the cold surface of the roller it is rapidly cooled and converted into a solid film. The film is scraped off the roller, and after being stored for about a day it is worked until it gains a smooth even

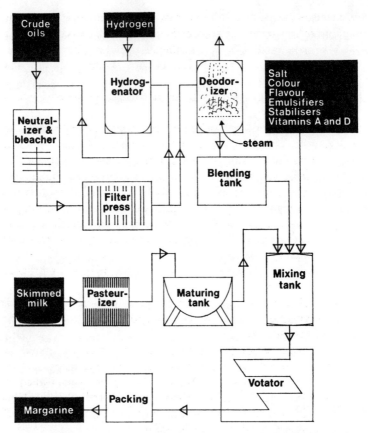

FIG. 6.5. Stages in the manufacture of margarine by the 'Votator' Method

texture. This involves breaking up the structure of the flakes of fat, by passing it through rollers and by kneading it.

In the more modern continuous process, using a machine known as a 'Votator', the emulsifying and processing stages follow one another directly and take place in closed machines. This enables a great saving in time to be made, and prevents the margarine from coming into contact with air.

All that remains to be done now is to pack the margarine, which in these days of prepacked foods and self-service stores involves weighing it into blocks, wrapping and labelling it. The label must state that the product is margarine and give the vitamin content and the butter content (if butter has been added).

A COMPARISON OF MARGARINE AND BUTTER. The objective of margarine manufacturers has always been to make a product closely resembling butter. The main factors to be considered in judging the degree of success that has been achieved are: colour, flavour, texture and nutritional value.

The difference in colour between butter and margarine is now so small that it is not noticeable.

The flavour of butter is very difficult to reproduce. It is considered to be partly due to *diacetyl*, $CH_3COCOCH_3$, which is formed in small quantities during the souring of milk. During margarine manufacture various flavourings are introduced in an effort to produce a butter-like flavour, and success in this respect has been considerable though not complete. The souring of the milk is carefully controlled and ripening is stopped when the desired degree of flavour has been produced. The flavour of the sour milk is reinforced by the addition of mixtures containing diacetyl.

The texture of margarine can be varied to suit particular requirements, and this gives it a distinct advantage over butter, the composition of which is not subject to accurate control so that it becomes inconveniently soft in warm weather, and too hard for spreading in cold weather.

Margarine produced by early methods was significantly inferior to butter in its vitamin content, and all table margarine now manufactured contains added vitamin A and D. The vitamin content is controlled by law so that it contains $900\mu g/100 g$ vitamin A (as retinol equivalent) and $8\mu g/100 g$ vitamin D. This means that the vitamin content of margarine is equal to that of summer butter.

The energy values of butter and margarine are very similar being about 3000 kJ/100 g. This figure applies to good fresh butter containing 85 per cent fat, and will be rather less if the moisture content of the butter is greater. The amount of water in butter is limited, however, the maximum allowed being 16 per cent; a similar limitation also applies to margarine.

In all respects, except perhaps flavour, margarine is as valuable a food as butter, and it is superior to butter in that its texture can be controlled more accurately. In spite of this, margarine was for many years regarded as a poor man's substitute for butter, rather than as a food in its own right. It is pleasing that this prejudice seems to have disappeared, and that the merits of margarine are now more fully appreciated. The inferiority of flavour of margarine, as compared with that of butter, has been remedied in some newer products now available. Some manufacturers attempt to improve the flavour of their product by the addition of butter, though the addition of more than 10 per cent butter is prohibited by law.

Cooking Fats

Cooking fats, or *shortenings* as they are sometimes called, differ from margarine in that they are pure fat products rather than solid emulsions. At the present time the oil blend is made up of about one third of each of the three types of oil—vegetable, animal and mineral—though the pattern is a constantly changing one. The most important individual oils used are palm oil, lard and fish oil. They are partially hydrogenated so as to give a product having the required plasticity and after refining and blending, the fat blend is cooled and processed in a 'votator'-type of machine, similar to that used in making margarine. After the oil blend has been cooled down it is a near-white solid but, during processing, air is sometimes incorporated and it is transformed into a pure white thick creamy liquid. While in a liquid condition it may be forced under pressure through a texturizing valve which ensures that on cooling the product sets into a smooth-textured soft mass.

SUPERGLYCERINATED FATS AND THEIR USE IN CAKE MAKING. Domestic cooking fats have a variety of uses but in the bakery trade cooking fats are often required for specific purposes, such as cake making, and these incorporate an emulsifier. Such fats are called *superglycerinated* or *high ratio* fats, the copyright of the latter term being held by the American company, Proctor and Gamble. The emulsifying agent most frequently used is glyceryl monostearate. The efficiency of such a fat is measured in terms of its creaming, emulsifying and shortening powers.

The creaming power of a fat is measured by its capacity for incorporating air bubbles when it is beaten up. This power is dependent upon the plastic properties of the fat which enable it to entrap air bubbles within its structure without loss of mechanical strength, which would certainly occur if it were in a liquid condition. In the first stage of making a rich type of cake, fat is warmed to increase its plasticity and then the softened fat is creamed with sugar by beating the two together until sufficient air becomes trapped in the mixture. This entrapped air assists the action of baking powder in the aeration of the cake during baking and has an important influence on the volume and evenness of texture of the final product.

When creaming of the fat and sugar is complete, eggs are usually beaten into the mixture and mixing is continued until the whole is light and foamy. The result is an emulsion, usually of the o/w type, because egg yolk tends to emulsify fat as an o/w emulsion. The emulsion is stabilized by the lecithin of the egg yolk and the GMS of the superglycerinated fat. The presence of the GMS greatly increases the stability of the emulsion and enables a large amount of water to be emulsified with the fat. As the amount of sugar that can be used depends on how much water there is to dissolve it, the use of high ratio fats enables cakes of high sugar and moisture content to be produced. Looking at it in another way a cake having a certain sugar and moisture content can be produced using less of a superglycerinated fat than of a normal cooking fat. This has led to the term 'fat extender' being used to describe such a fat.

After eggs have been beaten into the mixture, flour and baking powder (and milk if it is used) are added. A foam is created, each tiny air bubble being surrounded by an oil film which, at this stage, is not very strong. When the cake mixture is put into the oven, the air and water vapour trapped within the bubbles expand due to the rise in temperature. If the cake is to rise evenly during baking to give it the desired lightness of texture, the foam must be stable. Rupture of the oil films will produce the familiar 'sad' or 'sinking' effect. The protein of the egg white acts both as a *foaming* agent and a foam *stabilizer*. The protein becomes adsorbed on to the interface between the air and the oil film, and as the temperature rises and the bubble expands, the protein stiffens or coagulates, so forming a rigid wall round the bubble. This prevents the bubble from bursting and also prevents the production of very big bubbles which would spoil the evenness of the texture. If the ratio of fat to egg is too high, the foam structure is weak and during baking some bubbles break and the cake sinks.

As already indicated a fat must not only act as a creaming and emulsifying agent but also as a 'shortener'. This function is of primary importance in the production of biscuits and shortbread but is also an important factor in cake-making. Fat coats the starch and gluten of the flour with an oily film so breaking up the structure and preventing the formation of a tough mass. This leads to a cake which has a tender and 'short' crumb, whereas the use of too little fat produces a cake which is tough and of poor keeping quality. The greater the proportion of fat in the mixture the greater is the shortening effect.

If a cooking fat is to be an effective shortening agent it must have good plasticity because this enables it to spread over a large area of flour, coating the surface with a film of oil. Such a fat must be neither too hard, in which case it will have poor spreading power, nor too liquid as with an oil, in which case it tends to form globules rather than a film. In other words a soft fat is required; this may be achieved by suitable blending of the oils used in manufacture. Blends which contain a high proportion of unsaturated triglycerides have better shortening power than those composed of mainly saturated fats. The presence of monoglycerides, such as the GMS added to superglycerinated fats, and diglycerides, also improves shortening power.

DAIRY PRODUCTS

Milk

Milk is a food of outstanding interest. In the first place it is designed by nature to be a complete food for very young animals. Its extremely high nutritional value is a consequence of this and cow's milk—which is the only type to be discussed—is not only a complete food for young calves but is also an excellent food for babies and young children and a valuable food for adults. In the second place milk is an interesting and complex colloidal system, the properties of which are of great practical importance in making butter and cheese and in other ways of processing milk. The complexity of this colloidal system can be judged from the fact that, in spite of much research, there is still much that is not fully understood.

Milk is an o/w emulsion containing $3\frac{1}{2}$–4 per cent fat. In addition to milk fat the fat phase contains fat-soluble vitamins and the aqueous phase contains proteins, mineral salts, sugar (lactose) and water-soluble vitamins. The composition of different specimens of milk may show some variation with such factors as breed of cow, the nature of its food and the season of year. The figures which are given in Table 6.5 are, therefore, average values which refer to fresh summer milk. Winter milk contains only about half as much vitamin A as summer milk. The table also shows the percentage contribution made to the nutritional allowances of a man and a child by one pint of fresh milk each day, assuming that proteins contribute to energy. The figures given indicate the importance of milk as a source of calcium and riboflavine: they also show why milk is regarded as such a valuable food, for it makes contributions to every class of nutrient. The main nutrients in which fresh milk is deficient are iron, nicotinic acid and vitamin D, while milk as received by the consumer may also be deficient in ascorbic acid.

THE FAT OF MILK is in the form of minute droplets, most of which have diameters of 5–10 micron (1 micron is 10^{-4} cm). The oil droplets are so small that a single drop of milk contains several million of them and the fact that milk fat is so highly emulsified makes it particularly easy to

Table 6.5. Composition of Fresh Summer Milk and its Contribution to the Diet

Nutrient	Amount in 100 g milk	% Contributions to nutrient allowances by 1 pint of milk daily	
		Man with daily allowance of 12·6 MJ	Girl 3–4 years with daily allowance of 6·2 MJ
Energy	274 kJ	13	25
Protein	3·3 g	22	34
Carbohydrate	4·8 g	4	8
Fat	3·8 g	6	12
Water	88 g	—	—
Solids, not fat	8·8 g	—	—
Calcium	120 mg	86	69
Iron	0·01 mg	1	2
Vitamin A	44 μg	17	29
Thiamine	35 μg	17	33
Nicotinic acid	90 μg	4	9
Riboflavine	150 μg	48	95
Ascorbic acid	1 mg	55	75
Vitamin D	< 0·1 μg	—	3 (max.)

digest; it is digested more easily than any other fat. Milk fresh from the cow contains uniformly distributed oil droplets but when milk is allowed to stand the oil droplets, being lighter than the aqueous phase, tend to rise to the surface and form a layer of cream. As the oil droplets rise they coalesce and form larger droplets but the emulsion does not break down.

Milk may be *homogenized* by forcing it through a small hole under pressure. This breaks up the oil droplets and reduces their size to 1–2 microns. This may not sound like a dramatic reduction in size but it increases the number of droplets by a factor of about 500 and results in a tremendous increase in surface area of fat. Such treatment has a considerable effect on the properties of milk; for example it prevents the cream from separating out and it gives the milk a higher viscosity and richer taste. Homogenized milk coagulates more easily and has greater proneness to off-flavours and rancidity than unhomogenized milk.

Milk, whether homogenized or not, is a stable emulsion and the fat/water interface is stabilized by adsorbed natural emulsifiers present in the milk. The main emulsifer is protein which is adsorbed round each oil droplet forming a protective monolayer, but other emulsifiers such as phospholipids (e.g. lecithin) and vitamin A also play a part.

THE PROTEINS OF MILK consist of molecules which are so large that single molecules constitute colloidal particles dispersed through the aqueous phase of the emulsion, i.e. as a sol. The most important proteins in milk are *caseinogen* (2·6 per cent), *lactalbumin* (0·5 per cent) and *lactoglobulin* (0·2 per cent) all of which are of high biological value: a term discussed further on page 203.

Caseinogen is a complex material that probably contains at least 3 separate protein components as well as calcium, magnesium, citrate and phosphate. The colloidal particles of caseinogen are stabilized by a positive charge owing to the presence of bound calcium and magnesium ions. The charged particles are sensitive to changes of pH and to changes in concentration of surrounding ions. For example, during digestion milk becomes solid owing to the coagulation or 'clotting' of caseinogen. This is brought about by the enzyme *rennin* which, at the low pH prevailing in the stomach, converts caseinogen into a coagulated form called *casein*. The casein reacts with calcium ions to give a three-dimensional gel which is in the form of a tough clot called *calcium caseinate*.

The making of junket is also an example of clotting. When milk is warmed to blood-heat and *rennet* added, it slowly coagulates into a white solid and exudes a slightly yellow liquid called *whey*. The change in the milk which occurs on making junket is the same as that which occurs in the stomach. Rennet is obtained from a calf's stomach but its essential constituent is rennin which, as before, is responsible for the clotting of milk.

Lactalbumin and lactoglobulin are not coagulated by rennin but they are more easily coagulated by heat than caseinogen. Thus, when milk is heated, lactalbumin and lactoglobulin coagulate and form a skin on the surface. This skin is responsible for the way in which milk so easily 'boils over', for expanding bubbles are trapped beneath the skin and build up a pressure which eventually lifts the scum and allows the milk to boil over the sides of the pan.

THE CARBOHYDRATE OF MILK consists of the disaccharide lactose, also called milk sugar. Lactose is the only sugar manufactured by mammals and is distinguished by its lack of sweetness compared with other sugars.

As is well known, milk readily becomes sour when it is stored. This is because milk contains bacteria, called *lactic bacilli*, in which are enzymes that bring about the breakdown of lactose into the sour-tasting lactic acid:

$$C_{12}H_{22}O_{11} + H_2O \xrightarrow{\text{lactic bacilli}} 4CH_3CH(OH)COOH$$
$$\text{Lactose} \qquad\qquad\qquad\qquad \text{Lactic acid}$$

The pH of fresh milk is 6·4–6·7, the value being maintained within this narrow range by proteins, phosphate and citrate which act as buffers. As milk turns sour the pH drops and when it reaches 5·2 the milk *curdles* and the caseinogen is precipitated in the form of flocculent curds. It will be noted that curdling and clotting are not the same chemically, for in curdling caseinogen is merely precipitated, while in clotting a tough mass of calcium caseinate is formed. Although milk which has been kept for a period curdles naturally because of the presence of lactic acid, any acid will produce the same effect. Curdling is hastened by warmth and it is for this reason that care must be taken when preparing such dishes as tomato soup where the acidity of the tomato juice may be sufficient to curdle the hot milk. If conditions are sufficiently acid, curdling may occur in the cold, for example, when milk is added to acid fruit such as rhubarb.

THE MINERAL ELEMENTS OF MILK are either in the form of mineral salts or occur as constituents of the organic nutrients. Some are in solution and some are colloidally dispersed either as sol particles or combined with protein. As milk is the sole food of a young calf it contains all the mineral elements required by the animal for growth. It is particularly rich in calcium and phosphorus, both of which are needed to build bone and teeth. These mineral elements are found in milk combined together in the form of calcium phosphate, which is not soluble but is held in suspension in the form of fine particles. Combined phosphorus is also found in caseinogen and in phospholipids such as lecithin.

Many other mineral elements are present in small quantities; chlorine and iodine, for example, occur as soluble chlorides and iodides. Iron is present in milk but in such small quantities as to make it the one important mineral element in which milk is seriously deficient for human nutrition.

THE VITAMINS OF MILK are found either dissolved in fat globules or in aqueous solution. Vitamins A and D are both found in milk fat, the former in appreciable amounts, the latter in very much smaller quantities. The amount of both vitamins present in milk is greatest in summer when the cows are feeding on grass and receiving what sunshine our summers afford. The vitamin A value of milk is in part due to β-carotene and it is this substance which gives to milk its creamy colour.

Milk is particularly rich in riboflavine and it is a most valuable source of this vitamin. It also contains useful amounts of thiamine and ascorbic acid and a small amount of nicotinic acid. The actual amounts of these vitamins in milk when it reaches the consumer depends upon the treatment it has received. Both ascorbic acid and thiamine are destroyed by heat treatment, while exposure to light destroys ascorbic acid and riboflavinc.

Butter

Butter, no less than milk, is a complex colloidal system and although the conversion of cream into butter is an ancient art, complete understanding of the mechanism of the process is still wanting. Butter is made from cream by churning. The cream used contains 30–38 per cent milk fat and may be used fresh or allowed to go sour, a process which is known as *ripening* in which lactose is converted into lactic acid and flavour developed. After pasteurization the cream is agitated or churned at a controlled temperature in the range of 10–15° C. During churning the cream becomes increasingly viscous and eventually granules of solid butter appear. The liquid fraction, called buttermilk, is run off, salt (and usually colouring) is added and the butter is mixed or 'worked' until a suitable consistency is obtained. These steps are usually carried out separately, but more recently a continuous process has been developed.

The conversion of cream into butter involves 'breaking' the o/w cream emulsion and turning it into a w/o emulsion, a process which is known as *inversion*. The detailed mechanism of this change is not known but a simple outline can be given. At an early stage in churning air becomes trapped in the cream emulsion and a foam is formed. As already noted, natural emulsifiers present in cream stabilize the emulsion by being adsorbed at the oil/air interface. When air is trapped in the emulsion these emulsifiers become desorbed and spread out on to the surface of the air bubbles. The oil droplets lose their stability and coalesce into larger drops. Continued churning brings about collapse of the foam structure, and the coalescing fat particles appear as visible granules and separate out from the aqueous phase.

Although both o/w emulsion and foam structures have collapsed, further churning brings about dispersion of a small amount of water in the fat and a w/o emulsion is formed. The nature of the final product is affected by the proportion of solid to liquid triglycerides present in the fat phase. Some liquid oil droplets are dispersed in the continuous fat phase, though continued churning reduces the proportion of such dispersed oil. If the temperature of churning is lowered the proportion of crystalline triglycerides in the fat increases and a correspondingly harder butter is formed.

The composition of butter is variable. An average butter contains the following: 82·5 per cent fat, 12 per cent water, 2 per cent sugar (lactose), 2 per cent salt and 1·5 per cent protein (caseinogen). Butter is a natural product apart from the addition of salt as a preservative, and colouring matter. In addition to the constituents mentioned above, butter contains vitamins A and D, particularly the former. The actual vitamin content varies considerably, being much higher in summer when the cows feed on grass than in winter when no fresh food is available. The average vitamin content of butter is 995 μg of vitamin A (retinol equivalent) and 1·25 μg of vitamin D per 100 g. The statutory requirements for butter stipulate that it shall contain a minimum of 80 per cent milk fat and a maximum of 2 per cent milk solids other than fat and 1·6 per cent water. (In low salt butters the minimum for milk fat is 78 per cent.)

Milk fat contains a mixture of combined saturated and unsaturated fatty acids (see Table 6.1). One of the main acid components is oleic acid, and this causes butter fat to have a low melting point: others occurring are linoleic and linolenic acids. The other striking feature of the acid components of butter fat is the large amount of combined low molecular weight acids present. On hydrolysis, butter yields about 4 per cent butyric acid and smaller amounts of caproic, caprylic and capric acids.

Cheese

Although there are more than 400 different named cheeses the basic principles which govern their manufacture are the same. Milk is coagulated and the solid formed is cut into small pieces to allow the whey to drain off. The solid curd is dried, salt is added and the cheese pressed or moulded and allowed to ripen. Cheddar cheese, which is a typical and popular hard cheese, will serve as a convenient example in discussing the main stages of cheese manufacture which are summarized in Table 6.6.

Table 6.6. Stages in Making Cheddar Cheese

Stage	Description of physical and chemical changes
1 Pasteurization	Whole milk is pasteurized.
2 Ripening or souring	Lactic acid bacteria starter added. Lactose converted into lactic acid with consequent fall in pH.
3 Clotting or coagulation	Rennet added to sour milk at 30°C. Caseinogen converted into casein which forms a tough gel or clot of calcium caseinate known as curd.
4 Cutting	Curd is cut into small pieces.
5 Scalding and pitching	The temperature is raised to about 40°C, pH continues to fall and cutting is continued. Pieces of curd matt together and whey is run off.
6 Cheddaring or piling	Curd is cut into blocks and piled up. Whey drains off and curd forms solid mass with a firm soft texture.
7 Milling and salting	The dry curd is milled into small pieces and salt is added. More whey is lost.
8 Pressing	The soft cheese is put into moulds, pressure is applied and more whey expressed.
9 Maturing	After removal from the mould, the cheese is allowed to mature for 3 months or longer.

The essence of cheesemaking is the coagulation of milk and its conversion from a colloidal dispersion into a gel known as curd, and the subsequent release of water in the form of whey. The loss of moisture from a gel is known as *syneresis* and results in a fall in water content from 87 per cent in milk to less than 40 per cent in mature cheddar cheese. The control of this water loss constitutes a major part of the art of cheesemaking. The rate at which water is lost depends upon three factors, namely temperature, pH and the way the curd is cut, and in practice all three are controlled so as to give rapid syneresis. Reduction of water content is most important as it determines the hardness and keeping quality of the cheese. The changes in water content and pH during cheesemaking are shown in Fig. 6.6.

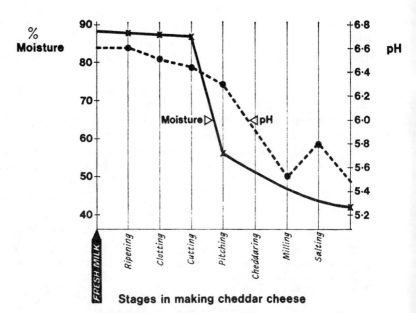

FIG. 6.6. The variation of water content and pH during cheesemaking

The chemical changes which occur during maturing of cheese are still not completely understood but are certainly brought about by enzymes. Lactic acid bacteria thrive in the immature acid cheese and the enzymes present in them bring about a number of chemical reactions which are responsible for the development of flavour and aroma. A week after manufacture is started all the lactose has disappeared, having been converted into lactic acid. Apart from lactose breakdown, maturing mainly involves breakdown of protein and fat. Protein is broken down by enzymatic hydrolysis brought about by rennin and other peptidases. Proteins are progressively broken down into smaller molecules such as peptones and ultimately into amino acids. Such soluble and low molecular weight nitrogen compounds certainly contribute to cheese flavour and in addition they bring about physical changes in the cheese, causing it to become softer and creamier. Fat, like protein, is broken down by enzymatic hydrolysis and is converted into glycerol and free fatty acids. Milk fat is relatively rich in low molecular weight fatty acids such as butyric, caproic and capric, which are released on hydrolysis and, being volatile and strong-smelling, contribute to cheese flavour.

Amino acids and fatty acids produced by breakdown of protein and fat may be further broken down by enzymes yielding low molecular weight molecules such as amines, aldehydes and ketones which being volatile and strong-smelling contribute to the flavour of mature cheese.

It is evident that the flavour of cheese is due to a very large number of different substances and that before they all become known much more research will be needed. After cheddar cheese has been stored for about three months it has developed its full flavour, although it may be stored for a year or longer.

The very large number of cheeses that are made makes it impracticable to do more than describe the main types and varieties, and this is done in Table 6.7. The main distinction is between soft cheeses which are not pressed and therefore have a high moisture content, and hard cheeses which are pressed and therefore have a lower moisture content and better keeping qualities. Soft cheeses have an open texture and provide suitable conditions for development of moulds, which require air for successful growth. The best known of the British mould-ripened cheeses in Stilton, the blue-green veins of which are caused by moulds. White Stilton is merely ordinary Stilton which has not been matured long enough for mould to develop.

Cheese has a high nutritional value as would be expected from the fact that a pint of milk produces only about 56 g cheese. Certain water-soluble nutrients of milk are lost in the whey, but most of them are retained in the curd. A hard cheese, such as Cheddar, consists of roughly one-quarter protein, one-third fat and one-third water. It is a rich source of calcium, phosphorus and vitamin A, and also contains useful quantities of other nutrients as shown in Table 6.8. It is a much more concentrated food than milk but is less complete because of its lack of carbohydrate. Soft cheeses retain a higher percentage of moisture than hard ones and, therefore, have a lower percentage of other nutrients. Cream cheeses, which are made from cream, are rich in fat but contain

Table 6.7. Types and Varieties of Cheese

Type	Varieties	Milk used	% Water	Nature
Very hard	Parmesan	Skimmed ripened milk	< 25	Dry cheese, excellent keeping qualities, matured > 1 year
Hard	Cheddar	Whole ripened milk	35	Mature, non-crumbly
	Cheshire	Whole ripened milk	38	Immature, crumbly, mild flavour
Semi-hard	Pecorino	Unripened sheep's milk	35–40	Soft, mild cheese (Italian)
	Edam	Unripened skimmed milk	35–40	Mild, firm, red colour (Dutch)
Soft	Cambridge	Unripened whole milk	> 40	Immature cheese, curd is not cut
Cream	Cream	Ripened cream	45–50	Soft, mild, rich flavour
Internal mould	Stilton	Ripened whole milk	33–35	Blue mould, mellow flavour, cured 4–6 months
External mould	Camembert	Ripened whole milk	45–55	Soft, creamy consistency (French)

much less calcium, phosphorus and vitamin A than Cheddar. The amount of water and milk fat in cheese is regulated by law and Cheddar cheese, for example, must not contain more than 39 per cent water and at least 48 per cent milk fat expressed on a dry basis.

The actual vitamin content of a cheese is very variable depending upon the quality of milk used in its production. Thus, Cheddar cheese which is particularly rich in vitamin A contains on average 420 μg per 100 g of cheese but in practice it may contain between nine and twenty-seven times as much vitaim A as the same amount of average summer milk.

Table 6.8. A Comparison of the Composition of Cheese and Summer Milk

Name	Energy (kJ) per 100 g	Nutrients per 100 g					
		g Protein	g Fat	g Carbohydrate	mg Calcium	mg Phosphorus	mg Iron
Cheddar	1708	25	34	0	810	545	0·6
Stilton	1990	25	40	0	362	304	0·5
Cream cheese	3406	3	86	0	30	44	0·1
Summer milk	274	3·3	3·8	4·8	120	100	0·1

FAT IN THE DIET

Fat in the diet is obtained in two forms, the 'visible' fats like butter and margarine and 'invisible' fats which occur in foods like milk and eggs where the fat is in a highly emulsified form. The amount of fat in different foods is shown in Table 6.9.

As fat has a higher energy value than either carbohydrate or protein, foods containing a high proportion of fat form a compact energy source. A man doing heavy work expends about 14 MJ per day. If he obtained all his energy from fat he would need to eat only 378 g—less than a pound—of fat. A less fatty diet containing a large amount of carbohydrate would be more bulky. A balanced diet always contains fat, though the proportion of fat varies according to circumstances. Countries like Britain, which have a high standard of living, have a higher proportion of fat in the diet than less industrialized countries where living standards are lower. Manual workers, whose energy requirements are great, can have a diet which is no more bulky than that of sedentary workers, if it contains a greater proportion of fat.

Table 6.9. The Fat Content of Foods

Food	% Fat	Food	% Fat
Lard	99	Eggs	11
Margarine	81	Beef	17
Butter	81	Milk	4
Bacon	40	Bread	2
Cheddar cheese	34	Rice	1
Pork sausage	32	Potatoes	0
Herring	18	Haddock	< 1

Fat in the Body

When fatty foods are eaten they pass through the digestive system in the manner described in Chapter 3. In the small intestine they are partly hydrolysed by lipase, one fatty acid molecule being split off from a fat molecule at a time, so that the result is a mixture of free fatty acids and mono- and diglycerides. As the hydrolysis is not complete, little free glycerol is produced. A proportion of the fat is not hydrolysed at all, but is absorbed directly into the blood in a highly emulsified form. Although the exact mechanism of the digestion and absorption of fat is not fully understood, it is certain that about two hours after a meal the blood becomes 'milky' in appearance due to the presence of emulsified fat, and that within another few hours this fat has disappeared from the blood.

It might be supposed that once fat has been absorbed it would be oxidized directly to produce energy while the surplus would be transferred to the 'reserve' and stored in the fat depots of the body. Modern evidence, however, suggests a rather different sequence of events. After absorption, most of the fat is transported to the fat storage cells of the body and is not oxidized immediately. This seems to occur even when the body is in urgent need of energy. The fat depots are not stable though; they are in a constant state of flux. In experiments carried out on rats fatty acids labelled with *deuterium* were fed to rats and within a week nearly half of the fat of the fat depots was found to contain deuterium. This method of tracing the path of molecules during metabolism by labelling certain atoms with isotopes is known as the *isotopic tracer* technique and is more fully described on page 200. The results show that fatty acids are rapidly interchanged between fats indicating that the latter are constantly being broken down and resynthesized.

When the body uses fat as a source of energy—which is mainly when there is a shortage of carbohydrate—the glycerol and fatty acids are oxidized. The breakdown of glycerol involves reaction with ATP (*adenosine triphosphate*) to form glycerol phosphate which is subsequently broken down, in a series of oxidation steps, to carbon dioxide and water. The oxidation of fatty acid molecules takes place in steps, a fragment containing two carbon atoms being removed in each step. If stearic acid is oxidized, for example, it is first broken down to palmitic acid, palmitic acid is then oxidized to myristic acid and so on, until butyric acid is reached. In each step the two carbon atoms removed from a fatty acid molecule appear as acetic acid:

$$C_{17}H_{35}COOH + O_2 \longrightarrow C_{15}H_{31}COOH + CH_3COOH$$
Stearic acid   Palmitic acid

The butyric and acetic acids formed are oxidized to carbon dioxide and water by a complex process. This simple picture of fatty acid oxidation was worked out many years ago, and although it is still believed to be essentially correct, modern research has filled in many of the details. For example, the oxidation process is not a spontaneous one and before it can proceed the necessary energy of activation must be supplied. The energy required is obtained from ATP—an energy-rich molecule—in the same way as during the oxidation of glucose which is considered in more detail in Chapter 8. The reaction is catalysed by the enzyme *thiokinase* in conjunction with coenzyme A which combines with the fatty acid to form a complex molecule that suffers enzymatic dehydrogenation, hydrolysis and further dehydrogenation which results in a two carbon atom unit being split off from the fatty acid molecule. This sequence of dehydrogenation, hydrolysis and dehydrogenation is repeated as each additional two carbon atom unit is split off from a fatty acid molecule. The fragment split off is in the form of acetyl coenzyme A, which is then oxidized in a complex cycle of reactions known as the citric acid cycle (or Krebs cycle, see p. 170). It appears that the final oxidation of both carbohydrate and fat follows the same pathway; also both nutrients finally yield the same products, namely carbon dioxide, water and ATP.

If energy is not required immediately, molecules of glycerol and fatty acid recombine and are deposited again as fat. There is, therefore, a dynamic equilibrium between the breakdown and rebuilding processes.

During normal fat metabolism a small amount of acetoacetic acid, CH_3COCH_2COOH, is formed and is further broken down in muscles and other organs. When fats are metabolized at an abnormally fast rate, acetoacetic acid accumulates faster than it can be removed and its concentration in the blood increases. Some of it is converted into acetone, CH_3COCH_3. Both these substances contain a carbonyl group and their accumulation in the blood is called *ketosis*. This condition may result from the use of diets containing too much fat and too little carbohydrate and also occurs during starvation and in people suffering from diabetes.

Dietary Fat and Health

Recent research has shown that there is a relationship between dietary fat and coronary heart disease. This disease is known to be related to high levels of *triglycerides* and *cholesterol* in the blood, which in turn are related to both the nature and amount of fat in the diet. It has been shown that whereas consumption of saturated fats raises levels of triglycerides and cholesterol in the blood, consumption of poly-unsaturated fats can lower them. A polyunsaturated fat is one which is rich in triglycerides containing several double bonds.

The evidence linking coronary heart disease with dietary fat is now sufficiently well established to make it prudent to recommend some changes to our diet. An authoritative report issued jointly by the Royal College of Physicians and the British Cardiac Society (1976) includes some dietary recommendations. It proposes that the amount of fat in the diet should be reduced from 40 per cent to 35 per cent of total energy requirement, and that this reduction should apply particularly to saturated fats. It also suggests that some saturated fats should be replaced by polyunsaturated fats. (It also notes that dietary control of fat to control obesity is important.)

Table 6.10 gives the main sources of saturated and polyunsaturated fats. In British diets the most important sources of saturated fats are meat (25 per cent of total intake), butter (18 per cent) and milk (11 per cent), while the most important sources of polyunsaturated fats are margarine and cereals each of which supplies about 20 per cent of the total intake.

In addition cholesterol is found in a number of foods, particularly egg yolk but also offal, shellfish and dairy products. (It should be noted that only about 25 per cent of blood cholesterol comes from the diet; the remainder being synthesized in the body.)

It needs to be emphasized that there is no proof that any single factor causes coronary heart disease. It is generally accepted that apart from consumption of saturated fats many other factors, including obesity, lack of exercise, smoking and possibly mental stress may be involved. At present we can only say that although there is much evidence linking consumption of saturated fat with coronary heart disease, there is much controversy as to its significance.

Table 6.10. Important Sources of Saturated and Polyunsaturated Fats

Saturated Fats	Butter, lard, suet, mutton fat, hard margarine, coconut oil, hard cheeses, cream
Polyunsaturated Fats	Corn oil, safflower oil, sunflower seed oil, peanut oil, soya bean oil, soft margarines made with a high proportion of polyunsaturated oils, most nuts (but not coconut or cashew)

SUGGESTIONS FOR FURTHER READING

ALPHA-LAVAL. *Dairy Handbook*. Alpha-Laval Co., 1980.

EDWARDS, G. *Vegetable Oils and Fats*, 2nd edition. Unilever Booklet, 1968.

FAO/WHO. *Dietary Fats and Oils in Human Nutrition*. HMSO, 1980.

HYDE, K. A. and ROTHWELL, J. *Ice-cream*. Churchill Livingstone, 1973.

KON, S. K. *Milk and Milk Products in Human Nutrition*, 2nd edition. FAO, 1972.

MEYER, A. *Processed Cheese Manufacture*. Food Trade Press, 1973.

MOORE, E. *Margarine and Cooking Fats*. Unilever Booklet, 1971.

MULDER, H. and WALSTRA, P. *The Milk Fat Globule. Emulsion Science as applied to Milk Products*. Commonwealth Agricultural Bureaux, 1974.

NATIONAL DAIRY COUNCIL, *A Handbook of Dairy Foods*, 3rd edition. National Dairy Council, 1974.

PORTER, J. W. G. *Milk and Dairy Foods*. Oxford University Press, 1975.

ROBINSON, R. K. (**Ed**). *Dairy Microbiology* (2 vols). Applied Science, 1981.

ROYAL COLLEGE OF PHYSICIANS. *Prevention of Coronary Heart Disease.* Report reprinted from Journal of Royal College of Physicians, 1976.

SCHMIDT, G. H. and VAN VLECK, L. D. *Principles of Dairy Science*. Freeman, USA, 1974.

SCOTT, R. *Cheesemaking Practice*. Applied Science, 1981.

WEBB, B. H. *et al. Fundamentals of Dairy Chemistry*, 2nd edition. Avi, USA, 1974.
A comprehensive book with extensive bibliographies.

Chapter Seven

Carbohydrates 1
Sugars

Carbohydrates constitute one of the three main classes of nutrients. They are found in all plants where they are produced from carbon dioxide and water. At the same time oxygen is evolved as shown in the equation for the formation of the simple carbohydrate glucose:

$$6CO_2 + 12H_2O \longrightarrow C_6H_{12}O_6 + 6O_2 + 6H_2O$$
$$\text{Glucose}$$

Water appears on both sides of this equation because it has been shown that all the oxygen evolved originates from the water. The oxygen atoms in the glucose and water molecules on the right-hand side of the equation are those which were originally combined with carbon in the carbon dioxide. The equation is a comparatively simple one but it shows only the starting materials and final products of a series of complex reactions.

The building up of carbohydrate molecules by plants is accomplished by photosynthesis. Energy is required to transform the carbon dioxide and water into carbohydrates and this is supplied by sunlight. Consequently, photosynthesis does not take place in the dark. Animals are unable to synthesize carbohydrates and this is one of the fundamental differences between them and plants.

The solar energy used in photosynthesis is stored as chemical energy and this may later be drawn upon by the plant, which, by oxidizing the carbohydrate back to carbon dioxide and water, is able to make use of the energy liberated. Alternatively animals, by eating the plant, may utilize the chemical energy stored in the carbohydrate molecules.

Plants can build up a variety of carbohydrates by photosynthesis. The sugars glucose and sucrose and the polysaccharides starch and cellulose, are important examples of carbohydrates built up by photosynthesis.

Carbohydrates contain only carbon, hydrogen and oxygen and, except in rare cases, there are always two atoms of hydrogen for every one of oxygen. Accordingly, carbohydrates have the general formula $C_x(H_2O)_y$, where x and y are whole numbers and it is from this formal representation as hydrates of carbon that the name carbohydrate is derived.

Many of the carbohydrates known, particularly the simple ones, do not occur naturally but have been obtained by synthesis in the laboratory. Only the naturally occurring carbohydrates are of interest from the point of view of food chemistry and those containing six, or multiples of six, carbon atoms are particularly important. Familiar examples are glucose $C_6H_{12}O_6$, sucrose $C_{12}H_{22}O_{11}$ and starch, the very large molecules of which are represented by the formula $(C_6H_{10}O_5)_n$.

The simpler carbohydrates, called sugars, are crystalline solids which dissolve in water to give sweet solutions. The simplest of these, such as glucose and fructose, are called *monosaccharides* and they are of great importance as the units or building blocks from which the more complex carbohydrates are built. *Disaccharides*, for example sucrose, maltose and lactose, contain two connected monosaccharide units which may be alike or different. Disaccharides can be hydrolysed by boiling with dilute acids, or by enzymes, to give the monosaccharides from which they are built up. Sucrose, for example, on hydrolysis gives equal parts of glucose and fructose. Like the monosaccharides, disaccharides dissolve in water to give sweet solutions and so are classified as sugars.

All soluble carbohydrates may be detected by *Molisch's test*. A solution of the substance being tested for the presence of carbohydrates is placed in a test-tube. A few drops of a 10 per cent solution of α-naphthol in alcohol are added and concentrated sulphuric acid is then poured carefully down the side of the tube to form a separate layer. A red-violet ring formed at once or after a few minutes standing indicates the presence of carbohydrates.

MONOSACCHARIDES

D-Glucose, Dextrose or Grape-Sugar

These are all names for the same sugar which is found in grapes and other sweet fruits. Onions and unripe potatoes also contain substantial amounts and honey contains about 35 per cent glucose. Glucose is formed during digestion by hydrolysis of starch and other carbohydrates.

Glucose, $C_6H_{12}O_6$, is a white solid (m.p. 146°C) which is less sweet than sucrose. It behaves as an aldehyde and this indicates the presence in the molecule of the $-CHO$ group. Like all aldehydes it is easily oxidized to the corresponding acid. Even mild oxidizing agents are sufficient to effect this change and they are, of course, reduced in the process. Because of the ease with which it will reduce oxidizing agents glucose is said to be a reducing sugar and this reducing action forms the basis of several tests for glucose and other reducing sugars. For example, glucose will reduce an ammoniacal solution of silver nitrate to metallic silver and an alkaline solution containing cupric ions, known as Fehling's solution, to cuprous oxide.

Glucose was originally given the structure shown. The carbon atoms are numbered so that reference can easily be made to them later.

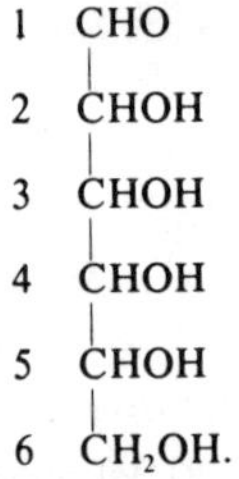

1   CHO
    |
2   CHOH
    |
3   CHOH
    |
4   CHOH
    |
5   CHOH
    |
6   CH₂OH.

Carbon atoms 2, 3, 4 and 5 are asymmetric and, as would be expected, glucose is optically active. It is dextrorotatory and this is indicated, as usual, by a (+) placed before the name. The prefix D is also often used; it indicates the disposition in space, or configuration as it is called, of the hydrogen atom and hydroxyl group on carbon atom 5. Ordinary glucose is D-(+)-glucose and using the projection formulae discussed in Chapter 4 it is represented:

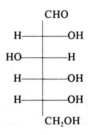

The mirror-image form, L-(−)-glucose, has been synthesized but it is not found naturally.

The sign indicating direction of rotation does not always correspond with the letter indicating the configuration at carbon atom 5 and, indeed, there is no reason why it should. For instance, D-fructose, another common naturally occurring monosaccharide, is laevorotatory and is correctly named D-(−)-fructose. These prefixes are often omitted unless it is necessary to draw attention to the configuration or sign of rotation.

All aldehydes give a pink colour when mixed with Schiff's reagent.

Glucose, however, does not affect Schiff's reagent and for this and other reasons it is now thought that glucose is not an aldehyde at all but that it is very easily converted into one during the course of many reactions. Glucose is now given the cyclic structure shown below.

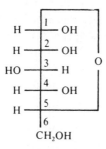

This is just a development of the formula on page 120. In this structure there is no aldehyde group at carbon atom 1 but a new hydroxyl group. Carbon atoms 1 and 5 are connected by an oxygen atom to give a six-membered ring, and the hydrogen atom which was formerly part of the hydroxyl group at carbon atom 5 is now part of the new hydroxyl group at carbon atom 1. This is a rather awkward method of writing the formula of glucose, because the ring and all the groups attached to it appear to lie in one plane. A semi-pictorial formula, such as that given below, provides a better idea of the actual shape of the molecule. The plane of the ring is supposed to be projecting from the plane of the paper with the thick edge towards the reader.

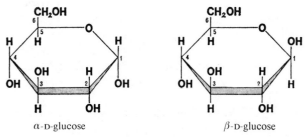

α-D-glucose   β-D-glucose

FIG. 7.1

The substituent groups lie above and below the plane of the ring.

It will be noted that carbon atom 1 is asymmetric in the above ring structure whereas in the open chain formula on page 120 it is not. Because of this, two isomeric forms of glucose are known which differ in the configuration at carbon atom 1. Ordinary glucose is α-glucose and the other form, β-glucose, can be obtained by crystallizing glucose from hot solvents. β-Glucose is of no importance from a practical point of view. If either α- or β-glucose is dissolved in water some of the molecules change into the other isomer and an equilibrium mixture is obtained which contains both forms. This conversion is believed to take place via the open chain aldehyde form and a small amount of the aldehyde form is probably always present in a solution of glucose. This explains why glucose behaves as an aldehyde in many reactions. The secondary alcohol group at carbon atom 1 is often called the *potential aldehyde group* or *reducing group*.

Nutritive sweeteners based on glucose are increasingly being used as a complete or partial replacement for sucrose in many manufactured foods. *Glucose Syrup* is the best known of these products and is made by hydrolysing maize starch by heating it under pressure with dilute hydrochloric acid. The composition of the sweet colourless syrup produced varies according to the degree of hydrolysis and is defined in terms of the reducing power of the syrup expressed as its *dextrose equivalent* (DE). For example, the carbohydrate content of a 43 DE syrup is about 20% dextrose, 17% maltose and 63% dextrins. Such syrups are particularly useful in sugar confectionery as they prevent crystallization on cooling (see p. 130). Glucose syrups with a higher DE value contain less dextrins and more glucose and maltose and are therefore sweeter than those with lower DE values. They are used particularly in jams and preserves.

More recently it has been found that if glucose syrups with a high DE value are treated with the enzyme *glucose isomerase* up to half the glucose is isomerized into fructose. The resulting high fructose glucose syrup is at least as sweet as sugar because of its high fructose content and has the additional advantage of enhancing fruit flavours. It is expected that such syrups will find extensive use in many products but particularly in soft drinks and jams and preserves.

D-Fructose, Laevulose or Fruit-sugar

Fructose is a laevorotatory sugar and is found with glucose in the juice of sweet fruits and in honey. It is obtained, with glucose, when sucrose is hydrolysed. Like glucose it is a powerful reducing agent. It is sweeter than both glucose and sucrose.

Fructose was originally given an open chain structure but, as in the case of glucose, this was found to be unsatisfactory and it has been superseded by a cyclic structure involving a six-membered ring. α and β forms are possible as with glucose.

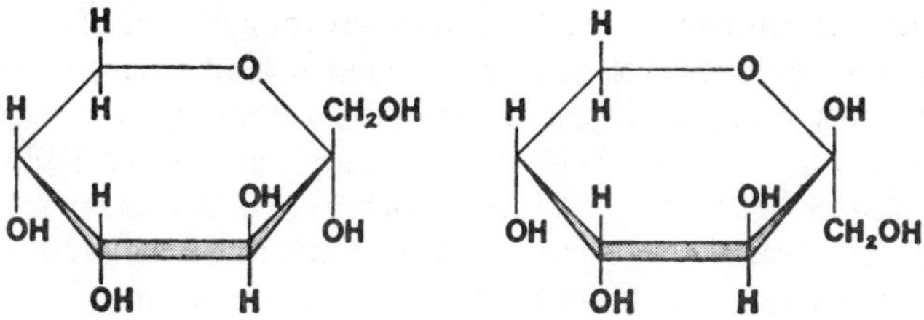

α-D-fructose   β-D-fructose

FIG. 7.2

DISACCHARIDES

Disaccharides are formed by the union of two monosaccharide molecules, with loss of water:

$$(C_6H_{11}O_5)O\underline{[H+HO]}(C_6H_{11}O_5) \longrightarrow (C_6H_{11}O_5)-O-(C_6H_{11}O_5)+H_2O$$

Two monosaccharide molecules   A disaccharide molecule

It is not possible to prepare disaccharides from monosaccharides in the laboratory by this process despite its apparent simplicity. Nature, however, accomplishes it without difficulty. Disaccharides are easily split into their component monosaccharides by enzymes or by boiling with dilute acids. Many disaccharides are known but the most important, and the only ones of interest in food chemistry, are maltose, lactose and sucrose.

Maltose or Malt Sugar

Maltose is obtained from starchy materials by the action of the enzyme diastase. The enzyme maltase hydrolyses maltose to glucose and this may also be accomplished by heating with dilute acid. D-Glucose is the only monosaccharide formed during these hydrolyses and this indicates that maltose contains two connected glucose units. Maltose is a reducing sugar and measurement of its reducing power shows that only one of the potential aldehyde groups is free, the other being involved in the formation of the link between the two D-glucose units. The link between the glucose units between carbon atom 1 in the first glucose unit and carbon atom 4 in the second.

Maltose can exist in α and β forms and this is why the configuration of carbon atom 1 in the second glucose unit has not been indicated. This is the potential aldehyde group responsible for the reducing power of maltose. Carbon atom 1 in the other glucose unit is in the α configuration.

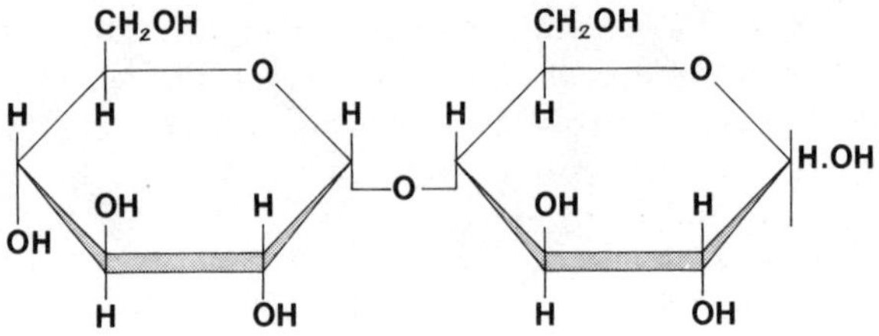

FIG. 7.3. Maltose

Lactose or Milk Sugar

Lactose is a white crystalline solid which is somewhat gritty in appearance. It occurs in the milk of all animals: cows' milk contains 4–5 per cent and human milk 6–8 per cent. On hydrolysis of lactose with the enzyme lactase or by boiling with dilute acid, equal quantities of D-glucose and the monosaccharide D-galactose are obtained and so the lactose molecule contains these two monosaccharides linked together. It is a reducing sugar hence at least one of the reducing groups is free. Lactose has the following structure:

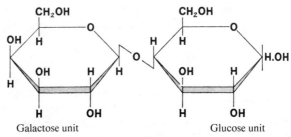

Galactose unit   Glucose unit

FIG. 7.4. Lactose

Sucrose, Cane Sugar or Beet Sugar

Ordinary sugar, whether obtained from sugar cane or sugar beet, is substantially pure sucrose. It is a white crystalline solid which dissolves in water to give a dextrorotatory solution. Sucrose is widely distributed in the vegetable kingdom in many fruits, grasses and roots and in the sap of certain trees; it is produced and consumed in far larger quantities than any other sugar. Over two million tons of sucrose are used annually in this country (which is roughly 41 kg per person per year) and of this about one-third comes from home-grown sugar beet.

On hydrolysis with dilute acids, or the enzyme sucrase, sucrose gives equal quantities of glucose and fructose, so the sucrose molecule must contain one glucose unit combined with one fructose unit. It is unable to reduce Fehling's solution or ammoniacal silver nitrate so the reducing group in each monosaccharide unit must be involved in the link between them. The fructose unit in sucrose does not have the usual six-membered ring but a five-membered ring:

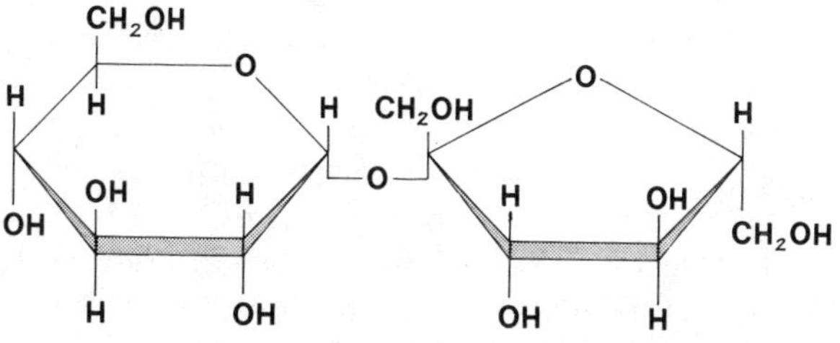

Glucose unit   Fructose unit

FIG. 7.5. Sucrose

Sucrose is very readily hydrolysed to glucose and fructose, the latter having the normal six-membered ring structure. Fructose is more strongly laevorotatory than glucose is dextrorotatory and so the mixture of glucose and fructose obtained on hydrolysis is laevorotatory. This change in the sign of rotation is called an *inversion*.

The mixture of glucose and fructose produced by the inversion is called *invert-sugar* and has been known in the form of honey for many centuries. Bees collect nectar, which is essentially sucrose, from flowers and it is inverted by enzymes during passage through their bodies. Honey is not pure invert sugar because it contains, in addition to glucose and fructose, some sucrose, about 20 per cent water and small quantities of extracted flavours peculiar to the flower from which it was obtained. When sucrose is used in the preparation of acidic foodstuffs a certain amount of inversion invariably takes place. For instance, if sucrose is used for sweetening fruit drinks it is completely inverted within a few hours. Jams and sweets also contain invert-sugar.

Sucrose is obtained commercially from sugar cane, which can only be grown in tropical countries, and sugar beet which can be grown in any temperate climate. Whichever is used, the same product is obtained; there is no difference between the sugar obtained from sugar beet and that obtained from sugar cane.

PRODUCTION OF RAW SUGAR FROM SUGAR CANE. The sugar cane is a type of giant grass which resembles bamboo and may grow to a height of 4·5 metres with a diameter of 3–5 cm. The sugar, which amounts to about 15 per cent of the weight of the cane, is found in a soft fibre in the interior of the cane. From three to eight tons of sugar are normally obtained from an acre of sugar cane. The sugar is extracted from the cane by crushing and spraying with water. The solution obtained contains about 13 per cent sugar and 3 per cent impurities, the rest being water. This solution is purified by boiling and adding lime which precipitates some of the impurities, while others coagulate and float on the surface as a scum. The lime and impurities are removed and the clear solution obtained is concentrated by evaporation under reduced pressure until a mixture of sugar crystals and mother liquor is obtained. The crystals are separated from the mother liquor by spinning the mixture very quickly in large drums. These drums have perforated sides through which the mother liquor, called molasses, is forced by centrifugal action, leaving the raw sugar behind. The molasses are used for the manufacture of rum and industrial alcohol.

PRODUCTION OF RAW SUGAR FROM SUGAR BEET. The sugar content of sugar beet is similar to that of sugar cane but only about two tons of sugar can be obtained from an acre of sugar beet. The sugar is extracted from the shredded beets by steeping them in hot water; it diffuses through the cell walls into the water, leaving behind most of the non-sugar solids. Batteries of specially designed diffusers are used to ensure that the maximum amount of sugar is removed by the minimum quantity of water. The solution obtained contains about 14 per cent sugar and 4 per cent impurities, the remainder being water. It is treated with slaked-lime, and carbon dioxide is passed through the solution. The carbon dioxide combines with the calcium hydroxide to give calcium carbonate which settles to the bottom of the solution, carrying with it most of the impurities. After removal of the precipitate the clear solution obtained is concentrated by evaporation under reduced pressure to give sugar crystals and molasses which are separated by centrifuging as described for cane-sugar. The raw sugar obtained is very similar to that produced from cane-sugar but may have a less attractive taste and smell.

SUGAR REFINING. Raw sugar, whether obtained from beet or cane, contains about 96 per cent sucrose. It consists essentially of sugar crystals coated with a layer of molasses. The first step in the refining process is to mix the raw sugar with sugar syrup to produce a stiff semi-solid mixture of syrup and crystals. This is centrifuged and the syrup is forced out, leaving the sugar crystals within the centrifuge. The sugar crystals are then washed with water to remove the adhering syrup. A considerable amount of sugar is contained in the syrup and wash liquors from the centrifuge and this is recovered by evaporation of the water under reduced pressure.

The sugar crystals are next dissolved in water and treated with milk of lime and carbon dioxide as was described for the production of raw beet sugar. This removes the bulk of the impurities and the remainder are removed by allowing the solution to percolate through a bed of bone charcoal some six metres deep. Before this treatment with charcoal the solution is brown in colour but the product, known as *fine liquor* is colourless, all the coloured impurities having been adsorbed by the charcoal.

All that remains to be done is to concentrate the fine liquor by evaporating the water, and crystallize the sucrose to produce uniform crystals of the correct size. The evaporation is carried out at reduced pressure in steam-heated 'vacuum pans' so that the water can be removed at a temperature much below the normal boiling point of the solution and this prevents any discoloration of the sugar. A small charge of fine liquor is first evaporated in the pan until it is super-saturated. This is then seeded with caster or icing sugar to produce a large number of tiny crystals which act as nuclei for subsequent crystallizations. This seeding operation is known as *graining* and when it is complete the evaporation is continued with gradual addition of more and more fine liquor until the crystals grow to the appropriate size for granulated sugar. By careful control the addition of fine liquor can be made continuous, the rate of addition being varied as required. The crystallizing process formerly depended mainly on the skill and experience of the person carrying it out but it is now largely controlled by instruments which maintain the degree of supersaturation within suitable limits.

At the end of the crystallization the sugar crystals are suspended in syrup. Spinning in centrifugal machines removes most of the syrup, the remainder being removed by spraying with hot water and centrifuging. The syrup and washings contain about 40 per cent of the sugar originally present in the fine liquor and most of this is recovered by decolorizing and recrystallizing. This can be repeated several times. Eventually, however, the colour and quality of the sugar recovered from the syrup do not conform to the high standards required. When this happens the syrup is used for the manufacture of Golden Syrup or is concentrated and crystallized to give a soft brown sugar.

Caster sugar is made in the same way as granulated sugar but the crystallization procedure is modified so that much smaller crystals are obtained. This is done by using a larger number of nuclei or by preventing the crystals from growing to granulated sugar size. Caster sugar is also obtained as a by-product of the production of granulated sugar and it is separated from it by sieving the dry sugar. The particle size in **icing sugar** is even smaller than in caster sugar and it is made by pulverizing granulated sugar to an extremely fine powder in special mills. **Brown sugar** is obtained by crystallizing from the syrup obtained at the end of the refining process. Such sugar, known as *pieces* or *yellows*, is slightly sticky because of the presence of a thin coating of mother liquor on each crystal. **Lump sugar** is made by vacuum evaporation of fine liquor as was described for granulated sugar but a special technique is used to produce two sizes of crystals, the larger of which provide the characteristic sparkle of lump sugar while the smaller bind the crystals together. The mass of crystals and mother liquor produced is run into special cylindrical moulds which are slowly cooled so that the contents set to a rigid mass of sugar crystals soaked in syrup. The moulds are so designed that they can be rapidly spun on centrifugal machines to remove excess syrup. The last traces of syrup are removed by washing with specially pure concentrated fine liquor, which is itself subsequently removed by centrifuging. The solid sugar is carefully dried to remove final traces of moisture and is then cut by machine into the familiar cubes.

SUGAR CONSUMPTION AND HEALTH

During the present century world consumption of sugar has tripled. In Britain annual sugar consumption per person which was only 2 kg in the early eighteenth century is now about 41 kg, roughly half of which is bought by the housewife as sugar, the other half being contained in a wide variety of manufactured foods. The present high level of sugar consumption must be considered undesirable on 3 main counts; it contributes to obesity because sugar not required for energy is converted into fat; it increases the rate of dental decay and it is possibly related to the high incidence of coronary heart disease.

There is a direct relationship between sugar consumption and dental decay. Decay starts through the formation of a plaque or film on the surface of teeth which adheres to the tooth through the action of *dextran*, a sticky, complex carbohydrate. It is now known that dextran is synthesized from sucrose with the aid of bacteria present in the mouth and this fact indicates the prime importance of sucrose in causing dental decay.

When carbohydrates are absorbed by the body there is not only an increase in the level of blood sugar but also in triglycerides and cholesterol. As pointed out on p. 115 the incidence of coronary heart disease is related to the high levels of these last two substances. Recent experiments have shown that sucrose (and fructose) are more effective in increasing triglyceride and cholesterol levels than other carbohydrates, such as starch and glucose. It should be noted that although there is some evidence relating high sugar consumption to coronary heart disease the validity of this evidence is questionable and only a minority opinion accepts that there is a direct link between them.

FOODSTUFFS MANUFACTURED FROM SUGAR

SUGAR CONFECTIONERY. The term sugar confectionery is used to describe the large range of confectionery we commonly call 'sweets'. Boiled sweets, toffees and caramels, the filling used as centres for chocolates, marshmallow, nougat, pastilles and gums are all examples of sugar confectionery. This great variety of tooth-decay accelerators have one thing in common—they are all produced by controlled crystallization of sucrose from a supersaturated solution. The differences that exist between them depend upon water content, the extent to which crystallization of sucrose has occurred, and the presence of fat or milk, which enables emulsions to be formed, and flavouring agents.

When a concentrated solution of sucrose—a syrup—is heated the temperature at which it will boil depends upon the amount of water present in the solution as shown in Fig. 7.6.

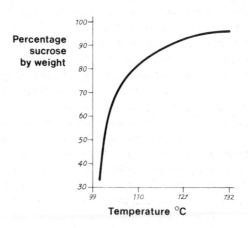

FIG. 7.6. The boiling points of sugar solutions

The water content of a sugar solution can be accurately determined from a knowledge of its boiling point. If boiling is allowed to continue the concentration of the solution increases as water evaporates and the boiling point increases. Soft sweets, such as toffee, are cooked to a lower temperature than hard sweets such as butterscotch or boiled sweets.

Boiled sweets are traditionally made by boiling sugar solutions with acidic substances to produce a certain amount of inversion. Boiling is continued until the temperature reaches 150 °C by which time almost all the water has been driven off and, on cooling, the mass solidifies as a glass-like solid—the familiar boiled sweet. At the end of the cooling period only a small amount of water (a few per cent) is present. The glucose produced by the inversion process prevents the sucrose from crystallizing when the mass is cooled down. It is said to 'cut the grain'. Glucose itself does not crystallize easily from water and in a mixed solution of glucose and sucrose the glucose inhibits the crystallization of the sucrose. The final product is a supersaturated solution of sucrose, with smaller amounts of glucose and fructose, in a very small quantity of water. The amount of invert-sugar produced during the boiling must be carefully controlled because too much will make the product prone to take up water from the air and become sticky. This is because the fructose in the invert-sugar is hygroscopic. On the other hand, if too little invert sugar is produced it will be insufficient to prevent crystallization of the sucrose. About 10–15 per cent invert-sugar is the amount required to give a non-sticky non-crystalline product.

Any acidic substance may be added to produce the inversion, and cream of tartar is commonly used. The amount of acid used depends upon several factors, including the hardness of the water, but it is quite small and, in the case of cream of tartar, is in the region of 0·15–0·25 per cent of the weight of sugar used. Boiled sweets are made commercially by heating a syrup of sucrose and glucose syrup (see p. 122) which prevents crystallization of the sucrose in the same way as invert-sugar. The amount of glucose syrup used can amount to 30–40 per cent but the product is not hygroscopic because it contains no fructose. Glucose syrup is less sweet than sucrose or invert-sugar and so the boiled sweets produced in this way are also less sweet. In addition, the dextrin in the glucose syrup is said to impart a certain toughness to the sweets and can sometimes cause cloudiness.

The creamy material used for filling soft-centred chocolates and by biscuit and cake manufacturers for decorative purposes is known as **fondant**. It consists essentially of minute sugar crystals surrounded by saturated sugar syrup.

Fondant is made by boiling a sugar solution and adding glucose syrup or an inverting agent as in the case of boiled sweets. No attempt is made to boil off all the water, however, and the mixture is only boiled to 116–121°C compared with 149–166°C in the case of boiled sweets. The syrupy solution obtained is cooled quickly to about 38°C by running on to a rotating water-cooled drum from which it falls into a beater. Here it is agitated violently to induce crystallization which occurs suddenly to produce a very large number of tiny crystals. Control of the water content of the syrupy solution is very important; if it is too low insufficient saturated syrup may be present to fill up the spaces between the sugar crystals in the fondant which may crack and craze as a result.

It is possible to make fondants containing only sucrose but they are rather hard and crystallize and dry out quickly. Moreover, fondants containing no glucose are susceptible to fermentation and may become mouldy because of the growth of yeast cells and moulds in the syrup surrounding the sugar crystals. It has been shown that fermentation cannot occur in syrup containing more than 78 per cent of sugar solids because the micro-organisms responsible cannot tolerate such concentrated solutions. A saturated solution of sucrose in water, however, contains only 66·5 per cent sucrose at normal temperatures and this is conducive to mould growth. In fondants containing glucose and fructose, whether produced by inversion of sucrose or added in the form of glucose syrup the concentration of sugars in the syrup is too high for the yeast cells to flourish and fermentation is not possible.

Toffee consists essentially of a dispersion of minute globules of fat in a supersaturated sugar solution. Fat, milk, sugar and glucose syrup are the main ingredients. Various grades of sugar are used, depending upon the recipe, from the best quality granulated sugar to raw sugars and treacles which contribute characteristic flavours to the product. As in the case of boiled sweets, sugars other than sucrose must be present to prevent graining. In home-made toffee an inverting agent such as vinegar or citric acid may be used to produce some invert-sugar from the sucrose, but in commercial practice it is usual to employ glucose syrup to prevent graining.

The milk used makes an important contribution to the flavour and is added as condensed milk, either full-cream or skimmed. The characteristic colour of toffee is largely due to caramelization of the milk solids during cooking. In addition the caseinogen of the milk acts as an emulsifying agent. Butter and various vegetable fats are used in the manufacture of toffee, and emulsifying agents, such as glyceryl monostearate or lecithin, may also be incorporated if insufficient milk solids and butter are present, to aid in the dispersion of the fat and produce a stable emulsion.

In toffee manufacture the ingredients are boiled together until the temperature reaches the required value. The temperature attained in the boiling process largely determines the consistency of the toffee produced because this depends, among other things, on the amount of water in the toffee. Very hard toffee such as butterscotch is heated to 146–154 °C, which gives a water content of 3–5 per cent. Ordinary toffees and caramels are heated to 118–132°C when the mixture contains 6–12 per cent water. Temperatures were formerly estimated by removing a sample, cooling it in water and examining it when cold. The temperatures are known by distinctive names such as 'soft-ball', 'hard-ball', 'soft-crack' and 'hard-crack' which refer to the consistency of the cold toffee. This method gives satisfactory results in the hands of experienced operators, but it is giving way to the thermometer with its more accurate indication of temperature. When boiling is complete the toffee is poured on to a slab, cooled and fed to machines which cut and wrap it for sale.

CHOCOLATE. The essential ingredients of chocolate are cocoa, cocoa-butter and sugar. The cocoa and cocoa-butter are both obtained from cocoa-beans which grow in pods on cocoa trees in tropical countries. The pods are egg-shaped, about eight inches long, and contain twenty to thirty beans embedded in a soft white starchy pulp. The pods are split open and the beans, with adhering pulp, are scraped out and allowed to ferment in a closed container for several days. A yeast fungus grows on the pulp and it liquefies owing to fermentation to alcohol. The liquid formed is allowed to drain away from the beans which during the process, change in colour from their original light violet to dark brown. After drying in the sun the beans are ready for shipment to the cocoa manufacturers.

In the manufacture of cocoa and chocolate, the beans are first roasted in revolving drums and are then broken into small pieces by passing through special rollers. At the same time the husk is removed, leaving behind the small pieces of roasted bean which are known as *nibs*. This roasting process is of great importance because it is at this stage that the characteristic chocolate flavour and aroma develop.

The nibs contain about 50 per cent of a fat known as cocoa-butter and during the next operation, in which the nibs are finely ground in mills, the heat generated melts the cocoa-butter to produce a viscous brown liquid as product. When the liquid, which is a dispersion of cocoa in cocoa-butter is cooled, a brown solid known as *cocoa-mass* is obtained. For the production of cocoa a proportion of the cocoa-butter is squeezed out in powerful hydraulic presses. The residue, containing 20–30 per cent cocoa-butter, is finely ground and sold as cocoa powder. It contains about 2 per cent theobromine and 0·1 per cent caffeine; both these compounds are alkaloids and they are responsible, at least in part, for the bitterness of cocoa and chocolate.

Chocolate is produced by mixing cocoa-mass with finely powdered sugar and the cocoa-butter expressed from cocoa-mass during the manufacture of cocoa powder. The amount of sugar used is large and plain chocolate may contain 50 per cent sugar. For milk chocolate, milk solids are incorporated, either as dried milk or as full-cream condensed milk. The mixing is carried out in special pieces of equipment known as *melangeurs* in which massive rollers rotate in contact with a revolving heated plate. On leaving the melangeurs the mixture passes to a refining machine, where it is pinched between rollers revolving at different speeds. To complete the mixing process the molten chocolate is next 'conched' for a long period of up to twenty-four hours. In the conching process heavy rollers subject the chocolate to severe mechanical treatment and blend all the ingredients into a uniform velvety mass. The manufacturing process is now complete and it only remains for the chocolate to be moulded into the familiar bars.

Chocolate for coating purposes, such as is used in covering 'centres' to make individual chocolates or in covering biscuits, contains a larger proportion of cocoa butter than ordinary block chocolate. The purpose of this is to increase the fluidity of chocolate when warm. Coated chocolate goods are made by passing the centre or biscuit to be coated through a curtain of molten chocolate in a machine called an *enrober*.

Chocolate and cocoa are highly nutritious as is shown by the following average figures:

Table 7.1. Composition of Cocoa and Chocolate

	Fat %	Carbohydrate %	Protein %	Energy value kJ/100 g
Cocoa powder	22	45	19	1860
Plain chocolate	33	59	4	2309
Milk chocolate	38	54	9	2411

In addition to these main constituents, chocolate also contains useful amounts of calcium, iron, vitamin A and the B vitamins.

JAM. Jam is made by boiling fruit with sugar solutions and is essentially a gel or semi-solid mass containing pulped or whole fruit. A gel is really a very viscous solution or dispersion which possesses some of the attributes, such as elasticity, of a solid. In the case of jam the gel is formed from the sugar, the acids present in the fruit, and a polysaccharide called *pectin* obtained from the fruit. The amount of pectin in the gel is quite small, usually less than 1 per cent of the weight of the jam. The sugar content, on the other hand, is very high and is usually about 70 per cent. Of the remainder, the bulk is water with a small amount of fibrous matter and seeds. In Great Britain jam must contain not less than 68·5 per cent soluble solids unless packed in hermetically sealed containers in which case it must contain not less than 65 per cent.

The quantity of pectin and acid in fruit for jam making is of great importance because gel formation only occurs when the concentrations of sugar and pectin and the pH of the mixture lie within certain limits. Some fruits such as currants, damsons, gooseberries, lemons and bitter oranges are rich in both acid and pectin and can easily be made into jam. Others, such as strawberries, blackberries, raspberries and cherries contain little pectin and some must be added before jam can be made successfully from them. A simple way of doing this is to add another fruit rich in pectin and acid, e.g. apple or a concentrated pectin preparation (see p. 143). As the percentage of pectin in a jam increases so does the firmness of the gel produced on cooling. A satisfactory gel is obtained with about 1 per cent pectin although for a given pH and sugar content the firmness of the gel is influenced by the 'quality' of the pectin as well as by the quantity present.

Pectin is a polysaccharide and its molecules consist of large numbers of simple sugar-like molecules connected together to form a long thread-like molecule. The length of a pectin molecule depends upon its source. During gel formation the long molecules link loosely together to form a three-dimensional network which gives the gel its stability. If the pectin molecules are too short the gel may lack strength and be runny or soft.

Anyone who has tried to make jam at home knows that the jam obtained from ripe fruit is not as good as that from fruit which is almost ripe. This is because pectin will not form a satisfactory gel until the pH is lowered to about 3·5 and unripe fruit is usually more acidic than ripe fruit. To decrease the pH of a jam mixture an acidic fruit juice, such as lemon juice, may be added or a small amount of citric acid, malic acid or cream of tartar. A low pH during the cooking period may cause inversion of too much sucrose, and also hydrolyse the pectin to some extent. As both these changes are detrimental the pH adjustment is often carried out at the end of the cooking period.

When fruit is boiled with sugar a certain amount of inversion occurs and this is of the utmost importance because invert-sugar prevents the crystallization of the sugar in the jam when it is kept. In addition, the presence of invert-sugar increases the amount of sugars (sucrose, glucose and fructose) which will remain dissolved in the jam to a level at which mould growth is impossible. Too much invert-sugar, however, is detrimental because it reduces the strength of the gel and may cause the jam to set to a honey-like mass on keeping.

Another reason why fruit used in jam making should not be over-ripe is that *proto-pectin*, from which pectin is formed during jam making, is present in maximum amount just before the fruit is ripe. If jam factories could make jam only when supplies of fresh fruit were available they would be able to work for only a very short period each year. Moreover, the great amount of fruit harvested during these periods would be far too large to be made quickly into jam by the existing number of jam factories. To overcome this difficulty large amounts of preserved fruits are used. The method of preserving the fruit is very simple; it is kept submerged in a weak solution of sulphur dioxide in water. Fruit can be preserved in this way either before or after cooking. In practice, strawberries, raspberries and blackberries are preserved raw whereas plums, currants and gooseberries are usually preserved as a cooked pulp because sulphur dioxide tends to toughen the skins of the uncooked fruit. The fruit is bleached by the sulphur dioxide during the preserving but the colour returns during the cooking. Almost all the sulphur dioxide is driven off during cooking and the finished jam must not contain more than 100 parts per million.

When jam is made at home the fruit is first cooked until tender. Pectin is extracted during this process and the length of the cooking period depends upon the fruit being used. Cooking is complete when a sample of the fruit forms a coherent pectin clot when allowed to stand for a few minutes with several times its volumes of methylated spirit. The clot should be strong enough to withstand pouring from one vessel to another without breaking. When a satisfactory pectin clot is obtained the sugar should be added and the mixture boiled as rapidly as possible. The duration of the boiling period will depend on the fruit used and the size and shape of the pan; it varies from about five to about twenty minutes. A shallow pan, in which a large surface area of the jam is exposed for evaporation is best because this permits rapid evaporation. The boiling period is usually complete when the temperature of the boiling mixtures reaches $104°C$. The exact temperature at which boiling should be stopped depends upon the acidity and pectin content of the fruit, however, both of which influence the setting properties of the jam. The point at which boiling should be stopped can be quite accurately judged by removing a sample and examining its behaviour on cooling. A sample of the jam placed on a cold plate should quickly form a skin which wrinkles on being touched. Alternatively, a sample is allowed to cool on a spoon which is then tilted so that the jam drops off. If the jam 'runs' in a continuous liquid stream, boiling is incomplete and should be continued. Jam which has been sufficiently boiled should leave the spoon in discrete flakes which break away cleanly from each other.

Jam making on a large scale is carried out in a much more scientific way than this. To begin with, the recipe is adjusted to give the correct amounts of sugar and pectin with the particular fruit being used and pH is also carefully controlled. Pre-cooked pulp is often used and the boiling is usually carried out in open pans holding about 180 litres of jam. The boiling time is very short and seldom exceeds ten minutes. This short boiling time preserves the gel-forming properties of the pectin and also keeps the amount of invert-sugar formed to between 25 per cent and 40 per cent. The time of boiling and hence the amount of invert-sugar formed can be controlled by altering the amount of water used. With too little invert-sugar, sucrose may crystallize, whereas with too much the gel obtained may be weak or the invert-sugar itself may crystallize as a pasty, honey-like mass.

The end of the boil can be judged as in home jam-making, from the behaviour of a sample of the jam taken on a shallow spoon or 'skimmer' and allowed to drip off. It can also be estimated from the boiling point of the solution; when this reaches 104–106°C the end of the boiling period is imminent. The boiling point is really an indication of the strength of the solution being boiled and this can be more accurately determined by means of a refractometer which measures the refractive index of the solution. From a knowledge of the refractive index the concentration of soluble solids in the solution can be accurately calculated. The soluble solids are added sugar and pectin together with sugars, acids and other materials extracted from the fruit. The soluble solids content aimed at varies from maker to maker but is usually about 70 per cent.

After boiling, the jam must be cooled as quickly as possible to prevent inversion continuing. After bottling, a waxed-paper disc is placed on the jam to prevent condensation of water on its surface. This would dissolve some of the sugar from the jam and produce an area of low sugar concentration conducive to mould growth. If the jars are hermetically sealed with a metal cover, or if the jam is canned, the waxed disc is not necessary because mould growth cannot occur in such containers.

SUGGESTIONS FOR FURTHER READING

BIRCH, G. G. *Glucose Syrups and Related Carbohydrates* (Symposium Report). Elsevier, 1970.

CAKEBREAD, S. *Sugar and Chocolate Confectionery*. Oxford University Press, 1975.

LEES, R. and JACKSON, B. *Sugar Confectionery and Chocolate Manufacture*. L. Hill, 1973.

McILROY, R. J. *Introduction to Carbohydrate Chemistry*. Butterworths, 1967.

MINIFIE, B. W. *Chocolate, Cocoa and Confectionary: Science and Technology*, 2nd edition. Churchill, 1980.

RAUCH, G. H. *Jam Manufacture*, 2nd edition. L. Hill, 1965.

YUDKIN, J. *et al. Sugar*. Butterworths, 1971.

YUDKIN, J. *Pure, White and Deadly; the problem of sugar*. Davis-Poynter, 1972.

Chapter Eight

Carbohydrates 2

Polysaccharides

Polysaccharides are carbohydrates of high molecular weight which differ from the sugars in being non-crystalline, generally insoluble in water and tasteless. A polysaccharide is built up from a large number of connected monosaccharide units which may be alike or different. As in the case of disaccharides one molecule of water is lost in the union between one monosaccharide molecule and the next. The polysaccharides which are of importance in food chemistry are all built up from monosaccharides containing six carbon atoms and are best formulated $(C_6H_{10}O_5)n$. The value of n varies, but in most cases is quite large. A single *cellulose* molecule for example can contain several thousand connected glucose units. Hydrolysis breaks down a polysaccharide molecule into smaller portions containing various numbers of monosaccharide units and may, if sufficiently drastic, convert the polysaccharide completely to monosaccharide:

$$(C_6H_{10}O_5)n + nH_2O \longrightarrow nC_6H_{12}O_6$$

Like the sugars, polysaccharides are built up by plants from carbon dioxide and water and it is probable that the sugars represent an intermediate stage in the photosynthesis of polysaccharides. It has already been mentioned that animals are unable to build up carbohydrates by photosynthesis and for this reason polysaccharides are found predominantly in plants. The polysaccharide *glycogen*, however, is elaborated by man from glucose, and several similar examples of animals synthesizing polysaccharides from monosaccharides are known. In man, glycogen constitutes a store of carbohydrate, starch performs a similar function in plants and glycogen is sometimes called animal starch. In plants, polysaccharides also serve as skeletal material and this is not paralleled in animals.

Cellulose

Cellulose is the chief structural carbohydrate of plants and, as such, is very widely distributed. All forms of plant life, from the toughest tree-trunk to the softest cotton-wool, contain cellulose and indeed the latter is almost pure cellulose. Whatever its origin the constitution of cellulose is the same. Because it is so widely distributed in the vegetable kingdom, cellulose is found, to a greater or lesser extent, in all foods of vegetable origin. It cannot be digested by man and most carnivorous animals because the enzymes present in their stomachs cannot rupture the β-1,4 link between the glucose units. For this reason cellulose has no nutritional value although it may serve a useful purpose as roughage. Much cellulose is removed in the processing of food; for example the husks of cereal grains, which are mainly cellulose, are usually removed. Cellulose can be digested by horses and by ruminants such as cows. The latter have auxiliary stomachs containing micro-organisms which produce enzymes capable of hydrolysing cellulose to glucose.

Cellulose can be hydrolysed by heating it with hydrochloric or sulphuric acid. The only monosaccharide obtained in this process is D-glucose. It has been shown that the glucose units in cellulose are β-glucose which are connected together to form very large, chain like molecules. The link between the glucose units is from carbon atom 1 in one unit to carbon atom 4 in another as shown in Fig. 8.1

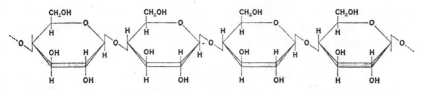

FIG. 8.1. Portion of a cellulose molecule showing 1–4 connected β-D-glucose units

The number of glucose units connected in this way to form a cellulose molecule varies with the origin of the cellulose, but it is always large and may amount to several thousand. Bundles of chains lying side by side are linked together to give cellulose fibres.

Starch

Starch is the chief food reserve of plants and is converted, as required, into sugars. It may be stored in the stems as in the sago palm, in the tubers as in potatoes or cassava, from which tapioca is made. Unripe fruits contain appreciable amounts of starch which is converted to glucose as the fruit ripens. It is especially abundant in seeds such as cereal grains and the pulses.

On microscopic examination, starch from various plant sources is found to consist of small granules, the shape and size of which are peculiar to the plant from which they have been obtained. The size of starch granules measured along their longest axis varies from 0·0002 cm to 0·015 cm. Particles of this size cannot be seen by the naked eye but are clearly visible on microscopic examination. Potato starch granules are among the largest and rice starch among the smallest. The granules of a particular type of starch need not all be of one size. In potato starch, for instance, the granules vary in size from 0·0015 cm to 0·01 cm. The size of the starch granules may influence the properties of the starch because large granules gelatinize more easily than small granules. It is difficult to generalize concerning the shape of starch granules but those from cereals such as maize or rice are angular, while spherical or ellipsoidal granules are characteristic of tuber and root starches such as tapioca, sago and potato starch.

Starch does not dissolve in cold water and it was formerly thought that this was because each granule was enclosed in an impervious cellulose envelope. It is now believed that the resistance to water is due to closer and more orderly packing of the starch particles at the surface of the granule than in its interior. If a suspension of starch in water is heated, water diffuses through the walls of the granules and causes swelling. This begins at about 60° C and by about 85° C the volume of the granules has increased by about five times and the starch sol is very viscous; a process known as gelatinization. Such a sol will set into a gel on cooling if sufficiently concentrated.

Uncooked starchy foods are not easy to digest because the starch granules are contained within the cell walls of the plant which the digestive juices are unable to penetrate. Cooking serves to gelatinize the starch granules; it also softens the cellulose of the cell walls and makes the pectin more soluble (see Fig. 8.2 on page 141).

Glucose is the only monosaccharide obtained on hydrolysis of starch. It was first thought that starch was composed, like cellulose, of strings of connected glucose units, the only difference between the two being that the glucose units in cellulose were the α-isomer and in starch the β-isomer. It is now known, however, that starch is a mixture of two substances called *amylose* and *amylopectin*. Both of these are polysaccharides and there is usually about four times as much amylopectin as amylose.

Amylose is responsible for the blue colour produced when starch reacts with iodine. It can be separated from amylopectin by formation of an insoluble complex with a suitable liquid such as butyl alcohol. The enzyme β-amylase, which is present in cereals, hydrolyses amylose almost completely to maltose. Amylopectin, on the other hand, gives a reddish-brown colour with iodine and only about half of it is converted

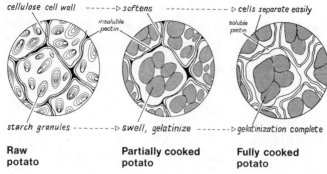

Fig. 8.2. Section of a potato as seen through a microscope

into maltose by β-amylase, the residue being referred to as a *dextrin*. Glucose syrup (p. 122) contains considerable quantities of dextrins, which are produced by incomplete hydrolysis of starchy materials. When dry starch is heated so-called pyro-dextrins are formed. These are brown in colour and soluble in water. Toast and bread-crust both derive some of their brown colour from pyro-dextrins.

The molecular weight of amylose varies from about 10 000 to about 50 000 and this corresponds to 70–350 glucose units. The glucose units are connected in a 1–4 manner to form a chain as in cellulose. Maltose is the only disaccharide obtained when amylose is hydrolysed and this shows that the glucose units are the α-isomer and not the β-isomer as in cellulose.

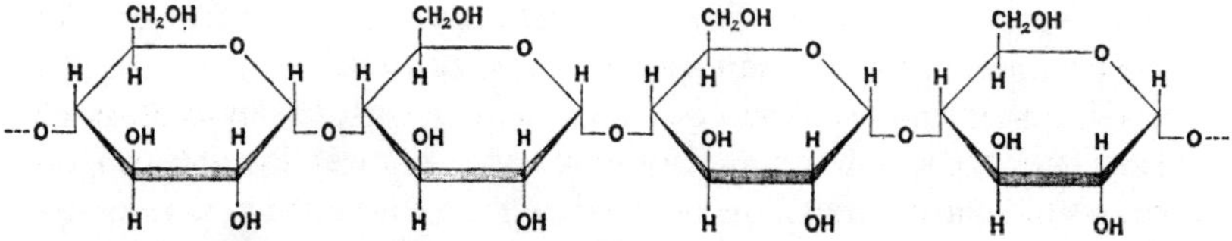

Fig. 8.3. Portion of an amylose molecule showing 1–4 connected α-D-glucose units

The structure of amylopectin is not as simple as that of amylose. To begin with the molecule is larger and may contain as many as 100 000 glucose units. It consists of a large number of comparatively short interconnected chains of glucose units. A portion of an amylopectin molecule can be represented diagrammatically as in Fig. 8.4 (p. 142). In this diagram each hexagon represents a glucose unit and AB and DE are the short chains of about 24 glucose units connected at BC and EF. The links connecting the chains are from the reducing group at the end

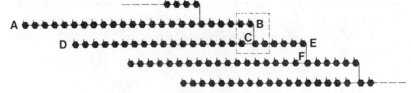

FIG. 8.4. Portion of an amylopectin molecule

of one chain to a primary alcohol group on another, i.e. from C_1 to C_6. The section of the above diagram enclosed in a broken line is shown in detail in Fig. 8.5.

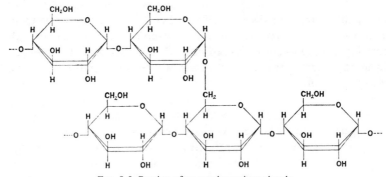

FIG. 8.5. Portion of an amylopectin molecule

In a single amylopectin molecule there are large numbers of these chains each containing 20–30 glucose units, depending upon the source of the starch. In the diagram above, only one 'branch' has been shown originating from each chain of glucose units. Most chains have more than one branching point, however, and a most complex three-dimensional structure can result.

Now that we know something of the structure of amylopectin it is possible to understand why β-amylase can only convert about half of it into maltose. The reason is that amylase splits off pairs of glucose units, in the form of maltose, from the free end of the chains of glucose units in the amylopectin molecule (i.e. the left-hand end in Fig. 8.4). When the chain has been degraded as far as a branching point the amylase is unable to split off further pairs of glucose units and the product is referred to as a β-limit-dextrin.

In addition to amylose and amylopectin, starch may contain small amounts of non-carbohydrate material such as phosphates and fats. The amount and composition of this extraneous material depend upon the source of the starch. Potato starch and wheat starch each contain about 0·5 per cent non-carbohydrate material and phosphates predominate: wheat starch, on the other hand, contains about 0·75 per cent made up largely of fats.

Pectin

Pectin is the name given to a mixture of polysaccharides found in fruits and some roots, which is responsible for the formation of gels in jam manufacture. Pectin can be isolated from fruits by extraction with hot dilute acids. Non-carbohydrate materials are extracted at the same time but the pectin can be separated from them by adding alcohol, which precipitates it.

Pectins from various sources differ considerably in composition but all of them contain *methyl pectate*, and two other complex polysaccharides called *araban* and *galactan*, which do not contribute to the gel-forming properties. The methyl pectate is responsible for the gel-forming properties of pectin: it consists of a chain of repeating esterified α-D-galacturonic acid units as shown in Fig. 8.6 although not all the carboxyl groups are esterified:

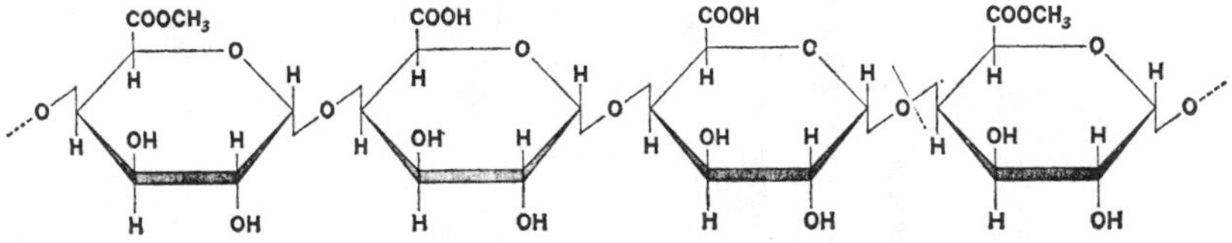

FIG. 8.6. Portion of a methyl pectate molecule

Several hundred of these esterified acid residues may be present in a single molecule of methyl pectate.

Concentrated pectin extracts can be bought for use in jam making (see p. 133). They are made either from citrus fruit residues or from the pulp remaining after the expression of juice from apples. The pectin is extracted by pressure cooking with water or very dilute acid. The extract is filtered, vacuum concentrated, and the pectin precipitated by adding alcohol.

Glycogen

This is the reserve carbohydrate of man and other animals. Glycogen has a molecular weight of 5 000 000 or greater. It differs from starch in being soluble in water and giving a reddish colour, not blue, with iodine. On hydrolysis the only monosaccharide obtained is glucose. The enzyme β-amylase converts glycogen to maltose in about 50 per cent yield and this is reminiscent of amylopectin. The structure of glycogen resembles that of amylopectin closely, but the repeating chains are much shorter and contain only 12 glucose units compared with 20–30 in amylopectin.

IMPORTANT CARBOHYDRATE FOODSTUFFS

Figure 8.7 shows some of the more important foods containing large quantities of carbohydrate (expressed as monosaccharide):

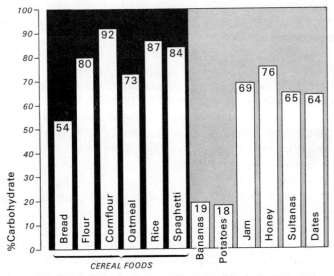

FIG. 8.7. The percentage carbohydrate content of foods

The most important cereals are wheat, oats, barley, rye, rice and maize. All cereals are cultivated grasses and the cereal grain is really the seed of the grass. Contained within the grain is a rich store of nutrients for the grass which should grow from it. Civilized societies in all parts of the world depend upon cereals for nourishment because they produce the maximum yield of food from a given area of ground. The cereal grains are obtained by threshing the harvested 'grass' to separate the grain from the chaff, which surrounds each grain, and the stalk which supports the ear.

It is clear from Fig. 8.7 that cereals are principally sources of carbohydrate. In addition, however, they contain substantial amounts of protein (from about 6 per cent in rice to about 12 per cent in oats and Canadian wheat) and because large quantities of cereal products are eaten this may constitute quite a large proportion of the total protein intake. Fats are also found in cereals (from about 1·5 per cent in wheat to about 5 per cent in oats). Cereal grains contain substantial amounts of vitamins of the B group though, as will become evident in the sequel, the quantity of these vitamins present in foods manufactured from cereals depends largely upon the degree to which the several parts of the grain have been separated in milling. The amount of moisture in cereal grains is quite small (from 7 per cent in oats to about 12 per cent in wheat) and this largely accounts for their good keeping qualities.

In the vegetable family the chief sources of carbohydrate are potatoes and the pulses such as peas, beans and lentils which are the seeds of leguminous plants.

Wheat

Wheat is by far the most important cereal as far as people in Great Britain are concerned. It was first grown in the Middle East but in the course of centuries its cultivation has spread and varieties of wheat suitable for cultivation in zones as climatically different as the tropics and the North European areas bordering on the Arctic Circle are now known. Some varieties of wheat, known as winter wheat, are sown in the autumn and harvested in the following August but spring wheat, which is sown and harvested in the same year, is grown in countries such as Canada, where the winters are severe. Winter wheat, such as English wheat, usually contains less than 10 per cent protein and gives a weak dough which bakes into small close-textured loaves. Flour from such wheat is said to be soft. Spring wheat, such as Canadian wheat, on the other hand, is rich in proteins and gives a strong flour from which a strong elastic dough can be made. Strong flours give doughs which produce bold well-risen loaves and they are very suitable for bread-making. English flour and other similar 'soft' flours are more suitable for the manufacture of cakes and biscuits and for household use. Flour used for breadmaking in this country is usually a blend of the two types.

Durum wheat, which is used for making macaroni and spaghetti is a particularly hard wheat of high protein content.

THE STRUCTURE OF A WHEAT GRAIN. A grain of wheat is normally about one centimetre long and half a centimetre broad. It is egg-shaped with a deep fissure or crease running along one side and a number of small hairs, called the beard, at one end. The grain is enclosed in an outer covering called *bran* which consists of several distinct layers and

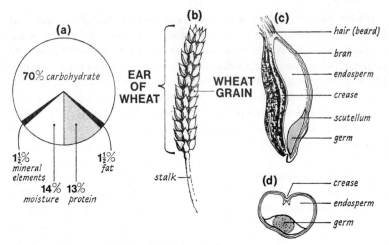

(a) The composition of wheat
(b) An ear of wheat
(c) Longitudinal section of a wheat grain
(d) Transverse section of a wheat grain

FIG. 8.8. The composition of wheat

constitutes about 15 per cent of the whole wheat. Bran contains a high proportion of B vitamins and about 50 per cent of the mineral elements present in the grain. Unfortunately bran consists largely of cellulose and hence is indigestible by humans. It is separated from the remainder of the grain during the production of flour (see below) and is used mainly for animal foods. The *germ*, which is situated at the base of the grain, is the actual seed or embryo and constitutes about 20 per cent of the whole grain. It is rich in fats, protein, vitamins of the B group, vitamin E and iron. The combined fatty acids present in the fats are mainly essential fatty acids. A membranous tissue called the scutellum separates the germ and the endosperm; it is exceedingly rich in the vitamin *thiamine* and contains about 60 per cent of all the thiamine present in the grain. The *endosperm* is mainly starch and is intended as a reserve of food for the germ. It is by far the largest component and makes up about 80–90 per cent of the wheat grain. The starch granules are embedded in a matrix of protein and the periphery of the endosperm is composed of a single layer of cells called the aleurone layer. This layer contains a higher proportion of proteins than the endosperm as a whole, but unfortunately it is removed with the bran during the milling of the wheat.

So many varieties of wheat are grown and climatic and other conditions are so variable that it is not possible to give precise figures for the composition of wheat. The figures given in Fig. 8.8 represent an average value.

FLOUR MILLING. Wheat grains are almost always reduced to flour before being eaten and this operation is known as flour milling. Archaeological evidence shows that flour was made in hand mills as long ago as 400 B.C. and in later times windmills or water mills were used in which the wheat was ground between two circular grooved stones the upper of which revolved while the lower stone remained stationary. The wheat was fed into the centre through a hole in the upper stone and was ground into flour during its passage to the periphery of the stones. In this process *all* the wheat grain was ground up so that the flour produced, called wholemeal flour, contained the germ, bran and scutellum as well as the powdered endosperm. Wholemeal flour is dark in colour and bread produced from it may be rather coarse, depending upon the extent to which the bran particles have been reduced in size.

Modern milling processes differ greatly from the age-old method just described. The milling is carried out using steel rollers in place of revolving flat stones and the germ, bran and scutellum are removed so that the flour produced consists essentially of powdered endosperm. The process is very complex but in essence it consists in separating the endosperm from the other constituents of the grain then gradually reducing the size of the endosperm particles by passing them through a series of steel rollers as shown diagrammatically in Fig. 8.9. Before milling, different varieties of wheat may be blended together so that the flour obtained from the blend is best suited to the purpose for which it is intended. After blending, the wheat is passed through a series of ingenious machines which remove stones, weed seeds and other extraneous materials, and may then be washed and brushed to remove adhering dirt.

Imported wheat is often too dry to be milled directly, and it must be 'conditioned' or brought to the optimum moisture content for milling. This can be done by storing the wheat in a moist condition for one or more days. The conditioning can be speeded up by passing the moist wheat through a machine known as a conditioner, in which it is heated to a temperature of 40–50°C for thirty to ninety minutes. Alternatively the wheat may be exposed to live steam for a minute or so, followed by rapid cooling in cold water. During the conditioning process the distribution of moisture through the grain becomes more uniform, the bran becoming tougher and the endosperm more friable. This makes easier the separation of endosperm and germ from the bran in the milling operations which follow. English wheat often contains more water than is desirable, and when this is so it must be dried before milling.

The conversion of grain to flour begins with the operation known as breaking, in which the grain, or grist as it is known, is passed through four or five pairs of rolls known as break rolls. These rolls, which are

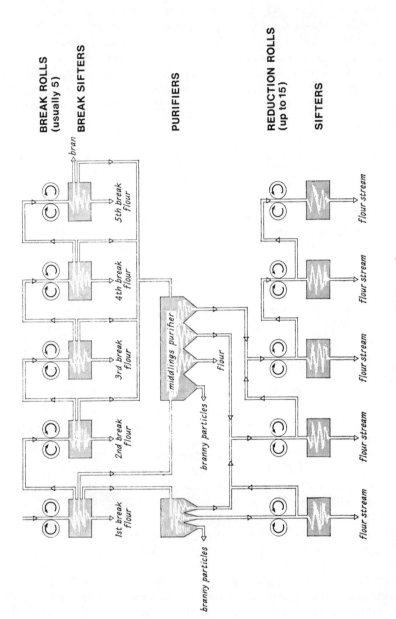

Fig. 8.9. Conversion of wheat to flour

made of steel, are corrugated and rotate at different speeds. The corrugations, which are arranged in a spiral fashion, break grain apart at the crease and scrape away the endosperm from the bran. After passing through the first break rolls the wheat is sieved through silk or fine wire gauze and separated into a small quantity of flour, known as first break flour, small particles of endosperm known as 'middlings' or 'semolina' and coarser particles of bran with adherent endosperm. The bran with its attached endosperm is passed on to the next set of break rolls. Each pair of break rolls is set closer together and has finer corrugations than the one before it and the branny residue from the final sifting is extremely thin with little or no attached endosperm.

The middlings produced at each set of break rolls are 'graded' or sized by further sieving in machines known as purifiers. These consist of enclosed reciprocating sieves through which a current of air is blown. The blowing removes particles of endosperm which are still attached to the bran, and these are treated in a separate part of the mill where the endosperm is scraped away from the bran by finely corrugated rolls similar to break rolls.

The graded semolina and middlings are converted to flour by a series of smooth rolls called reduction rolls. There are usually from ten to fifteen sets of reduction rolls and as with the break rolls, the clearance between the rolls decreases from one set of rolls to the next. The reduction rolls crack the semolina particles and gradually produce smaller and smaller fragments without damaging the starch grain themselves. If the endosperm were simply crushed to a fine powder by being passed through a pair of rolls set very closely together the starch granules would be badly damaged and the resulting flour would be of very poor quality. The product from each set of reduction rolls is sieved to remove the flour, and the residue is divided into two parts; the finer of these two fractions is sent to one of the succeeding reduction rolls, and the less fine is sent back down the reduction system. The germ is not friable and so it is flattened rather than powdered by the reduction rolls, and is easily separated in the sifting operations.

Flour 'streams' are obtained at each of the break rolls and reduction rolls and these differ markedly in composition. They may be mixed in various proportions to give flour suitable for special purposes, or they may all be combined to give what is known as a straight-run flour.

The milling technique described above can be modified to produce more or less flour from a given amount of wheat. The percentage of flour produced is termed the extraction rate of the flour. Wholemeal flour, which contains all the bran, germ and scutellum and endosperm of the wheat grain has an extraction rate of 100 per cent. An extraction rate of

70 per cent, on the other hand, produces flour which is composed almost exclusively of crushed endosperm.

SPECIAL FLOURS. *High and low protein flours.* The starch particles present in a sample of ordinary flour vary in size from below 5 microns to about 12 microns in diameter (1 micron = 10^{-6} m). The larger particles, of diameter greater than about 35 microns, consist of starch granules embedded in a protein matrix. Particles of size between 17 and 35 microns are, in the main, free starch granules and little protein matrix is present. Below about 17 microns the particles are mainly small starch granules, fragments of free protein and small particles of protein matrix with adherent fragments of starch. If flour is subjected to a further size-reducing process in an impact mill many of the larger particles consisting of starch embedded in protein matrix can be broken down and more separate starch granules and protein fragments released. By separating the flour produced into three fractions it is possible to obtain two high-protein flours and one low-protein flour as shown in Table 8.1.

Table 8.1. Protein Contents and Yields from an English Wheat Flour
(Parent flour = 9·5 % protein content)

Particle size range in microns	Yield %	Protein content %
35–120	43	11·5
17–35	45	6·0
less than 17	12	15·6

Because the sizes of the flour particles are so small it is not possible to separate the fractions by conventional sieving operations, but this can be done by using a piece of equipment known as an air classifier. In the classifier flour particles in air are subjected to powerful centrifugal forces by being made to follow a spiral path at high speeds and at the same time, of course, each particle is experiencing frictional drag. The centrifugal force on each particle is proportional to its weight whereas frictional resistance varies with particle size and not with weight. Because of this difference the coarser particles migrate to the outside of the spiral path and finer particles accumulate in the centre. The fraction of largest particle size is noticeably coarser, because of the absence of fine particles, than normal flour and it has been used for biscuitmaking and for self-raising flour. The intermediate low-protein fraction is valuable as a high-ratio cake flour (see p. 102) because of its fine and even particle size.

Enzyme-inactivated Flour. Wheat contains amylases and if the wheat has begun to sprout, as it may do if harvested under damp conditions, the α-amylase content may be relatively high. When a dough made from such flour is kept, considerable starch breakdown occurs and a sticky dough may be produced. In the case of flours for use in gravies, thickening agents, and powdered soups a high α-amylase content may be particularly undesirable because if the gravy or soup is made and kept hot the α-amylase may break down the starch to such an extent that it is no longer able to act as a thickening agent. Enzyme-inactivated flour is now available for special purposes such as this and it is made from wheat which has been steam treated so that its temperature reaches 100° C. The wheat is subsequently dried and converted into flour in the usual way. Enzyme-inactivated flour is not suitable for breadmaking because the elastic properties of the gluten are destroyed by the steaming process.

Agglomerated Flour. When ordinary flour is added to water the particles float on the surface and tend to stick together to form lumps which are difficult to disperse. An 'instant' flour which is easily wetted by water and can be dispersed in water without difficulty is manufactured by allowing flour to fall through jets of steam. The outer surfaces of the flour particles are wetted and if they are then allowed to fall through cold jets of air the particles stick together or agglomerate. The moisture content of the clusters is adjusted by passing the flour through heated chambers and oversize particles are reduced to a uniform particle size. As well as being easily dispersible in water, agglomerated flour, or instant flour, is free flowing and dust free because it consists of small clusters of flour particles above 100 microns in diameter. When agglomerated flour is added to water the clusters are penetrated by water as a result of capillary action and the wetted particles sink. Agglomerated flour is especially useful in soup and gravy powders or as a thickening agent, but it is likely to find many other applications in convenience foods.

FLOUR IMPROVERS. It was formerly the practice to store flour for several weeks after milling before it was used for breadmaking. During this period its breadmaking characteristics improved, as a result of the action of atmospheric oxygen on the proteins which form gluten during doughmaking. The gluten obtained from 'aged' flour is stronger and more elastic than that obtained from freshly milled flour. It has been discovered that this ageing period can be dispensed with if the flour is treated with a minute quantity of one of a number of oxidizing agents which are called flour improvers. It is now common practice to treat all flours with one of these improvers. Some of the compounds employed as flour improvers and the proportions in which they are used are listed in Table 8.2 below.

Table 8.2. Flour Improvers

Name	Formula	Parts improver used per million parts flour
Chlorine	Cl_2	400
Chlorine dioxide (Dyox)	ClO_2	35
Sulphur dioxide (for biscuits only)	SO_2	200 (maximum)
Benzoyl peroxide	$(C_6H_5CO)_2O_2$	50 (maximum)
Potassium bromate	$KBrO_3$	20
Ammonium persulphate	$(NH_4)_2S_2O_8$	200
Ascorbic acid	$C_6H_8O_6$	20–80

The first four of the improvers listed increase the whiteness of the flour by bleaching the *carotene* and *xanthophyll*, which are always present and give the flour a slight yellow tinge. When other improvers are used the miller may also employ a bleaching agent, such as nitrogen peroxide, to produce the desired change of colour.

The way in which improvers perform their functions is not fully understood though many theories have been advanced to explain it. It is possible, however, that the improvers produce some cross-linking between adjacent protein molecules by the formation of disulphide links from neighbouring sulphydryl (–SH) groups as shown in Fig. 8.10. The

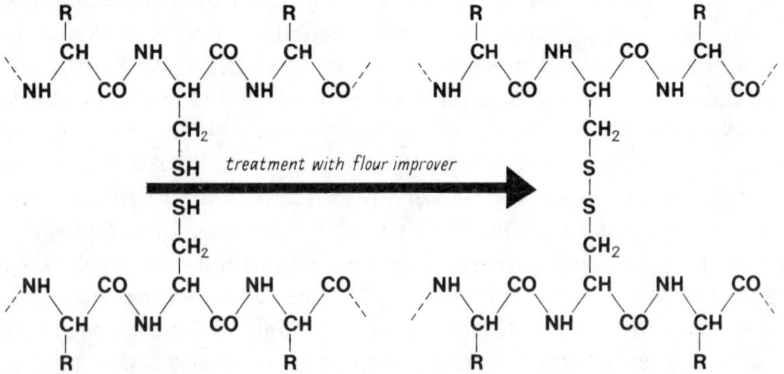

Two protein molecules with adjacent sulphydryl groups.

One larger protein molecule formed by cross-linking.

FIG. 8.10. Action of flour improvers

sulphydryl groups belong to the amino acid cysteine which forms part of some protein molecules (see Chapter 9 and Table 9.1). The increase in molecular weight and molecular complexity produced by such a process of cross-linking would be expected to produce a corresponding increase in the strength and elasticity of the gluten formed on treatment with water. This, of course, is the characteristic effect produced by flour improvers.

THE ENZYMES OF FLOUR. Wheat flour contains α- and β-amylases which are capable of hydrolysing the amylose and amylopectin of starch. The hydrolysis does not occur to any significant extent in dry flour but begins immediately a dough is made. β-amylase attacks the damaged starch grains inevitably present as a result of milling and hydrolyses some of the amylose to maltose. It can also hydrolyse amylopectin and produce maltose by splitting off pairs of glucose units from the ends of the chains. With amylopectin, only the 'free' ends of the chains can be attacked and hydrolysis ceases before the glucose unit which connects two chains together is reached. The links between the chains cannot be hydrolysed by β-amylase and a high molecular weight dextrin, which is not susceptible to further attack by β-amylase, is ultimately obtained. α-Amylase, which is present in flour made from sprouting wheat, attacks amylopectin in an entirely different way; it splits the links between the chains to produce low molecular weight dextrins. These dextrins differ in structure, as well as in size, from those produced by β-amylase. They consist, like amylose, of strings of connected glucose units whereas the dextrins produced by β-amylose are branched and three-dimensional like amylopectin.

The dextrins produced by α-amylase can be hydrolysed to maltose by β-amylase. Conversely, α-amylase can attack the dextrins produced by β-amylase to produce simpler dextrins which can be further hydrolysed to maltose by β-amylase. Clearly, by acting in conjunction, α- and β-amylase can produce a far greater quantity of maltose than either acting alone. The presence of much α-amylase in flour can have a disastrous effect when it is made into bread: the low molecular weight dextrins present cause marked crumb-stickiness and may lead to collapse of the loaf. α-Amylase is active up to about 60°C and so its action may continue for some time after the bread has been put in the oven.

Flour also contains peptidases and it is believed that these play a part in the 'ripening' of the dough. Peptidases also make available much α- and β-amylase which is combined with protein and would otherwise be unavailable. Lipases and lipoxidases also occur in flour and act upon the fats present. Lipases catalyse the hydrolysis of fats to glycerol and fatty acids whereas lipoxidases catalyse oxidation. Flour which has been stored for a long period may have a tallowy smell and flavour owing to the presence of oxidation product of fats. Phytase is another important enzyme present in flour. It splits up phytic acid and phytates (see p. 162) and is active during the fermentation and early stages of baking.

Breadmaking

A type of bread, known as unleavened bread, can be made by mixing flour with water and then baking it. Historically this is the forerunner of modern bread, but the product is hard and unattractive to most palates and the resemblance to bread, as we know it, is slight.

Bread is made from flour, water, salt and yeast. It has a honeycomb structure and may be regarded as a solid foam (see Table 6.3) with a multitude of pockets of carbon dioxide distributed uniformly throughout its bulk. Sugars naturally present in flour and the maltose made available by the action of amylases, are hydrolysed to glucose and this is fermented by zymase present in the yeast. Alcohol and carbon dioxide are formed and the latter aerates the dough. The reactions concerned are identical with those discussed on page 60. They are summarized below:

$$\underset{\substack{\text{starch}}}{(C_6H_{10}O_5)_n} \xrightarrow[\text{flour}]{\text{amylases in}} \underset{\text{maltose}}{C_{12}H_{22}O_{11}} \xrightarrow[\text{yeast}]{\text{maltase in}} C_6H_{12}O_6 \xrightarrow[\text{yeast}]{\text{zymase in}} C_2H_5OH + CO_2$$

Most of the alcohol formed during fermentation is driven off during baking and many thousands of gallons of alcohol enter the atmosphere daily from bakeries. In all, about 7 per cent of the nutrients originally present in the dough are lost as a result of the fermentation process. Small amounts of carboxylic acids are produced during the fermentation period as well as carbon dioxide and alcohol. The acids formed lower the pH of the dough and this affects the colloidal state of the gluten (see below) and assists in ripening the dough. The carbon dioxide retained by the dough also lowers the pH and so, in addition to its leavening function, it has a beneficial effect on the gluten structure. Some protein breakdown occurs during the fermentation period owing to the presence of proteolytic enzymes. During this period the yeast cells multiply and the yeast contributes substantially, together with the fermentation products, to the flavour of the loaf.

Two of the proteins present in flour—*gliadin* and *glutenin*—become hydrated and form an elastic complex called *gluten* when flour is kneaded with water. It is the presence of this elastic gluten which makes the manufacture of bread possible, because it forms an interconnected network which contains the carbon dioxide within the loaf and prevents its escape. The gluten is uniformly distributed throughout the dough and the carbon dioxide becomes trapped as small pockets of gas. As gas production continues the gluten strands are stretched and it is thought that bonds between adjacent protein molecules are broken and reformed to produce an elastic gas-retaining three-dimensional network. A ripe dough, that is one which is ready for baking, is springy and elastic and it can be fairly easily stretched out and shows a capacity to recover its former shape. An under-ripe dough is extensible, i.e. it can be stretched, but lacks elasticity. If fermentation is allowed to continue unhindered the dough becomes over-ripe and, as dough in this condition cannot be stretched far without breaking, its power to retain carbon dioxide is lost.

The salt used in doughmaking influences the rate at which fermentation takes place and enables the baker to control the development of the dough. In addition, it has a strengthening and toughening action on the gluten, which may be due to its inhibiting action on protein-splitting enzymes which, in the absence of salt, would cause a certain amount of degradation of the gluten. The third and most important function of the salt is to improve the flavour of the bread which, without it, has a flat insipid taste. The weight of salt added is about 2 per cent of the weight of flour used, although this figure varies slightly, more salt being used in the North of England than in the South. The amount of water needed to make a dough varies with the quality of the flour, but it is roughly half the weight of the flour used. Its temperature must be adjusted so that the fermented dough has a temperature of $24-27°C$. The quantity of yeast needed depends upon the time and temperature of fermentation but is usually about $0.3 - 1.0$ per cent of the weight of the flour used. When bread is baked the carbon dioxide expands, the starch gelatinizes, and the gluten coagulates to produce a more or less rigid loaf. The changes which occur during baking are considered in more detail on page 158.

Bulk Fermentation. In the traditional method of breadmaking all the ingredients are mixed together to form a dough which is allowed to ferment for a period. This is referred to as bulk fermentation. Several techniques of doughmaking are employed; in some cases a 'sponge' or very fluid dough made from some of the yeast, salt, water and about a quarter of the flour is allowed to ferment overnight before being added to the main bulk of the ingredients for a further shorter period of fermentation. The 'straight dough' technique is probably the most important method of bulk fermentation used in England, however. A typical recipe would be as follows: flour, 127 kg (i.e. 1 sack); yeast, 1.36 kg; salt, 2.27 kg; fat, 0.91 kg; water, 72.6 kg (i.e. 72 litres). The yeast is suspended in a little of the water and all the ingredients are thoroughly mixed by a mechanical mixer until a homogeneous dough is obtained.

This is covered to prevent the formation of a skin, and allowed to ferment for a period of one hour or longer depending upon the quantity of yeast used and the temperature of the dough. Yeast functions best in doughmaking at a temperature of about $26°C$ and the dough should preferably be kept at or about this temperature. The dough is then thoroughly kneaded or 'knocked back' to expel some of the carbon dioxide and tighten up the dough. This has the effect of bringing yeast cells into contact with a new environment and assists further fermentation. The dough is then covered again and allowed to ferment for a further period—usually about two and a half hours but, as before, this depends upon the amount of yeast used and the ambient temperature—at the end of which it is divided into pieces of the required weight which are shaped into balls. A good deal of carbon dioxide is lost during the dividing and moulding process and the dough is given a further period of fermentation referred to as first proof or intermediate proof to allow more carbon dioxide to be formed. During this period the gluten fibres recover after the rather harsh treatment they have received during dividing and shaping. After the first proving period of 10–15 minutes is over the dough is moulded to its final shape and after placing in baking tins, or on baking sheets, is given a final proof of about forty-five minutes at a somewhat higher temperature (usually $32–35°C$) during which it becomes fully inflated with carbon dioxide and assumes its final shape.

In a modern bakery the mixing, knocking back, dividing and moulding to shape are carried out mechanically and the proving periods are often spent on conveyor belts passing through temperature controlled chambers. Because of the fairly long fermentation period, however, a considerable weight of dough is being dealt with at any one time in a large bakery and this has to be man-handled from place to place and, of course, it occupies considerable space. In modern bread-making methods the fermentation period is replaced by a short period of intensive mixing (see below) and this overcomes one of the main drawbacks of the traditional breadmaking process.

Mechanically Developed Doughs. It has been found that if freshly-mixed dough is subjected to a short period of very intensive mixing the bulk fermentation period may be omitted. During this process of 'mechanical development' the mixing machine rapidly stretches the protein fibres of the gluten and this replaces the stretching brought about by gas evolution in the bulk fermentation process. It is thought that bonds between adjacent protein units are ruptured during the mechanical treatment and this is followed by a rapid redisposition of the protein molecules. At this point mechanical work must cease and a period of re-formation of chemical bonds takes place to give the required network structure. If mixing is continued beyond this point an inferior product results. It has been found by experiment that the optimum amount of development is that produced by the expenditure of about 0·14 kilowatt minutes per kg of dough or, expressing this in electrical units of work, 11 watt hours per kg. This is about five to eight times the amount of energy used in a normal breadmaking process.

Yeast is still used in mechanically developed doughmaking although one of its jobs—the stretching and re-orientation of gluten fibres—is done mechanically. The yeast is still required for producing carbon dioxide, which aerates the bread in the usual way, and for flavouring.

There are a number of methods of making mechanically developed dough but one process which has become important is that developed at the British Baking Industries Research Association at Chorleywood which has become known as the Chorleywood bread process. In this method a normal breadmaking recipe can be used except that somewhat more yeast and water than usual are required (about 2·3 kg of yeast are required per sack of flour compared with about 1·4 kg for bulk fermentation and about 7 per cent more water). Ascorbic acid and fat must also be present. Ascorbic acid is perhaps more familiar as vitamin C but it is used here as an oxidizing agent or improver, and not as a vitamin supplement. It may be worth pointing out that ascorbic acid itself is a reducing agent but in the dough it is enzymically oxidized to dehydroascorbic acid (see p. 246) and it is this which functions as the effective oxidizing agent. About 75 ppm of ascorbic acid are required and this is about 10 g per sack of flour. The inclusion of about 0·9 kg of fat per sack of flour is essential and this should preferably be a high melting point fat.

Almost any flour can be used in the Chorleywood process and good bread can be obtained from weak flour. This means that English flour may be used, whereas for the normal bulk fermentation methods the use of a strong flour is necessary. The reason for this is that a certain amount of protein is lost during the bulk fermentation period and this does not occur to any extent with mechanically developed doughs. The fact that there is little or no nutrient loss is important to the baker for economic reasons and it also explains why more water must be used when mixing a mechanically developed dough. The water content of the final product— the baked loaf—is the same as usual. Control of temperature is less important in the Chorleywood process than in bulk fermentation methods and good results can be obtained throughout the range 27– 32°C. Because of the large amount of energy expended during development of the dough its temperature may increase by 11–14°C during the process.

The ingredients for the dough are fed into a powerful mixing machine which is equipped with a meter to indicate how much energy is expanded during the development period. The mixing and development are completed in as short a time as possible—usually about five minutes—and when the appropriate amount of energy has been expended the machine switches off. The dough is then divided into pieces of the correct weight for the loaves required and these are shaped into balls and given a first proof period of six to ten minutes before being moulded to shape and being placed in baking tins. After a second proving period of about fifty to sixty minutes the bread is ready for baking in the normal way.

The advantages of the Chorleywood bread process compared with a normal bulk fermentation process are summarized in Table 8.3.

Table 8.3. Advantages of the Chorleywood Bread Process

Time	Less than 2 hours including baking—a saving of about 60 per cent.
Premises	Dough-room areas are reduced by 75 per cent. Temperature and humidity control not required.
Materials	Flour of low protein content may be used. No fermentation losses.
Product	Variability of product reduced. Bread has a lower staling rate.

Changes during Baking. Bread is baked at a temperature of about 232°C for a period of from 30 to 50 minutes depending upon the type of bread and the size of the loaf. During baking, the dough first rises rapidly because the pockets of carbon dioxide in the loaf expand as the temperature increases. At first there may also be some slight increase in the activity of the yeast, resulting in increased production of gas, but this diminishes as the temperature increases, until at a temperature of about 54°C the yeast is killed and fermentation ceases. As the temperature increases, the water present causes the starch granules to swell and gelatinize, and during this period the starch probably abstracts some water from the gluten. Hot gluten is soft and devoid of its characteristic elasticity, and gelatinized starch now supports the structure of the loaf. The gluten begins to coagulate at about 74°C and the coagulation continues slowly to the end of the baking period. The temperature of the interior of the loaf never exceeds the boiling point of water, in spite of the high temperature of the oven. Water and much of the carbon dioxide and alcohol formed during the fermentation escape during baking. Considerable dextrin formation occurs at the outside of the loaf as a result of the action of heat and steam on the starch; the sugars formed are converted to caramel which imparts an attractive brown colour to the crust.

Bread Quality. A loaf of bread has certain characteristics by which its quality is judged. The dough should rise to produce an upstanding loaf, the interior of which should be uniform in porosity and firm and elastic in consistence. The crust should be golden-brown in colour and should be crisp and brittle rather than tough, because this would make it difficult to cut and chew. A dough which has been insufficiently fermented will give a starch gel which is too stiff to permit expansion and a small, dense loaf will result. In a dough which has been over-fermented, starch breakdown will have occurred to such an extent that the strength of the starch gel is reduced to a point where it is unable to stand the increased internal gas pressure which occurs during baking. Individual gas cells will coalesce to form large pockets and gas escape at the surface will prevent the loaf from rising properly. In addition, such a loaf will contain larger quantities of dextrins than are found in a properly fermented loaf, and this will cause the interior of the loaf to be darker in colour.

It is common knowledge that when bread is kept it becomes stale. The crust becomes soft and leathery and it loses its appealing flavour. This is due largely to the diffusion of water from the interior of the loaf to the crust. Such 'crust-staling' occurs more rapidly with wrapped bread than with unwrapped because the moisture is unable to escape. At the same time the interior of the loaf becomes stale and this crumb-staling is associated with loss of water and is characterized by a hardening of the crumb structure and deterioration of flavour. Crumb-staling is not due entirely to loss of moisture and it has been known for over a hundred years that bread stales even when kept in conditions which preclude loss of moisture. Such stale bread which has retained its moisture can be made fresh again by heating to a temperature of 160°C or higher. This heating process can often be applied with advantage to bread and other flour products which have become stale under ordinary conditions though it is ineffective in producing freshness if the moisture content has fallen below 30 per cent.

It is now known that crumb-staling is caused by a change in the nature of the amylopectin in the bread from an amorphous, partly gelatinized, form to a more crystalline modification. During this process the amylopectin molecules become more closely oriented and aggregated as a result of hydrogen bonding. To put this more simply we may say that in fresh bread the amylopectin molecules, and the chains of glucose units of which they are built up, are arranged in a completely haphazard and random manner in partially swollen starch granules. In stale bread, on the other hand, many amylopectin molecules may be arranged in a cluster and the chains of glucose units lie parallel to each other almost as if they had been combed into position. The presence and absence of order in stale and fresh bread respectively has been confirmed by X-ray studies. During the change from partially gelatinized starch to the more or less crystalline form, water is released and is absorbed by the gluten and crust.

Staling can be prevented by drying, because bread containing less than about 16 per cent moisture does not stale. Surprisingly, excess moisture can also prevent staling and wet bread remains fresh for long periods. Neither of these methods is of any practical importance, however. Temperature can play an important part and bread kept under controlled moisture conditions remains fresh above 60°C and below −10°C. At temperatures between these extremes bread becomes stale with a maximum rate of staling at about 0°C. This discovery has been put to practical use in the preservation of bread and sponge-cakes (which normally stale in the same way as bread) by deep-freezing. It has long been recognized that wrapped bread stays fresh longer than unwrapped, although crust staleness may develop more quickly. This is undoubtedly due to moisture retention which prolongs the period for which the crumb remains soft.

Another method of delaying staling is by the incorporation into the bread of emulsifying agents though it is not yet clear how these substances delay the onset of staling. The use of emulsifying agents in bread is controlled by the Bread and Flour Regulations, 1963, and only stearyl tartrate or partial glycerol esters, such as glyceryl monostearate, may be used for this purpose.

Types of Bread. Table 8.4 summarizes those sections of the Bread and Flour Regulations (1963) which define the main types of bread offered for sale in Great Britain. The percentages quoted are calculated by weight on the dry matter of the bread.

BREAD AS A FOOD. White bread, which is made from flour of about 70 per cent extraction rate, contains approximately 54 per cent carbohydrate, 8 per cent protein and 1·7 per cent fat. As far as these nutrients are concerned the composition of bread is similar to that of the flour from which it is made if allowance is made for the difference in water content. Like all other foods produced from cereals, bread is eaten primarily as a cheap source of energy, but it also contains valuable

Table 8.4. Types of Bread

White bread	Composed of dough, made from flour, yeast and water and subsequently baked. May contain a fairly wide range of added ingredients including salt, fats, sugar, milk and milk products, rice and soya flour wheat germ, oats, enzyme-active preparations, bleachers and improvers, preservatives, emulsifiers and stabilizers.
Brown bread	As white bread but must contain not less than 0·6 per cent fibre and may be coloured by caramel.
Wholemeal bread	Made from flour obtained by grinding up the whole of the wheat berry—including the bran and germ. No bleach or improver may be used.
Wheatgerm bread	Contains at least 10 per cent processed wheat germ, e.g. *Hovis*. Characteristic flavour.
Malt bread	Contains 5–15 per cent of ground malt or malt extract. Darker in colour and sweeter than ordinary bread. Rather sticky texture.
Milk bread	Contains at least 6 per cent of whole milk solids.
Skimmed milk bread	Contains at least 6 per cent of skimmed milk solids.
Butter bread	Contains at least 6 per cent of added milk fat.
Protein bread	Contains at least 22 per cent protein.
Gluten bread	Contains at least 16 per cent protein.
Starch reduced bread	Contains not less than 50 per cent carbohydrate.

amounts of protein, iron and vitamins. Bread made from flour of 70 per cent extraction rate has an energy value of about 1070 kg/100 g. A small white loaf will provide 4777 kJ; this is a considerable fraction of the 12 000 kJ required daily by a moderately active man. A pound loaf also contains over 38 g of protein, which is nearly half the recommended daily allowance for a moderately active man.

Because the nutrients in wheat grains are not present in the same proportions in all parts of the grain, a change in the extraction rate produces a change in the composition of the flour obtained. In particular, flour of low extraction rate contains less thiamine and mineral elements than flour of high extraction rate because these nutrients are mainly concentrated in the germ, bran and scutellum, all of which are removed in the production of low extraction-rate flour. This difference is clearly shown in Table 8.5 although it must be stressed that such figures are only of value if they refer to straight-run flour (p. 149) as by appropriate variations in milling technique several flour streams of different composition can be obtained for a given overall extraction rate.

Riboflavine and nicotinic acid, which are members of the B group of vitamins, are both present in greater concentrations in flour of high

Table 8.5. Effect of Extraction Rate on Composition of Flour

Extraction rate	English flour		Canadian flour	
	100%	70%	100%	70%
Protein g/100 g	9·10	8·10	13·9	13·1
Calcium mg/100 g	36·0	19·0	28·0	13·0
Iron mg/100 g	3·10	1·40	3·90	1·80
Thiamine μg/100 g	294	87·0	363	69·0

extraction rate than in 'white' flour, though the difference is not so marked as with thiamine.

From a consideration of these facts it would appear that wholemeal bread is better, from a purely nutritional point of view, than bread produced from flour of lower extraction rate. This is not necessarily so, however, because although the nutrients listed above may be present in larger amounts in wholemeal flour than in flour of lower extraction rate it does not follow that they are also absorbed by the body in larger amounts. Flour of 100 per cent extraction rate may contain as much as 2·6 per cent fibre compared with 0·2 per cent for flour of 70 per cent extraction rate and there is evidence to show that the incorporation of much roughage with foods leads to a decrease in the amount of nutrients absorbed because of the increased peristalsis it produces. Most so-called wholemeal bread sold today, however, is of about 95 per cent extraction rate, the coarsest bran particles having been removed from the flour. Again, although calcium, iron and phosphorus are present in larger amounts in wholemeal flour than in flour of lower extraction rate they may not be completely absorbed. This is because the phosphorus is present in the form of a complex acid called phytic acid which combines with calcium, and also with iron, to form insoluble salts, called phytates, which are not absorbed by the body. However, phytases present in the flour break down much of the phytic acid during breadmaking and so make it available to the body. In bread made from flour of 70 per cent extraction rate about 85 per cent of the phytic acid is broken down compared with only 30 per cent in bread made from flour of 95 per cent extraction rate. Whether or not the body is able to make full use of all the nutrients in wholemeal bread it remains true that vitamins and minerals are lost from wheat during the milling of flour of low extraction rate. In order to compensate for these losses, at least in part, it is now obligatory for millers to add certain nutrients to all flour other than wholemeal flour of 100 per cent extraction rate. Sufficient iron, thiamine, nicotinic acid and purified chalk must be added to ensure that 100 g of the flour will contain not less than 1·65 mg of iron, 0·24 mg of thiamine, 1·60 mg of nicotinic acid or nicotinamide and between 235 mg and 390 mg of calcium carbonate. The iron is added as ferric ammonium nitrate or, rather surprisingly, as metallic iron produced in a finely divided state by reducing ferric oxide with hydrogen. Flour of any extraction rate may be produced provided that the above nutrients are present in the stated amounts.

BISCUITS. Biscuits are made from flour with the addition of other ingredients such as salt, fat, sugar and flavouring agents. Baking powder is sometimes added to make them rise a little and some biscuits, such as cream crackers, are leavened with yeast in much the same way as bread. The dough is rolled to a thin sheet, cut into appropriate shapes and quickly baked at a high temperature. The water content of biscuits is only about 3 per cent compared with about 39 per cent in bread. The energy value of sweet biscuits may be twice as high as that of bread because of their low water content and the extra sugar and fat they contain.

SEMOLINA. In addition to being used in flour milling (see p. 149) the name semolina is given to a wheat product obtained wholly from the endosperm of Durum wheat (which is rich in gluten). It is made by milling wheat grains but the particle size is much greater than that of flour.

MACARONI, SPAGHETTI AND VERMICELLI. These are all made from semolina of high protein content. The semolina is mixed to a doughy mass with water and is then thoroughly kneaded. The kneaded dough is next transferred to a press where it is extruded through a hole of the desired size and shape, to give tubes or threads which are afterwards dried for a long period. These wheat products are cooked by immersion in boiling water, and during this process they may absorb as much as three times their own weight of water. Because of this high water content large quantities of these foods are required to provide a sustaining meal, and they are usually supplemented by other more nutritious foods such as cheese.

SHREDDED WHEAT AND PUFFED WHEAT. These are breakfast foods prepared from whole wheat grains. The former is made from shredded, cooked wheat grains and the latter from wheat grains which have been cooked under pressure. At the end of the cooking period, the pressure is released and the grains become inflated or 'puffed' by the air and steam within them.

Other Cereals

Oats, rye, barley, maize and rice are all important cereals but their contribution to the British diet is much less than that of wheat.

OATS. Oats are richer in fats and mineral elements than other cereals and their protein content is also high. Flour made from oats is not suitable for making bread, however, because the proteins it contains do not form an elastic complex like the gluten of wheat when mixed with water.

Oats are prepared for human consumption by cleaning them and then drying and storing for a period. This facilitates the removal of the closely adherent husk. The product, known as *groats*, can be ground to produce oatmeal or rolled into flakes after being partially cooked by steam. The rolling ruptures the cell walls and flattens the grains and this makes subsequent cooking easier.

Oatmeal contains roughly 12 per cent protein, 73 per cent carbohydrate and 9 per cent fat. Consequently, oatmeal and rolled oats are nutritious foods, oatmeal having an energy value of 1692 kg/100 g. It must be remembered, however, that porridge made with water contains only about one-eighth of its weight of oatmeal. The phosphorus content of oatmeal is relatively high and it is mainly present in the combined form as phytic acid which, as has already been pointed out in connection with wheat, combines with calcium and iron and prevents their absorption by the body.

RYE. Rye can be grown in areas where the climate is too severe for wheat. The nutrients in rye are present in roughly the same amounts as in wheat. It is much less valued that wheat, however, because the proteins it contains do not give a strong gluten during doughmaking and, while large quantities of bread are made from rye flour, the product differs markedly from bread as we know it. Rye flour gives stodgy loaves which are unattractive to those accustomed to wheat bread. However, rye-bread is still a staple article of diet in Northern Europe, especially among the poor classes. Rye-bread may contain substantial proportions of wheat flour and this improves the appearance of the loaves obtained. It is not eaten to a large extent in this country, but crisp rye-biscuits (e.g. 'Ryvita') made from crushed whole rye grain are quite popular.

BARLEY. Barley is not eaten as a cereal in this country but is grown extensively for the manufacture of malt for brewing and for animal fodder. Bread is never made from barley because its proteins do not form a gluten when mixed with water and an aerated loaf cannot be obtained.

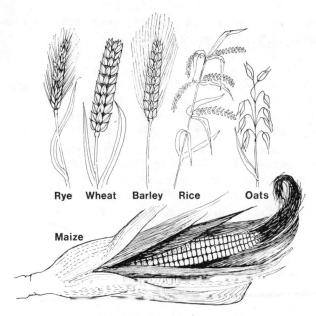

Rye Wheat Barley Rice Oats

Maize

FIG. 8.11. Cereal grains

MAIZE. Maize is not widely used as a food for human consumption in this country. In other countries, particularly America and South Africa, it forms an important part of the diet. It cannot be used for making bread because its proteins do not form a gluten. As a provider of energy maize is as efficient as the other cereals, but in other respects it is less desirable. The phosphorus in maize is present in combined form as phytic acid this can interfere with the absorption of calcium and iron by the body. The quantity of the vitamin nicotinic acid present is also small, and the deficiency is made more serious by the fact that the essential amino acid *tryptophan*, which can be converted by the body to nicotinic acid is also present in only small quantities. The deficiency disease pellagra is associated with high consumption of maize, but it should not occur if adequate amounts of other foods are eaten.

Corn-on-the-cob, which is becoming popular as a vegetable in this country, is a special variety of maize. The popular breakfast food called cornflakes, and cornflour, used in custards and blancmange powders, are also maize products. Cornflour consists of little but starch and is made by washing away the protein and fat from maize flour with dilute alkaline solutions. *Sago, tapioca* and *arrowroot* are similar food products containing little except starch, but they are not made from cereals. Sago is produced from the pith of the sago palm, tapioca from the roots of the cassava plant and arrowroot from the underground stem or rhizome of the West Indian maranta.

RICE. This is the main cereal of oriental countries though it is not important in British diets. It is the poorest of all cereals in protein, fat and mineral elements and can hardly be called a nutritious food although, like all cereals, it is a valuable source of energy. Rice has an energy value of 1530 kg/100 g and to provide the 12 MJ required daily by a moderately active man almost 900 g of rice would be required. This would weigh nearly 4 kg after cooking because of the large quantities of water absorbed by rice during boiling.

When harvested, rice grains are enclosed in thick husks which are removed during its preparation as a food for human beings. The grains are then polished to remove a thin skin called silverskin. The layers removed, particularly the silverskin, contain thiamine, and polished rice is completely lacking in this important vitamin. Consumption of polished rice as a main article of diet may produce the disease beriberi, which is caused by a deficiency of thiamine.

Potatoes

The potato is not a true root like the carrot, but is a swollen underground stem or tuber which contains a store of food for the plant.

Potatoes contain about 15–20 per cent starch, the remainder being mainly water with small quantities of proteins, mineral elements and vitamins. Potatoes are primarily a cheap source of energy, their energy value being about 324 kg/100 g. They are not, however, such a rich source of energy as cereal products and bread provides about three times as much energy as an equal weight of potatoes. Potatoes contain about 0·35 per cent nitrogen and of this, about half is present as protein. About 10 per cent of the nitrogenous compounds present are amino acids and these are as valuable, from the nutritional point of view, as proteins. In addition to their importance as an energy source potatoes also provide valuable quantities of ascorbic acid. Raw, new potatoes contain about 30 mg/100 g of this vitamin and some 60 per cent of this may remain in peeled boiled potatoes. The concentration of ascorbic acid is lower in the skin of the potato than in the interior, but the tissue immediately beneath the skin, which is usually removed when potatoes are peeled before cooking, contains about 15 per cent of the total ascorbic acid content of the tuber. When potatoes are cooked in their skin the peel removed afterwards is much thinner and less ascorbic acid is lost.

CARBOHYDRATES AS FOODSTUFFS

Foodstuffs rich in carbohydrates are of value primarily as sources of energy. Weight for weight, proteins provide roughly the same amount of energy as carbohydrates, and fats provide twice as much. Of the three, however, carbohydrates are by far the cheapest and the most easily digested and absorbed. It has already been mentioned that over-indulgence in foods rich in sugar may lead to obesity and to under-consumption of other foods containing essential nutrients. These remarks apply equally to over-consumption of foods containing polysaccharides because these are hydrolysed to monosaccharides before absorption. If more monosaccharide is produced than is required the excess is converted into fat and stored in fat depots until it is required for provision of energy in time of restricted food intake.

In the absence of sufficient carbohydrate the energy requirements of the body can be met by protein and fat, and it is possible to live on a diet containing little carbohydrate. Eskimos, for example, live almost exclusively on protein and fat. In Japan, on the other hand, about 80 per cent of the total energy intake is supplied by carbohydrate. A diet which is low in carbohydrate is not recommended for persons in normal health, however, because carbohydrate 'spares' protein. The body can make best use of ingested protein if carbohydrate is eaten at the same time.

Carbohydrates in the Body

During digestion the carbohydrates contained in food (with the exception of cellulose), are hydrolysed by enzymes to their component monosaccharides. The process starts in the mouth, where saliva, which contains salivary amylase, is intimately mixed with the food and begins to hydrolyse the starch to maltose. The hydrolysis continues in the stomach until the food is acidified by mixture with the gastric juice. The food passes from the stomach to the small intestine, where pancreatic amylase continues the conversion of starch to maltose. Maltase present in the intestinal juices hydrolyses the maltose so formed to glucose. Lactase and sucrase, which are also present, convert lactose and sucrose to glucose, galactose and fructose, as explained in Chapter 7. The monosaccharides pass from the small intestine into the bloodstream and are carried to the liver (where fructose and galactose are enzymically converted to glucose) and the muscles.

The liver and muscles are able to convert glucose to glycogen which serves as a reserve of carbohydrate for the body. Glycogen is re-converted to glucose as required to meet the energy requirements of the muscles and other tissues. The muscles of a well nourished man may contain as much as 250 g of glycogen and up to 100 g, which is sufficient to satisfy his glucose requirements for about six hours, may be present in his liver. When the muscles and liver can accommodate no more glycogen the surplus glucose is converted by the liver into fat which is stored in fat depots as the body's second line of defence against food shortage. A small amount of glucose circulates in the blood for transport to tissues drawing upon the liver's carbohydrate stocks or for transport to the liver to be converted to glycogen. After eating a meal the blood may contain up to 0·14 per cent glucose but this figure falls to about 0·08 per cent some three or four hours after eating. This is quite a small amount and is equivalent to only about 5 g of glucose.

The Oxidation of Glucose

The Body obtains energy by converting fats, proteins and carbohydrates to glucose and oxidizing that to simpler molecules and ultimately to carbon dioxide and water. The overall process may be likened to the release of energy from fossil fuels by burning them in a power station or boiler. Metabolic oxidation is infinitely more subtle and impressive, however, and man's most sophisticated fuel burning appliances are primitive compared with nature's delicately balanced and controlled complex of interdependent reactions.

The living cell has to function in an aqueous environment at a constant pH and at a comparatively low and essentially constant temperature. It cannot use heat energy to do work and bearing in mind the limitations mentioned it may seem surprising that any energy is made available at all. In fact, however, as we shall see below, almost half the energy locked up in the glucose molecule is captured by the body and this is a better conversion rate than that achieved by the most modern fuel-burning power station.

When glucose is completely oxidized to carbon dioxide and water by burning in oxygen a large amount of heat is evolved:

$$C_6H_{12}O_6 + 6O_2 \longrightarrow 6CO_2 + 6H_2O + 2820\,kJ$$

In the body, however, oxidation does not take place in one step but by a complicated and elegant series of nearly thirty reactions, each of which releases only a fraction of the energy which would be made available by complete oxidation of the glucose molecule. Many of the oxidative steps in this sequence of reactions do not involve direct reaction with oxygen at all but are simple dehydrogenation reactions which can be represented by a general equation:

$$AH_2 \xrightarrow{\;-2[H]\;} A$$

In many of these reactions the two hydrogen atoms removed are transferred to a coenzyme, e.g. Coenzyme 1, (NAD, i.e. nicotinamideadenine dinucleotide) or Coenzyme 11 (NADP, i.e. nicotinamideadenine dinucleotide phosphate) which act as hydrogen acceptors. The transfer is catalysed by oxidases which are highly specific in the sense that a particular oxidase will only work with one substrate-coenzyme pair.

There are two main stages in the oxidation of glucose by the body. In the first stage it is converted by a series of reactions to pyruvic acid:

$$C_6H_{12}O_6 \xrightarrow{-4[H]} 2CH_3COCOOH \qquad \text{No oxygen required}$$

33 kJ energy made available to the body.

In the second stage the pyruvic acid is oxidized by a further series of reactions to carbon dioxide and water:

$$CH_3COCOOH \xrightarrow{+5[O]} 3CO_2 + 2H_2O \qquad \text{Oxygen required}$$

About 126 kJ energy made available to the body.

The first stage is called *glycolysis* or, since it can take place in the absence of oxygen, *anaerobic glycolysis*. The amount of energy made available by glycolysis is small compared with that released during the second stage. Energy for violent physical exercise—such as running to catch a bus—is required instantly and as the bloodstream may be unable to supply oxygen sufficiently quickly to permit complete oxidation of glucose, anaerobic glycolysis takes place preferentially. The pyruvic acid produced is reduced to lactic acid and this is carried by the bloodstream to the liver where part of it is oxidized to provide energy for reconversion of the remainder to glycogen and glucose. The cyclic conversion of glucose to pyruvic acid, lactic acid and back to glucose is known as the Cori cycle after its discoverers. Normally, when energy is not required so quickly, it is obtained by complete oxidation of glucose to carbon dioxide and water via pyruvic acid and about 75 per cent of the cell's energy requirements are provided by the second stage. Conversion of pyruvic acid to carbon dioxide and water occurs by a cyclic process involving citric acid which is often referred to as the citric acid cycle or, in deference to Sir Hans Krebs, who worked out the details of the process, the Krebs cycle. Fig. 8.12 summarizes the changes which occur during the digestion absorption and oxidation of carbohydrates by the body.

The biochemical oxidation of glucose is a complex and involved process and it took over fifty years to work out exactly how it occurs. All the separate reactions are enzyme-controlled, ten enzymes being required for the conversion to pyruvic acid and another ten for the

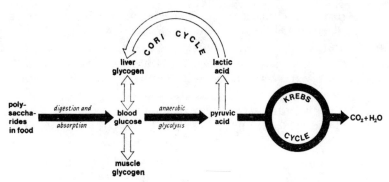

FIG. 8.12. Digestion, absorption and oxidation of carbohydrates

second stage of the oxidation to carbon dioxide and water. The whole sequence is of great importance and beauty but many readers will be relieved to learn that we do not intend to give complete details of it here. One aspect of the oxidation process, which is common to both the first and second stages, and is indeed a feature of many other biochemical energy transformations, deserves further attention however. This is the way in which a compound with the intimidating name of *adenosine triphosphate* (ATP for short) can behave as an energy-bank or energy store-house for the body. ATP is built up from one molecule of the purine derivative adenine, one molecule of the sugar ribose (which together form the nucleotide *adenosine*) and three molecules of phosphoric acid.

In the body the phosphate groups may be split off successively from an ATP molecule to yield first *adenosine diphosphate* (ADP), then *adenosine monophosphate* (AMP), and finally adenosine itself. The adenosine part of the molecule is unchanged in this series of reactions and if we represent it by A we can represent the series of reactions as follows:

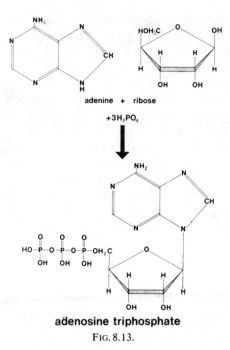

adenine + ribose

$+3H_3PO_4$

adenosine triphosphate

FIG. 8.13.

The importance of the series of reactions (shown on p. 170) is the fact that the two terminal phosphate groups are attached by high-energy phosphate bonds (shown in dark print in the equations) and conversion of 1 mole of ATP to ADP or one mole of ADP to AMP is accompanied by the release of 33 kJ. Conversion of AMP to adenosine, on the other hand, only yields 12·6 kJ. In the reverse reactions the same amounts of energy are absorbed:

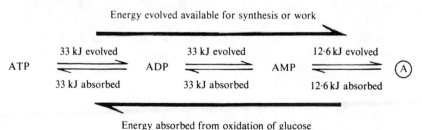

Energy evolved available for synthesis or work

ATP   33 kJ evolved / 33 kJ absorbed   ADP   33 kJ evolved / 33 kJ absorbed   AMP   12·6 kJ evolved / 12·6 kJ absorbed   (A)

Energy absorbed from oxidation of glucose

The energy-rich phosphate bonds function as energy stockpiles for energy released during oxidation of glucose in the cell. The energy is available for re-use on demand, for muscular contraction or to make possible the synthesis of some other molecule by the body or for any other purpose. When this occurs ATP is converted to ADP or AMP which are then re-available for conversion to ATP at a time when surplus energy is available.

During the complete oxidation of one mole of glucose by the body thirty-six moles of ATP (or their equivalent in related compounds) are formed from ADP and the energy absorbed in this process and hence available for further use is $36 \times 33 = 1188$ kJ. This compares with the 2820 kJ evolved when glucose is burned in oxygen and from this we see that the body is able to capture about 43 per cent of the energy of the glucose molecule. The residue is either used up in making other molecules during the oxidation process or appears as heat.

The complicated series of reactions involved in the assimilation and utilization of glucose by the body are controlled by several hormones the best known of which is *insulin*, which is secreted by the pancreas. In the disease *diabetes mellitus* insufficient insulin is produced by the pancreas and as a result glucose circulates in the blood in abnormally large amounts and is not taken up by the liver or muscles for conversion to glycogen or for oxidation. The body is thus unable to utilize carbohydrate foods and has to resort instead to fats and proteins to make up its energy deficiencies. Unfortunately, increased utilization of fat in this way leads to accumulation of certain poisonous products of fat metabolism in the liver and the bloodstream and this can have serious consequences. Diabetes mellitus can be controlled by careful attention to the diet and in more severe cases by regular injections of insulin.

Dietary Fibre

The term fibre is hard to define; it is not simply cellulose (p. 138) for it includes other polysaccharides, hemicelluloses and lignin (p. 266). Some foods, such as lean, stringy beef from old animals and old root vegetables such as carrots contain fibre that is coarse. Other foods, however, such as wholemeal bread and young root and leafy vegetables contain fibre which is much finer. Both the quality and quantity of fibre in the diet is important and it is the fine fibre that produces beneficial effects in the body. The term dietary fibre is usually taken to mean the indigestible parts of leaves, stems, roots, seeds and fruit of plants, but excludes the coarse fibres of meat and fish.

Until recently the fibre or roughage content of the diet was regarded simply as that part of food which could not be digested and which, apart from its ability to produce soft, bulky stools, passed through the body unchanged. It is now believed, however, that the low fibre content in the diet of Western industrialized communities may contribute to a number of diseases including diverticulosis of the colon, coronary heart disease and cancer of the bowel.

Although fibre is not digested in the body it is not simply an inert material, for it has a number of important effects. The best known of these is the laxative effect of fibre, especially wheat fibre in the form of bran, caused by the water-holding capacity of fibre in the large intestine. Apart from this, fibre reduces the absorption of certain nutrients, particularly mineral elements, it alters the effect of microbes in the colon and it can absorb some toxic materials. Certain types of fibre e.g. pectin can lower blood cholesterol.

During the last hundred years extensive refining of cereals, particularly in industrialised countries, has gradually reduced the amount of cereal fibre in the diet. This is now a matter of concern and while much research remains to be done it would seem a prudent precaution to increase the content of fine fibre, particularly cereal fibre, in the diet.

SUGGESTIONS FOR FURTHER READING

AYKROYD, W. R. *Wheat in Human Nutrition.* FAO (United Nations), 1970.

BIRCH, G. G. and SHALLENBERGER R. S. *Developments in Food Carbohydrate—I.* Applied Science Publishers, 1979.

CANDY, *Biological Functions of Carbohydrates.* Blackie, 1980.

FANCE, W. J. *The Students' Technology of Breadmaking and Flour Confectionery,* 2nd edition. Routledge and K. Paul, 1966.

FAO/WHO, *Carbohydrates in Human Nutrition.* HMSO, 1980.

KENT, N. L. *Technology of Cereals,* 2nd edition. Pergamon, 1975.

KENT-JONES, D. W. and AMOS, A. J. *Modern Cereal Chemistry,* 6th edition. Food Trade Press, 1967.

ROYAL COLLEGE OF PHYSICIANS, *Medical Aspects of Dietary Fibre.* Pitman Medical, 1980.

SPILLER, G. A. and AMEN, R. J. (Eds). *Fibre in Human Nutrition.* Plenum Press, 1976.

SPILLER, G. A. and AMEN, R. J. (Eds). *Topics in Dietary Fibre Research.* Plenum Press, 1978.

TAYLOR, R. J. *Carbohydrates.* Unilever Booklet, 1975. A well presented fairly advanced chemical review of the structure of carbohydrates.

WILLIAMS, A. (Ed). *Breadmaking, the Modern Revolution.* Hutchinson Benham, 1975.

Chapter Nine

Amino acids and proteins

Previous chapters have been concerned with substances containing the elements carbon, hydrogen and oxygen, and it has been shown that these elements combined in the form of fats and carbohydrates are of fundamental importance in food science. In addition to these elements there is a fourth, namely nitrogen, which also plays a vital role in human life and which, when combined in the form of amino acids and proteins, constitutes a third group of compounds which are of basic importance in food and nutrition.

There is a definite relation between elementary nitrogen on the one hand and the complex proteins required by man on the other. The way in which nitrogen is built up by stages into animal protein and then degraded in further stages back again into nitrogen is summed up in the nitrogen cycle.

Elementary nitrogen occurs in almost limitless quantities in the atmosphere, while combined nitrogen is widely distributed in the soil in the form of salts and, in the form of organic compounds, is found in all living matter. Combined nitrogen forms an essential part of the structure of the body, which requires a continuous supply of nitrogen in a suitable form. Unfortunately the body is unable to synthesize its nitrogen compounds starting from elementary nitrogen; indeed, it is unable to perform such syntheses, even when it is provided with a supply of inorganic nitrogen compounds. This means that man must be supplied with nitrogen which has already been converted into suitable organic form.

This produces the paradoxical situation that though nitrogen is abundant in its elementary form, nitrogen compounds which can be utilized by man are scarce. The explanation of this is to be found in the character of the element, which is noted for its inertness. This lack of reactivity makes it difficult to convert the element into its compounds, a process which is called *fixation*.

Fixation of nitrogen into ammonia and subsequently into soluble ammonium salts is carried out commercially, but the amounts of fixed

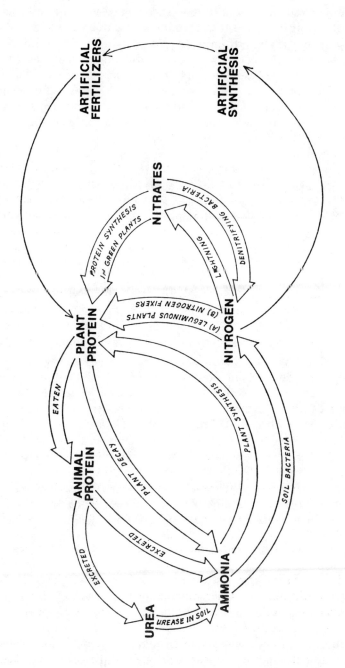

Fig. 9.1. The nitrogen cycle

nitrogen thus produced are infinitesimal compared with the amounts required by living things. Fortunately, nitrogen fixation carried out with difficulty by chemists is performed with ease in nature, aided by micro-organisms such as *Rhizobium*, which enable leguminous plants such as peas and beans to synthesize protein from nitrogen. Other green plants synthesize protein from nitrates present in the soil. Synthesis of protein is opposed by destructive processes which break down protein by stages into nitrogen, thus completing the cycle which is summarized in Fig. 9.1.

Amino Acids

Amino acids contain an amino group $-NH_2$ and a carboxyl group $-COOH$. The simplest example of such an acid is amino acetic acid, called *glycine*, in which one of the hydrogen atoms of the methyl group of acetic acid has been replaced by an amino group. Amino acids of interest in nutrition have the amino group attached to the carbon atom next to the carboxyl group and may be represented by the general formula:

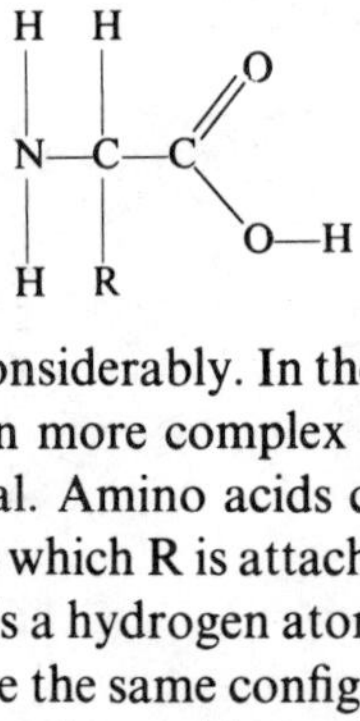

The nature of R may vary considerably. In the simplest case of glycine it is a hydrogen atom while in more complex amino acids it may be an aliphatic or aromatic radical. Amino acids can exist in stereoisomeric forms as the carbon atom to which R is attached is asymmetric except in the case of glycine where R is a hydrogen atom. The asymmetric carbon atom has been found to have the same configuration in all the naturally occurring optically active amino acids and this configuration is designated the L-form.

CLASSIFICATION OF AMINO ACIDS. More than twenty amino acids have been obtained from food and body proteins. They may be classified as being either neutral, basic or acidic. Neutral amino acids are those, like glycine, which contain one amino and one carboxyl group, basic amino acids contain one carboxyl but more than one basic group, while acidic amino acids contain one amino and two carboxyl groups. Table 9.1 gives the amino acids of most interest in nutrition. Those amino acids marked by the letter E are essential amino acids, a term which is explained on page 190.

PROPERTIES OF AMINO ACIDS. Amino acids are white crystalline substances which are soluble to some extent in water but which are mostly

Table 9.1. Structure of Amino Acids, $H_2NCHRCOOH$

Name (E) = essential	Abbreviation	R	Isoelectric point
Neutral			
Glycine	Gly	H–	6·0
Alanine	Ala	CH_3-	6·0
Valine (E)	Val	$(CH_3)_2CH-$	6·0
Leucine (E)	Leu	$(CH_3)_2CHCH_2-$	6·0
Isoleucine (E)	Ileu	$CH_3CH_2CH(CH_3)-$	6·0
Norleucine	Nor	$CH_3(CH_2)_3-$	6·1
Phenylalanine (E)	Phe	$C_6H_5CH_2-$	5·5
Tyrosine	Tyr	$C_6H_4(OH)CH_2-$	5·7
Serine	Ser	$HOCH_2-$	5·7
Threonine (E)	Thre	$CH_3CH(OH)-$	5·6
Cysteine	CySH	$HSCH_2-$	5·1
Cystine	CySSCy	$HOOCCH(NH_2)CH_2S_2CH_2-$	4·8
Methionine (E)	Met	$CH_3SCH_2CH_2-$	5·7
Tryptophan (E)	Try		5·9

Basic			
Ornithine		$H_2N(CH_2)_3-$	9·7
Arginine	Arg	$HN=CNH(CH_2)_3-$ (with NH_2 above)	10·8
Lysine (E)	Lys	$H_2N(CH_2)_4-$	10·0
Histidine	His		7·6

Acidic			
Aspartic acid	Asp	$HOOCCH_2-$	2·8
Glutamic acid	Glu	$HOOC(CH_2)_2-$	3·2

insoluble in organic solvents. The amino group, as its name suggests, is related to ammonia and like ammonia it has basic characteristics while the carboxyl group is acidic. The combination of an amino group and a carboxyl group in the same molecule results in it being able to act as an acid or a base; such a substance is said to be *amphoteric*.

The formulae shown in Table 9.1 show the arrangement of covalent bonds in amino acids but they do not show the ionic character which amino acids display in solution. In solution amino acids may be more correctly represented as follows:

$$\overset{+}{N}H_3—CH—\overset{-}{COO}$$
$$|$$
$$R$$

This formula shows the ionic character of an amino acid and that it contains both a positive and a negative group. Amino acids are weak electrolytes and they ionize according to the pH of the system. We can represent this ionization as:

$$\overset{+}{N}H_3-CH-COOH \overset{+H^+}{\underset{acid}{\longleftarrow}} \overset{+}{N}H_3-CH-COO^- \overset{-H^+}{\underset{alkali}{\longrightarrow}} NH_2-CH-COO^-$$
$$\quad\; | \qquad\qquad\qquad\qquad\quad | \qquad\qquad\qquad\qquad | $$
$$\quad\; R \qquad\qquad\qquad\qquad\quad R \qquad\qquad\qquad\qquad R$$
positive ion $\qquad\qquad$ zwitterion $\qquad\qquad$ negative ion

Thus if acid is added to a neutral solution of an amino acid a positive ion is formed, whereas if alkali is added a negative ion is formed. Therefore an amino acid may be neutral or positively or negatively charged according to the pH of the system.

When an amino acid is neutral, that is when the positive and negative charges are equal, it is said to be at its *isoelectric point* and it is called a *zwitterion* or dipolar ion. Such zwitterions are effective buffers because of their capacity to combine with both acids and bases, thus preventing the change of pH that would otherwise occur. The buffering action of amino acids is very important, particularly in living cells where the cell can only function provided that the pH is maintained within a narrow range.

The isoelectric points of a number of amino acids are shown in Table 9.1. The isoelectric point is important because at this pH many properties have either a maximum or minimum value; for example, electrical conductivity, solubility and viscosity are all a minimum. The reason why electrical conductivity is a minimum is fairly obvious—the nett charge on each molecule is zero—but the reason why solubility should also be a minimum is rather less obvious. Although at the isoelectric point the over-all charge on amino acid molecules is zero, a dipole exists and this results in strong electrostatic attraction between neighbouring molecules which results in the molecules packing closely together. Other factors, such as hydrogen bonding, may also accentuate the close-packing effect and the resultant close-packing of amino acid molecules reduces the possibility of interaction with solvent molecules and therefore reduces solubility to be a minimum.

Although amino acids containing one amino and one carboxyl group are neutral in reaction, yet it will be noted from Table 9.1 that their isoelectric point is not at pH 7. This is because the dissociation constants of the two groups are not equal. Amino acids containing more amino groups than carboxyl groups are basic and have isoelectric points above pH 7, while those with more carboxyl than amino groups are acidic and have isoelectric points below 7.

Glutamic acid is an example of an amino acid containing two carboxyl groups and one amino group. It is a white crystalline solid which has an acidic reaction in water and an isoelectric point of pH 3·2. It is of particular interest in that it is produced in large quantities for conversion into its sodium salt which is used in food preparation as a seasoning agent. The free acid was first isolated in 1866 by hydrolysing wheat gluten which yields 36 per cent glutamic acid. This forms the basis of one modern method of extraction, the hydrolysis being carried out using hydrochloric acid. The resulting products are neutralized, filtered and subjected to fractional crystallization, when glutamic acid crystals are obtained as one of the fractions.

MONOSODIUM GLUTAMATE. When glutamic acid is dissolved in water and the solution is neutralized with sodium hydroxide, *monosodium glutamate* is formed and after purification and crystallization it is obtained as a white, odourless solid. Although the pure salt has only a faint flavour of its own, it enhances the natural flavour of many substances to which it is added. For this reason it is now added to a large range of foods, usually in amounts of 0·1–0·3 per cent. It is notably successful in bringing out the natural flavour of meat, fish and vegetable foods and is now added to many canned foods, particularly to fish and meat products but also to some soups, such as mushroom and chicken noodle. It is also used to enhance the flavour of dehydrated vegetable foods and is found in many soup powders. The powdered salt can be used with fresh food, being added before cooking or sprinkled on afterwards as a condiment. Although previously regarded as harmless recent evidence suggests that a small proportion of people may suffer unpleasant effects when relatively large amounts are ingested, as has sometimes happened in Chinese restaurants.

Glutamate occurs both in foods and in the body either free or as part of proteins. For example, proteins of foods such as milk, cheese and meat are rich in glutamate while some vegetables, notably mushrooms, tomatoes and peas, have high levels of free glutamate. The body contains glutamate both free and as part of the protein; about one-fifth of body protein is glutamate.

Peptides

When two amino acid molecules combine, the acid group in one molecule reacts with the basic group in the other with the elimination of water:

$$\overset{+}{N}H_3CHCOO^- + \overset{+}{N}H_3\overset{\overset{R^2}{|}}{C}HCOO^- \longrightarrow \overset{+}{N}H_3CHCONH\overset{\overset{R^2}{|}}{C}HCOO^- + H_2O$$

$$\underset{R^1}{|} \qquad\qquad\qquad\qquad \underset{R^1}{|}$$

The product formed is a *dipeptide* and contains the group –CONH– which is the peptide linkage. Substances of relatively small molecular weight containing this group are called *peptides*.

A dipeptide still contains an amino and a carboxyl group and may react with another amino acid molecule to form a *tripeptide*. Theoretically this procedure may be repeated again and again with the formation of *polypeptides*. In practice, amino acids do not react together in this way, but dipeptides, tripeptides and polypeptides may be synthesized indirectly. For instance, in 1907 Emil Fischer, in a classical synthesis, made a polypeptide from fifteen glycine molecules and three leucine molecules, and other polypeptides of even greater complexity have been synthesized since then.

Proteins

Proteins are the most complex substances known to man. This fact can be simply illustrated by comparing the molecular weights and formulae of proteins with those of other types of substance. A simple monosaccharide such as glucose has a molecular weight of 180 and a formula of $C_6H_{12}O_6$, whereas a simple protein has a molecular weight reckoned in thousands and a correspondingly complex formula. The protein *lactoglobulin*, for instance, has a molecular weight of about 42 000 and a formula approximating to $C_{1864}H_{3012}O_{576}N_{468}S_{21}$. Large protein molecules are much bigger than this and have molecular weights of several million.

STRUCTURE OF PROTEINS. The way in which the structure of proteins has been determined constitutes one of the most significant scientific advances of recent years. The problem is one of awe-inspiring difficulty, but a notable step forward was made when, in 1956, the structure of the protein *insulin* was announced. It is a relatively small simple protein built up from only 51 amino acid units, whereas large proteins may contain over 500 such units. Nevertheless, since then, encouraged by this initial breakthrough, research has been intensified and has been crowned with increasing success. The structures of a number of proteins have been worked out with the aid of X-ray diffraction measurements and calculations involving advanced computer techniques. The structure of several enzymes, such as papain (211 units), chymotrypsin (246 units) and carboxypeptidase (307 units), and of large proteins containing over 500 amino acid units, such as haemoglobin (574 units) are now known.

Following success in determining the structure of insulin and other more complex proteins a great deal of research has been directed towards synthesizing proteins from their component amino acids and recently the first successful syntheses have been reported. As might have been expected the protein to be synthesized first was the smallest—insulin. This was followed in 1969 by an even more significant event; the synthesis of the first enzyme—*ribonuclease*. This enzyme contains 124 amino acid units and its synthesis confirms much of the evidence as to the structure of proteins discussed below.

Besides the elements carbon, hydrogen, oxygen and nitrogen, proteins often contain sulphur and sometimes phosphorus. On hydrolysis, proteins break down to polypeptides and eventually to amino acids, a single protein producing up to about twenty different amino acids. It is, therefore, clear that amino acids are the building units of which proteins are composed, but how are these units joined together to form a protein molecule? Much evidence is now available to indicate that the amino acids in proteins are joined together by peptide linkages. For example, though protein molecules contain few free amino or carboxyl groups, on hydrolysis about equal numbers of these groups are produced, as would be expected if peptide links are being broken. Also, some synthetic polypeptides are identical with polypeptides produced by partial hydrolysis of proteins.

Protein molecules, it is now believed, are composed of large numbers of up to twenty different amino acids joined together by peptide linkages. X-ray analysis gives some indication of how the peptide chains are arranged in protein molecules. Such chains have a zigzag structure with the R-groups protruding alternately in opposite directions as shown in Fig. 9.2a. The first major problem in working out protein structure is that of determining the sequence of amino acid units R_1, R_2, R_3 constituting the chain.

When it is considered that there are hundreds, and sometimes thousands, of amino acid units in a single protein molecule and that there are over twenty *different* amino acids available to choose from, it is clear that the number of different molecules which can be constructed is almost limitless. It has been calculated that for a medium-sized protein containing 288 amino acid units and 12 *different* amino acids there are 10^{300} different possibilities. The magnitude of this number may perhaps be appreciated from the fact that there are less than 10^{10} people living on the earth! In spite of the difficulty of solving this problem, the amino acid sequence of a number of amino acids is now known, that of insulin—the simplest and the first to be worked out—being shown in Fig. 9.2c.

The determination of the sequence of amino acids in polypeptide chains reveals what is known as the *primary* protein structure, but this is only the beginning of the problem of working out the complete structure

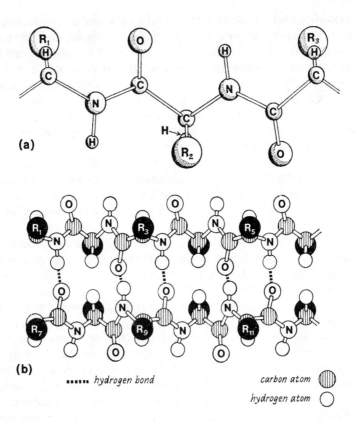

FIG. 9.2. (a) The zigzag structure of a polypeptide chain showing its three dimensional nature. (b) Polypeptide chains joined by hydrogen bonds in a protein molecule. (c) Sequence of amino acids in insulin, showing how two chains are joined by disulphide links

of a protein. In a protein molecule polypeptide chains are linked together in a number of different ways giving rise to molecules of definite shape; this constitutes the *secondary* protein structure. Many of the R-groups in polypeptide chains contain reactive groups (see Table 9.1) which couple with reactive groups in adjacent chains so joining the chains together by cross-linking.

The most important R-group involved in cross-linking is that of *cysteine* which contains the SH-group. When two cysteine units in different polypeptide chains are adjacent, a disulphide bridge—S—S— may be formed between them by oxidation of the SH-groups, thus joining the chains together. Fig. 9.2c shows how two such chains are joined together at two different points in insulin. It also shows how an internal disulphide bridge can be formed between cysteine units occuring in the same chain.

In addition to strong covalent cross-linking through disulphide bridges other weaker types of cross-link also play a part in protein structure. For example, when neighbouring R-groups in different polypeptide chains contain free $\overset{+}{N}H_3$ and $CO\bar{O}$ groups the resulting electrostatic attraction holds the chains together, although the strength of the attraction depends upon the pH of the system. Cross-links are also formed by salt formation between basic groups in one chain and acidic groups in another and by ester formation between hydroxyl groups in one chain (e.g. threonine and serine) and groups such as phosphate in another. Cross-links may also be produced by the formation of *hydrogen bonds*, though such links formed between hydrogen in one chain and, for example oxygen in a neighbouring chain are much weaker than true chemical bonds. Fig. 9.2b illustrates how such bonds are formed between adjacent polypeptide chains.

Structurally, proteins are said to be either *fibrous* or *globular* according to their shape. Fibrous proteins, which are simpler than globular proteins, are divided into elastic and inelastic types. The inelastic type, of which *collagen* of connective tissue and *fibroin* of silk are typical examples, consists of zigzag polypeptide chains which are held together by cross-links. Thus they have the form of an extended chain which cannot be stretched further whereas the elastic type has a similar extended form but also has an unstretched form in which the chain is compressed until it is like a coiled spring. The particular form of the coil is an α-helix, the loops of the coil being maintained in position by internal hydrogen bonds as shown in Fig. 9.3a, or by disulphide cross-links. *Keratin* of hair and wool, *elastin* of tendons and arteries and *myosin* of muscle are important examples of elastic proteins.

Globular proteins are more complex than fibrous proteins because the

α-helix chain is folded in various ways to form molecules having an
irregular but bulky shape. The particular way in which folding takes
place depends upon the points in adjacent coils at which disulphide and
other cross-links are formed. One of the complexities of determining the
structure of globular proteins is that no general pattern of folding seems
to exist and that the exact nature of folding—called the *tertiary*
structure—needs to be determined for each protein individually. Fig.
9.3b gives an impression of how the α-helix is folded in the *myoglobin*

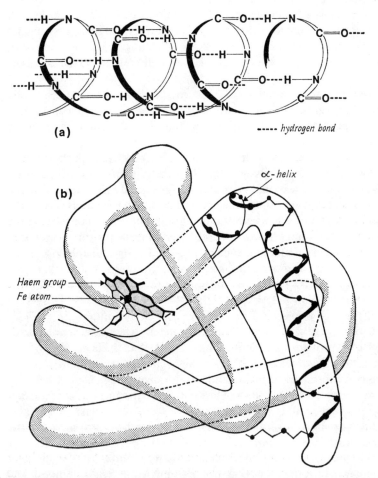

Fig. 9.3. (a) An α-helix showing how the links of the coil may be held in position by
hydrogen bonds and (b) an impression of a molecule of *myoglobin* showing the helical
nature of a section of the chain and the way in which the chain is folded (after R. E.
Dickerson)

molecule, about three-quarters of the chain being in the form of an α-helix. It can be seen that the structure is complex and non-symmetrical, though the overall shape is approximately spherical. Globular proteins are very important in the body as they include all proteins found within body cells and many food proteins.

PROPERTIES OF PROTEINS. The molecular weight of an average protein is about 60 000, and they are without characteristic melting points. Some have been obtained in crystalline form. The solubility of proteins in different solvents may show wide variations, especially in water, salt solutions and alcohol, and this is used for classifying them. Although we talk about the solubility of proteins they do not give true solutions but, because of their large size, they form colloidal dispersions or sols. The colloidal character of proteins is important in many foods as we have already seen in connection with the colloidal food systems, such as milk, butter and ice-cream, discussed in Chapter 6.

The properties of proteins are similar in many ways to those of the amino acids from which they are constructed. For example, they contain free amino and carboxyl groups at the ends of the polypeptide chains and as these carry a positive and negative charge proteins form zwitterions; consequently they are amphoteric and they act as buffers. The nett charge on protein molecules varies with pH and is zero at the isoelectric point. The isoelectric point is important in considering the behaviour of food proteins because at this pH many properties are either a maximum or minimum; some values are shown in Table 9.2.

Table 9.2. Molecular Weights and Isoelectric Points of Some Food Proteins

Protein	Source	Molecular weight	Isoelectric point
Caseinogen	Milk	34 000	4·6
β-Lactoglobulin	Milk	35 000	5·1
Ovalbumin	Eggs	44 000	4·6
Gliadin	Wheat	27 000	6·5
Gluten	Wheat	39 000	7·0
Gelatin	Bones	Variable	4·9
Myosin	Meat	850 000	5·4

The properties of fibrous proteins are distinct from those of globular proteins. The former are relatively insoluble, being resistant to acids and alkalis, and they are unaffected by moderate heating whereas the latter are soluble and are affected by acids, alkalis and heating. Globular proteins are very sensitive to chemical and physical conditions on account of the weak cross-links that hold the folded α-helix chains in position. A small change of pH or a small rise in temperature is sufficient to disrupt such cross-links and cause the chains to unfold, a process which is known as *denaturation*. When proteins are denatured their properties are completely altered; biological activity is destroyed, solubility decreased and viscosity increased. Moreover the change is irreversible.

Denaturation may be brought about by controlling pH and occurs most readily at the isoelectric point when proteins are least stable. For example *caseinogen*, which is the main protein of milk, has an isoelectric point of 4·6, and this explains why, when milk turns sour and the pH drops, it curdles so easily. It also explains why milk is coagulated or clotted in the stomach so easily by rennin, for the pH is low and not far removed from the isoelectric point of caseinogen. The denaturation of milk proteins is discussed in more detail on page 106.

Many proteins are denatured by heat. For instance, if egg white is heated, coagulation begins at about 60°C when the protein *ovalbumin* starts to separate out as a solid. As the temperature is raised, coagulation continues until the whole mass is completely solid. It is clear that coagulation occurs in the cooking of protein foods. For example, the proteins in lean meat coagulate on heating. Coagulation starts at about 60° C as with albumin and if cooking temperatures are kept somewhat below 100° C, coagulation is slow and the coagulated protein is not too hard. In this state protein is most digestible. However, if a temperature of 100° C or over is used, as in boiling and roasting, coagulation is more rapid and the denatured protein forms a hard solid mass which is more difficult to digest than lightly coagulated protein. This explains the old saying that 'a stew boiled is a stew spoiled'.

Partial coagulation of proteins may be brought about by beating them into a foam. For example, when egg white is beaten the foam which is formed is stabilized by the partial coagulation of the ovalbumin. If such a foam is heated it becomes rigid due to further coagulation of the ovalbumin. Such foaming occurs most readily at the isoelectric point when the ovalbumin is least stable and it may be promoted by addition of an acidic substance which lowers the pH to a value near the isoelectric point.

Proteins are precipitated out of solution by certain salts such as ammonium sulphate, sodium chloride, mercuric chloride and lead acetate. Thus, the presence of mineral salts affects the denaturation of proteins by heat treatment. The fact that lead acetate causes precipitation of ovalbumin in egg white explains why white of egg is used in cases of lead poisoning, for by reaction with egg white a soluble lead salt is rapidly converted into an insoluble compound which is not assimilated.

TESTS FOR PROTEINS. In order to detect the presence of nitrogen (and sulphur) in a substance *Lassaigne's* test may be used. The substance to be tested is heated with sodium which reacts with nitrogen and sulphur, forming sodium cyanide and sodium sulphide respectively. Sulphide ions give a purple colour on addition of sodium nitroprusside solution and cyanide ions give a blue precipitate or colour with a mixture of ferrous and ferric ions.

Lassaigne's test detects the presence of nitrogen in a substance, but further tests are required to determine whether the compound containing nitrogen is a protein. Proteins may be detected by means of colour tests. For example, in the *Biuret* test proteins give a characteristic purple colour when they are heated in the presence of strong alkali and copper sulphate solution. A similar colour is given by any substance containing more than one −CONH− grouping so that the test is not specific for proteins but is also positive for all polypeptides.

Most proteins give a positive result in the *Xanthoproteic* reaction in which the suspected protein is heated with concentrated nitric acid. In the presence of protein the solution turns yellow and, on the addition of alkali, orange. *Millon's* reaction may be used to detect proteins which on hydrolysis yield *tyrosine*. The only common protein which does not give a positive result in this test is gelatin. The substance is warmed with Millon's reagent (which contains mercurous and mercuric nitrates in nitric acid), and if a protein is present a white precipitate turning red is obtained.

GELS AND GELATIN. Gels are remarkable colloidal systems in which large volumes of liquid are immobilized by small amounts of solid material, the liquid constituting the dispersion medium and the solid the disperse phase. Gels are of considerable importance in food preparation on account of the rigidity which such a system possesses. For example, gels formed by polysaccharides—such as pectin gels in jam and starch gels in cooked starchy foods—have been discussed in Chapters 7 and 8. Proteins also form gels and the gel formed by *gelatin* is of particular importance in food preparation.

Gelatin is made from another protein called *collagen* which occurs in the skin and bone of various animals. The molecules of collagen are made up of three chains of α-helices, the chains being intertwined and held in position by covalent cross-links and other weaker links. When collagen is treated with hot water and acid or alkali all the weak cross-links and, according to the harshness of the treatment, a proportion of the covalent cross-links are broken down. The resulting product, commercial *gelatine*, is soluble and contains a range of protein molecules and about 12 per cent water and 1 per cent mineral salts. It is produced in granular form and in thin sheets, the former being the more common.

When cold water is added to gelatin it swells owing to the absorption of water. This is because the different protein molecules that constitute gelatin are in the form of zigzag polypeptide chains that are weakly linked together to form a three dimensional network. Water becomes entangled and immobilized in this network in much the same way as water is held by a sponge. Additional water is bound to the gelatin by hydrogen bonding. If hydrated gelatin is heated with water above 35° C it liquefies and forms a sol. On cooling, the sol 'sets' and becomes solid, a process which is known as *gelation*. As little as 1 per cent gelatin is sufficient to produce such a gel. The gel formed is semi-rigid though its rigidity disappears on heating or shaking; the solution thus formed is not coagulated by heat.

The setting powers of gelatin are utilized in the preparation of food. Commercial table-jellies are made from syrups of glucose and sucrose. Gelatin is added to the hot syrup and, after it has dissolved, acid (usually citric), flavouring and colouring are added and the mixture is cooled until it sets. Gelatin is also responsible for the setting of stews and of broth prepared by boiling bones. If a gelatin sol is cooled until it is viscous but not firmly set, it can be beaten into a foam. A foam is most easily formed at the isoelectric point of gelatin (see Table 9.2) when the galatin particles adhere to each other most strongly. During beating, air is incorporated into the mixture and because the gelatin at this stage has a certain elasticity it is able to stretch and surround the air bubbles without breaking. Whipped cream and flavouring may be added to such foams in making gelatin desserts.

Gelatin is also used as a stabilizing agent for emulsions, and its use in this connection was discussed with reference to ice-cream on page 98.

CLASSIFICATION OF PROTEINS. As proteins cannot be classified according to their chemical structure, they are divided into groups according to their general character, these main groups being subdivided principally by their differing solubilities in various solvents. The main groups are Simple, Conjugated and Derived proteins (see Table 9.3).

Simple proteins are those which on hydrolysis produce amino acids or their derivatives, while conjugated proteins are those which on hydrolysis produce amino acids and a non-protein molecule called a *prosthetic group*, e.g. on hydrolysis haemoglobin splits into the protein *globin* and

Table 9.3. Classification of Proteins

Simple proteins	Characteristics	Example and source
Albumins	Soluble in water Coagulated by heat	Ovalbumin (egg) Lactalbumin (milk)
Globulins	Insoluble in water Coagulated by heat	Edestin (wheat) Tuberin (potato)
Glutelins	Insoluble in water and neutral salts Coagulated by heat	Glutenin (wheat) Oryzenin (rice)
Prolamines	As for glutelins but also soluble in 70–80% alcohol	Gliadin (wheat) Zein (maize)
Albuminoids	Insoluble except in strong acids and alkalis	Collagen (skin and bones) Elastin (arteries and tendons)
Basic Proteins	Soluble in water and dilute acids	Globin (red blood corpuscles) Myosin (muscle)

Conjugated proteins	Prosthetic group	Example and source
Nucleoproteins	Nucleic acid	Thymonucleic acid (thymus gland)
Chromoproteins	Coloured group containing a metal	Haemoglobin (blood) Myoglobin (meat)
Phosphoproteins	Phosphate	Caseinogen (milk)
Glycoproteins	Carbohydrate	Mucin (saliva, egg white)

Derived proteins	Characteristics	Example
Primary protein derivatives	Insoluble in all reagents	Denatured proteins (e.g. coagulated)
Secondary protein derivatives	Soluble in water Not coagulated by heat	Proteoses Peptones Peptides

the red-coloured prosthetic group *haeme*. Derived proteins are produced by the action of acids, alkalis or enzymes on proteins. Primary derived proteins are produced by denaturation, secondary derived proteins by hydrolysis.

PROTEIN FOODS

There are thousands of different plant and animal proteins the exact structures of which are unknown. Fortunately this knowledge is not needed when considering the value of protein foods, because such foods are hydrolysed during digestion, liberating the constituent amino acids.

As only about twenty different amino acids are liberated by hydrolysis, consideration of the value of protein foods is simplified into diagnosis of the amounts and the nature of the various amino acids so produced. Of the amino acids obtained from protein only 8 are essential to adults. This means that there are 8 amino acids which cannot be manufactured by the body (or which the body makes too slowly for normal metabolism), whereas it can make sufficient of the other amino acids for itself if it is provided with suitable starting materials. A diet containing the 8 essential amino acids will provide an adult with suitable material with which to build all the amino acids needed. In addition *histidine* is regarded as essential for the growth of infants. Essential amino acids are marked with the letter E in Table 9.1 on p. 177.

PROTEIN QUALITY. The quality of protein food may be judged by its protein content, the number and amounts of essential amino acids it contains and the degree to which its protein is digested and absorbed by the body. The highest quality protein foods are those which provide all 8 essential amino acids in the proportions needed by man (see Table 9.4). Such proteins have high nutritive value (sometimes described as 'biological value' on the basis of feeding experiments—see p. 203).

On the whole animal proteins are of better quality than plant proteins. In particular, cereal proteins are low in *lysine*, which is therefore called the *limiting amino acid* because it is the one most below human requirements (see Wheat in Table 9.4). Exceptions to this generalization include the animal protein gelatin which is of low quality (*tryptophan* is the limiting amino acid) and the plant protein of soya beans which is of high quality (*methionine* is the limiting amino acid).

Table 9.4. Essential Amino Acid Content of Proteins (mg/g protein)

Amino acid	Eggs	Milk	Beef	Wheat Flour	Suggested pattern for adults*
Isoleucine	54	47	53	42	18
Leucine	86	95	82	71	25
Lysine	70	78	87	20	22
Methionine and cystine	57	33	38	31	24
Phenylalanine and tyrosine	93	102	75	79	25
Threonine	47	44	43	28	13
Tryptophan	17	14	12	11	6·5
Valine	66	64	55	42	18

* FAO/WHO report, 1973, assuming a safe level of protein intake for adults of 0·55 g per kg body weight.

Protein quality of a food can be evaluated in chemical terms by comparing its amino acid content with that of a reference protein (usually whole egg protein). The result is known as the *chemical score* of the protein.

Chemical scores: egg, 100; milk, 95; beef, 93; soya beans, 74; rice, 67; wheat, 53; maize, 49.

Chemical score values are found to match up fairly well with biological values.

In terms of diet we normally eat a mixture of proteins and the fact that any one protein is of high or low biological value is of no great significance. The important dietary requirement is that the total protein intake should supply all the essential amino acids in suitable proportions for our needs. Thus although a certain protein may be of low quality because it lacks a particular amino acid, yet if it is eaten together with a second protein which lacks a *different* essential amino acid, the mixture is of high biological value. Such amino acids are said to *supplement* or *complement* each other.

The principle of supplementation is illustrated by a mixture of gelatin and bread. The limiting amino acid of wheat is lysine whereas that of gelatin is tryptophan. As gelatin is relatively rich in lysine the two complement each other. Examples of other complementary proteins are fish and rice and maize and beans.

The general conclusion reached is that diets should contain a wide variety of protein sources in which case the total mixture will have high biological value. Only where 70 per cent or more of dietary proteins comes from one staple food such as wheat or maize need there be concern that protein quality will fall below an acceptable level. The protein content of a range of foods is shown in Table 9.5.

Table 9.5. The Protein Content of some Animal and Vegetable Foods

Animal foods	% Protein	Vegetable foods	% Protein
Cheddar cheese	25	Soya flour	40
Raw meat	20–25	Peanuts	28
Raw fish	14–18	White bread	8
Bacon	10–15	Rice	6
Eggs	12	Fresh peas	6
Milk	3	Old potatoes	2
Butter	<1	Bananas, oranges	1

Meat

Lean meat is the flesh or muscular tissue of animals. Its composition is different from that of the internal organs, such as kidneys and liver, which are referred to collectively as offal. The composition of the flesh of different animals shows considerable variation and the composition of even a single type of meat, such as beef, varies according to breed, type of feeding and the part of the animal from which the meat has come.

Muscle tissue consists of about three-quarters water and one-quarter protein together with a small variable amount of fat, 1 per cent mineral elements and some vitamins. Structurally the tissue is composed of microscopic fibres, each of which is made up of cells. The main constituent of the cells is water in which the proteins and other nutrients are either dissolved or suspended. Numbers of fibres are held together by connective tissues to form a bundle. A quantity of such bundles is enveloped by a tough sheath of connective tissue which forms a tendon joining the muscle to the bone structure.

The cells of the muscle fibres contain a number of proteins, the most important being *myosin* (7 per cent) and *actin* (2·5 per cent). Myosin is a relatively large elastic protein which can exist in stretched and un-stretched forms and which is classified as a basic protein (Table 9.3). Actin has two forms; a small globular form of molecular weight about 70 000 and a fibrous form in which a series of globular units are arranged in a double chain. The cells also contain ATP (adenosine triphosphate) which, as we saw in Chapter 8, provides the energy used when muscle fibres contact. After death ATP is broken down and in its absence myosin and action combine to form rigid chains of *actomyosin*. In this state, known as *rigor mortis*, meat is rigid and tough and it is therefore not consumed until, after a period of storage known as *conditioning*, the stiffness has diminished and tenderness and flavour have improved.

The changes that occur during conditioning are complex as might be expected from the protein nature of meat; moreover, they are affected by a number of variables of which temperature, pH and length of storage are all important. Although the changes that constitute conditioning are complicated and still not completely understood it is a very important process resulting in the conversion of the muscular tissue of animals into the 'meat' of our diet. After death the glycogen present in muscular tissue is broken down by stages to lactic acid with consequent fall in pH. The final pH is usually about 5·5, which is close to the isoelectric point of the main muscle proteins (isoelectric point of myosin is 5·4). As we have already noted proteins are least stable and most readily denatured at the isoelectric point, and during conditioning proteins of muscular tissue are denatured, though the proteins of connective tissue are not. Denaturation is followed by some breakdown of denatured proteins resulting in the formation of peptides and amino acids and an increase in tenderness. A further important change results from the fact that the solubility of proteins is a minimum at the isoelectric point and hence during conditioning some water is lost from meat.

During conditioning the colour of meat changes from reddish to brown and this is associated with the conversion of the main muscle pigment *myoglobin* into *metmyoglobin*. The myoglobin molecule consists of a protein part, consisting of folded chains of α-helices as shown in Fig. 9.3b together with a non-protein coloured *haem* group containing an iron atom in the ferrous state. During conditioning myoglobin is denatured and oxidized, ferrous iron being converted into ferric iron, and the resulting metmyoglobin is brown in colour.

The connective tissue of meat which surrounds the bundles of muscle fibres is mainly *collagen*, while the walls of the muscle fibres are mainly *elastin*. As we have already seen both these proteins are classified as albuminoids in Table 9.3, and both are fibrous proteins, collagen containing inelastic polypeptide chains joined by cross-links and elastin having an unstretched α-helix form. Collagen and elastin, being insoluble and tough, are difficult to digest. However, when meat is cooked in the presence of moisture the collagen is converted into gelatin, which is soluble in water. This makes the digestion of connective tissue much easier, and enables the digestive juices to come into intimate contact with the myosin of the muscle fibres. The greater the age of the animal and the more active its life, the greater is the amount of connective tissue and the thickness of the walls of the fibres. Thus, meat of old animals is more difficult to digest than that of young ones and muscular tissue of active animals is more difficult to digest than that of inactive ones.

Embedded in the connective tissue is a variable amount of 'invisible' fat. This makes the digestion of meat more difficult because it coats the muscle fibres with a thin oily film which resists the action of the digestive juices. In addition to the invisible fat there is a much larger amount of visible fat which is stored in the fat depots of the animal's body. Such fat is mainly found under the skin and around internal organs and is, therefore, not a part of lean meat.

Apart from protein and fat, meat contains small quantities of mineral elements and vitamins, but is notable for its lack of carbohydrate, in which respect it resembles eggs. Meat is rich in phosphates and potassium but is a poor source of calcium. It contains a small but valuable amount of iron, though certain organs, such as liver, are richer sources of this element. Meat is a useful source of the B group of vitamins, notably nicotinic acid. The amount of thiamine in meat is not large except in the case of pork, which contains about 0·6 mg per 100 g of meat. Riboflavine occurs in useful quantities especially in internal organs such as the kidneys. Lean meat contains very little vitamin A, and practically no vitamin D or ascorbic acid.

Finally, the extractives of meat deserve a mention because they impart to it most of its characteristic flavour and because they aid digestion by stimulating the secretion of saliva and gastric juice. They are so named because they are dissolved out of meat, or extracted, when it is put into boiling water. The extractives contain soluble inorganic salts, lactic acid and various nitrogenous compounds which are not proteins, the most important of which are *creatine* and *creatinine*. These constituents do not, however, account for the flavour of the extractives, the basis of which remains largely unknown.

Summing up it may be said that meat is a valuable protein food. As normally eaten, it also contains a considerable proportion of visible fat. It is also a significant source of iron and phosphorus and the B group of vitamins, especially nicotinic acid and riboflavine. The composition of meat is very variable and the figures gives in Table 9.6 are average values for the carcass as a whole. Lean meat contains less fat and more water than the figures given. The amount of fat in the carcass varies greatly, but present trends are towards slaughter of animals when relatively young having a lower fat content than before.

Table 9.6. Composition of 100 g Edible Portions of Meat and Fish

	Meat			Fish		
	Beef	Lamb	Pork	Haddock	Herring (Jan.– (Aug.)	Sardines (canned)
kJ Energy	940	1388	1364	321	970	906
g Protein	18	16	16	17	17	20
g Fat	17	30	30	0.7	18	14
g Water	64	53	54	82	64	58
mg Calcium	7	7	8	16	33	550
mg Iron	1·9	1·3	0·8	0·3	0·8	2·9
μg Vitamin A	0	0	0	0	45	30
μg Thiamine	60	90	580	8	0	40

Fish

Fish, like meat, is of value mainly as a source of protein, the amount of protein in fish being about the same as in lean meat. Fish protein differs from that of meat in having less connective tissue and no elastin. The absence of tough elastin and the conversion of collagen into gelatin which occurs during cooking, make the protein of cooked fish easily digestible. Fish contains rather more water and waste matter than meat.

Fish may be divided into two classes: white fish, such as haddock, cod, whiting and plaice, which contain very little fat (usually less than 1 per cent), and fat fish such as herring, trout and salmon, which usually contain 10–25 per cent fat. This fat is 'invisible' fat, being dispersed in the flesh and not deposited in fat depots. The difference in the fat content of three representative fishes, haddock, herring and sardines, is clearly shown in Table 9.6 as are also differences in the content of other nutrients and energy values.

Table 9.6 shows clearly that fat fish have a much higher nutritional value than white fish. Fish are good sources of phosphorus, though not of calcium unless the bones are eaten. They are not usually a rich source of iron though sardines are an exception. Sea fish are a valuable source of iodine. Fat fish are valuable sources of the fat-soluble vitamins A and D, fish-liver oils being exceptionally good sources of these vitamins. They also contain useful amounts of the B group of vitamins. White fish do not contain vitamins A and D, and usually contain less of the B vitamins than fat fish.

Eggs

The hen's egg, which is the only variety to be discussed here, is a most interesting food because it is designed to accommodate a living organism. It contains a sufficient store of nutrients to supply a developing chick embryo with all that it needs during its early stages of growth. It is, therefore, a complete food for a growing chick embryo and although it is not a complete food for humans, it is, nevertheless, a valuable one.

The egg consists of three main parts—the shell, the white and the yolk—and these are shown in Fig. 9.4. The outer shell forms a hard protective layer composed mainly of calcium carbonate and as it is porous it allows a developing embryo to obtain a supply of oxygen. The colour of the shell may vary from white to brown though, contrary to popular opinion, this gives no indication as to the quality of the contents of the egg. Inside the shell is a viscous colourless liquid called egg white which in a fresh egg is divided into regions of thick and thin white and which accounts for about 60 per cent of the total egg weight. It is a dilute aqueous solution, being about one-eighth protein and seven-eighths water. The main protein is *ovalbumin*, though smaller quantities of several others are present, including *mucin* which accounts for the viscosity of the liquid. Also present are small quantities of dissolved salts and the vitamin riboflavin. In the centre of the egg is the yolk, which is a

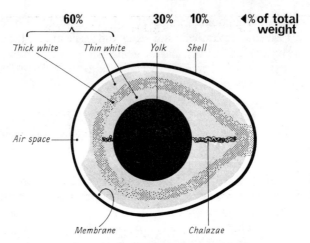

Fɪɢ. 9.4. The structure of a hen's egg

thick yellow or orange o/w emulsion stabilized by lecithin. It is suspended in the white, being held in position by the *chalazae*, and it is a rich source of nutrients, being much more concentrated than egg white. It is roughly one-third fat, one-half water and one-sixth protein; It also contains a supply of mineral elements and vitamins.

The only type of nutrient not present in an egg is carbohydrate. Its presence might be expected, because it would provide a ready source of energy for the growing chick. However, the size of the egg is limited and fat, which weight for weight has more than twice the energy value of carbohydrate, forms the sole source of energy.

The proteins of eggs, particularly those of egg white, have been intensively studied. Nine proteins have been identified in egg white and the nature and properties of the principal ones are summarized in Table 9.7. In addition to those mentioned in the table two globulins, identified as G_2 and G_3, and a small amount of a protein called *avidin* are also present. Avidin is of some nutritional importance as it combines with the vitamin *biotin*, rendering it unavailable to the body. The main proteins of egg yolk are the phosphoproteins *lipovitellin* and *lipovitellenin* which comprise about 30 per cent of the total egg yolk solids. The phosphorus content of these proteins is in the form of phosphoric acid esterified with the hydroxyl groups of hydroxy amino acids. They also contain a lipid part as their names suggest, and this is mainly lecithin.

The proteins of an egg are of high nutritional value and because of the quantity present—about 12 per cent of the edible part—eggs must be considered as a valuable protein food. Moreover, the properties of egg

Table 9.7. The Principal Proteins of Egg white

	Ovalbumin	Conalbumin	Lyso-zyme	Ovomucin	Ovomucoid
% of total protein	70	9	3	2	13
Type	Albumin	Albumin	Globulin	Conjugated	Conjugated
Molecular weight	44 000	74 000	15 000	8 000 000	28 000
Non-protein part	Phosphate, Carbohydrate	None	None	Carbohydrate	Carbohydrate
Isoelectric point	4·6–4·8	5·6–6·0	10·5–11·0		3·9–4·5
If coagulated by heat	Yes	Yes	No	No	No

proteins, particularly the ease with which they coagulate, cause eggs to be used in many methods of food preparation. Thus, eggs are used in cake mixtures where their coagulation during baking helps to 'fix' the shape of the cake, they are used as thickening agents in sauces and custards, as binding agents and as coatings to hold the outside of crumbly foods together during cooking. The use of egg-white for entrapping and stabilizing foams has already been discussed in Chapter 6.

The rate at which egg proteins coagulate depends upon conditions such as pH, salt concentration and temperature. Egg white coagulates readily into a white solid on heating and at its normal pH of around 9 coagulation starts at about 60° C. At higher temperatures the rate of coagulation increases until eventually it is nearly instantaneous. Egg yolk coagulates less readily than the white and does not coagulate appreciably below 70° C. As coagulation proceeds the viscosity of the yolk increases until eventually it breaks up into a powder.

The nutritional value of an egg may be summed up by saying that it supplies the diet with valuable amounts of iron, phosphorus and protein of high nutritional value and useful amounts of fat, vitamin A and calcium. It also supplies some vitamin D, riboflavine, thiamine and biotin.

PROTEINS IN THE BODY

During digestion proteins are broken down into amino acids. Their degradation is brought about progressively by peptidases as explained in Chapter 3. Peptidases are hydrolysing enzymes which operate by catalysing the hydrolysis of the peptide links in the protein molecule, so breaking down the protein into smaller units.

In the stomach the gastric glands secrete pepsinogen which, at the low pH of the gastric juice, becomes activated forming the enzyme pepsin. The action of pepsin is extremely specific; it catalyses the hydrolysis of only those peptide links which are joined to particular groupings. Moreover, it is an endopeptidase and acts only on inner peptide links of polypeptide chains. Fig. 9.5 shows part of a protein molecule, and the only point at which pepsin could act is indicated. As a result of the action of pepsin, proteins are broken down into smaller peptone units. The enzyme rennin is also present in the gastric juice and brings about the coagulation of the caseinogen of milk.

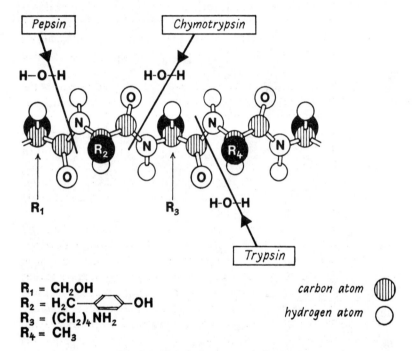

R_1 = CH_2OH

R_2 = H_2C—⟨⟩—OH

R_3 = $(CH_2)_4NH_2$

R_4 = CH_3

carbon atom ⦷

hydrogen atom ◯

FIG. 9.5. Hydrolysis of a protein fragment

In the small intestine, endopeptidases such as trypsin and chymotrypsin continue the hydrolysis of proteins and complete their breakdown into peptones. The action of these enzymes is just as specific as that of pepsin, each enzyme attacking only a certain type of link. The points at which they could attack a typical protein fragment are illustrated in Fig. 9.5. Peptones are further broken down by a group of exopeptidases, called erepsin, which are present in the intestinal juice. These enzymes catalyse the hydrolysis of peptones into dipeptides which are broken down into amino acids by a series of dipeptidases. Proteins are thus completely hydrolysed to amino acids before passing from the small intestine into the blood. The amino acids are, however, rapidly removed from the blood by all the cells of the body, but particularly by the liver.

ENZYMES. The supreme importance of enzymes in the body and their protein nature have already been emphasized in Chapter 2. Now that the structure of proteins has been considered it is possible to gain a clearer insight into the nature and mechanism of enzyme activity. It must be admitted, however, that in spite of the success of current research we still have a great deal to learn about the way enzymes act, though this is hardly surprising considering the complexity of protein structure. Moreover, the results of recent research show that few generalizations may be made in this field and that each enzyme needs to be investigated individually.

Enzymes are globular proteins which, as we have already seen, are the most complex proteins known and consist of folded α-helix chains, the method of folding being irregular and dependent on the nature of the cross-links formed between adjacent helical coils. Such structures are very sensitive to both chemical and physical conditions on account of the ease with which such cross-links are broken. This explains why enzymes are so sensitive to changes of temperature and pH. Moreover, the zwitterion structure of enzymes enables them to resist changes of pH in living systems by acting as buffers.

The lock and key theory of enzyme action was outlined in Chapter 2 and this theory has the merit of extreme simplicity. Modern developments have confirmed the essential correctness of this theory but have shown that the details are a good deal more complicated. It appears that the lock should be regarded as being flexible and that a substrate must not only fit the enzyme lock exactly but that it must also induce a change in the enzyme structure thus causing a reorientation of the enzyme groups involved in catalysis. Thus the specificity of an enzyme is due not only to a good fit between lock and key but also to the ability of the key to bring about certain structural changes in the lock. The structures of the enzymes lysozyme, ribonuclease and carboxypeptidase have been determined and show that these molecules are folded in such a way as to contain a jaw-like groove into which substrate molecules fit. In the case of carboxypeptidase it has further been shown that the substrate protein brings about structural changes in the enzyme molecule which are essential to its catalytic activity. Not all enzyme molecules possess jaw-like grooves, however, and in such cases (e.g. chymotrypsin) some other mechanism must operate.

GROWTH, MAINTENANCE AND REPAIR OF TISSUES. The present picture of protein metabolism is quite different from earlier. theories which assumed that the proteins of living tissues were stable and only required replacement after a long period of service. It is now believed that for from being stable, body proteins are in a constant state of flux and are continually being degraded and resynthesized in an analogous manner to fat molecules. On the one hand there are the complete body proteins, and on the other a reservoir of amino acids derived partly from food and partly from degraded body proteins. During life the proteins and amino acids are in dynamic equilibrium with each other. Such an equilibrium involves the continual hydrolysis of the peptide links of protein molecules and the continual resynthesis of proteins from amino acids, these changes being controlled by a group of enzymes known collectively as *cathepsins*.

The problem of discovering the mechanism of protein metabolism is largely one of finding out what happens to amino acids supplied to the body from protein food. The technique of utilizing *isotopic tracers* has been largely responsible for elucidating the facts. Isotopes are chemically identical, but because their mass is different they differ physically from one another. Because of their chemical equality the body cannot distinguish between them. The atomic weight of nitrogen is 14·008, this figure being the average of the mass numbers (the nearest whole number to the atomic weight) of the different isotopes present. One nitrogen isotope has a mass number of 15 and is written N^{15}. If the body is supplied with an amino acid containing N^{15} it treats it in exactly the same way as a 'normal' one. The isotopic tracer technique as applied to protein metabolism involves, therefore, the labelling of amino acids supplied to the body with N^{15}. After a period of time the whereabouts of the labelled atoms may be found by a physical form of analysis which distinguishes between atoms of different mass.

By using the tracer technique it has been found that when a labelled essential amino acid is supplied to the body it is rapidly incorporated in all body proteins. What is more remarkable is that the N^{15} atoms of the labelled amino acid are found distributed among the other amino acids in the body, showing that there must be a continual transfer of nitrogen from one amino acid to another.

Body proteins are, therefore, involved in rapid and ceaseless change, being continually split into amino acids which are then built up again into reconstituted protein molecules. In addition, the nitrogen atoms of amino acids are being constantly interchanged. The rapidity of these changes is great, as can be seen from the fact that half of the liver protein of a rat is resynthesized in a week.

PROTEIN AS A SOURCE OF ENERGY. Although the primary function of food proteins is the provision of amino acids for the production and maintenance of body proteins (including enzymes), they are ultimately broken down to urea with the liberation of energy. The secondary role of proteins is, therefore, as a supplementary energy source.

The first step in the breakdown of amino acids is normally *deamination* in which the amino group is removed from the amino acid as ammonia. Often this is accompanied by enzymic oxidation, so that the amino acid is coverted into a *keto acid* which is a carboxylic acid containing a keto group. A general example is given below:

$$2RCH(NH_2)COOH + O_2 \xrightarrow{\text{enzyme}} 2RCOCOOH + 2NH_3$$

Amino acid   Keto acid

The keto acid produced in deamination may act as an energy source, for it may be used in the formation of glucose which may subsequently be converted to glycogen. The conversion of a keto acid into a carbohydrate is accompanied by liberation of energy which is available for use by the body.

The ammonia formed in deamination is poisonous and is rapidly converted into urea, which is then excreted by the kidneys in urine. Both ammonia and carbon dioxide are required to produce urea, the formation of which may be represented very simply:

$$CO_2 + 2NH_3 \longrightarrow CO(NH_2)_2 + H_2O$$

Although carbon dioxide and ammonia are the starting materials and urea the final product, a whole cycle of stages is involved in the reaction. The ammonia and carbon dioxide are used in the formation of arginine, which is then broken down to urea and ornithine by enzymic hydrolysis catalysed by the enzyme *arginase*:

$$H_2N \begin{vmatrix} CNH \\ \| \\ NH \\ + \\ H_2O \end{vmatrix} (CH_2)_3CH(NH_2)COOH \xrightarrow{\text{Arginase}} CO(NH_2)_2 +$$

                       Arginine $H_2N(CH_2)_3CH(NH_2)COOH$

                                                 Ornithine

NITROGEN EQUILIBRIUM. It is now possible to build up a complete picture of protein metabolism. Protein foods are hydrolysed within the body to amino acids which become part of the amino acids reservoir. Amino acids are removed from the reservoir to reconstruct body proteins and to build enzyme molecules. In an adult only small amounts of amino acids are needed for the construction of growing tissues such as hair and nails, and the formation of new tissue, such as skin. Amino acids are also constantly being removed from the reservoir and degraded with the release of energy, the breakdown products being excreted mainly as urea. In a normal healthy adult the total intake of nitrogen from food is equal to the total nitrogen which is excreted. The body is then said to be in *nitrogen equilibrium*.

The tendency for the body to maintain nitrogen equilibrium has been taken as a sign that it cannot store protein. Although it is true that protein cannot be stored on the same scale as fat, nevertheless, the fact that an increased protein intake does not lead to an immediate increase in the rate at which nitrogenous breakdown products are excreted suggests that some protein can be stored. In such a case nitrogen equilibrium is eventually regained, indicating that in the interim protein has been stored but that finally the increased nitrogen intake is balanced by an increased rate of nitrogen excretion. It is now established that protein may be stored by the body mainly in such organs as the kidneys and liver.

During the period when some protein is being stored, nitrogen equilibrium is upset, the nitrogen excreted being less than the nitrogen intake. The body is then said to have a positive balance. A positive nitrogen balance also occurs during growth, when a considerable amount of new body protein is being formed. If the intake of protein becomes low a negative introgen balance results because the intake of nitrogen is less than that excreted. In such circumstances, stored protein can be utilized and is broken down to amino acids and finally to simple products, such as urea, which are excreted.

Protein Requirement

In considering how much protein should be supplied to the body in the diet, account must be taken of its nature; consequently it is much more difficult to estimate the optimum dietary intake of protein than of carbohydrate or fat. All carbohydrate in the diet, except cellulose, furnishes the body with glucose, and so it is a simple matter to estimate the amount of carbohydrate food required to produce a certain quantity of glucose. In the case of protein foods, however, such calculations are more difficult to make because a single protein produces a number of amino acids during digestion. Whereas a certain amount of protein of high nutritional value may satisfy the body's protein requirements a much larger amount of low quality protein will be needed. It is, therefore, only possible to calculate the minimum protein intake necessary for health on the assumption that this amount of protein furnishes the body with the minimum of essential amino acids which it requires.

Many studies of protein requirement have been undertaken and the Food and Agriculture Organization (FAO) and the World Health Organization (WHO) have published a comprehensive report of protein needs (1973, with additional reports in 1975 and 1978). These reports provide estimates of safe levels of protein intake for groups of people with different physiological needs, the safe level being defined as the amount of protein considered necessary to meet the physiological needs and maintain the health of nearly all individuals in a specified age/sex group.

Assessment of protein can only be done in terms of the quality of the protein consumed. Quality of protein can be measured in a number of ways and expressed as *chemical scores* (see p. 191) or *biological value* (BV) or *net protein utilization* (NPU).

MEASUREMENT OF BIOLOGICAL VALUE. Biological value is measured in feeding experiments using young rats which are fed a low protein (10 per cent) diet so that all the dietary protein is needed for growth. Any protein not used for growth, therefore, is of too poor quality to be of any use and is oxidized and excreted in the urine as urea. By measuring the the amount of urea excreted, the amount of protein retained in the body can be calculated. The percentage of absorbed protein that is retained in the body is known as its *biological value*. If the digestibility of the protein is taken into account we have a measure of the percentage of protein eaten that is retained in the body and this is known as the *net protein utilization*.

As between 90 and 95 per cent of protein is digested in a normal diet values for BV and NPU are often similar.

> **Biological values:** egg, human milk, 100; cheese, meat, fish 75; soya flour, 70; bread, 50; maize, 36.

The FAO/WHO believe that protein quality in rich countries has a chemical score of about 80 per cent and in poor countries about 70 per cent. The safe levels of protein intake recommended for different levels of protein quality are given in Table 9.8.

In the UK the recommended daily amounts (RDA) of protein recommended by DHSS (1979) are somewhat higher than the FAO/WHO figures. It is considered that a diet that provided less than 10 per cent of total food energy as protein would be likely to be unpalatable to most people in the UK. In addition such a diet might be deficient in other nutrients such as easily absorbable iron, vitamin B_{12}, riboflavine, nicotinic acid and trace elements, such as zinc, which are often

Table 9.8. FAO/WHO Safe Levels of Daily Protein Intake in g in Terms of Different Protein Quality

Age range		Chemical score of protein			
		100	80	70	60
Infants	6–11 months	14	17	20	23
Children	7–9 years	25	31	35	41
Males	16–19 years	38	47	54	63
	Adult	37	46	53	62
Females	16–19 years	30	37	43	50
	Adult	29	36	41	48
	Pregnant	38	47	54	63
	Lactating	46	55	62	71

associated with protein. The RDA of protein given in Table 12.8 on p. 274 are set therefore at a level that provides 10 per cent of total food energy on the assumption that dietary protein has an NPU of 75.

Effects of protein deficiency are most noticeable in children, and include poor growth, damage to the brain and liver and a deficiency disease known as *kwashiorkor* prevalent in Africa. In adults protein deficiency is relatively rare but it may lead to *anaemia*; if associated with general starvation conditions the condition of blood and muscles deteriorates and the body becomes swollen.

NOVEL PROTEIN FOODS. Animal protein, particularly meat, is expensive and—on a world-wide basis—in short supply. For both these reasons, and because an expanding world population will increase the demand for protein, new forms of protein foods are being actively developed. The two types of novel protein being investigated are those produced (1) by processing of conventional foods and (2) from sources not previously used as a food including (a) plants and (b) micro-organisms.

The most important novel proteins produced so far are those derived from soya beans, which unlike most vegetable proteins are of high quality. Such products are often made to simulate meat and are intended as a cheaper alternative to it; a comparison of the amino acid pattern of soya beans with beef (Table 9.9) shows that the former is low in methionine which is the limiting amino acid, but otherwise they are broadly comparable.

Soya beans (and soya bean flour) have been a valuable source of protein in the diets of China and Japan for many centuries, and they are now being cultivated increasingly in other countries, particularly in the USA. They are grown primarily as a source of vegetable oil and production of soya beans is now greater than that of any other oilseed. Soya beans contain a substance that inhibits the enzyme activity of tripsin and this inhibitor must be destroyed when the beans are converted into defatted soya flour; a process involving extraction with a hydrocarbon solvent. The protein content of the flour produced is about 50 per cent.

The conversion of soya flour into products having a meat-like texture is now carried out on a large scale. The simplest way of doing this is to convert the flour into a dough, heat under pressure above 100° C and extrude through a nozzle into atmospheric or reduced pressure. The sudden drop in pressure causes the material to expand and achieve the desired texture. The material is cut into pieces and dried. It can either be used in its natural form or flavours and colours may be added to the dough so that the final product has a meaty colour and texture. In America the product is known by its trade name *textured vegetable protein* (TVP). TVP is available in many sizes and shapes including chunks, flakes and granules in both flavoured and unflavoured forms.

Another type of product, known as *spun vegetable protein* is made by extracting the protein from soya flour, dissolving it in alkali and forcing the resulting solution through the tiny holes of a spinneret to give many fine threads of spun material. The threads of precipitated protein are stretched and twisted into bunches of fibres having a meat-like texture to which additives such as colour, flavour, fat and protein binders may be added. The final product may be dried or frozen and commercial products of this kind are made in the UK. Spun products have a more fibrous texture than textured ones, but are more expensive to produce.

Vegetable proteins are regularly used in schools, hospitals and canteens usually as a meat extender to replace part of the meat in traditional dishes. It is recommended (Food Standards Committee, 1974) that in the UK not more than 10 per cent of meat should be replaced by vegetable protein, though in the USA the limit is 30 per cent. Vegetable proteins are also being used as components of simulated meat products such as stews, curries and burger and burger-style dried mixes. Although previously found mainly in Health Food Stores such products are now available in supermarkets.

Large amounts of plant materials are grown as a source of vegetable oils. In addition to soya beans, groundnuts, cotton seed and others are used (see p. 84) and after the oil has been extracted a protein-rich residue remains. Concentrated protein can be extracted not only from such oil seeds but also from grass and other indigestible, but often abundant, vegetable material and also from fish. At present such processes are only carried out on a small scale.

Micro-organisms such as yeast, fungi, bacteria and algae are being developed as sources of edible protein usually known as *single cell protein*. The advantages of using unicellular organisms as a protein source are (1) that they can be grown in media which are cheap, such as industrial waste materials, and (2) they grow very rapidly indeed. The media used must contain a suitable source of carbon which may be a cheap carbohydrate, such as molasses or a waste hydrocarbon produced during oil refining, and a cheap source of nitrogen, such as liquid ammonia or ammonium or nitrate salts. In addition they need a supply of oxygen, water and small quantities of mineral elements, sulphur, phosphorus and possibly vitamins.

Table 9.9. Essential Amino Acid Content of Novel Proteins (mg/g Protein) Compared with Beef

Amino acid	Beef	Soya	Grass	Yeast	Fungi	Bacteria
Isoleucine	53	62	93	45	43	43
Leucine	82	79	130	70	55	68
Lysine	87	53	72	70	51	59
Methionine*	38	16	21	18	10	24
Phenylalanine†	75	49	93	44	39	34
Threonine	43	37	67	49	25	46
Tryptophan	12	11	21	14	21	9
Valine	55	53	103	54	60	56

* with cystine   † with tyrosine

From Table 9.9 it can be seen that compared with beef single cell proteins are low in methionine but otherwise their amino acid patterns are fairly similar. The commercial exploitation of single cell protein is under active development. For example, species of micro-fungi such as *Fusarium graminearum* are being grown on starch waste, yeasts are being grown on petroleum oil and bacteria are being grown on methane and methanol. For the present it is intended that these protein concentrates should be used as animal feedstuffs but eventually it is hoped that they will help meet the need for new protein foods for humans.

SUGGESTIONS FOR FURTHER READING

ALTSCHUL, A. M. *New Protein Foods, Vol.* 1, *Technology.* Academic Press, 1974.

BENDER, A. E. *et al.* (Eds). *Evaluation of Novel Protein Products.* Pergamon, 1970.

DAVIS, P. (Ed). *Single Cell Protein.* Academic Press, 1974.

DHSS. *Foods which Simulate Meat: Nutritional aspects.* HMSO, 1980.

FAO/WHO *Energy and Protein Requirements*. Reports, 1973, 1975, 1978.

FORREST, J. C. *et al*. *Principles of Meat Science*. Freeman, USA, 1975.

GERRARD, F. *Meat Technology*, 5th edition. Northwood Publications, 1977.

JONES, A. *World Protein Resources*. Medical and Technical Publishing Co., 1974.

LAWRIE, R. A. *Meat Science*, 3rd edition. Pergamon, 1979.

MINISTRY OF AGRICULTURE, FISHERIES AND FOOD. *Food Standards Committee Report on Novel Protein Foods*. HMSO, 1974.

STADELMAN, W. J. and COTTERILL, O. J. (Eds). *Egg Science and Technology*. Avi, USA, 1977.

TAYLOR, R. J. *The Chemistry of Proteins*, 2nd edition. Unilever Booklet, 1969.

TAYLOR, R. J. *Plant Protein Foods*. Unilever Booklet, 1976.

WOLF, W. J. and COWAN, J. C. *Soya Bean as a Food Source*. Blackwells, 1975.

Chapter Ten

Water and mineral elements

WATER

Without water there could be no life; water is essential to the life of every living thing from the simplest plant and one-cell organism to the most complex living system known—the human body. Moreover, while living things may exist for a considerable time without the other essential nutrients, they soon die without water. Living things contain a surprising amount of water, never less than 60 per cent of their total weight and sometimes as much as 95 per cent. About two-thirds of the body is water and all the organs, tissues and fluids of the body contain water as an essential constituent. Only a few parts of the body, such as bones, teeth and hair contain little water.

During life, water is continually being lost from the body, partly in the urine, partly from the surface of the body as sweat and partly as water vapour in the gases expelled in respiration. Small amounts of water are also lost in the faeces. If the body is to function successfully the water that is lost must be replaced, and a balance maintained between intake and output. The main source of water for the body is food and drink, though some is produced when nutrients are oxidized. The balance between input and output for an adult in a temperate climate is roughly as shown in Table 10.1.

Water is unlike the other essential nutrients in that most of it does not undergo chemical change within the body. Whereas proteins, for example, are broken down into amino acids during digestion, most water passes through the body unchanged. The functions performed by water are mainly due to physical action and depend upon its ability to transport nutrients through the body, to dissolve substances or hold them in colloidal suspension and, above all, to remain liquid over a wide range of temperature. This latter property enables water to provide a liquid medium in which the thousands of reactions necessary to life can occur.

Although most of the water in the body is involved in physical

Table 10.1. Water Balance in the Body

Source	Water intake cm^3/day	Source	Water loss cm^3/day
Food	850	Urine	1500
Drink	1300	Lungs	400
Oxidation of		Skin	500
nutrients	350	Faeces	100
Total:	2500	Total:	2500

changes, some is also concerned with chemical changes. Some chemical changes, such as the enzymic and hydrolytic breakdown of nutrients during digestion, involve the uptake of water whereas others, such as the oxidation of absorbed nutrients to provide the body with energy, release water. Apart from the water involved in such chemical reactions in the body, water is also required by all plants in order to synthesize carbohydrate during photosynthesis.

The Structure of Water and Ice

A water molecule contains two atoms of hydrogen covalently linked to an atom of oxygen, the bond angle being about 105° as shown in Fig. 10.1a. The electronegativity of oxygen, that is its attraction for electrons, is greater than that of hydrogen. This results in unequal charge distribution over the molecule, the oxygen atom carrying a partial negative charge $(\delta -)$, balanced by partial positive charges $(\delta +)$ on the hydrogen atoms. Such polar molecules attract each other and in water hydrogen bonds are formed between adjacent molecules as shown in Fig. 10.1b. It will be noted that, because of the shape of water molecules, such intermolecular attraction results in water molecules grouping together to form tetrahedral structures in which water molecules are linked to four others.

As was mentioned in Chapter 4, hydrogen bonds are weak electrostatic links which are easily broken, and in water such bonds are constantly being formed, broken and re-formed. If water is heated the thermal energy of the molecules is increased, and their resulting increased motion favours the breaking, rather than the formation, of hydrogen bonds. In water vapour no hydrogen bonds are present and the water molecules exist as single units. On the other hand, if liquid water is cooled the loss of thermal energy by the water molecules favours the formation of hydrogen bonds and in ice hydrogen bonding is so

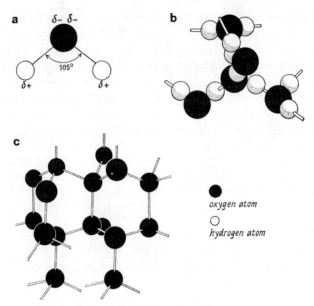

FIG. 10.1. (a) A water molecule showing its polar character and bond angle; (b) hydrogen bonding in water gives rise to tetrahedral structures; (c) hydrogen bonding in ice gives rise to hexagonal ring structures (only oxygen atoms are shown; the lines joining them represent hydrogen bonds).

extensive that all the water molecules are linked together by hydrogen bonds so forming a rigid and regular structure. The tetrahedral structure of groups of water molecules is preserved, but the tetrahedra are further linked together to form layers of hexagonal rings which are joined to give a very open structure as shown Fig. 10.1c. The open structure of ice compared to that of water explains why ice has a larger specific volume and smaller density than water.

The Physical Characteristics of Water

Water is the commonest of all liquids and perhaps for this reason it is often considered to be unremarkable. Because it is ubiquitous its presence, like that of air, is taken for granted. Yet it is fortunate that water is so readily available for, in reality, it is a most remarkable liquid, having properties which make it uniquely suited for the endless purposes for which it is used, including the support of life itself.

Water is a colourless, odourless and tasteless liquid which, under normal atmospheric conditions, boils at 100°C and freezes at 0°C. These facts are well known and cause no surprise. Yet in view of its low molecular weight it is surprising that water should be a liquid at all.

Oxygen, sulphur, selenium and tellurium belong to the same family of chemical elements and it is to be expected, therefore, that their hydrides would be similar to each other. For example, it would be expected that their boiling points and melting points would increase with increasing molecular weight and yet, as Table 10.2 shows, although water has the lowest molecular weight, it has a higher melting point and boiling point than any of the others. Of the four hydrides, water is the only one to be liquid at normal temperatures and, moreover, it remains liquid over a much wider temperature range than the others. This latter point is important because it means that water remains liquid over the temperature range at which plant and animal systems operate. The reason for the anomalous behaviour of water is that, because of hydrogen bonding, its effective molecular weight is much greater than 18.

Table 10.2. The Melting and Boiling Points of Four Hydrides

	H_2O	H_2S	H_2Se	H_2Te
Molecular weight	18	34	81	130
Melting point (°C)	0	− 86	− 64	− 57
Boiling point (°C)	100	− 61	− 42	− 2
Liquid range (°C)	100	25	22	55

Although water boils at 100°C at normal atmospheric pressure, its boiling point decreases or increases as the pressure is lowered or raised. At the top of Mount Everest, for example, its boiling point is about 72°C, whereas in a pressure cooker working at considerably above atmospheric pressure, it boils at 120°C. The temperature at which water boils is also affected by the presence of dissolved substances. These increase the boiling point by an amount which is proportional to their molecular concentration. Thus in jam making, when fruit is cooked in water containing dissolved sugar, the boiling point is greater than 100°C. If boiling is continued the concentration of the solution increases and consequently the boiling point rises. Indeed, as mentioned on page 135, the end of the boiling period can be judged from the boiling point, a knowledge of which enables the composition of the mixture to be determined.

The freezing point of water is lowered by the presence of dissolved solids, the lowering being proportional to the molecular concentration of dissolved material. Thus water in plant tissues and foods does not freeze until below 0°C. This fact must be taken into account when preserving foods by cold storage, where temperatures of $-18°C$ are often used to ensure that the water in the food is frozen. When water freezes its volume increases due to an increase in hydrogen bonding and the formation of an hexagonal structure which is very open. This causes ice to float on water thereby conserving the heat of the water beneath; this has important consequences because it enables aquatic plant and animal life to continue beneath the ice. It has many other important consequences among which may be mentioned the bursting of plant tissues which occurs when the plant sap freezes, and the breakdown of the tissues of frozen food which occurs if large ice crystals are allowed to form.

The specific heat and the latent heat of vaporization of water are high compared with their values for other liquids. In liquids containing no hydrogen bonding all the thermal energy supplied increases the kinetic energy of the molecules and hence the temperature. In water, however, some of the thermal energy supplied is used in breaking hydrogen bonds and therefore more heat energy must be supplied to obtain a given temperature rise than in liquids containing no hydrogen bonds. This is important in the body because the high specific heat allows water to act as a heat reservoir, preventing its temperature from rising quickly when heat is absorbed. The latent heat of vaporization of water is high for a similar reason, namely that energy is required to break hydrogen bonds, making necessary a greater supply of heat to vaporize a given mass of water than would be needed for the same mass of a non-hydrogen bonded liquid. The high latent heat value of 2.3 kJ/g means that 2.3 kJ are required to vaporize a gram of water at a given temperature. Thus, when sweat evaporates from the surface of the body a relatively large amount of heat is absorbed from the skin, which is thereby kept cool.

WATER AS SOLVENT. Water has been called the 'universal solvent' and, though this is not a completely accurate description, it does have unique solvent properties which enable it to dissolve a very large number of substances. It is sometimes called an ionizing or polar solvent because it will dissolve electrovalent substances such as acids and salts. It will also dissolve some covalent compounds, such as sugar and urea, though others, such as fat, do not dissolve. The importance of the solvent action of water cannot be emphasized too strongly; it enables water to dissolve a large number of substances which are essential to plant and animal life. These dissolved substances can then be transported through the organism to places where they are needed. In the absence of water, or some other solvent, they could not be utilized by living things.

The explanation for the excellent solvent properties of water is to be found in the nature of the molecule itself: to be more specific it depends upon the polar character of the water molecule. Water is so highly polar that it is strongly attracted to all ions in solution. Indeed this polar attraction is so strong that ions cannot exist free in aqueous solution; they are always *hydrated*, in which form they are firmly bound to surrounding water molecules.

Salts, which are insoluble in most liquids, are often dissolved by water. Salts are difficult to dissolve because they are ionized in the solid state and it will be recalled from Chapter 4 that crystalline sodium chloride, for example, exists entirely as ions, and that these ions are held together by strong electrostatic attarraction. In order to dissolve such substances the ions must be separated by the solvent and this is difficult because it requires a large amount of energy. Water is able to effect this because it hydrates the ions, and the energy liberated in hydration is sufficiently great to compensate for the energy required to separate them.

$$Na^{\oplus} Cl^{\ominus} + n\,kJ \longrightarrow Na^{\oplus} + Cl^{\ominus}$$
$$\text{ions separated}$$

$$Na^{\oplus} + Cl^{\ominus} + \text{water} \longrightarrow Na^{\oplus} \cdot xH_2O + Cl^{\ominus} \cdot yH_2O + n\,kJ$$
$$\text{ions in solution}$$

In other words the overall process of dissolving a salt in water, that is separating and hydrating the ions, requires little if any energy, and therefore occurs readily.

Water is also a good solvent for substances which, although they are not ionic, contain polar groups and which are able to form hydrogen bonds and other weak electrostatic links with water molecules. Thus low molecular weight alcohols—which contain polar hydroxyl groups—are readily soluble in water, though as molecular weight increases and the proportion of non-polar hydrocarbon chain increases, solubility decreases. Molecules which contain a number of hydroxyl groups, such as simple sugars, are very readily soluble in water because the greater number of polar groups they contain increases attraction between them and water. The fact that water can dissolve covalent substances providing that they contain a reasonable proportion of polar groups is very important in the body. It means that after food has been broken down during digestion into relatively small polar molecules, such as simple sugars and amino acids, it is dissolved by the body fluids, which are mainly water, and transported through the body in solution.

Apart from its capacity for promoting the ionization of other substances, water itself ionizes to a very small extent as described in Chapter 5;

$$H_2O \rightleftharpoons H^+ + OH^-$$

It will be recalled that in water, and indeed in any aqueous system, the product of the concentration of hydrogen and hydroxyl ions is constant;

$$[H^+][OH^-] = 10^{-14}.$$

Thus in pure water the hydrogen ion concentration is 10^{-7} g ions/l and the pH is 7. This value of pH defines the neutral point of the pH scale.

Water Supplies

There is no such thing as pure natural water. Rain water, which is the purest form of natural water, contains small amounts of dissolved gases, such as oxygen, carbon dioxide and, near industrial areas, sulphur dioxide. It also contains small quantities of dust. Other types of natural water, such as spring and river water contain, in addition to the impurities of rain water, dissolved salts and in the latter case additional impurities from vegetation and drainage.

An adequate supply of clean, wholesome water is one of the essentials of modern life and water for domestic consumption must be carefully treated before use so that it is not injurious to health. A considerable proportion of the water supply in Great Britain is obtained from reservoirs which receive their water from moorland catchment areas. The water which is withdrawn from such reservoirs is treated in a number of ways before being supplied to the consumer. The essential stages are settlement, filtration and sterilization. Some water used for drinking is now also treated by fluoridation as described on page 228. Water which has been treated in these ways is wholesome and suitable for human consumption, although for industrial purposes it may also require to be softened.

Water which needs to be softened is said to be *hard* because it does not easily give a lather with soap. The hardness of water is due to the presence of certain mineral salts—chiefly the sulphates and bicarbonates of calcium and magnesium—and because of this, hard water makes good drinking water. For industrial purposes, however, hard water is unsatisfactory both because of its poor lathering properties and because the mineral salts tend to precipitate out and form insoluble deposits in boilers, water pipes and other equipment. Consequently water required for industrial purposes is often softened and this is done by removing the calcium and magnesium ions by a process of *ion-exchange* in which these ions are exchanged for sodium ions which do not form insoluble salts.

STERILIZATION. Natural water always contains organic matter and dissolved oxygen and is, therefore, a natural breeding ground for bacteria. Typhoid fever, cholera and jaundice are caused by the infection of water supplies, and in order that bacteria causing these and other diseases may be eliminated, water which is to be used for human consumption is usually sterilized before use.

Water is normally sterilized by adding $0 \cdot 5$ ppm of chlorine; this small concentration is sufficient to kill all bacteria but not to impart a taste to the water. Water which is to be used for canning or bottling may be sterilized by adding 1 or 2 ppm of ozone. This treatment is more expensive than chlorination but has the advantage that ozone breaks down into oxygen which has no taste.

Sources of Water for the Body

The body can survive for several weeks without solid food, but in the absence of water it cannot survive for more than a few days. The reason for this is that normal functioning of the body involves a continual loss of water which, because the body cannot store water, must be balanced by a continual supply. Water is supplied to the body in three ways which are, in order of importance; water and beverages, solid food, and water formed within the body.

WATER AND BEVERAGES. For a sedentary person living in a temperate climate and eating a normal diet, about a litre of water must be taken in liquid form each day. This figure is a minimum and can, with advantage, be increased. A daily fluid intake of two litres might become necessary in warm weather when the amount of water lost through the sweat glands is increased above the average. The whole of this water could be supplied directly, but in a normal diet a considerable proportion is taken in the form of such fluids as tea, coffee, cocoa, fruit juices and alcoholic beverages.

Tea and coffee are best considered as flavoured water unless drunk with milk and sweetened with sugar, whereas the other beverages mentioned have a definite nutritional value and are dealt with elsewhere.

TEA. Tea leaves, which are the basis of the familiar beverage, grow on an evergreen shrub which is grown extensively in India, China and Ceylon as well as in other countries. The tea shrub is kept small by pruning and only the bud and the two youngest leaves are picked in preparing good quality tea (Fig. 10.2). Fresh tea leaves contain a number of water-soluble constituents including polyphenols, which account for about 30 per cent of the dry weight, amino acids (4 per cent), caffeine (4 per cent) and traces of sugars and mineral elements. Of these

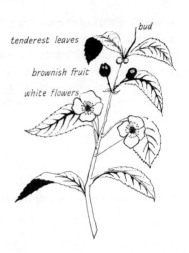

FIG. 10.2. A branch of the tea shrub showing the tenderest leaves and bud, which are used for making good quality tea

caffeine is the most important as it gives tea its mild stimulating action. Caffeine is a *purine* and its structure is given below:

Caffeine

Tea leaves also contain insoluble materials, mainly fibrous material (e.g. cellulose), proteins and pectins and a very small quantity, about 0·01 per cent, of essential oils which contain a large number of volatile components that contribute to flavour and aroma.

After being picked, tea leaves are dried and in addition to loss of moisture this brings about some chemical changes, including an increase in caffeine content and amino acids. The dried leaves are broken up by passing them between rollers and this process releases enzymes, principally *polyphenol oxidase*, which are responsible for the so-called 'fermentation' that follows. Ideally 'fermentation' is carried out at 25° C at which temperature enzyme activity is at a maximum. The leaves are spread out in layers and in the presence of oxygen in the air polyphenol oxidase catalyses the oxidation of some polyphenols to o-quinones which subsequently react to form coloured compounds, particularly the brownish substances generally known as *thearubigins*. The exact nature of the chemical changes taking place during fermentation are exceedingly complex and remain largely unknown. After fermentation the leaves are dried further at a temperature which inactivates all enzymes, caramelizes sugars and reduces the moisture content to about 3 per cent.

The popularity of tea as a beverage depends mainly on the mild stimulating effect produced by caffeine, although a high-grade tea is also prized for its fragrant aroma and delicate flavour. When boiling water is added to tea leaves, the resulting infusion contains a proportion of the soluble constituents of the leaves. After five minutes about 80 per cent caffeine and 60 per cent of other soluble matter are extracted, and after half an hour all the caffeine and about 85 per cent of other soluble matter are extracted. Tea is best drunk after it has been infused for about five minutes; after that time extraction of caffeine is slow, volatile constituents are lost and bitterness increases. Quality further deteriorates when an infusion is kept hot due to changes in the thearubigins. When an infusion is cooled, caffeine reacts with the thearubigins and other coloured substances to give a precipitate or 'cream' which serves as an indicator of the quality of the tea.

COFFEE. The coffee plant, like the tea plant, is an evergreen shrub. It is cultivated in many tropical countries, particularly Brazil. The fruit is like a cherry in appearance and contains two seeds, called 'coffee beans', enclosed in a tough skin. In order to extract the beans, the outer pulpy part of the fruit is removed and the beans, still surrounded by their skin or husk, are dried in air. Husks are then removed by rolling, so liberating the beans.

The chemical composition of coffee beans is exceedingly complex, over 200 constituents having been identified, and because of this complexity the chemical basis of coffee flavour and aroma remain largely unknown. The most important constituent of coffee beans is undoubtedly caffeine although the amount present, 1–2 per cent, is less than in tea leaves. Other water-soluble constituents of coffee beans include about 5 per cent *chlorogenic acid*, 1 per cent *trigonelline*, which is structurally related to nicotinic acid, 5 per cent sucrose, 3 per cent protein and 5 per cent mineral elements, mainly potassium. The water-soluble components of coffee account for about 25 per cent of the total, the major insoluble constituent being polysaccharides together with much small amounts of 'coffee oil'.

Coffee beans are roasted before use; this removes much of the moisture, converts some of the sugar into caramel and develops flavour and aroma. Roasting has little effect on caffeine but both chlorogenic acid and trigonelline are largely broken down, the latter forming a certain amount of nicotinic acid;

Trigonelline   Nicotinic acid

The fragrant aroma associated with coffee-roasting is due to volatiliz-ation of essential oils and other easily vaporized flavouring matter. The roasted beans, now dark brown in colour, are brittle and this makes subsequent grinding easier. After grinding the flavour and aroma of the powder rapidly diminishes in air; if the coffee is not used immediately it should, therefore, be stored in an airtight container.

The roasted beans are ground because in this form the constituents are more easily extracted by hot water, up to 35 per cent of the constituents of the bean going into solution. The actual amount extracted depends on the fineness of the coffee grounds, the temperature of the water used and the time of infusion. Caffeine is rapidly extracted, especially if very hot water is used; at 95° C 80 per cent is extracted after two minutes and 90 per cent after ten minutes. Coffee is best made using very hot water (95° C) and a short (two minutes) time of extraction as this favours extraction of caffeine but not of substances that contribute to bitterness. Coffee produced in this way contains about twice as much caffeine as is contained in tea.

Coffee may be adulterated by the addition of chicory, only the root of the plant being used. Chicory, which is roasted before use, contains no caffeine but it does contain caramel and adds to the colour and flavour of the infusion. The main reason for its use is that it is much cheaper than coffee.

'Instant' coffee is made by extracting the water-soluble components of roasted coffee beans with hot water and concentrating the resulting liquid extract and converting it to a powder either by spray-drying or, more recently, by freeze-drying (see Chapter 13). Improving techniques have resulted in the production of 'instant' coffees which retain most of the flavour and aroma constituents of the roasted beans.

SOLID FOOD. Nearly all solid food contains water, the only exceptions being pure chemical substances, such as sugar and salt. The amount of water contained in food varies from a small percentage in 'dry' foods such as dried milk, biscuits, cheese, and chocolate to a large percentage in 'moist' foods such as vegetables and fruit. Some foods usually classed as dry also contain a large proportion of water; white bread, for example, contains about 40 per cent water. Fig. 10.3 shows the percentage of water in some foods, and it will be noted that fruit and vegetables head the list, usually containing 80–90 per cent water. An average of rather less than a litre of water ($1\frac{1}{2}$ pints) is taken into the body each day in the form of so-called solid food, and it is evident that this source of water makes an appreciable contribution to the total water requirement.

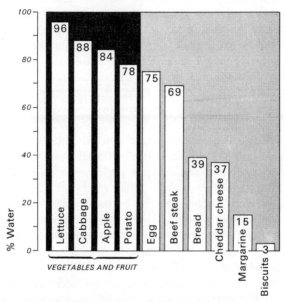

Fig. 10.3. The percentage of water in various foods

WATER FORMED WITHIN THE BODY. If absorbed nutrients are oxidized within the body to produce energy, they are eventually broken down into carbon dioxide and water. The oxidation of glucose, for example, is shown in the equation:

$$C_6H_{12}O_6 + 6O_2 \longrightarrow 6CO_2 + 6H_2O$$
$$180\,g \qquad\qquad\qquad 6 \times 18\,g = 108\,g$$

One gram molecular weight of glucose produces six gram molecular weights of water. If more familiar quantities are used it means that a kg of glucose produces just over half a litre of water. In an average daily diet the amount of water produced by oxidation of food is nearly an eigth of a litre. Oxidation of energy-producing foods is thus the least important way in which the body obtains its water requirement.

MINERAL ELEMENTS

The term mineral elements refers to elements other than carbon, hydrogen, oxygen and nitrogen; that is those elements which normally form salts and, as far as the body is concerned, which remain after the body has been cremated and converted into ash. The main elements found in the ash, which accounts for about 4 per cent of the total body weight, are shown in Table 10.3. It will be noted that the amounts of calcium and phosphorous in the body vary considerably from person to person. Apart from the major elements shown in the table, very much smaller amounts of others are also found and these are known as *trace elements*. Though trace elements are present in only minute quantities, they are just as essential to human life as elements, such as calcium, which are present in relatively large amounts. In addition to the essential trace elements, minute amounts of other mineral elements are found in the body but their significance is not yet clear and they will not be considered in this book.

It may be noted from Table 10.3 that the main mineral elements of the body have low atomic numbers. This is partly because such elements tend to form soluble salts which can readily be taken up from the soil by plants and partly because they are the ones most widely found in foods. Once such elements have been taken into the body as part of the diet they must be absorbed before they can be used by the body. Those elements, such as sodium, potassium and chlorine, which form simple soluble compounds exist in solution as free ions and as such are readily absorbed. Other elements, such as calcium, phosphorus and magnesium, which often form complex insoluble compounds, are much less readily absorbed by the body. The assessment of the dietary needs of the latter is therefore rather difficult because the amount actually available to the body is less than that supplied in the diet. In such cases an allowance has to be made for the proportion of the intake which is not available to the body.

Mineral elements are used by the body in a great variety of ways but these uses may be considered under three main headings, namely: as part of the rigid body structure, as part of soft body tissues and as part of body fluids. The main use of each mineral element is summarized in

Table 10.3. The Principal Mineral Elements in the Body

Element	Atomic number	Average amount in adult (g)	Recommended adult allowance (mg) in UK	Where mainly found in body
Sodium	11	80	—	Body fluids as Na^+
Magnesium	12	25	(200–300)	Bone
Phosphorus	15	600–900	(800)	Bone as $Ca_3(PO_4)_2$
Sulphur	16	170	—	Amino acids, e.g. methionine
Chlorine	17	120	—	Body fluids as Cl^-
Potassium	19	135	(800–1300)	Cell fluids as K^+
Calcium	20	1000–1500	500	Bone as $Ca_3(PO_4)_2$
Iron	26	4	{ Men, 10 Women, 12	Blood as haem

Table 10.3. Calcium, phosphorus and magnesium are very largely used to form the bone structure of the body, indeed as much as 99 per cent of the calcium in the body is used in this way. Other elements, for example potassium, are mainly used in soft tissues and potassium ions help to control the pH of intracellular fluids and maintain osmotic pressure within the cell. Phosphates are also important in cell fluids and in addition to their buffering and osmotic functions they are concerned with energy release in cells.

The main mineral elements present in body fluids—that is fluids outside cells—are sodium and chlorine. Mineral elements in body fluids are present as ions and it is important that their concentration is controlled so as to preserve the electrolyte balance in the body. For example, if large amounts of salt are eaten in the diet there is a natural tendency for the concentration of these ions in the blood to increase. In these circumstances the body restores the concentration of chloride and sodium ions to their original level by withdrawing them to the kidneys whence they pass out of the body in the urine. The pH of body fluids must be maintained within narrow limits and this is achieved by the buffering activity of the ions present. For example, the pH of blood must be maintained close to 7·4 and this is done mainly by the carbonate/bicarbonate buffer system though phosphates and proteins also contribute to the total buffering effect.

CALCIUM AND PHOSPHORUS. These two elements account for about 75 per cent of the total weight of mineral elements in the body, and both have a number of essential functions to perform. Hence, the body must receive a sufficient supply of each of them if it is to remain healthy.

No less than 99 per cent of the total calcium content of the body is found in bones and teeth, mainly as calcium phosphate, $Ca_3(PO_4)_2$. When a baby is born its bones are soft and mainly consist of collagen. Bone only becomes hard on calcification, which occurs when minute crystals of calcium phosphate are deposited in the soft organic framework of the bone. Calcification requires the presence of calcium, phosphorus and vitamin D (see p. 252) and a deficiency of any one or all of these results in badly formed teeth and bone, poor growth and in extreme cases development of rickets.

Small amounts of calcium are also found in body fluids either as calcium ions or in combination with protein. Although the concentration of calcium ions in the blood is small, about 10 mg per 100 ml plasma, it must be maintained at a fixed level. This is done by using calcium phosphate of bones as a calcium reservoir. If there is a shortage of calcium in the blood, bones are decalcified and calcium ions pass into solution. The calcium in bone is very labile and there is a constant interchange of calcium between bone and blood. This interchange is facilitated by the very large surface area of bone crystals, calculated to be over one hundred acres in an adult man, which is in contact with blood. Shortage of calcium in the diet, therefore, affects the structure of the bones, which become weakened.

Calcium ions are needed in the blood, for in their absence blood cannot clot and a small cut is liable to result in excessive bleeding, which if not prevented may lead to death. The actual mechanism of coagulation is complicated but the main result is that in the presence of calcium ions the soluble protein *fibrinogen* is converted into *fibrin* which forms the blood clot. The part played by vitamin K in this process is discussed on page 253. Calcium ions are also necessary in the body fluids for the successful functioning of nerves and muscles.

Phosphorus, like calcium, is mainly found in the calcium phosphate of bones and teeth, about 85 per cent of the phosphorus in the body being involved in this way. The remaining 15 per cent is distributed through the cells and fluids of the body. Phosphorus is essential to the structure of every cell in the body and it is also an essential constituent of the body fluids.

Phosphoric acid and its salts form buffer mixtures in the blood, and thereby preserve its pH at 7·4. Phosphorus, in the form of phosphate groups in adenosine triphosphate, plays a vital part in the complex process whereby energy is obtained from the oxidation of nutrients, and this important process is discussed on page 170.

It is difficult to estimate the amount of calcium needed by the body and it is found that the body can maintain a balance between the calcium taken into the body and the amount excreted even when the amount of calcium in the diet varies between wide limits. The American National Research Council (NRC) recommends a daily intake of 800 mg calcium for a normal adult on the basis that 320 mg/day are lost from the body and that only about 40 per cent of the calcium in the diet is absorbed. This value is almost certainly above the minimum requirement and the World Health Organization (WHO) recommend that 400–500 mg/day would serve as a 'practical allowance' for a normal adult. They recommend higher allowances for those with special needs, e.g. children and pregnant and nursing women. The Department of Health and Social Security (DHSS) have adopted the WHO figures as recommended intakes for the UK and the upper limits in each range are given in Table 12.8 on page 274. The requirement for phosphorus is usually taken as being the same as that for calcium.

Phosphorus occurs extensively in many foods and is unlikely to be lacking in a normal diet. There is a real possibility, however, that a diet may not supply sufficient calcium because significant amounts of calcium are found in a relatively small range of foodstuffs. It is for this reason that calcium, in the form of calcium carbonate, is now added to all flour except wholemeal flour at the rate of 235–390 mg/100 g.

Table 10.4. Calcium and Phosphorus Content of Foods

Food	Calcium mg/100 g	Phosphorous mg/100 g
Dairy products and eggs		
Milk	120	95
Butter	15	24
Cheese, Cheddar	810	520
Eggs	54	218
Meat and fish		
Beef	7	156
Liver	6	313
Haddock	16	242
Sardines, canned	550	683
Cereals		
Bread, white	100	81
Bread, brown	88	240
Flour, 70% extraction	138	84
Rice	4	99
Vegetables and fruit		
Potatoes, old	8	40
Cabbage, Savoy	57	54
Spinach	70	93
Apples	4	9
Oranges	41	24

Table 10.4 gives a comparison of the calcium and phosphorus content of some foods. It is clear that cheese is a particularly valuable source of both elements. Cheese, milk, fish of which the bones are eaten and bread are all valuable sources of calcium; milk, cheese and flour products together account for over four-fifths of the calcium in British diets. In addition to calcium obtained from food, small additional amounts are supplied by hard water containing calcium salts, though even very hard water does not contribute more than 5 per cent of the total allowance.

It does not automatically follow that all the calcium in food is available to the body. As pointed out in Chapter 5 much of the calcium in spinach is not available, because it is in the form of *calcium oxalate* which is not absorbed into the blood. The calcium in any food containing equivalent amounts of oxalic acid and calcium is not available. In a similar way foods containing phytic acid render calcium unavailable by forming insoluble *calcium phytate*. Phytic acid occurs in flour, for instance, and may render its calcium unavailable (see Chapter 8). In general, less than half the calcium taken into the body is absorbed and available for use.

IRON. Iron accounts for about $0 \cdot 1$ per cent of the mineral elements in the body and the total amount of iron in the body is only about 4 g. 60–70 per cent of the iron is found in the haemoglobin of red blood cells which transport oxygen from the lungs to the tissues. Red blood cells have a life of about four months and it has been estimated that some ten million of these cells are withdrawn from circulation every second. If the iron contained in these cells passed out of the body it would be difficult to replace it from food. Fortunately most of the iron which is released is conserved and is used to form the new red corpuscles which are produced in the marrow of the bones. In this way the iron involved in the formation of haemoglobin is used repeatedly.

A small proportion of iron in the body, about 10 per cent, occurs in body cells, and some cell enzymes, such as the *cytochromes*, contain iron. The remainder of the iron in the body is stored in the liver, spleen and bone marrow in the form of a complex containing iron, phosphate and protein and known as *ferritin*. Although ferritin acts as reserve store of iron, free iron can only be released from the complex slowly and so is not available to supply iron in emergencies.

In the UK the daily intake of iron for an adult male recommended by the DHSS (1979) is 10 mg (see Table 12.8). Women who lose blood through menstruation require a larger intake, probably about 12 mg per day. For pregnant women 13 mg per day and for nursing mothers 15 mg per day are recommended. This iron is mainly supplied by food, but water may also make a small contribution and utensils used in preparing food may also contribute. For example, the iron content of beef could be doubled by mincing it in an iron mincer! The iron content of a number of foods is shown in Table 10.5. It will be noted that even those foods which are richest in iron contain only very small quantities.

10.5. Average Iron Content of Foods

Food	Iron (mg/100 g)	Food	Iron (mg/100 g)
Kidney	6	White bread	1·7
Liver	11·4	Flour, 70% extraction	2·1
Oatmeal	4·1	Haddock	0·3
Sardines	2·9	Cabbage	0·6
Spinach	3·2	Potatoes, old	0·7
Beef	1·9	Cheddar cheese	0·6
Eggs	2·1	Apples	0·3
Brown bread	2·5	Milk	0·1

The proportion of dietary iron that is absorbed by the body is remarkably small. Adults absorb about 10 per cent of the iron in their diet, though people who have special need for iron, such as growing children and pregnant women, are able to absorb more. The fate of iron in the body has been studied by labelling iron in food using a radioisotope of iron having atomic weight 59 and determining the amount of the isotope in the blood and excreta by measuring their radioactivity. It has been found that iron which is absorbed into the bloodstream is in the form of ferrous iron, whereas most of the iron in food is in the form of ferric iron. Therefore, during digestion some ferric iron must be reduced to the ferrous state. Reduction takes place in the stomach and is promoted by protein and ascorbic acid in the presence of hydrochloric acid. Ascorbic acid also protects the reduced iron from oxidation. Apart from ascorbic acid, a number of other factors affect the absorption of iron, two of which have already been mentioned, namely the presence of phytic acid and oxalic acid in food. These two acids render iron unavailable by forming an insoluble phytate and oxalate respectively.

Iron is one of the mineral elements which may be lacking in an average diet, and for this reason it is now added to all flour in the UK, except wholemeal, so that its iron content is at least 1·65 mg per 100 g of flour. In an average British diet cereals provide nearly 40 per cent, meat 25 per cent and vegetables almost 20 per cent of the total iron intake. Eggs provide an additional 5 per cent.

An insufficiency of iron compounds in the body shows itself as anaemia.

Trace Elements

In addition to the major mineral elements already considered, the body also requires minute quantities of certain other elements known as trace elements. A number of such elements, known as *essential trace elements*, are essential to human life and these are as follows; cobalt, copper, manganese, molybdenum, zinc, selenium, fluorine, iodine, chromium, nickel, tin, silicon and vanadium. The exact role that these elements play in the body is often not fully known, though most of them form an integral part of vitamins, enzymes or hormones. Very minute amounts of these elements are required in the diet and any normal diet will contain sufficient for the body's needs. Table 10.6 summarizes the main facts about these elements.

Table 10.6. Some Essential Trace Elements

Element	Probable requirement mg/day	Form in the body	Good sources
Cobalt	< 0·1	Vitamin B_{12}	Liver, meat
Copper	1–3	Enzymes	Liver, meat, shell fish, nuts
Manganese	3–5	Enzyme activator	Cereals, peas, beans, nuts
Molybdenum	Trace	Enzyme	Peas, beans
Zinc	10–20	Enzyme	Oysters, kidney, liver
Selenium	Trace	Associated with vitamin E	Wheat
Iodine	0·06–0·15	Hormone	Sea fish, fish oils, iodized salt
Fluorine	1–2	Bones and teeth	Sea fish, water, tea

The metallic elements are particularly associated with enzyme activity and are usually an integral part of the enzyme. Zinc, for example, is part of the enzyme *carbonic anhydrase* found in red blood cells where it assists quick liberation of carbon dioxide in the lungs. Copper forms part of several enzyme systems including *cytochrome oxidase*, and *tyrosinase*. Copper, and all the other metallic essential trace elements except zinc, have a variable valency and this enables them to take part in oxidation-reduction reactions in the body. In cytochrome oxidase copper is associated with iron and catalyses oxidation-reduction mechanisms concerned with tissue respiration. Tyrosinase is concerned with the oxidation of tyrosine and seems to be unique in that it can catalyse the reaction even when tyrosine is part of an intact protein. Manganese activates the enzymes *alkaline phosphatase* and *arginase* which are concerned with bone and urea formation respectively.

The amount of essential trace elements in the body is very small indeed and therefore the amount needed in the diet is minute. For example, the total amount of copper in the body is 100–150 mg and the daily intake required is only about 2 mg. Normal diets supply sufficient of all the essential trace elements except possibly iodine and fluorine. For this reason these two elements warrant separate consideration.

IODINE. Iodine is the heaviest member of the halogen group which comprises the chemically related elements fluorine, chlorine, bromine and iodine. They all occur in nature in the form of salts and are all found in sea-water. All the halogens are found in the body and they are all essential except bromine. Iodine is carried round the body in blood as iodide and is absorbed in the thyroid gland, oxidized to iodine, combined with tyrosine and the compound formed converted into the hormone *thyroxine*.

Small amounts of iodine may be supplied in drinking water, but it is mainly obtained from food, sea-foods being the richest source. Thus cod, salmon and herring are all useful sources of iodine, though the best source is cod liver oil. The importance of fish as a source of iodine is shown by the fact that in an average British diet it supplies over a quarter of the total domestic consumption, while milk and cereals each supply about one-fifth. Sea-weeds extract iodides from sea-water and are, therefore, a useful reservoir of combined iodine. In remote coastal areas, such as occur in the Highlands of Scotland for example, sheep are often to be found eating sea-weed at low tide, thereby gaining a valuable supply of iodides. In some parts of the world certain sea-weeds are regarded as valuable foods for man; for instance, cooked sea-weed food, known as laverbread, is eaten in southwest Wales.

The body normally contains only about 20–50 mg iodine and the amount required daily by the diet is very small indeed, about 0·07 mg being sufficient for normal needs. In spite of this minute requirement people in many parts of the world exist on diets which are deficient in iodine. In Derbyshire, for example, people suffer from goitre (which in consequence is often called 'Derbyshire neck') because their diets lack sufficient iodine. Goitre is widespread in America, Switzerland, Yugoslavia and many other countries.

In areas where the iodine content of the diet is low a satisfactory way of increasing the intake of iodine is to use 'iodized salt'. Iodized salt is prepared by adding potassium iodide to salt, the proportion used in

Great Britain being 1 part of potassium iodide to about 40 000 parts of salt. Potassium iodide is soluble in water and is rapidly absorbed into the blood, any surplus being quite harmless. The use of iodized salt is, therefore, to be recommended as a simple and harmless way of supplementing the iodine obtained from food. In addition to iodide, small quantities of magnesium carbonate may also be added to 'Table Salt' to improve its free-running properties.

FLUORINE. Fluorine is the lightest and most reactive member of the halogen group and in the body it is found in bones and teeth, although there is as yet no direct evidence to prove that it is essential to the body. It appears to harden teeth enamel by combining with calcium phosphate in teeth. It has been shown that traces of combined fluorine are beneficial in protecting teeth against decay, the protective effect being most noticeable in children under eight years of age. However, if the amount of fluorine compounds present increases teeth may become mottled in appearance.

Minerals containing combined fluorine have a wide distribution in nature, though they only occur in small quantities. Small amounts of fluorine compounds are, therefore, usually present in natural water. In Great Britain water nearly always contains traces of fluorides, though their concentration rarely exceeds one part per million (ppm) parts of water. Drinking water is the main source of fluorine in the diet as very few foods contain more than 1 ppm, the main exceptions being sea fish, which contain 5–10 ppm, and tea.

The DHSS report (1979) does not attempt to indicate any requirement for fluoride but notes that the average daily intake of fluoride in the UK from food and beverages is about $0.6 - 1.8$ mg. In areas where drinking water contains very little or no fluoride the intake of fluoride may be so low that dental decay results. This situation can be remedied if controlled amounts of fluoride are added to drinking water. Treatment may be carried out by adding sodium fluoride or sodium silicofluoride, Na_2SiF_6, or hydrofluosilicic acid in such quantities that the total fluoride content of the water is 1 ppm. The amount of fluorine added must be carefully controlled because if the amount of fluorine present exceeds 1.5 ppm teeth may become mottled in appearance.

Experiments carried out over many years in the USA, Britain and other countries prove beyond any doubt that fluoridation of water to increase the fluorine content to 1 ppm reduces the incidence of dental caries, particularly in young children. An authoritative report by the Royal College of Physicians (1976) concludes that allegations linking fluoridation of water supplies with various medical disorders are without any foundation. The report presents four main conclusions:

1 The presence of fluoride in drinking water substantially reduces dental caries throughout life.
2 A level of 1 ppm of fluoride in drinking water is completely safe irrespective of the hardness of the water.
3 Alternative methods of taking fluoride, such as toothpaste or tablets, are less effective than fluoridation of water supplies.
4 Fluoridation does not harm the environment.

At present fluoridated water is available to less than 10% of the population of the UK and the report recommends that where the natural fluoride content of water supplies is less than 1 ppm, fluoride should be added to bring it to this level.

TRACE ELEMENTS AND FOOD PROCESSING. Trace elements may become incorporated into food during processing and although minute amounts of such elements may be beneficial or even essential to the body, slightly larger amounts are frequently toxic. Modern analytical techniques such as flame photometry and atomic absorption spectrophotometry enable concentrations of less than 1 ppm of many elements to be determined and have paved the way for legislation which lays down limits for a number of elements. The ability to measure concentrations of less than 1 ppm and the improvement in processing techniques is making it possible to reduce such limits. For example, the general limit for lead has been reduced from 2 ppm to 1 ppm (1979). Table 10.7 summarizes the position and gives examples of specific and general limits that are applied.

The inclusion of traces of some elements in foods during processing can have an adverse effect on quality and this is an additional reason for measuring and controlling the amounts of trace elements entering food in this way. Copper, for example, even in concentrations of less than 0·1 ppm, can lead to the development of rancidity in milk and butter.

Water. Supplies and Health

As pointed out on page 214 a clean, wholesome water supply is one of the essentials of modern life. In Britain we are fortunate to have such a supply. However, the mineral content of water varies considerably over the country; in some areas the water is soft while in others it is hard and contains mineral elements which are valuable for health. Where water lacks fluoride this may be added to water in controlled amounts as already discussed.

There has recently been much discussion about the relation between

Table 10.7. Limits for Trace Elements in Food

Element	General limit		Examples of specific limits (ppm)
	Statutory or recommended	Limit in ppm	
Lead	Statutory	1	Dried herbs and spices, 10; Corned beef, tea, 5; canned fish, 3; canned foods, 2; Baby foods, 0·2
Arsenic	Statutory	1	Spices, 5; Chicory, 4; ice-cream, soft drink concentrates, fruit juices and beer, 0·5
Fluorine	—	—	Baking powder, 15; self-raising flour, 3
Copper	Recommended	20	Tea, 150; chicory and gelatine, 30; beer and wines, 7
Zinc	Recommended	50	Gelatine, 100; ready-to-drink beverages, 5
Tin	Recommended	250	Canned foods only

soft water and health. There is some evidence to suggest that the incidence of coronary heart disease (CHD) is linked with soft water supplies. Soft water contains less calcium carbonate, magnesium and sulphate and more sodium than hard water. Soft water may also be deficient in vanadium. In addition, soft water picks up traces of zinc, cadmium, iron, copper and lead from pipes. It seems possible that incidence of CHD may be related to a deficiency of calcium, magnesium and vanadium and/or an excess of copper and cadmium.

Much more evidence needs to be obtained before any link between CHD and soft water supplies can be regarded as established.

SUGGESTIONS FOR FURTHER READING

HARLER, C. R. *The Culture and Marketing of Tea*, 3rd edition. Oxford University Press, 1964.

MATZ, S. A. *Water in Foods*. Avi, USA, 1965.

ROYAL COLLEGE OF PHYSICIANS. *Fluoride, Teeth and Health*. Pitman Medical, 1976.

TAYLOR, R. J. *Water*. Unilever Booklet, 2nd edition. 1969.

URQUHART, M. *Cocoa*, 2nd edition. Longmans, 1961.

WHO. Report on Trace Elements in Human Nutrition. HMSO, 1973.

Chapter Eleven

Vitamins

Until 1912 it was supposed that a diet containing adequate amounts of protein, carbohydrate, fat, mineral elements and water would be sufficient for maintaining health. In that year Gowland Hopkins found, however, that animals fed on an artificial diet containing only these nutrients did not thrive and it is now known that small quantities of certain other nutrients called vitamins are required in addition.

Vitamins are organic compounds found in small amounts in many foods; their presence in the diet is essential because, with a few exceptions, the body is unable to synthesize them from other nutrients. In the case of most vitamins a deficiency will cause a check in the growth of children and this is usually aggravated by a loss of appetite. Various diseases, called deficiency diseases, are also associated with shortages of specific vitamins; these will be described later. Deficiency diseases have been the cause of much suffering and death for many centuries but today they can be prevented and cured by ensuring that the diet contains a sufficient quantity and variety of vitamins. The important of vitamins cannot be over-emphasized. Indeed, the discovery of the existence of vitamins and the subsequent exploitation of this knowledge has been called the greatest advance in nutrition in the twentieth century.

Most vitamins are very complex chemically; they do not belong to one chemical family but are all quite different from each other. However, the structures of all of them are known and, with one exception, they can be prepared synthetically. Before their structures were determined the vitamins were designated by letters as vitamin A, vitamin B and so on. They are now known by names which give some indication of their chemical structure and in general these names are used in preference to the letters. In some cases, however, it is more convenient to use the letter by which they were originally known.

Foods contain only very small quantities of vitamins, but these small amounts carry out some most important tasks in the body. Members of the B group of vitamins, for example, form part of several coenzyme molecules which are absolutely necessary for the maintenance of good health. The other vitamins are essential, though in some cases their exact job in the chemistry of the body is not known.

Only small amounts of vitamins are needed by the body and the minute quantities present in foods are usually sufficient for man's needs. They are, however, distributed among many types of food, and to ensure that all the vitamins are represented in the diet it is important that a variety of different foods is eaten. The vitamin content of a food can vary quite considerably. This is especially so with fruit and vegetables, where the vitamin content depends, among other things, on the freshness and variety of the fruit or vegetable and climatic conditions during its growth. The figures for the vitamin content of foods given in this chapter are average values and this must be borne in mind when consulting them.

It is so important that sufficient quantities of vitamins are consumed that in some cases extra vitamins are added to food. Examples have already been encountered in connection with flour, to which the vitamins thiamine and nicotinic acid are added to replace what has been lost during milling and margarine, to which vitamins A and D are added. In these cases the synthetic vitamins are used and this demonstrates how useful a knowledge of their structures is because otherwise synthesis would be impossible.

The main sources and functions of the more important vitamins are summarized in Table 11.1.

The measurement of the vitamin content of food was originally difficult because, at the time when the effects of vitamins were discovered, the pure vitamins themselves could not be isolated. In order to overcome this international standards were agreed. Vitamin A, for example, occurs in cod liver oil and so a sample of this oil was used as a standard. The vitamin content of the oil was expressed as an arbitrary number of international units (iu) per gram and the vitamin A content of any other food could then be compared with the standard by means of feeding experiments. This was done by noting the effects of a definite amount of the standard oil on a laboratory animal, usually a rat, and observing how much of the food in question was needed to produce the same effects.

All the known vitamins have now been isolated in a pure form and international units can be precisely defined in terms of the weight of pure vitamin. Vitamin C, for example, has been prepared in crystalline form and the international unit defined as 0·05 mg of the pure vitamin. Similarly, vitamin content of any food can be expressed in mg or μg per unit weight of food so that the need to express vitamin content in iu no longer exists and they are now rarely used.

Table 11.1. Vitamins

Name	Main sources	Functions in the body and effect of shortage
Vitamin A	Green vegetables, milk, dairy products, margarine, fish liver oil	Necessary for healthy skin and teeth and also for normal growth and development. Deficiency will slow down growth and may lead to disorders of the skin, lowered resistance to infection and disturbances of vision such as night blindness.
The B Vitamins	Bread and flour, meat, milk, potatoes, yeast extract	Function as co-enzymes in many of the reactions involved in making use of food. Shortage causes loss of appetite, slows growth and development and impairs general health. Severe deficiency may lead to a deficiency disease such as pellagra or beriberi.
Vitamin C	Green vegetables, fruits, potatoes, blackcurrant syrup, rosehip syrup	Necessary for the proper formation of teeth, bones and blood vessels. Shortage causes a check in the growth of children and if prolonged may lead to the disease scurvy.
Vitamin D	Margarine, butter milk, fish liver oils, fat fish	Necessary for the formation of strong bones and teeth. A shortage may cause rickets and possibly dental decay.

The recommended daily intakes of vitamins are shown in Table 12.8 (p. 274).

Retinol or Vitamin A

This is a pale-yellow, fat-soluble solid. It is only very slightly soluble in water and has the structure shown:

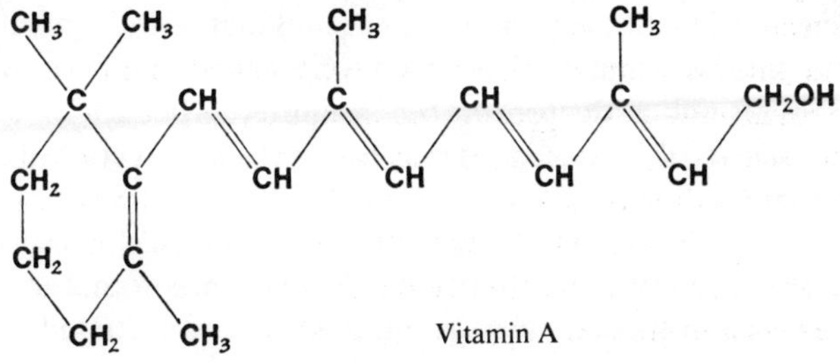

Vitamin A

Vitamin A is an unsaturated alcohol and in spite of its intimidating formula it behaves like all other alcohols. It has been synthesized and is now produced industrially on a fairly large scale for the enrichment of margarine.

Vegetables contain no vitamin A as such but pigments called carotenes are present which are converted to vitamin A in the wall of the small intestine during absorption and hence vegetables have considerable vitamin A activity. Several carotenes are known; the most important is β-carotene which is often referred to as pro-vitamin A. β-carotene is a red solid which was first isolated from carrots; indeed, it owes its name to this relationship. Solutions of β-carotene are yellow in colour and it is used for colouring margarine. The molecule of β-carotene is almost exactly twice as big as that of vitamin A but it is a hydrocarbon, not an alcohol, and has the structure shown:

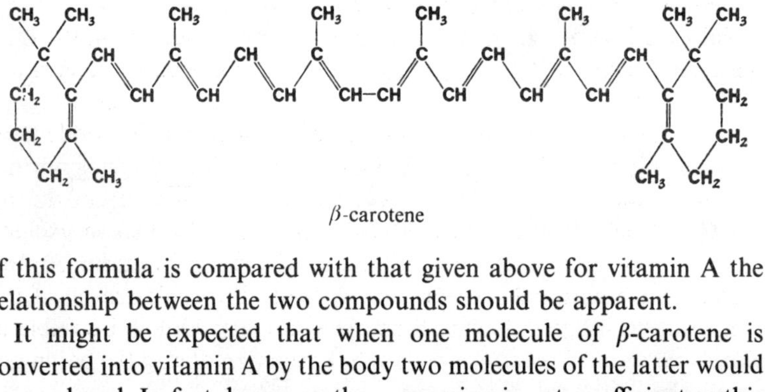

β-carotene

If this formula is compared with that given above for vitamin A the relationship between the two compounds should be apparent.

It might be expected that when one molecule of β-carotene is converted into vitamin A by the body two molecules of the latter would be produced. In fact, however, the conversion is not as efficient as this and β-carotene is only about one sixth as effective as an equal weight of retinol. Other carotenoids present in vegetable foods are converted to retinol even less efficiently and may be taken as having half the activity of β-carotene. Vitamin A intakes are best expressed in terms of retinol equivalents; 1 μg of retinol is equivalent to 6 μg of β-carotene or 12 μg of other biologically active carotenoids. The international unit of retinol is equivalent to 0·33 g of the pure substance and that of β-carotene to 1·0 μg of the pure substance. Thus to convert *weights* of β-carotene to weights of retinol a divisor of 6 is required whereas to convert *international units* of β-carotene to international units of retinol a divisor of 3 must be used.

SOURCES OF VITAMIN A AND CAROTENES. Vitamin A is found in animal tissues and as fish liver oils are the most concentrated source, consumption of cod liver oil or halibut liver oil is a simple way of ensuring that a sufficient supply of the vitamin is obtained. Carotenes are found in plant tissues and about one third of the vitamin A activity of British diets is contributed by carotenes. β-carotene is present in green vegetables, in carrots and in yellow fruits such as apricots. When vegetables are eaten, not all the carotene is absorbed and only a small fraction of that absorbed may be converted into vitamin A. The source of the carotene may affect its availability; for example, carotene is obtained from green vegetables more easily than from carrots, which have a comparatively fibrous structure. Milk and milk products are also good sources of vitamin A but the amount present depends upon the amount of carotene or vitamin A in the food eaten by the cow and so dairy produce is usually a richer source of the vitamin in summer, when fresh grass is available, than in winter. Cod liver oil or synthetic vitamin A is incorporated into many animal feeding stuffs, however, and so the difference is not as great as one would expect.

Table 11.2 shows the main sources of vitamin A activity in the diet. Because of their highly unsaturated nature vitamin A and carotenes are easily destroyed by oxidation, especially at high temperatures. They are much more susceptible to oxidation after extraction from foods than when in animal or plant tissues. Losses due to oxidation during normal cooking processes are small, but considerable loss may occur during storage of dehydrated food if precautions are not taken to exclude oxygen. Apart from this sensitivity to oxidation, vitamin A and carotenes are reasonably stable and are only slowly destroyed at the temperatures used in cooking food. They are also almost insoluble in water and so there is little or no loss by extraction during the boiling of vegetables.

REQUIREMENTS AND RECOMMENDED INTAKES OF VITAMIN A. The amount of vitamin A required for the maintenance of normal health depends largely upon age and the recommended daily intakes are as shown in Table 12.8 (page 274). The recommendations are expressed in terms of retinol equivalents to allow for the fact that much of the vitamin A activity of a mixed diet is provided by carotenes. The recommended intake for adults is 750 μg of retinol equivalents daily. During lactation the intake should be increased to 1200 μg daily. A smaller intake is recommended during childhood and adolescence.

A condition known as 'night blindness' is caused by a deficiency of vitamin A. Sufferers from this experience difficulty in adjusting their vision from conditions of good illumination to those in which light is subdued. A severe deficiency may cause development of an eye disorder

Table 11.2. Average Values of Vitamin A Activity of Foods

Food	Retinol equivalents (μg per 100 g food)
Foods supplying retinol	
Halibut-liver oil	900 000
Cod-liver oil	18 000
Liver, ox	17 270
Herring	45
Sardines (canned)	30
Butter	995
Margarine	900
Cheese	420
Eggs	140
Milk	0
Foods supplying carotene	
Red palm oil	20 000
Carrots	2 000
Spinach	1 000
Tomatoes	117
Bananas	33
Foods with negligible vitamin A activity	
Potatoes	
Cooking fats, lard and suet	
Bacon, pork, beef (trace) and mutton (trace)	
Bread, flour and other cereals	
Sugar, jams and syrups	
White fish	

known as xerophthalmia in which the cornea of the eye becomes dry and subsequently thickened. Blindness is a common sequel to xerophthalmia. Dryness of the skin accompanied by numerous horny pimples may also accompany a deficiency of vitamin A. There is also some evidence that lack of vitamin A may cause a lowered resistance to infection. Shortage in infancy during the formation of teeth may produce poor teeth and even after formation lack of vitamin A may affect the enamel. As vitamin A is not soluble in water an excess above need is not excreted in the urine but accumulates in the liver. (This is why animal liver is such a valuable source of vitamin A.) For this reason an excessive intake should be avoided. Mothers who give their babies vitamin A supplements in the form of fish liver oil should take particular care not to exceed the stated dose.

The B Group of Vitamins

The B group of vitamins comprises several vitamins which have similar functions and which are often found together in foods. In the body the B vitamins are largely concerned with the release of energy from food. The B vitamins are all soluble, to a greater or lesser extent, in water and since the body lacks the capacity for storing them any excess over immediate requirements is excreted in the urine. The more important members of the B group of vitamins are:

1 *Thiamine* or vitamin B_1.
2 *Riboflavine* or vitamin B_2.
3 *Nicotinic acid* or *Niacin* and its amide *nicotinamide*.

Other less important members are:

4 *Pyridoxine* or vitamin B_6.
5 *Pantothenic acid*.
6 *Biotin*.
7 *Cobalamin*, formerly called vitamin B_{12} or *cyanocobalamin*.
8 *Folic acid*.

Thiamine or Vitamin B_1

This is a white, water-soluble crystalline solid. A thiamine molecule contains a pyrimidine and a thiazole ring; it also contains a primary alcohol group and an amino group. It has the structure shown:

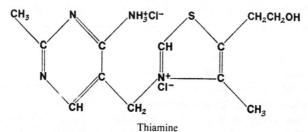

Thiamine

The amino group is combined with hydrochloric acid as a salt and one of the other nitrogen atoms is also in this quadricovalent, unielectrovalent condition. Thiamine owes its water solubility to the presence of these two electrovalencies. The alcohol group can form esters in the usual way and before thiamine is utilized by the body it is esterified with pyrophosphoric acid.

Thiamine has been synthesized and is made on quite a large scale for the enrichment of flour (see Chapter 8). The pure substance is now so readily available that the international unit (3 μ g) is rarely used.

SOURCES OF THIAMINE. Thiamine is widely distributed in foodstuffs as Table 11.3 shows. Most of the thiamine in an average diet comes from cereals, meat and vegetables.

Table 11.3. Average Values for Thiamine Content of Foods in mg/100 g

Yeast extract	3.00	Bread (white)	0.18
Pork (roast, fried or grilled)	0·66	Mutton or lamb (cooked)	0·10
Oatmeal (raw)	0·50	Eggs (raw)	0·09
Porridge	0·05	Potatoes (boiled)	0·08
Bacon (fried)	0·40	Beef (roast)	0·05
Peas (boiled)	0·25	Beef (corned)	0·01
Kidney	0·39	Cheese (Cheddar)	0·04
Bread (Hovis)	0·29	Milk (pasteurized)	0·04

Because thiamine is so soluble in water, as much as 50 per cent may be lost when vegetables are boiled. Potatoes boiled in their skins retain 90 per cent of their thiamine compared with a retention of 75 per cent in the case of boiled peeled potatoes. Thiamine decomposes on heating though it is fairly stable at the boiling point of water and little loss occurs at this temperature in acid conditions. In neutral or alkaline conditions breakdown is more rapid. Foods which have been subjected to higher temperatures, as in roasting, or in 'processing' during canning, may have a large proportion of their thiamine destroyed. Meat loses about 15–40 per cent of its thiamine when boiled, 40–50 per cent when roasted and up to 75 per cent when canned. When bread is baked some 20–30 per cent of the thiamine present in the flour may be destroyed by the moist heat. In cakes made with baking powder all the thiamine may be destroyed by reaction with the baking powder. Some preservatives also destroy thiamine and sulphites, which may be used in sausages, are particularly prone to cause thiamine breakdown.

The deficiency disease beriberi, which is caused by a deficiency of thiamine, is almost unknown in Great Britain, but it is still common in Far Eastern countries, where the standard of living is very low. In these countries the main article of diet is polished rice, which contains little thiamine. The husk and silverskin of the rice grains are removed to improve its palatability and keeping properties. Unfortunately, however, this process also removes most of the thiamine. If the rice grains are parboiled before the husks are removed much of the thiamine is absorbed and retained by the endosperm. Loss of thiamine occurs in the same way during the milling of wheat to produce flour of low extraction rate and it is for this reason that synthetic thiamine is now added to all such flour produced in Great Britain. Enriched flour provides about 25 per cent of the thiamine in the average diet in Britain.

REQUIREMENTS AND RECOMMENDED INTAKES OF THIAMINE. It has been found that thiamine is esterified with pyrophosphoric acid in the body to give *thiamine pyrophosphate* or cocarboxylase which is an essential coenzyme involved in the utilization of carbohydrates. In the absence of sufficient thiamine, carbohydrate metabolism is upset and this produces a check in the growth of children together with a loss of appetite and other symptoms such as irritability, fatigue and dizziness. Prolonged and severe deficiency can cause the disease beriberi. Several types of this disease are known but all of them are associated with loss of appetite, leading to reduced food intake and, in time, emaciation and an enlargement of the heart occur. The nervous system is badly affected and this may produce partial paralysis and muscular weakness.

The amount of thiamine needed in the diet depends upon the quantity of carbohydrate consumed. Persons subsisting on a diet which consists largely of carbohydrate require more thiamine than those on a properly balanced diet and because of this dependence on carbohydrate intake it is difficult to estimate the daily requirements of thiamine. The situation is made more complicated because some thiamine may be synthesized by bacteria in the large intestine and the amount available from this source may vary from person to person and from time to time. Estimates of thiamine requirements range from 0·2 mg to 0·5 mg per 4·2 MJ per day. The recommended thiamine intakes given in Table 12·8 (p. 274) vary from 0·3 mg for children under 1 year old to 1·3 mg for very active men.

In common with other water-soluble vitamins thiamine is not stored by the body and any excess over immediate requirements is rapidly excreted in the urine. A *regular* and adequate supply of the vitamin is thus essential.

Riboflavine or Vitamin B$_2$

This is a yellowish-green fluorescent solid with the structure shown:

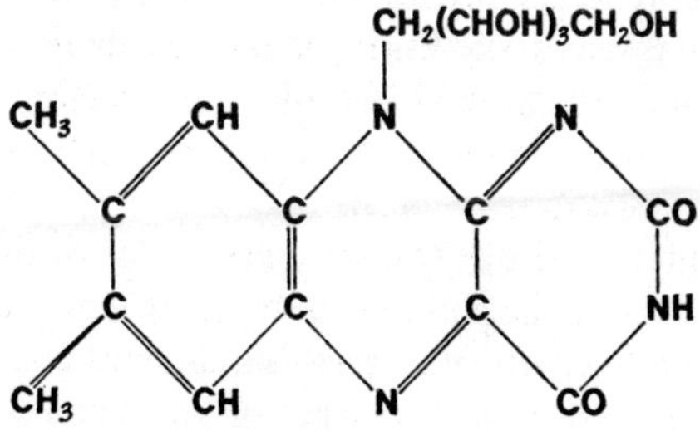

Riboflavine

The molecule contains a complex heterocyclic ring system combined with the sugar ribose. Riboflavine is synthesized commercially and is used in some countries for enrichment of food.

SOURCES OF RIBOFLAVINE. Riboflavine is widely distributed in plants and animal tissues and the more important sources are shown in Table 11.4. Riboflavine is only very slightly soluble in water and losses by solution during cooking are small except in alkaline conditions. Heating causes little breakdown of riboflavine and little or no loss occurs during canning. Meat loses about one-quarter of its riboflavine during roasting. The vitamin is sensitive to light and three-quarters of the riboflavine in milk may be destroyed by exposure to direct sunlight for three and a half hours.

Table 11.4. Average Values for Riboflavine Content of Foods in mg/100 g

Marmite	5·90	Beef	0·19
Liver (fried)	3·10	Milk	0·15
Kidney	1·90	Potatoes (boiled)	0·04
Cheese (Cheddar)	0·50	Beers, ales and stout	0·05

REQUIREMENTS AND RECOMMENDED INTAKES OF RIBOFLAVINE. In the body, riboflavine is esterified with phosphoric acid or pyrophosphoric acid and forms part of two coenzymes concerned in a variety of oxidation-reduction processes in living cells. A deficiency of riboflavine produces a check in the growth of children and lesions on the lips and cracking and scaliness at the corners of the mouth may occur. The tongue and eyes may also become irritated.

When riboflavine is eaten it is stored temporarily in the liver until it is needed by the body. It is not possible to store large amounts in this way, however, and it is necessary for regular and adequate amounts to be eaten. The quantity of riboflavine needed for the maintenance of health is not known with certainty but the recommendations in Table 12.8 (p. 274) should prove ample in all circumstances. The recommended daily intake for an adult man is 1·7 mg and for an adult woman 1·3 mg. During pregnancy and lactation the recommended intake is increased by 0·3 and 0·5 mg respectively. The riboflavine in the diet may be supplemented to a small extent by that produced by bacterial synthesis in the large intestine but not all of this is absorbed.

Nicotinic Acid or Niacin

Nicotinic acid is a pyridine carboxylic acid which, unlike most other vitamins of the B group, has a relatively simple structure:

Nicotinic acid   Nicotinamide

Nicotinic acid was first prepared, long before its importance as a vitamin was realized, from nicotine. In food, however, it is not derived from nicotine nor is it produced during tobacco smoking. It was thought that the name nicotinic acid would give to the general public an undesirable impression of close relationship to nicotine and so the name *niacin* is now widely used, especially in the United States of America. Large quantities of nicotinic acid, which is used for enriching flour, are prepared synthetically.

SOURCES OF NICOTINIC ACID. Nicotinic acid has been recognized as a vitamin only since 1937 and it was first isolated as a chemical from rice polishings. It is present in animal tissues mainly as the amide nicotinamide in which the amide group appears in place of the carboxyl group of nicotinic acid. Little or no free nicotinic acid or nicotinamide is present in cereals, the vitamin being bound in a complex called niacytin from which it is unavailable to man. For this reason, therefore, unfortified cereal products cannot be regarded as sources of nicotinic acid in the diet. The amino acid tryptophan, which is present in cereals, is converted by the body to nicotinic acid but the amount of nicotinic acid made available from cereals in this way is normally small. Some nicotinic acid equivalents (see below) are given in Table 11.5. The large amounts supplied by meat and fish are worthy of note. In Britain flour is enriched with synthetic nicotinic acid and about 23 per cent of the total intake of the vitamin is provided by bread and flour products.

Nicotinic acid and nicotinamide are not easily decomposed by heating. They are only moderately soluble in water and losses in cooking are small.

REQUIREMENTS AND RECOMMENDED INTAKES OF NICOTINIC ACID. Nicotinamide occurs in the body as part of two essential coenzymes concerned in a large number of oxidation processes such as are involved in the

Table 11.5. Average Values for Nicotinic Acid Equivalents of Foods in mg/100 g

Meat extract	67·7	Salmon (canned)	10·7
Coffee (instant)	45·7	Herring (raw)	7·1
Liver (fried)	20·7	Cod (raw)	4·8
Pork (cooked)	11·0	Bread (white)	2·6
Ham (boiled)	8·0	(wholemeal)	1·9
Beef	8·1	Beer	0·7
Kipper	6·9	Potatoes (boiled)	1·2
Mutton (roast)	9·2	Cabbage (boiled)	0·5
Bacon (fried)	9·2	Milk	0·9
		Sardines (in oil)	12·4

utilization of carbohydrates, fats and proteins by living cells. The amount required for the maintenance of health is difficult to estimate because it depends upon the quantity of tryptophan also present in the diet and the extent to which bacterial synthesis of nicotinamide occurs within the large intestine. To allow for the presence of tryptophan in the diet nicotinic acid intakes may be expressed in terms of nicotinic acid equivalents and for this purpose 60 mg of tryptophan are taken to be equivalent to 1 mg of nicotinic acid. The recommended intakes of nicotinic acid expressed in this way are given in Table 12.8 (p. 274). The recommended daily intake for an adult man is 18 mg nicotinic acid equivalents and for an adult woman 15 mg nicotinic acid equivalents. During pregnancy and lactation an increased intake of 3 and 6 mg nicotinic acid equivalents respectively is recommended.

A severe deficiency of nicotinic acid can cause the disease pellagra which is characterized by dermatitis, diarrhoea and symptoms of mental disorder. Less severe deficiencies can produce one or more of these symptoms. Pellagra has long been associated, like many other deficiency diseases, with a low standard of living. In particular, pellagra results from subsistence on a diet consisting mainly of maize and for this reason it has in the past been particularly common in the Southern States of the USA, where maize is a staple food. Maize contains only small amounts of nicotinamide and its proteins are deficient in tryptophan which can be converted by the body into nicotinamide. Pellagra is not associated solely with consumption of maize, however, and it may occur whenever the intake of nicotinamide, or its precursor tryptophan, is insufficient. Some nicotinamide may be synthesized by microbial action in the large intestine but the amount absorbed is small.

Pyridoxine or Vitamin B$_6$

Pyridoxine is the name given to a group of three simple pyridine derivatives which have the structures shown:

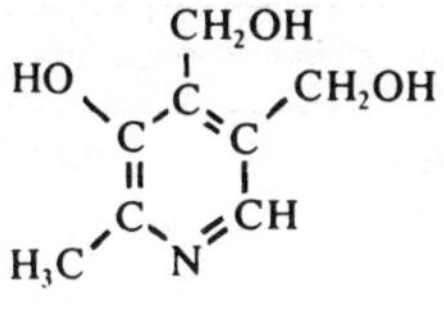

Pyridoxol 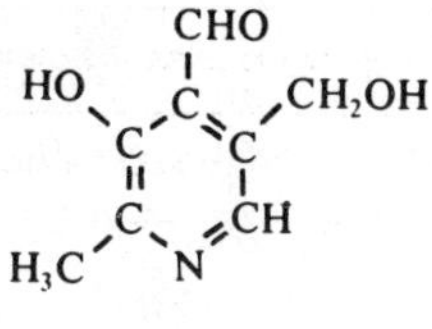   Pyridoxal 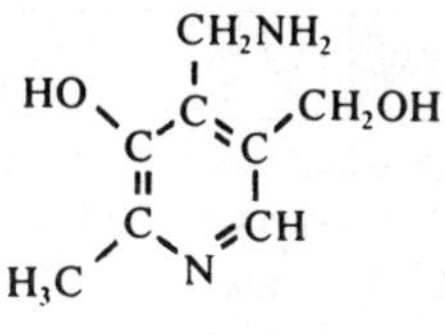   Pyridoxamine

All three compounds have been synthesized and are equally potent as vitamins. Vitamin B_6 is found in foods which contain the other B vitamins. The best sources are meat, liver and the germ and bran of cereal grains.

Symptoms of vitamin B_6 deficiency in animals can be produced by maintaining them on a diet devoid of the vitamin. It is not easy, however, to do the same thing with humans although various skin lesions are reputed to be caused by vitamin B_6 deficiency. Infants fed on milk powders deficient in vitamin B_6 were found to suffer from convulsions but responded rapidly to treatment with the vitamin. It is believed that pyridoxine and pyridoxamine are converted in the body to pyridoxal, the phosphate of which functions as a coenzyme in protein metabolism. The precise function of vitamin B_6 in the maintenance of good health is not well established, however.

It is difficult to stipulate a recommended daily intake of vitamin B_6 because so little is known of its functions and the effects of a deficiency. However, it is distributed widely and a varied diet should provide 1 to 2 mg per day which appears to be sufficient for most people.

Pantothenic Acid

This vitamin is a pale yellow oil with the structure shown:

$$HOCH_2C(CH_3)_2CHOHCONHCH_2CH_2COOH$$
Pantothenic acid

It is found in a wide variety of plant and animal tissues; indeed the name is derived from Greek words meaning 'from everywhere'. It is soluble in water and is rapidly destroyed by treatment with acids or alkalis or by heating in the dry state.

Pantothenic acid is an essential constituent of coenzyme A which is concerned in all metabolic processes involving removal or addition of an acetyl group $(-COCH_3)$. Such processes are of great importance in the many complex transformations occurring within the human body.

Pantothenic acid is undoubtedly of fundamental importance as a coenzyme and symptoms of deficiency of the vitamin have been produced in numerous species of animals and also in man by diets devoid of pantothenic acid. The daily requirements of pantothenic acid are thought to be about 5—10 mg per 10 MJ calories but no hard and fast recommendations are given. It is so widely distributed that a normal diet which contains 10—20 mg, should be adequate and there is no danger of a deficiency.

Biotin

Biotin has the structure shown. In food and animal tissues it is combined with proteins from which it is set free by enzymic hydrolysis during digestion.

Liver and kidney are good sources of biotin and smaller amounts are found in egg yolk, milk and bananas.

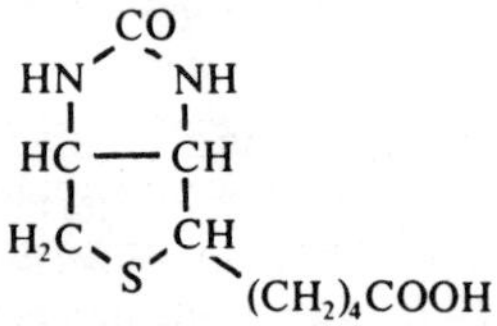

$$
\begin{array}{c}
CO \\
HN^{\diagup} \ \diagdown NH \\
| \qquad | \\
HC \!-\!\!-\! CH \\
| \qquad | \\
H_2C \diagdown \ _{S} \diagup CH \\
(CH_2)_4COOH
\end{array}
$$

Biotin

Raw egg white contains a protein or protein-like substance called *avidin* which combines with the biotin of the yolk to form a stable compound. This is not absorbed from the intestinal tract and so the biotin is not available to the body. Avidin can also render unavailable the biotin in other foods. Biotin was first discovered when rats fed on a diet in which the only source of protein was uncooked egg whites developed skin lesions and rapidly lost weight and died. Humans fed on a diet which was low in biotin and which contained large amounts of raw egg whites developed skin changes followed by loss of appetite, lassitude and slight anaemia. Consumption of biotin without accompanying raw egg white caused an immediate disappearance of the symptoms. This avidity for biotin is not shown by cooked egg white.

Apart from the artificially induced deficiencies of biotin referred to above there has been no other indication of the human need for biotin, and normal diets presumably provide ample quantities of it. It is assumed that biotin, like the other B vitamins, acts as a coenzyme in vital metabolic processes.

Cobalamin or Vitamin B_{12}

Cobalamin is a deep red crystalline substance first isolated in 1948. It has the most complex structure of any vitamin having the formula $C_{63}H_{90}O_{14}N_{14}PCo$. In view of this complexity it is perhaps not surprising that it is the only vitamin never to have been synthesized. The presence of cobalt in the molecule is a noteworthy feature.

Vitamin B_{12}, folic acid and iron are all required by the body for the formation of red blood cells. If either vitamin is not present in the diet, or is not absorbed by the body, anaemia results. Cobalamin is found in very small quantities in a variety of animal foods and it is unlikely that there will be a deficiency in a normal diet; any such deficiency is much more likely to be caused by poor absorption in the body. A deficiency of cobalamin causes pernicious anaemia. As there is little chance of a dietary deficiency there are no recommended allowances but it is believed that an adult requires 5–6 μg daily except for pregnant women who need about 8 μg daily.

Liver is the richest source of cobalamin; ox, calf and lamb liver contain respectively 110, 100 and 84 μg per 100g. Kidney is another good source (ox kidney contains 31 μg per 100 g) and fatty fish and egg yolk both contain useful amounts. Cobalamin is stable in most cooking processes, only 8 per cent being lost when liver is boiled for 5 minutes. Losses are considerable, however, in milk. For example, if milk is boiled for 2–5 minutes, about 30 per cent cobalamin is destroyed.

Folic Acid

Folic acid is the group name given to several closely related compounds the chemical name of the pure compound being *pteroylmonoglutamic acid*. Folic acid, which is a yellow crystalline substance, was first isolated and synthesized in 1946. Commercially it is extracted from yeast or liver or made synthetically. It is essential in the body for the formation of deoxyribonucleic acid (DNA) and hence for producing red blood cells. A deficiency of folic acid produces anaemia. Its function is closely related to that of cobalamin.

Folic acid is found in very small quantities in a wide variety of foods particularly in liver but kidney, green vegetables, wheat bran and yeast extracts are also good sources. Liver contains from 110 (pig) to 590 (chicken) μg folic acid/100 g, kidney from 31 (lamb) to 77 (ox) μg/100 g, while among green vegetables endive (330 μg/100 g) and spinach (140 μg/100 g) are good sources. Folic acid is easily destroyed and there are therefore considerable losses in cooking. For example, about 30 per cent is lost when liver or kidney is stewed or boiled and 20–40 per cent when green vegetables are boiled.

It is believed that the human requirement for folic acid is about 200 μg daily, and that about 50 per cent is absorbed from food. The WHO accordingly recommend an intake for adults of 400 μg daily. In the UK the DHSS recommend an intake of 300 μg daily for adults, except for pregnant women for whom 500 μg daily is suggested (see Table 12.8 on p. 274). There appears to be a danger that certain vulnerable groups in the community may suffer from a dietary deficiency of folic acid, and it is estimated that 10 per cent of elderly people and 30 per cent of pregnant women do suffer from such a deficiency. Folic acid tablets are available as a supplement to dietary sources for these vulnerable groups.

Ascorbic Acid or Vitamin C

Ascorbic acid, or vitamin C, is a white water-soluble solid of formula $C_6H_8O_6$. In spite of the name ascorbic acid the molecule does not contain a free carboxyl group. It is really a *lactone* formed from the free acid by loss of water between a carboxyl group on one carbon atom and a hydroxyl group on another. It has the structure shown:

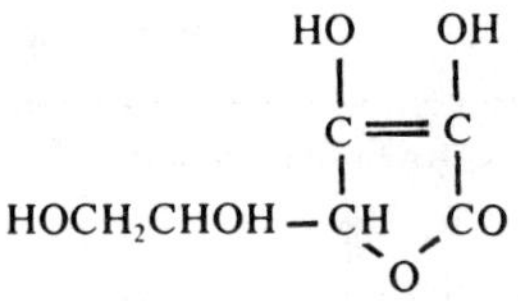

Ascorbic acid

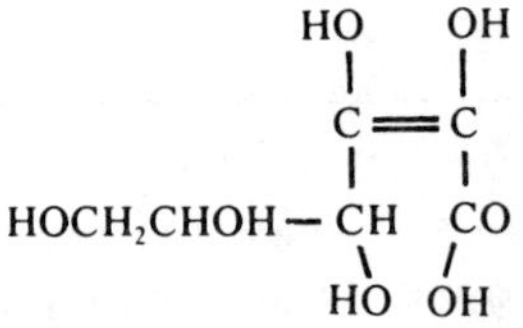

Free acid corresponding to ascorbic acid

Lactones behave much like acids and for many purposes can be regarded as acids. Ascorbic acid has the sharp taste usually associated with acids and will form salts. It is optically active and is dextrorotatory; laevorotatory ascorbic acid is also known but it has only about one-tenth the vitamin activity of its optical isomer. Ascorbic acid is a good reducing agent and consequently it is easily oxidized. The oxidation product *dehydroascorbic acid* is easily reconverted into ascorbic acid by mild reducing agents and because this reduction can be accomplished by the body it is as active as ascorbic acid itself. It is, however, less stable than ascorbic acid and only small amounts are present in foods.

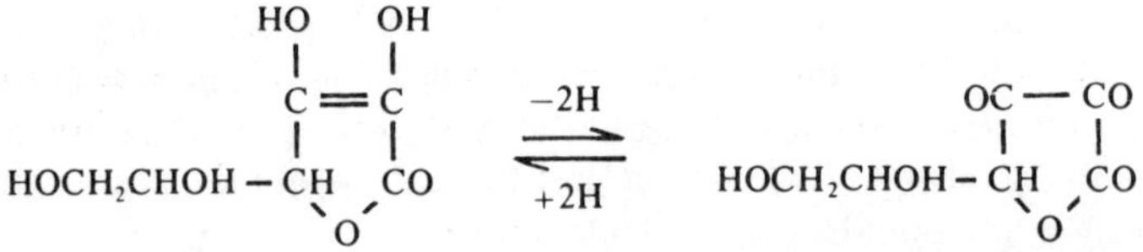

Ascorbic acid   Dehydroascorbic acid

Of all the vitamins, ascorbic acid is the most easily destroyed by oxidation, and in extracts, juices and foods with cut surfaces, it may be oxidized by exposure to air. The oxidation is catalysed by oxidases which are contained within the cells of foodstuffs and are set free on cutting, chopping or crushing. The rate of oxidation is greatly accelerated by heat (if the temperature is not high enough to destroy the oxidases), by alkalis and especially by traces of copper which catalyses the oxidation. The rate of oxidation is diminished in a weak acid solution and by storage in the cold.

SOURCES OF ASCORBIC ACID. Ascorbic acid occurs mainly in vegetable foods. Fruits are usually good sources but many popular eating apples, pears and plums supply negligible amounts. Green vegetables and potatoes are the most important sources of ascorbic acid in the diet in Great Britain. Table 11.6 lists the average ascorbic acid content of the more important sources of this vitamin.

Table 11.6. Average Values for Ascorbic Acid Content of Foods in mg/100 g

Blackcurrants	200	Potatoes, raw, new	30
Rose-hip syrup	175	" Oct.–Nov.	20
Sprouts (raw)	87	" Dec.	15
(boiled)	41	" Jan.–Feb.	10
Cauliflower (raw)	64	" March on	8
(cooked)	20	Apples, eating, raw	5
Cabbage (raw)	53	Lettuce (raw)	16
(boiled)	23	Bananas (raw)	10
Spinach (raw)	60	Beetroot (boiled)	5
(boiled)	25	Onions (raw)	10
Watercress (raw)	60	(boiled)	6
Strawberries	60	Carrots (raw)	6
Oranges (raw)	50	(boiled)	4
Lemons (raw)	50	Plums (raw)	3
Grapefruit (raw)	40	(stewed)	2
Peas (raw)	25	Pears (raw)	3
(boiled)	15	(stewed)	2
(dried boiled)	trace	(canned)	1
Tomato (raw or juice)	20	Cows' milk (fresh)	2
		Human milk	5

The amount of ascorbic acid present in vegetables is greatest in the periods of active growth during spring and early summer. Storage decreases the ascorbic acid content and this can be clearly seen in the figures given for potatoes in the table above.

Potatoes contain less ascorbic acid than green vegetables but such large quantities of them are eaten that they constitute an important source of this vitamin. A normal serving of boiled new potatoes provides about 90 per cent of the recommended daily intake of ascorbic acid. It is estimated that about 35 per cent of the total ascorbic acid intake in Great Britain is obtained from potatoes. The incidence of scurvy in Europe has progressively diminished since the introduction of the potato from the 'New World' in the sixteenth century.

As much as 75 per cent of the ascorbic acid present in green vegetables may be lost during cooking. This loss can be avoided by eating raw green vegetables in salads but the amounts which can conveniently be eaten in this way are comparatively small and more ascorbic acid may be obtained by eating a larger quantity of cooked vegetables. For example 25 g of lettuce, which is a convenient serving, provides 4 mg of ascorbic acid compared with 23 mg provided by 100 g of cooked cabbage. Raw cabbage is a much better source of ascorbic acid than lettuce; 25 g provides about 13 mg of the vitamin.

Cows' milk has only about one-quarter or one-third the ascorbic acid content of human milk and some of this is destroyed during pasteurization. Exposure of milk to sunlight also causes diminution of its ascorbic acid content and this change is brought about by lumiflavine which is produced by the action of sunlight on riboflavine. It is important that babies, and particularly those fed on cows' milk which has been boiled, should be provided with other sources of the vitamin. Concentrated orange juice, rose-hip syrup or blackcurrant juice are attractive additional sources of the vitamin. When babies progress to a mixed diet there is less need for such supplements and at two years of age the normal diet should provide sufficient ascorbic acid.

Canned fruits and vegetables vary considerably in their ascorbic acid content but some, for example tomatoes, are good sources of the vitamin. Some loss of ascorbic acid is inevitable in canning but good-quality canned fruits and vegetables often contain more of this vitamin than 'fresh' fruit and vegetables cooked at home. This is because they are canned while absolutely fresh and cooked under carefully controlled conditions.

Foods such as yeast, egg yolk, meats and cereals, which are rich in B vitamins are usually devoid of ascorbic acid. It is also absent in dried peas and beans although special methods of dehydration and storage can conserve 60–80 per cent of the ascorbic acid originally present.

LOSS OF ASCORBIC ACID IN COOKING. It has already been mentioned that losses of ascorbic acid occur during storage of fruits and vegetables. Some loss also occurs during the preparation and cooking of foods. This is due partly to oxidation and partly to solution in the water used for cooking. To avoid undue losses of this vitamin, vegetables and fruit should not be crushed or finely chopped before cooking, as this sets free oxidases which catalyse the oxidation of ascorbic acid by the air. There is evidence to show that loss of ascorbic acid is greater when vegetables are cut with a blunt knife than with a sharp one, presumably because the former ruptures more cells by crushing and hence sets free more oxidases than the latter.

If vegetables are put in cold water which is brought to the boil the dissolved oxygen in the water will, in the presence of the oxidases, destroy a substantial amount of the ascorbic acid present. The oxidases are most active at about 60–85° C and above this temperature are quickly inactivated. It is best to place vegetables in boiling water because this contains no dissolved oxygen and the oxidases are rapidly destroyed at this temperature. With potatoes, for example, it has been found that cooking in this way causes only half the reduction in ascorbic acid content experienced with the normal method of cooking.

The minimum quantity of water should be used when cooking vegetables so that large amounts of the vitamin are not dissolved. This is particularly important with leaf vegetables, such as cabbage, because of the large surface area from which the vitamin can be lost. Vegetables which are completely immersed in water when being cooked may lose up to 80 per cent of their ascorbic acid. If they are only one quarter covered by water only about half as much ascorbic acid is lost. With potatoes, which have a smaller surface area per unit weight, and in which gelatinization of the starch prevents diffusion of the ascorbic acid, the quantity of water used in cooking does not greatly affect the amount of ascorbic acid lost. Alkaline conditions should be avoided during cooking and the addition of bicarbonate of soda has little to recommend it though small quantities may be used to reduce the sourness of acid fruits without serious diminution in the ascorbic acid content.

Finally, cooked food should not be kept hot longer than is absolutely necessary before serving because this can destroy almost all the ascorbic acid. It has been shown that a loss of 25 per cent of the ascorbic acid of cooked food occurs on keeping hot for fifteen minutes and 75 per cent on keeping hot for ninety minutes. This is likely to be the greatest cause of loss of ascorbic acid in restaurants and hotels and in canteens where cooked food is received from a central kitchen.

REQUIREMENTS AND RECOMMENDED DAILY INTAKES OF ASCORBIC ACID. The functions of ascorbic acid in the body are not known with certainty but it has been shown to be necessary for the formation of the intercellular connecting protein collagen. The cells of the body concerned in the formation of bone and the enamel and dentine of teeth, lose their normal functional activity in the absence of ascorbic acid. A lack of ascorbic acid in the diet causes a condition known as scurvy, which is characterized by haemorrhages under the skin and in other tissues and swollen and spongy gums from which the teeth are easily dislodged or may fall out. Scurvy in infants is associated with great tenderness and pain in the lower limbs together with changes in the bone structure which are not found in adult scurvy. The disease has been known for hundreds of years and was formerly rife among sailors and other persons forced to subsist on a diet deficient in ascorbic acid. The cause of the disease was not known but in the course of time it was noted that consumption of fresh foods, particularly vegetables and fruits, could prevent and cure it. Scurvy is almost unknown in Great Britain at the present time although occasional instances occur among people, who for economic or other reasons, are living on a restricted diet.

A deficiency of ascorbic acid not severe enough to cause scurvy is thought to increase the susceptibility of the mouth and gums to infection and to slow down the rate at which wounds and fractures heal. Increased susceptibility to many kinds of infection, including the common cold, has been attributed to a shortage of ascorbic acid, but though this is known to be so in the case of guinea-pigs it is not at all certain that the same applies to human beings. It is known, however, that increased amounts of the vitamin are needed by the body when suffering infectious diseases and there is some evidence that common colds last longer if insufficient amounts of ascorbic acid are ingested. Ascorbic acid is also thought to assist in the absorption of iron by promoting its reduction to the ferrous state.

The amount of ascorbic acid needed for the maintenance of good health has been a subject of much controversy. An intake of 10 mg per day has been found to be sufficient to protect adults against symptoms of scurvy. Experiments with animals, indicate, however, that a three-to-fourfold increase in ascorbic acid requirements occurs during periods of stress and the recommended daily intake of ascorbic acid for adults is 30 mg. During pregnancy and lactation it is recommended that the intake should be increased to 60 mg per day. The recommendations for other age groups are shown in Table 12.8 (p. 274). In some other countries the recommended daily intakes of ascorbic acid are much greater than the British recommendations; in the USA, for example, the recommended daily intake is 60 mg for adults.

Cholecalciferol or Vitamin D

Naturally occurring vitamin D is called vitamin D, or cholecalciferol. It is a white crystalline solid, soluble in fats and oils but insoluble in water. One μg of vitamin D is equal to 40 iu though this latter unit is now little used.

It is believed that cholecalciferol is formed in the tissues of mammals from the pro-vitamin 7-dehydrocholesterol during exposure to sunlight:

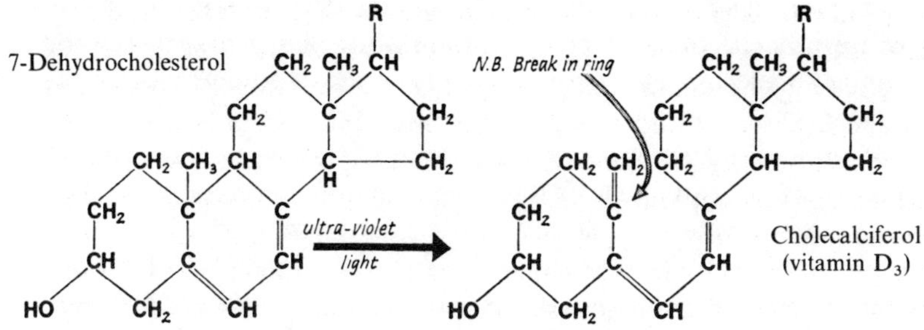

7-Dehydrocholesterol

N.B. Break in ring

Cholecalciferol (vitamin D_3)

$$R = -CH(CH_3)(CH_2)_3CH(CH_3)_2$$

Synthetic vitamin D differs slightly in structure from cholecalciferol. It is called ergocalciferol or vitamin D_2 and is made by irradiating the compound ergosterol with ultra-violet light.

$$\text{Ergosterol} \xrightarrow[\text{light}]{\text{ultra-violet}} \text{Ergocalciferol (vitamin } D_2)$$

Except for the side chain R, which has the structure $-CH(CH_3)CH=CHCH(CH_3)CH(CH_3)_2$, ergosterol and ergocalciferol have the same structure as 7-dehydrocholesterol and cholecalciferol respectively. As far as human beings are concerned, cholecalciferol and ergocalciferol are equally effective as vitamins and in what follows the term vitamin D will be used to refer to either or both of them.

SOURCES OF VITAMIN D. Vitamin D is not widely distributed in foodstuffs and is found almost exclusively in animal foods. Fish liver oils are the most important natural sources. Egg yolk and dairy products also contain some but the quantity these contribute to the diet is small. Synthetic vitamin D is added to all margarine sold in Great Britain, except that used by the baking industry, and also to many baby foods. Table 11.7 summarizes the important sources of vitamin D.

Table 11.7. Vitamin D Content of Foods in μg/100 g

Halibut liver oil	up to 10 000	Butter	up to 2
Cod liver oil	200–750	Eggs, whole	1–1·5
Herrings, sardines	5–45	Cheese	0·3
Salmon	4–30	Milk (Summer)	0·05
Margarine	2–9	Egg yolk	4–10

Vitamin D is not destroyed to any significant extent during normal cooking processes.

REQUIREMENTS AND RECOMMENDED INTAKES OF VITAMIN D. Vitamin D is concerned with the absorption of calcium and phosphorus by the body. In the absence of the vitamin the body is unable to make use of these elements and they are lost in the faeces. Phosphorus and calcium are both needed to form bones and deficiency of vitamin D causes rickets in the young and osteomalacia in those in whom bone growth has ceased. The disease rickets is characterized by curvature of the bones in the limbs and other distressing symptoms of improper bone formation. It was formerly very common in this country and one hundred and twenty years ago one-third of all the children of school age in London were sufferers from severe rickets. Now the incidence of rickets in children in this country is rare except in children of Asian immigrants in whom it is a continuing problem.

It has been recognized for about ninety years that rickets is more prevalent in industrial areas in the temperate regions where sunlight is deficient. The disease has been successfully treated by exposure to the maximum amount of sunlight and later it was shown that any other source of ultra-violet light (e.g. a 'sun-lamp') is also efficient. The reason for this is now clear; it is because the ultra-violet light converts the pro-vitamin, 7-dehydrocholesterol, present in the tissues of the skin into the active vitamin, which is then able to carry out its function.

Rickets is often, though not always, found in conjunction with dental caries and it is now realized that vitamin D is necessary for proper calcification of teeth no less than for bones. Not only does vitamin D assist in the formation of healthy teeth but it can also help to prevent the development of dental caries in existing teeth though other factors are also involved. Adults who do not receive sufficient vitamin D may develop the disease osteomalacia, which is similar to rickets. In these cases, however, there is always a deficiency of calcium as well. Growing children should take a fish liver oil or vitamin D supplement at least until bone growth has ceased.

The chief source of vitamin D is not diet but the action of ultra-violet light on the skin; there are therefore no recommended daily amounts (RDA) for adults. There are, however, certain vulnerable groups for whom RDA are given and for whom food containing vitamin D or a vitamin D supplement are a safeguard against insufficient exposure to sunlight. For babies under 1 year old the RDA is $7 \cdot 5 \mu g$ daily, and for children 1–4 years old and for pregnant and nursing women the RDA is $10 \mu g$ daily; and the same amount is suggested for those who are housebound.

If the body receives more vitamin D than it requires, the excess is stored in the liver. An excessive intake of vitamin D is poisonous and may result in unpleasant symptoms such as vomiting and loss in weight; eventually death may result. There is a particular danger that babies who are given extra vitamin D in the form of fish liver oil in their milk could suffer an excessive intake unless the stated dose is carefully observed.

Other Less Important Vitamins

VITAMIN E. This is a light yellow oil of formula $C_{29}H_{50}O_2$. It is not of great importance nutritionally, though its structure is known and it has been synthesized. It is found in eggs and in oils obtained from cereals such as maize oil and wheat-germ oil. Fish-liver oils, which are so richly endowed with vitamins A and D, two other fat soluble vitamins, are almost devoid of vitamin E.

Lack of vitamin E renders male rats sterile. Female rats deficient in vitamin E can conceive but the pregnancy is interrupted and no live young are born. There is no conclusive evidence that vitamin E influences human fertility though various claims have been made. A state of vitamin E deficiency has not yet been recognized in man and so there is no recommended daily intake. Vitamin E may, however, play an important part in the diet as an antioxidant in 'protecting' easily oxidized substances such as unsaturated fatty acids, carotene and ascorbic acid from being oxidized.

VITAMIN K. This is an oil formula $C_{21}H_{46}O_2$. The structure of vitamin K is known and it has been synthesized. It is essential for normal clotting of the blood. In the absence of vitamin K the liver is unable to perform its usual task of synthesizing *prothrombin* which is the precursor of the actual clotting agent thrombin.

A similar but simpler substance called vitamin K analogue is known. This assists the clotting of the blood in the same way as vitamin K but is about twice as powerful. Vitamin K analogue is much cheaper to produce than the actual vitamin and is normally used when administration of vitamin K is required.

There is little danger of vitamin K deficiency in a person who eats a normal diet and there are no recommended daily intakes. It is widely distributed in foods and fish liver oils and green vegetables are good sources. It is probable that bacterial synthesis in the large intestine provides human beings with vitamin K in addition to that obtained from foodstuffs.

SUGGESTIONS FOR FURTHER READING

BIRCH, G. G. and PARKER, T. (Eds). *Vitamin C* (Symposium Report). Applied Science
    Publishers, 1974.
MARKS, J. *A Guide to the Vitamins—their role in health and disease.* Medical and Technical
Publishing Co., 1975.
STEIN, M. (Ed). *Vitamins.* Churchill Livingstone, 1971.
    A valuable review of the nature of vitamins, their uses and losses occurring in processing.
TAYLOR, R. J. *Micronutrients.* Unilever booklet, 1972.
    Mainly concerned with vitamins and including some fairly advanced chemistry.

Chapter Twelve

Cooking and diet

Now it is time to consider the practical application of food science; namely to consider the cooking of food and the nature of our diet. Nutrition is very much concerned with assessing what constitutes a healthy diet and with ways of improving our diet. Over recent years there has been a growing concern about diet and health and a growing realization that many social and other factors affect our choice of food and our food habits. *Social or Community Nutrition* is now an important area of research. Social Nutrition has been defined by J. C. McKenzie as 'the study of the social, psychological and economic factors that determine food habits, and of the means by which future choice may be influenced in the interests of better nutrition'. There is now widespread appreciation that we need to develop our understanding of the causes of changes in food habits and the way in which we may initiate change in the interests of better nutrition. In this chapter we shall discuss cooking and what constitutes an adequate and healthy diet.

COOKING

Cooking not only improves the taste, smell and appearance of foods but it may also improve its digestibility. Tough meat, for example, may be made more tender if it is cooked by an appropriate method and this makes it easier to chew and digest. Cooking may also improve the keeping qualities of food by killing moulds, yeasts and bacteria that promote decay, though cooking needs to be distinguished from the use of heat treatment to preserve food—a subject which is dealt with in the next chapter.

Cooking may be simply defined as the heat treatment of foods carried out to improve the palatability, digestibility and safety of foods. Table 12.1 summarizes the principal methods of cooking food and it also indicates the different ways in which heat is transferred to the food. These methods will now be considered individually, particular attention being paid to the effect that different methods of cooking have on the nutrients in the food.

Table 12.1. Methods of Cooking

Method	Examples	Description	Method of heat transfer
Dry heat	(1) Baking and roasting	Cooking in an oven or other closed vessel	Hot air and reflected radiant heat
	(2) Grilling and broiling	Direct heating	Radiation and some convection
Moist heat	(1) Boiling	Cooking in boiling water	Conduction
	(2) Steaming	Cooking directly by steam (or in a steam-heated vessel)	Conduction (and convection)
	(3) Pressure cooking	Cooking by steam under pressure	Conduction
	(4) Stewing and simmering	Cooking in water below its boiling point	Conduction
Hot fat	(1) Frying	Food partly or completely immersed in heated fat	Conduction
	(2) Braising	Brief frying in shallow fat followed by stewing	Conduction
Microwave		Food subjected to microwave radiation in an oven	Heat generated in food

Moist Heat Methods

Moist heat methods of cooking employ relatively low temperatures and destruction of nutrients by heat is therefore not great. Cooking times at such low temperatures tend to be long, however, and this results in extensive loss of water-soluble nutrients into the liquid used for cooking. Vitamin C is the nutrient which is most easily destroyed in cooking and hence loss of this vitamin may be taken as an index of the severity of the cooking process; if little vitamin C is lost it may be taken that the cooking process is a mild one and that there will have been little loss of other nutrients. The results of experiments on the retention of vitamin C during the cooking of vegetables by moist heat methods are shown in Table 12.2. The results indicate that pressure cooking results in a smaller loss of vitamin C than boiling or steaming.

Table 12.2. % Retention of Vitamin C in Vegetables Cooked by Moist Heat Methods

Vegetable	Boiling	Steaming	Pressure cooking
Brussels sprouts	77	91	97
Cauliflower	81	77	92
Peas	70	68	98
Spinach	70	72	80

after McIntosh et al

It needs to be emphasized that nutrient losses quoted in the literature should be treated with caution. The figures quoted for a given food may show considerable variation and this is because nutrient losses depend to a large extent on the way in which the cooking is carried out and also on the physical state of the food. For example, the treatment that the food receives before it is cooked, the time of cooking, the amount of liquid used, the extent to which air is excluded and the time for which the food is kept hot before it is consumed all affect the extent to which nutrients are lost. Figures quoted for nutrient loss during cooking must therefore be considered in conjunction with the conditions of the experiment. Unless this is done much data in the literature appear to be contradictory.

In moist heat cooking, nutrients may be lost in a variety of ways. The most important source of loss is the leaching of water-soluble nutrients, primarily vitamins and mineral elements, into the cooking water. Nutrients are also lost by the action of heat in the presence of air; vitamin C, for example, is very sensitive to such oxidative loss. The action of oxidizing enzymes also causes loss of nutrients and again vitamin C is easily lost being rapidly destroyed by such oxidases in the presence of oxygen in the cooking water. As enzymes are destroyed by heat—ascorbic acid oxidase is rapidly destroyed at $100°$ C—loss of nutrients by enzymes is greatly reduced if food, particularly vegetables, is put into boiling water rather than being put into cold water which is then heated.

BOILING. Boiling is a common method of moist heat cooking; it utilizes the fact that because water has a high specific heat it is an efficient heat reservoir and therefore is a convenient medium in which to transfer heat to food. Its ready availability is another important factor. One disadvantage of water as a medium for heat transfer is that, because of its good solvent action, food cooked in it may lose a considerable proportion of its soluble matter. Vegetables, for example, are commonly cooked by boiling and this results in an inevitable loss of some mineral elements and vitamins, the loss of the latter being the more important from a nutritional point of view. Although little or no carotene is lost when vegetables are boiled, considerable amounts of thiamine and ascorbic acid are destroyed as both these vitamins are water-soluble and easily destroyed by heat. In general about one-third of the thiamine and two-thirds of the ascorbic acid are lost, though as discussed below the amount lost varies considerably with changing conditions.

Although some loss of water-soluble nutrients by leaching is inevitable during boiling, the extent of this loss is governed to some extent by the amount of water used. The loss of both mineral elements and water-soluble vitamins increases as the amount of water used increases. For example, in a series of experiments it was found that cabbage, which lost 60 per cent ascorbic acid when cooked in a small volume of water, lost 70 per cent when cooked in a larger amount. Losses of thiamine, which are important when boiling cereal foods, follow a similar pattern and, for example, it was found that rice which lost about 30 per cent thiamine when cooked in a small volume of water, lost 50 per cent when cooked in a larger amount.

Table 12.3. Relation Between Cooking Time and Retention of Vitamin C

Cooking time (min)	% Retention of vitamin C			
	Brussels sprouts	Cabbage	Carrots	Potatoes
20	49	—	35	—
30	36	70–78	22	53–56
60	—	53–58	—	40–50
90	—	13	—	17

The time for which foods are boiled also affects nutrients loss. For example, there is a drastic loss of ascorbic acid when prolonged cooking times are used as can be seen from Table 12.3 which shows the way ascorbic acid loss increases with cooking time for a number of vegetables. Another factor affecting nutrient loss is the treatment that the food receives before it is boiled. For example, the greater the surface area of a food the greater is the loss of water-soluble nutrients into the cooking water. Crushing, chopping, slicing and shredding of food not only increase the surface area but also set free enzymes that cause further loss. Table 12.4 shows what effect size has upon the loss of nutrients that occurs during the boiling of vegetables, such as carrots, swedes and sprouts. Peeling vegetables before cooking also increases loss of nutrients and it has been found that whereas whole unpeeled potatoes lost about one-third ascorbic acid when boiled, peeled potatoes lost an additional 10 per cent.

Table 12.4. Effect of Size on % Nutrient Loss Occurring in Boiled Vegetables

Nutrient	Large pieces	Small pieces
Ascorbic acid	22–33	32–50
Mineral salts	8–16	17–30
Proteins	2– 8	14–22
Sugars	10–21	19–35

STEAMING. This method of cooking involves using the steam produced from boiling water. As the contact between the food and water is less than in boiling there is smaller loss of soluble matter but, as a longer time of cooking is required, the amount of ascorbic acid which is decomposed by heat is increased.

The rate of cooking in steaming may be increased by the use of steam under pressure, this being the principle of the pressure-cooker. As increase of pressure raises the temperature at which water boils, the cooking temperature is greater than 100°C, e.g. when a pressure-cooker is used at its highest working pressure the boiling point is 120°C. It is found (see Table 12.2) that the amount of ascorbic acid lost because of the increased temperature is more than compensated for by the amount conserved due to the shorter cooking time. The use of pressure-cookers is valuable, therefore, in conserving the ascorbic acid in fruit and vegetables as well as reduing cooking time.

STEWING. Stewing involves cooking food in hot water, the temperature of which is kept below its boiling point. The changes which occur in stewing are, therefore, similar in character to those which occur during boiling though they occur at a slower rate. Stewing, being a slow method of cooking, involves considerable loss of soluble matter. For example, in stewing fish, a third of the mineral salts and extractives may be lost as well as water-soluble vitamins. Stewed fish, therefore, lacks flavour and has less nutritional value than when it is raw. However, if the liquor in which the food has been cooked is used for making a sauce or soup, then the passage of nutrients into the cooking water involves no loss of nutritional value and the liquor retains the flavour lost from the stewed food.

One of the advantages of stewing is that, because of the low temperature used, protein is only lightly coagulated and is, therefore, in its most digestible form. Another advantage of stewing is that it exerts a tenderizing effect on protein food because insoluble tough collagen is converted into soluble gelatin by prolonged contact with hot water. Stewing is, therefore, a particularly suitable method for cooking tough meat.

Many fruits, such as strawberries and melons, are best eaten raw but others, such as rhubarb and damsons, are undoubtedly improved by cooking. Fruit may be cooked by stewing in water to which sugar has been added. Dried fruits are soaked before cooking to allow maximum absorption of water by osmosis, and less sugar is added to the cooking water because, during soaking, sugar diffuses out of the fruit. During stewing, cellulose is softened, protein is lightly coagulated and soluble matter is lost to the cooking liquor. At the same time, where stewing is done in syrup, sugar is absorbed by the fruit. Because of the low temperature used and the presence of fruit acids, which maintain pH below 7, destruction of thiamine and ascorbic acid is small, though, due to their solubility, they gradually diffuse into the surrounding liquor.

Dry Heat Methods

Dry heat methods of cooking use higher temperatures than moist heat methods and loss of nutrients which are sensitive to heat is correspondingly greater. Apart from mineral salts, which are stable to heat, all nutrients are affected to some extent by dry heating. Fats are stable to moderate heating and, although they darken, little breakdown occurs unless they are heated to high temperatures when they start to decompose with the formation of *acrolein*, which has an unpleasant acrid odour (see frying). Carbohydrates are affected by dry heat: starch is converted into pyrodextrins which are brown in colour and which contribute colour to toast and breadcrust; sucrose is converted into dark-coloured caramel in a complex multi-stage reaction that involves its initial breakdown into monosaccharides and its final polymerization into coloured substances.

Dry heat cooking destroys those vitamins which are unstable to heat, notably ascorbic acid, which as we have already noted, is destroyed at quite low temperatures. Of the B vitamins, thiamine, is the most readily destroyed while riboflavine is relatively stable, little being lost provided that the pH of the food is below 7. Nicotinic acid is stable to heat and any losses that occur are due to leaching into the liquid lost from the food during heating. Table 12.5 gives a comparison of the extent of retention of these B vitamins that occurs in dry heating methods (and frying) using meat as an example. Vitamins A and D are stable to heat and are not lost in dry heat cooking.

Table 12.5. % Retention of B Vitamins in Cooked Meat

Meat	Cooking method	Thiamine	Riboflavine	Nicotinic acid
Pork	Roasting	40–70	74–100	65–85
	Grilling	70	100	85
	Frying	50–60	77	75–97
Beef	Roasting	41–64	83–100	72
	Grilling	59–77	77–92	73–92
	Frying	89	98	92

Proteins, as we saw in Chapter 9, are extremely sensitive to heat but their nutritive value is not significantly affected unless they are heated to a fairly high temperature, such as occurs in roasting. Loss of nutritive value depends not only on the cooking temperature but also on the time of cooking and the presence of other nutrients, particularly carbohydrates.

Amino acids are only destroyed at high temperatures such as are employed in roasting and even then the loss of protein is small and confined to the surface of the food. A much greater loss of nutritive value results from a change in protein structure which affects the linkages between amino acids in such a way that they become resistant to enzymic hydrolysis. Amino acids affected in this way—notably aspartic acid, glutamic acid and lysine—cannot be released by enzymes during digestion and are therefore unavailable to the body.

When protein and carbohydrate exist together in the same food an additional loss of nutritive value may occur due to *non-enzymic browning* also called the *Maillard reaction*. Reaction occurs between amino groups projecting from a protein chain or peptide or amino acid and the carbonyl group of a reducing substance such as glucose. The details of the reaction are not completely understood but it involves a number of steps, the first of which is an addition reaction between the amino and carbonyl groups, and the last is a polymerization to form a brown substance. Several amino acids undergo this reaction, notably lysine and methionine. The reaction results in the formation of substances which cannot be hydrolysed by enzymes, and the proteins affected are thus unavailable to the body.

Non-enzymic browning occurs particularly at high temperatures and at pH values of seven and above: a certain amount of moisture is also necessary. The reduction in nutritive value of protein due to non-enzymic browning has been studied intensively in terms of the loss of lysine during cooking. For example, it has been found that bread loses 10–15 per cent lysine during baking, a further 5 per cent during staling and a further 5–10 per cent during toasting. Some lysine is also lost during the roasting of meat, though in home cooking the loss has been found to be small.

Apart from producing some loss in the nutritive value of proteins during dry heat cooking, non-enzymic browning is also responsible for producing some desirable changes in the flavour, colour and aroma of food during roasting, baking and toasting. For example, it improves the quality of bread during baking and toasting, and of nuts and coffee beans during roasting. It is also partly responsible for the flavour of such diverse products as meat extract, biscuits and breakfast cereals.

Frying

Frying is a convenient method of cooking where a high temperature and rapid cooking are desired. Fat is the medium used in frying to provide the necessary high temperature. It is chosen because of its high boiling point and because it can be heated almost to its boiling point without much decomposition occurring. There are two methods of frying, the most important being *deep frying*.

Deep frying, as the name suggests, is done in a deep pan, the food being lowered into the fat when it is very hot, normally between 175° C and 200° C. As soon as the food comes into contact with the hot fat there is a violent bubbling as the water on the surface of the food is vaporized. Cooking proceeds so rapidly that loss of mineral salts and nitrogenous substances is reduced to a minimum. Cooking is complete when the outside of the food is crisp and usually golden-brown in colour.

The second method of frying is *shallow-frying*, which is done in a shallow pan, the bottom of which is covered with fat. The main role of the fat is to prevent the food from adhering to the pan, the cooking being done mainly by direct conducted heat. In this method of cooking, heat is applied only to one surface of the food at a time, so that uneven cooking may result unless the food is turned regularly.

Fats used for frying must be pure because impurities are likely to decompose at the high temperatures employed, producing unpleasant flavours and odours. Vegetable oils, providing that they have been carefully refined, may also be used for frying and such oils can often be heated to higher temperatures than the more conventional fats without decomposition occurring. When using a fat or oil for deep frying the temperature of the fat should be checked with a thermometer and it should not be allowed to rise above the value recommended. This is because if the temperature used is too high the *smoke point* of the fat may be reached, at which temperature blue smoke appears indicating incipient decomposition. If the temperature is raised above the smoke point the rate of decomposition increases rapidly.

If the frying temperature is sufficiently high to cause any fat to be hydrolysed, glycerol and free fatty acids are formed, and the glycerol may undergo dehydration with the formation of *acrolein*. This is a simple unsaturated aldehyde having an unpleasant acrid odour. It is probably present in small quantities in the smoke from the fat:

$$CH_2OHCHOHCH_2OH \longrightarrow CH_2 = CHCHO + 2H_2O$$

Glycerol   Acrolein

However, provided that the fat is not overheated and that no particles of food become mixed with it, it should be possible to use it many times before a fresh supply is needed.

Other factors which affect the choice of fat for frying are flavour and spattering properties. Spattering is due to the presence of water in the fat; the water vaporizes on heating and causes the fat to bubble and froth. When the bubbles burst, the fat is said 'to spatter'. Pure cooking fats do not contain water and so give smoother frying than butter and margarine. Efforts are usually made to reduce the spattering properties of margarine by the addition of lecithin, which also improves emulsification.

When food is fried some changes in its nutritional value occur. For example, it absorbs some of the fat used for frying and this results in an increase in its energy value. As already mentioned fat is usually very hot before food is added to it, and this results in extremely rapid evaporation of water and natural juices from the food thus reducing losses due to leaching to a minimum. Losses of nutrients which occur during frying have not been extensively investigated but in general they appear to be similar to losses which occur during roasting. Vegetables suffer a greater loss of vitamins when fried than when they are boiled. The loss of ascorbic acid in potatoes which are fried has been investigated but the results show considerable variation according to the conditions. Retention of ascorbic acid was found to be greatest when the potatoes were cooked rapidly in deep fat and lowest when they were cooked slowly in shallow fat. When meat is fried some loss of B vitamins occurs and some results are included in Table 12.5.

Microwave Cooking

The advent of microwave cooking introduces a new principle into cooking methods. Whereas in conventional cooking heat is applied to food from an outside heat source, in microwave cooking heat is generated within the food. The dramatic reduction of cooking time which results provides the main attraction of this new and potentially important method of cooking.

The electromagnetic radiation used in microwave cooking has a wavelength in the region $0.1 - 10$ cm; such radiation has a much greater wavelength than the more familiar visible or infrared regions of the electromagnetic spectrum. In microwave cooking the food is cooked in an oven of conventional size, the walls of the oven being lined with aluminium or stainless steel to reflect microwaves. The food to be cooked is placed on an oven shelf which is made of heat-resistant glass or a suitable plastic and microwaves, which are generated outside the oven in a type of valve known as a *magnetron*, pass into the oven through an opening in the roof or sides of the oven. When food molecules absorb microwave radiation they start to oscillate and because this induced oscillation opposes intermolecular forces molecular friction results and causes energy to be dissipated as heat.

The degree to which microwaves are absorbed by substances depends upon the dielectric constant of the material. Materials with a high dielectric constant absorb microwaves to a greater extent than those with low dielectric constants. Water has a particularly high dielectric constant compared with solid materials and thus in microwave cooking it is the water in the food which mainly absorbs the microwave radiation. Hence foods with a high water content cook more rapidly than those containing less water. Some materials, such as glass, plastic, china and earthenware have very low dielectric constants and absorb very little microwave radiation. In consequence they are heated to only a small extent by microwaves and so make suitable containers for food which is cooked by microwaves.

Microwaves penetrate food to a depth of 3–5 cm depending on the composition of the food. Thus when small pieces of food are exposed to microwaves the radiation completely penetrates it and heat is generated throughout the food resulting in rapid cooking. Larger pieces of food are cooked more slowly because those parts of the food which are not penetrated by microwaves are heated by conduction from the outer layers which have been penetrated by the radiation. Similarly, foods having an irregular distribution of water do not heat up uniformly as the water is heated rapidly by microwaves and surrounding regions are then heated more slowly by conduction.

Food cooked by microwave heating differs in some respects from food cooked by conventional methods. For example, the cooking time required when using microwaves is so short that slow chemical changes, which are important in slow cooking methods, do not have time to occur. Thus food cooked by microwaves does not turn brown or develop crispness, but it does retain most volatile substances; consequently the food has a different flavour from usual and this may make it unacceptable.

The particular merit of microwave cooking is the short cooking time required. For example, a fish fillet is cooked in only 30 seconds, a chop in 1 minute, a chicken in 2 minutes and a baked potato in 4 minutes. The rapidity with which microwaves heat food makes them very useful as a means of quickly re-heating pre-cooked foods—a process which takes only a few seconds—and for cooking frozen foods. In canteens, restaurants and hospitals cooked food often has to be kept hot for long periods, with consequent loss of flavour and nutritional value, before it is eaten. In these circumstances the use of microwaves enables cooked food to be reheated rapidly just before it is eaten, thus eliminating the need for keeping the food hot.

The nutritional losses incurred in microwave cooking have been compared with those which occur in conventional methods, particularly with respect to vitamins and little significant difference has been found. As ascorbic acid and thiamine are very sensitive to heat it was thought that the very short cooking times employed in microwave cooking might result in lower losses of these vitamins than occur in conventional methods. However, in experiments on some meats and vegetables, the results of which are recorded in Table 12.6, this was not found to be so. Although some differences were found these are not usually significant, though for pork microwave cooking gave better retention of thiamine than conventional methods. No clear pattern emerged for retention of ascorbic acid; for potatoes retention was greater using boiling rather than microwaves whereas with cabbage the position was reversed. In general the loss of ascorbic acid in vegetables depends more on the volume of water used and the cooking time than on the method of cooking used.

Table 12.6. Comparison of Vitamin Retention in Conventional and Microwave Cooking

Food	% Retention of ascorbic acid		% Retention of thiamine	
	Conventional	Microwave	Conventional	Microwave
Beef	—	—	81–86	70–80
Pork	—	—	80	91
Ham loaves	—	—	91	87
Potatoes	76	31	83	91
Cabbage	42	59	53	62
Carrots	80	83	81	91

Effects of Cooking on Vegetable Foods

The cell wall of all vegetable foods encloses a variety of nutrients, notably starch in potatoes and pulses (such as peas, beans and lentils) and mineral elements and vitamins in leafy vegetables, such as cabbage and spinach, and fruits. All cells contain water and a small amount of protein.

Cooking causes the starch granules to swell and gelatinize. At the same time the protein in the cells coagulates, cellulose is softened and pectin becomes more soluble. The boiling of potatoes illustrates this process (Fig. 8.2). Groups of starch grains in raw potatoes are enclosed within the walls of the plant cell which is made of cellulose together with some pectin in and between the cell walls. As the potatoes are heated starch grains swell and gelatinize, cellulose is softened and pectin becomes more soluble. Further heating completes gelatinization, giving the potatoes a soft texture; also loss of pectin causes the cells to separate easily, so making the potatoes easier to eat.

Fruit and leafy vegetables behave rather differently to potatoes on cooking, mainly because they contain less starch. On heating, the cells are killed and the proteins of the cell walls are denatured so that water flows in and out of the cells easily; this makes leafy vegetables flabby. The softening and increasing solubility of pectin is important because it allows the cells to separate easily. In addition to cellulose and pectin some vegetables, such as carrots (particularly when old), contain a woody non-carbohydrate material called *lignin*. As lignin is not affected by cooking, such vegetables retain a hard rather woody texture, even after long cooking.

Cooking may also have an effect on the colour of vegetable foods. When vegetables are boiled in water a proportion of the acids present passes into the cooking water thus reducing its pH. Under conditions of lowered pH and heating, chlorophyll is converted into *pheophytin* and the colour changes from green to a much duller brownish green. Chemically this change is due to the replacement of a magnesium atom in the centre of the large chlorophyll molecule by two hydrogen atoms. The rate at which the change takes place depends on pH, the cooking temperature and the cooking time. It was found, for example, that boiled broccoli lost about one-third of its chlorophyll if cooked for a normal period of 10 minutes, but that if it was cooked for twice as long twice as much chlorophyll was lost. The colour of cooked vegetables is improved by the addition of sodium bicarbonate as this raises the pH, but if too much is added the loss of ascorbic acid by oxidation is greatly increased. It is clear therefore that the addition of sodium bicarbonate, except in very small amounts, is not to be recommended.

Effects of Cooking on Animal Foods

The most important foods of animal origin are meat, fish, eggs and milk and the effects of cooking on the first three of these will now be considered. The effects of heat-processing milk are discussed in the next chapter.

MEAT. Meat is cooked to make it palatable, tender and safe, and all the methods of cooking discussed earlier may be used. Meat is of most importance in the diet as a source of protein and B vitamins and the effect of cooking on these nutrients is therefore of particular importance. In general the loss of protein is small except under extreme conditions of heating while loss of B vitamins varies from about one-third for thiamine, biotin and cobalamin to less than one-tenth for riboflavine and nicotinic acid.

Dry heat methods of cooking meat may be considered first. When the temperature reaches 60°C some proteins start to coagulate. If the temperature remains low, coagulation is slow and the protein will be in its most digestible form. On the other hand, if high temperatures are used coagulation is more complete and the protein becomes harder and less digestible. Heat alone does not increase tenderness very much because, apart from coagulation, the tough elastin remains unchanged and conversion of collagen into soluble form is slow. Thus dry heating methods are best used for cooking meat which contains little connective tissue. At high temperatures some protein may be destroyed by heat and some may be rendered unavailable by reaction with carbohydrate (non-enzymic browning) as described earlier. One of the amino acids liable to be rendered unavailable in non-enzymic browning is lysine and the loss of this amino acid which occurs during the cooking of meat has been studied under a variety of conditions. For example, it has been found that beef cooked for 3 hours lost one-fifth of its lysine at a cooking temperature of 120°C, but that when the temperature was raised 40°C, the amount lost increased to one-half.

When the temperature rises a little above 60°C meat starts to shrink because of the contraction of the proteins of the connective tissue. Shrinkage results in some of the 'juice' in the meat being squeezed out and the higher the cooking temperature the greater is the shrinkage and loss of juice. In roasting, for example, shrinkage causes the weight of meat to decrease by about one-third. The juice is mainly water but it also contains mineral salts, extractives and small amounts of water-soluble vitamins. During roasting in open containers, water reaching the surface of the meat rapidly evaporates, leaving behind the non-volatile material. This causes the brown outer layer of the meat to have a good flavour but also to be dry. Occasional basting of the meat with hot fat can be used, however, to prevent dryness. In closed containers and at lower temperatures the rate of evaporation is much slower and the juice drips from the surface of the meat, so reducing its flavour. However, where such methods are used the juice is usually collected and eaten with the meat as gravy.

Fat near the surface of the meat melts during cooking and most of it passes into the cooking vessel, though a small proportion of melted fat penetrates the lean meat. The greater the cooking temperature the greater is the loss into the cooking vessel and if too high a temperature is used some fat may become charred.

Some B vitamins are lost when meat is heated and the amounts of thiamine, riboflavine and nicotinic acid lost during the cooking of pork and beef are shown in Table 12.5. The loss of thiamine is particularly important as meat supplies us with about one-quarter of our intake of this vitamin. The loss of thiamine is directly proportioned to the cooking temperature though cooking time is also important. In general 40–50 per cent thiamine is lost during frying and 30–60 per cent on roasting.

In moist heat cooking methods several differences may be noted. In stewing, for example, the temperature of the meat remains well below 100 ° C, so preventing over-coagulation of protein; thus the protein is in its most digestible form. Tenderness of meat is also improved by the action of water and heat because these bring about the conversion of collagen into soluble gelatin, so allowing the muscle fibres to separate from each other. The other protein of connective tissues, elastin, remains unchanged, so that parts of an animal containing a high proportion of this protein, such as the neck, never become tender no matter how long cooking is continued.

The other main difference between the two methods of cooking concerns the loss of water-soluble matter. In moist heat methods, such as stewing, the surface of the meat is in contact with the cooking water. When protein shrinks, juice is forced to the surface of the meat and soluble matter dissolves in the water. Thus, mineral salts, extractives and thiamine are lost from the meat, which in consequence has less flavour and less nutritional value than if it had been cooked by a dry heat method. However, as such meat is normally eaten with the liquor in which it has been cooked this is not important from a nutritional point of view.

Finally a few words about the use of 'tenderizers' in cooking meat. It is known that certain enzymes are able to improve the tenderness of meat, Juice from the papaya fruit, for example, contains the peptidase *papain* (pronounced pap-ay-in) which acts on protein in a similar way to natural digestive peptidases in the body. Moreover, this enzyme retains its catalytic power at higher temperatures than would be tolerated by body enzymes. This enables papain to be used in the cooking of meat at low temperatures, its catalytic powers being greatest in the temperature range 55–75° C. The enzymes *bromelin*, obtained from pineapples and *ficin*, obtained from figs, may also be used to tenderize meat. At present, domestic use of tenderizers is negligible though in America tenderizers are used commercially in the preparation of processed meat.

FISH. When fish is cooked the changes which take place are similar to those which occur during the cooking of meat. As there is less connective tissue in fish than in meat and no elastin, cooking is not required to make the fish tender but only to render it as palatable and digestible as possible. There are less extractives in fish than in meat, and fish should therefore be cooked in such a way that as much flavour as possible is preserved. During cooking, proteins coagulate, collagen is converted into gelatin and some shrinkage occurs. Shrinkage, however, is less than with meat because of the smaller amount of connective tissue. Shrinkage causes water and soluble matter to be squeezed out of the fish and in moist heat methods of cooking, water, extractives and soluble mineral salts are lost. In boiling, for example, over a third of the extractives and soluble salts are lost, so that fish cooked in this way is rather tasteless. Dry heat cooking, on the other hand, causes rapid evaporation of water from the surface of the fish while the non-volatile soluble matter remains behind. Thus, fish cooked in this way has much more flavour than fish which has been boiled or steamed.

Table 12.7. Percentage Loss of B Vitamins when Eggs are Cooked

Vitamin	Boiled	Fried	Poached	Omelette or scrambled
Thiamine	10	20	20	5
Riboflavine	5	10	20	20
Folic acid	10	30	35	30

EGGS. When eggs are cooked there is little loss in nutritional value except that, some B vitamins are destroyed as shown in Table 12.7. There is little change in the nutritional value of protein, the main change being the coagulation of proteins in the white and yolk. This results in the whole contents of the egg becoming solid if cooking is continued for more than a few minutes.

Raising Agents

The baking of a dough or batter used in making bread, cakes or buns involves the use of an aerator which causes the mixture to rise during baking to give a product of even texture and, in the case of bread and sponge cakes, of large volume and open cellular structure.

Sometimes enough air may be incorporated by mechanical mixing to produce sufficient aeration during baking. Usually, however, carbon dioxide is used as an additional aerating agent. In breadmaking, carbon dioxide is normally produced by fermentation, but in making other types of baked confectionery carbon dioxide is produced by a chemical *raising agent* or *baking powder*.

The simplest raising agent is *sodium bicarbonate* or 'baking soda' which produces carbon dioxide when it is heated:

$$2\,NaHCO_3 + HCl \xrightarrow{heat} Na_2CO_3 + H_2O + CO_2$$

It will be seen from the equation that the sodium bicarbonate is converted into sodium carbonate or 'washing soda'. If sodium carbonate is present in appreciable quantities it imparts to the product an alkaline taste and a yellow colour. This unfortunate result is sometimes noticeable in home-made scones in which too much baking soda has been used. For this reason sodium bicarbonate is only used in making products like gingerbread and chocolate cake, which have a strong flavour and colour of their own.

A baking powder is a mixture of substances which, when mixed with water and heated, produces carbon dioxide. For most purposes a baking powder is a more suitable aerator than baking soda. It consists of three ingredients: sodium bicarbonate as the source of carbon dioxide, an acid or acid salt to liberate the gas from the bicarbonate, and some form of starch, often cornflour or ground rice, as an inert filler to absorb moisture. A typical baking powder might contain 20 per cent sodium bicarbonate, 40 per cent acidic material and 40 per cent filler.

The action of a baking powder is most simply illustrated by the reaction of a solution of hydrochloric acid with sodium bicarbonate. On mixing, carbon dioxide is given off in the cold without any unpleasant-tasting residue being left behind:

$$NaHCO_3 + HCl \longrightarrow NaCl + H_2O + CO_2$$

In practice this mixture is not used, because reaction is so rapid that much gas would be lost before baking started. Also the use of an acid in solution is inconvenient and the amount of acid needed would have to be most carefully controlled, so that no free acid remained in the product after baking.

If hydrochloric acid is replaced by tartaric acid the evolution of gas, which occurs when water is added to the baking powder, is rather slower. On reaction with sodium bicarbonate, tartaric acid is converted into the harmless salt, sodium tartrate. In modern baking powders the acid is replaced by the acid salt, potassium hydrogen tartrate, better known as cream of tartar. This salt is less soluble in cold water than the acid, so that when the baking powder is mixed with water very little reaction occurs; when the mixture is warmed, however, a copious stream of gas is produced;

$$\begin{matrix} \text{CHOHCOOH} \\ | \\ \text{CHOHCOOK} \end{matrix} + \text{NaHCO}_3 \xrightarrow{\text{heat}} \begin{matrix} \text{CHOHCOONa} \\ | \\ \text{CHOHCOOK} \end{matrix} + \text{CO}_2 + \text{H}_2\text{O}$$

Cream of tartar   Sodium potassium
                                           tartrate

A baking powder containing cream of tartar keeps better than one containing tartaric acid, because exposure to moisture has less effect. Also it is more convenient to use because carbon dioxide is not evolved in large quantities until the dough reaches the oven. As both the acid and the acid salt cost approximately the same, cream of tartar is normally preferred.

In Great Britain two other acid salts are sometimes used in place of cream of tartar. *Calcium hydrogen phosphate*, $CaH_4(PO_4)_2$, often called acid calcium phosphate (ACP), has the virtue of cheapness but, like tartaric acid, it reacts slowly with sodium bicarbonate in the cold when moisture is present; hence baking powders containing it have poor keeping qualities. *Disodium dihydrogen pyrophosphate*, $Na_2H_2P_2O_7$ usually referred to as acid sodium pyrophosphate (ASP) is preferred because of its superior keeping qualities. It is the acid salt of pyrophosphoric acid, $H_4P_2O_7$. Sometimes the two salts are used together.

Recently *glucono-delta-lactone* (GDL) has been tried as the acid component in baking powder. It slowly hydrolyses in water or in a dough at room temperature producing *gluconic acid* and the rate of hydrolysis, and hence the rate of production of carbon dioxide, is markedly increased at higher temperatures.

The effectiveness of an acidic component of baking powder is measured in terms of its 'neutralizing value' or 'strength' and is defined as the parts of sodium bicarbonate neutralized by 100 parts of the acidic component. On this basis the strength of acidic substances used is as follows:

ACP 80, ASP 74, cream of tartar 45 and GDL 45

Instead of adding a calculated amount of baking powder to flour it is sometimes more convenient to use a self-raising flour, which is flour to which sodium bicarbonate and an acid substance are added in such proportions that on reaction the correct amount of carbon dioxide is produced to aerate the flour. One of the advantages of self-raising flour is that because the baking powder and flour are present in the correct proportions, there is no danger of too much or too little aeration, and unpleasant tastes are avoided.

The acid substances added to self-raising flour are the same as those used in baking powders. Both acid calcium phosphate and acid sodium pyrophosphate are used to a large extent, both singly and together. The large excess of flour present absorbs any moisture and so prevents the deterioration of the acid calcium phosphate.

The use of baking powder or self-raising flour causes some loss of nutritive value, notably of thiamine, during baking. Thiamine is stable at low pH values but at pH values of 6 or above it is rapidly destroyed by heat. Baked goods involving the use of self-raising flour or baking powder usually have a pH of about 6·8 − 7·3 and at this pH thiamine is rapidly destroyed during baking. Losses of thiamine may be very high in such baked goods, and during the baking of cakes, for example, all the thiamine may be destroyed.

DIET

There is no such thing as a perfect or complete food, which means that there is no single food that provides sufficient of all the essential nutrients to keep us healthy. It follows that we need to eat a variety of foods to nourish us; also because different foods have widely differing nutritional contents we need to select the foods we eat in such a way that they provide us with a satisfactory or balanced diet. The information given in other parts of this book will not be of great practical value unless it can be applied so as to establish the nature of satisfactory patterns of eating. A discussion of diet therefore forms a practical and logical conclusion to the principles of nutrition discussed earlier.

Before considering diet itself it will be useful to specify what is meant by nutritional need, for unless this is known it is impossible to plan balanced diets. It must be emphasized that nutritional need can only be quantified in terms of nutrient intakes or 'allowances' and not nutritional 'requirements'. The term 'requirement' implies a measurement of the minimum of a nutrient needed to maintain health but such a measurement would only apply to the person for whom the measurement was made and even if such levels could be determined accurately enough they would not be valid for large groups of people. Recommended values of nutrient intake are average values designed for nations or other large groups of people and must therefore make allowances for individual variations. They are calculated on the basis of certain assumptions and aims and in applying them care must be taken to observe the nature of these. It is important, for example, to understand the principles which governed the Department of Health and Social Security (DHSS) in formulating their recommended daily amounts (RDA) of nutrients for the United Kingdom (1979). If the figures recommended—which are reproduced in Table 12.8—are used without reference to the explanations as to how and why they were selected, some confusion and error can result.

The RDA of nutrients shown in Table 12.8 are defined as being 'the average amount of the nutrient which should be provided per head in a group of people if the needs of practically all members of the group are to be met'. It is important to emphasize that the RDA of nutrients is distinct from requirement; the amounts represent a judgement of the average requirement plus a margin of safety. For energy, on the other hand, the recommended amount for a group is identical with the estimate of the average requirement of the group.

Compared with earlier DHSS recommendations (1969) the RDA show little difference except that food energy (and hence protein) amounts are slightly reduced in line with the trend of decreased energy expenditure both at work and during recreation, and RDA for vitamin D are no longer given (except for children and pregnant women) as most people will receive sufficient by exposure to sunlight. RDA for folic acid are given for the first time.

The recommended amount of nutrients given in the report are for *healthy* people—they make no allowance for additional needs resulting from any type of disease. Moreover the amount recommended for any particular nutrient is based on the assumption that the needs for all other nutrients and for energy are satisfied. When the recommended amount of nutrients is used to plan diets that are nutritionally adequate, or for interpreting the results of dietary surveys, allowance must be made for any sort of wastage because the recommendations refer to food that is actually eaten. The report also emphasizes that, because all nutrients can be stored in the body for at least a few days, it is not essential to consume the recommended amount every day.

The foregoing paragraphs give the general principles used in formulating the recommended amount given in Table 12.8. The principles used in formulating the amount of individual nutrients are discussed in the chapter concerned with that nutrient. Apart from the recommended amount given by the DHSS, a number of national and international bodies have produced sets of recommended nutrient allowances, among the most important of which are those of the National Research Council (NRC) of the USA and the international standard compiled by the Food and Agricultural Organization (FAO) of the United Nations.

Table 12.8. Recommended daily amounts of food energy and some nutrients for population groups in the UK (1979)

Age range years	Occupational category	Energy		Protein	Thiamine	Riboflavine	Nicotinic acid equivalents mg	Total folate µg	Ascorbic acid	Vitamin A retinol equiv-alents µg	Calcium	Iron
		MJ	Cal	g	mg	mg		µg	mg	µg	mg	mg
Boys												
under 1		(a)	(a)	(a)	0·3	0·4	5	50	20	450	600	6
1		5·0	1200	30	0·5	0·6	7	100	20	300	600	7
2		5·75	1400	35	0·6	0·7	8	100	20	300	600	7
3–4		6·5	1560	39	0·6	0·8	9	100	20	300	600	8
5–6		7·25	1740	43	0·7	0·9	10	200	20	300	600	10
7–8		8·25	1980	49	0·8	1·0	11	200	20	400	600	10
9–11		9·5	2280	57	0·9	1·2	14	200	25	575	700	12
12–14		11·0	2640	66	1·1	1·4	16	300	25	725	700	12
15–17		12·0	2880	72	1·2	1·7	19	300	30	750	600	12
Girls												
under 1		(a)	(a)	(a)	0·3	0·4	5	50	20	450	600	6
1		4·5	1100	27	0·4	0·6	7	100	20	300	600	7
2		5·5	1300	32	0·5	0·7	8	100	20	300	600	7
3–4		6·25	1500	37	0·6	0·8	9	100	20	300	600	8
5–6		7·0	1680	42	0·7	0·9	10	200	20	300	600	10
7–8		8·0	1900	47	0·8	1·0	11	200	20	400	600	10
9–11		8·5	2050	51	0·8	1·2	14	300	25	575	700	12
12–14		9·0	2150	53	0·9	1·4	16	300	25	725	700	12
15–17		9·0	2150	53	0·9	1·7	19	300	30	750	600	12

Men												
18–34	Sedentary	10·5	2510	63	1·0	1·6	18	300	30	750	500	10
	Moderately active	12·0	2900	72	1·2	1·6	18	300	30	750	500	10
	Very active	14·0	3350	84	1·3	1·6	18	300	30	750	500	10
35–64	Sedentary	10·0	2400	60	1·0	1·6	18	300	30	750	500	10
	Moderately active	11·5	2750	69	1·1	1·6	18	300	30	750	500	10
	Very active	14·0	3350	84	1·3	1·6	18	300	30	750	500	10
65–74 }	Assuming a	10·0	2400	60	1·0	1·6	18	300	30	750	500	10
75+ }	sedentary life	9·0	2150	54	0·9	1·6	18	300	30	750	500	10
Women												
18–54	Most occupations	9·0	2150	54	0·9	1·3	15	300	30	750	500	12
	Very active	10·5	2500	62	1·0	1·3	15	300	30	750	500	12
55–74 }	Assuming a	8·0	1900	47	0·8	1·3	15	300	30	750	500	10
75+ }	sedentary life	7·0	1680	42	0·7	1·3	15	300	30	750	500	10
Pregnancy		10·0	2400	60	1·0	1·6	18	500	60	750	1200	13
Lactation		11·5	2750	69	1·1	1·8	21	400	60	1200	1200	15

Note. (a) See Table 12.12.

By courtesy of H. M. Stationery Office

Where the amount of a nutrient recommended by the DHHS is markedly different from that of other bodies—as in the cases of protein and vitamin C—this is indicated in the relevant chapter.

Relation of Nutrients to the Diet

The estimates of the DHSS give the daily amount of energy and nutrients recommended for the maintenance of health, but the question of how these nutrients can best be supplied still remains. The most obvious way of forging this important link between recommended nutrient intakes and their practical application in terms of diet is to carry out dietary surveys and to relate diets which are nutritionally satisfactory to the analysis of nutrients contained in them. In Great Britain such surveys are carried out each year, diets being analysed not only in terms of nutrient content but also in terms of geographical and sociological differences. The results are summarized in the Annual Report of the National Food Survey Committee which provides valuable information on the way diet is changing in the country as a whole, in different regions of the country and in different classes of society. It also makes it possible to relate such diets to the recommended nutrient intakes and to check whether they are nutritionally satisfactory. The data contained in Tables 12.9 and 12.10 are obtained from this source.

A study of food habits of different races in different parts of the world reveals the fact that though nutritional needs remain essentially the same, the ways in which those needs may be met are unlimited. Diets may vary in an infinite number of ways and yet each diet may supply adequate amounts of the essential nutrients. Many variable factors, such as standard of living, custom, local abundance of certain foods and religious taboos all influence diet.

In highly industrialized countries such as Britain a wide variety of foods is available, whereas in less developed parts of the world the choice of foodstuffs may be more restricted. Such restricted diets, however, may be satisfactory and supply adequate amounts of all the nutrients. For example, a Central African tribe called the Masai exist on a diet which is largely composed of milk, meat and blood. These items are supplemented by concoctions made from barks of trees and certain roots which are drunk as beverages. This may seem a spartan and even repulsive diet to our more sophisticated taste, yet it keeps the tribe in good health and no deficiency diseases have been noted.

Another example from Britain itself illustrates the same point and shows that there is a remarkable difference in food habits even in such a small country as Britain. A survey carried out on the island of Lewis in the Hebrides some years ago revealed that the main articles of the diet were milk, fish, oatmeal, potatoes and turnips. To a town dweller this must seem an unbearably frugal diet, but its monotonous character was dictated by necessity not by choice. The poor soil and lack of sun allowed only such undemanding crops as oats, potatoes and turnips to be grown successfully, while the lack of good grazing no doubt restricted livestock to a few cows which were, therefore, used mainly for milk. The resources of the sea were easily tapped to provide a varied supply of fish. In spite of its lack of variety the satisfactory nutrient content of this diet was shown by the fact that the inhabitants, both children and adults, were completely healthy.

In 1940, when great efforts were being made by Britain to reduce food imports, a simple diet which would have been adequate nutritionally and would have required a minimum of imported food, was worked out. The main articles of this diet were milk, wholemeal bread and green vegetables. Scientifically such a diet would have been quite satisfactory but it was never adopted because it was thought that it would have been too unattractive for a modern industrialized nation.

These examples are not intended to show that diets restricted to a few foods only have some special virtue but they do make it clear that such diets may be nutritionally satisfactory, provided that the foods selected are chosen with care. It will be noted that the only food common to the three diets quoted above is milk. This is not accidental, for milk, more than any other food, approaches the ideal of a complete food; it is not a perfect food, however, chiefly because it contains insufficient iron, ascorbic acid, vitamin D and nicotinic acid for human needs.

A relatively complete food such as milk may be contrasted with one like sugar which provides only one nutrient. It is clear that a diet composed of foods each of which provides only one or two nutrients must be based on a much larger number of foodstuffs than one which utilizes more complete foods. Meat, fish and wholemeal bread, each of which features in one of the restricted diets mentioned above, all supply a range of nutrients, though none approaches the excellence of milk in this respect. Eggs are also valuable as suppliers of a variety of nutrients.

Nutrient Content Compared with Nutritional Value

It is very important to make a clear distinction between the nutrient content of a food and the nutrient contribution which that food makes to our diet. Some examples may help to make the point more emphatically. Dried peas have a high energy value (1150 kJ/100 g) and are rich in protein (21·5 per cent) and some vitamins, notably thiamine (0·6 mg/100 g). Yet the quantity of dried peas consumed in an average diet is so small that their contribution to our nutritional needs is very small indeed. Moreover, it is misleading to consider the nutrient content of dried foods if, before being consumed, such foods are soaked in water. When dried peas are cooked their water content increases by about 60 per cent with accompanying decrease in energy value to 420 kJ/100 g. The contribution of all pulses (peas, beans and lentils) to an average diet is only 0.3 per cent of the energy, 0.8 per cent of the protein and 1.9 per cent of the thiamine.

Compared with peas the nutrient content of potatoes is small. Old potatoes have an energy value of only 365 kJ/100 g and contain little protein (2 per cent) or vitamin C (10–20 mg/100 g). Yet because we eat considerable quantities of potatoes—on average about $1\frac{1}{4}$ kg/week—potatoes contribute 5 per cent of the energy, 4 per cent of the protein and 24 per cent of the vitamin C in an average diet. Similarly no one would claim potatoes as a food rich in iron. Potatoes contain only $0\cdot7$ mg/100 g of iron compared with a food such as liver which is relatively rich in iron and contains 11 mg/100 g. Although the iron content of liver is sixteen times that of potatoes, liver contributes only about 3 per cent of the iron in an average diet whereas potatoes contribute about 7 per cent.

The Adequacy of the British Diet

In considering the average British diet it is convenient to group the wide variety of foodstuffs consumed into six main categories, namely; (a) milk, cheese and eggs, (b) meat and fish, (c) cereals, (d) fruits and vegetables, (e) fats and (f) sugar and preserves. It is true that not all the items of our diet are included within these groups but excluded items, such as beverages, make a negligible contribution to the diet as a whole. The contribution of these food groups to the energy, proteins, fat, calcium and iron in an average British diet is shown in Table 12.9, and their contribution to vitamins in Table 12.10.

Table 12.9. % **Contributions made by Important Food Groups to an Average British Diet**

Food group	Energy	Protein	Fat	Calcium	Iron
Milk, cheese, eggs	16	27	22	62	8
Meat, fish	18	36	29	—	26
Cereals	39	24	10	23	37
Fruits, vegetables	11	10	2	8	22
Fats	15	<1	36	<1	<1
Sugar, preserves	—	—	—	<1	1

The importance of the group containing milk, cheese and eggs is evident from these tables and of this group fresh milk makes by far the

Table 12.10. % **Vitamin Contributions to an Average British Diet**

Food group	Vitamin A	Thiamine	Ribo-flavine	Nicotinic acid	Vitamin C	Vitamin D
Milk, cheese, eggs	17	15	50	3	8	28
Meat, fish	37	16	20	45	2	15
Cereals	1	45	13	23	—	5
Fruits, vegetables	25	21	9	20	87	—
Fats	20	—	—	—	—	49
Sugar, preserves	—	—	—	—	1	—

greatest contribution providing 10 per cent of the energy, 16 per cent of the protein, 13 per cent of the fat, 45 per cent of the calcium and 36 per cent of the riboflavine in an average diet. Meat and fish make a major contribution to all the nutrients shown in the tables except calcium and vitamin C. These two groups of foods account for half the cost of an average diet and provide it with one-third of its energy, half its fat and nearly two-thirds of its proteins as well as making significant contributions to mineral elements and vitamins, with the notable exception of vitamin C.

Cereals, being mainly carbohydrate, are major contributors to energy, and bread supplies 15 per cent of the total energy of our diet. More surprisingly they are also important sources of protein and bread supplies about 14 per cent of our total protein intake. Bread is a major item of our diet, average consumption being about 900 g a week, and as explained in Chapter 8 certain nutrients—calcium, iron, thiamine and nicotinic acid—are added to flour to make up for nutrient losses which occur during milling. This explains why bread is such an important source of these nutrients; it provides 12 per cent calcium, 20 per cent iron, 21 per cent thiamine and 5 per cent nicotinic acid to an average diet.

Fruits and vegetables are important mainly for their contribution to our intake of vitamins; a glance at Table 12.10 makes this fact plain and also shows their special significance as the source of almost 90 per cent of our vitamin C intake. As already pointed out potatoes provide 24 per cent of our supplies of vitamin C and they are by far the most important single source of this vitamin in our diet. Other important sources of vitamin C are citrus fruit (mainly oranges) which contribute 12 per cent of our intake, green vegetables which contribute a further 11 per cent and tomatoes (6 per cent) and apples and pears (5 per cent). Among other fruits and vegetables carrots are notable as providing 16 per cent of our vitamin A intake.

Fats, sugar and preserves are important as sources of energy, though fats have the additional importance that they often contain fat-soluble vitamins and so provide us with a considerable proportion of our intake of vitamins A and D. In order to ensure that those people who eat margarine in place of butter receive adequate amounts of these two vitamins, they are added to all table margarine. In an average diet butter provides 11 per cent of our intake of vitamin A and 5 per cent vitamin D while the corresponding figures for margarine are 9 per cent vitamin A and 43 per cent vitamin D.

The adequacy of an average British diet may be determined by comparing the actual energy value and nutrient intake with the RDA. Care is needed in interpreting such figures for several reasons, chief of which is the fact that the figures are average ones for the population as a whole and therefore, because of the variation of individual needs, cannot be applied to individuals or even to special groups. Moreover, as mentioned earlier, if the intake of a nutrient is less than 100 per cent of the DHSS recommendation it does not necessarily mean that the diet is deficient in that nutrient because recommended amounts contain a considerable margin of safety. The interdependence of certain nutrients must also be taken into account when interpreting the figures. For example, an apparently satisfactory intake of calcium in children cannot lead to proper bone formation unless the diet also contains adequate amounts of vitamin D.

Table 12.11. Energy and Nutrient Values of an Average British Diet

	Consumption per day	*% of DHSS RDA*
Energy (kJ)	9500	100
Protein	73 g	130
Fat	106 g	—
Calcium	990 mg	174
Iron	11 mg	102
Vitamin A (retinol equiv.)	1490 μg	194
Thiamine	1·2 mg	132
Riboflavine	1·9 mg	138
Nicotinic acid	30 mg	195
Vitamin C	54 mg	188
Vitamin D	2·6 μg	—

The consumption figures quoted in Table 12.11 reveal that for nutrients the amounts recommended by the DHSS are exceeded in all cases. In general the data given in Table 12.11 confirm other evidence that supports the view that the British diet is nutritionally adequate.

The food energy intake is the same as the recommended value when allowance is made for wastage and for meals not eaten at home. Carbohydrates contribute just under half the total food energy intake, fat just over 40 per cent and protein the remainder. The amount of protein consumed is more than adequate both as regards quantity and quality; about 65 per cent being from animal protein of high biological value.

The apparently high intake of vitamin C calls for some comment. The DHSS recommended intake of 30 mg per day for an adult, differs markedly from the recommended allowances of some other bodies. The NRC allowance of this vitamin is based on an entirely different criterion, namely that to maintain good health the body should maintain a body pool of 1500 mg vitamin C. On the basis that absorption of vitamin C is only about 85 per cent efficient, the NRC. RDA is 60 mg per day, i.e. double the DHSS value.

Trends in the British Diet

Since the end of the Second World War in 1945 there have been some notable changes in the British diet. The amount of carbohydrate in the diet, for example, has decreased mainly due to less bread and potatoes being eaten. This overall reduction conceals, however, an increase in the consumption of one carbohydrate—sugar. Sugar consumption has increased considerably over the past 100 years reaching a peak in 1960 and then declining somewhat to a current figure of just over 40 kg per person per year.

The proportion of fat in the diet has increased due to greater amounts of meat, butter, margarine, cooking fats and cream being eaten. While the total amount of protein in the diet has remained about the same, the amount of animal protein foods consumed—meat, milk, and cheese—has increased while the amount of vegetable protein foods—especially bread and potatoes—has decreased. Overall there has been a small reduction in food energy intake.

Finally it is worthy of note that the proportion of alcohol in the diet has doubled since the 1950s, and alcohol now represents 6 per cent of the average daily food energy intake.

The British diet is typical of the diet of an affluent country and as such is further discussed on page 287.

Dietary Needs of Vulnerable Groups

Although the British diet is satisfactory, there are groups—notably young children and elderly people—which are particularly prone to suffer from poor nutrition and in which deficiencies certainly exist.

There are other groups of people with special dietary needs, such as those who are ill, those who for reasons of health or fashion are slimming and those who for reasons of conscience or preference are vegetarians. Three examples of the nutritional needs of special groups are given below.

DIET OF BABIES. Mothers milk is the ideal food for babies; the amount and composition of the nutrients present is ideal for the healthy growth of the baby. It is to be hoped that the decline in breast feeding in the UK over recent years will be reversed with the appreciation that breast feeding is the best method for the young baby. It is generally recommended that babies are breast fed for a minimum of 2 weeks and preferably for the first 4–6 months of life.

The advantages of breast feeding are well documented. As mentioned above mothers milk provides the correct balance of nutrients for the baby's needs. The infants requirements of energy and protein (see Table 12.12) over the first 6 months of life are provided naturally and easily by breast feeding, and no nutrient supplements should be required provided that the mother is receiving an adequate diet. Nursing mothers are advised to take vitamin D supplements to increase their intake to the RDA of 10 μg daily.

Table 12.12. Recommended Daily Amounts (RDA) of Food Energy and Protein for Infants

Age range	Body weight (kg)		RDA food energy (kJ)		RDA protein (g)	
in months	Boys	Girls	Boys	Girls	Boys	Girls
0–3	4·6	4·4	2200	2100	13	12·5
3–6	7·1	6·6	3000	2800	18	17
6–9	8·8	8·2	3700	3400	22	20
9–12	9·8	9·0	4100	3800	24·5	23

Another advantage of breast feeding is that the milk is available at the right temperature and in the right quantity. Also with breast feeding the risk of infection is much less than in bottle feeding; the young baby is protected by antibodies and other protective substances in the mother's milk at a time when its own protective defences are not properly developed. Breast feeding reduces the risk of diarrhoea from contaminated milk because the milk passes direct from mother to baby without any external contact. Non-nutritional advantages of breast feeding include the fostering of a close physical relation between mother and baby and a beneficial effect on the health of the mother. Finally it is worth mentioning that babies are less likely to become obese when breast fed than when they are bottle fed because in the latter method there is a tendency to make feeds too strong and to add cereal foods to the milk.

Bottle Feeding: For many mothers there may often be a good reason why they cannot or should not breast feed, in which case they will bottle feed their baby using a commercial baby milk. Cows' milk has a composition very different from that of human milk and on its own is an incomplete food for babies; hence many attempts have been made to modify it so as to make it equivalent to breast milk. Although such attempts have not been completely successful many commercial products are available that are satisfactory.

Commercial baby milks are normally in concentrated form—either dried, evaporated or condensed—and are reconstituted by the addition of water. Cows' milk may be modified in a number of ways, but the main objects are to reduce the electrolyte and protein contents and to increase the lactose content. The manufacturer also adds vitamins A, C and D and iron in the form of non-toxic iron salts. Much research had gone into producing commercial baby milk that resembles human milk as closely as possible. For example there are *filled milks*, where animal fat is replaced by vegetable oils; milks with added lactose and milks where lactose is replaced by malto-dextrins.

Solid Food. Early weaning—as early as the third or fourth weeks— became fashionable in the fifties and sixties but it is now generally recommended that the use of solid foods should be discouraged before about 4 months or, as a better criterion, a weight of about 6 kg is reached. There is no sound nutritional reason for an earlier introduction to solid foods and indeed there are positive dangers related to early weaning. For example, early addition of solids to feeds can produce obesity in babies and the early use of cereal foods containing wheat gluten can predispose the baby to an allergy known as *coeliac disease*.

When solid foods are introduced babies can be given most of the foods eaten by the rest of the family (apart from strongly spiced ones) provided that they are minced or sieved. Such ordinary food is to be preferred to commercial baby foods which are often sweetened and salted. When babies start to drink ordinary cow's milk they should start receiving vitamin supplements, particularly of vitamin D if there is too little exposure to sunlight to synthesize the babies needs. Cod-liver oil will supply vitamins A and D and orange juice will supply vitamin C. Alternatively all three vitamins may be supplied as a vitamin supplement given in the form of drops. Such supplements should be continued for at least a year and preferably for two.

In spite of the availability of suitable vitamin supplements the diets of some babies and young children are lacking in these vitamins and in a very small minority this deficiency is sufficiently serious to produce rickets and scurvy. It should be emphasized, however, that the number of children suffering from vitamin deficiency diseases in Great Britain is extremely small. With increasing understanding of the dietary needs of the young, better dissemination of such knowledge to mothers and better availability of vitamin supplements and fortified foods, rickets, which at the beginning of the century was a common disease among children, is now uncommon among British children though unfortunately it is not uncommon among the children of Asian immigrants.

Apart from vitamins the main nutrient likely to be lacking in an infants' diet is iron. At birth babies have a reserve supply of iron which lasts for several months and this, together with the iron received from human or cows' milk, supplies their needs for some 4–5 months. After this time, however, they need to be given foods containing iron, sieved green vegetables, minced meat and eggs all being suitable. Although severe iron deficiency resulting in anaemia is not common in British children it is frequently found among immigrant children from countries, such as the West Indies, in which the traditional infants' diet is lacking in iron.

DIET OF THE ELDERLY. Elderly people may suffer from an inadequate diet for a variety of reasons such as loneliness, poverty, reduced enjoyment of food due to loss of taste and smell, mental and physical lethargy, or illness and inability to chew and digest food properly. In addition, elderly people often lack an understanding of the principles of nutrition. For these and other reasons elderly people more often suffer from malnutrition than the population as a whole. As the proportion of elderly people in Great Britain is increasing, the task of ensuring that they receive an adequate diet is of increasing importance.

Although the DHSS recommendations deal to some extent with elderly people their nutritional needs require further investigation. It is known that energy needs decrease with age because of the reduction in physical activity and the DHSS has made recommendations concerning the levels of food energy intake appropriate to different age groups (see Table 12.8).

Several studies have recently been carried out on the diet of the elderly. These conclude that the number of mal-nourished people was probably small and did not constitute a serious problem; it is believed that it is disease rather than malnutrition which is the primary problem. Some 3 per cent of elderly people suffer from malnutrition, the nutrients most likely to be deficient being the B vitamins, vitamin C and iron.

There are some particular hazards for older people. For example, old people who have difficulty in peeling fruit or cooking potatoes may lack sufficient vitamin C, while the housebound will have little or no chance of being in the sunshine and consequently may lack vitamin D. A vitamin D supplement may well be beneficial for older people, particularly in winter. Finally, old people suffer from loss of calcium from bone called *osteoporosis*. Although this condition cannot be prevented by diet, foods which are rich in calcium such as milk or cheese should be included in diets for the elderly.

SLIMMING DIETS. Many people slim for the simple reason that it is fashionable to be slim, but it is becoming increasingly recognized that many people are too fat and that this is objectionable not only for aesthetic reasons but for health reasons as well. People who are overweight impose a strain on the heart and other organs and they are more likely to suffer from mechanical disabilities, owing to the strain put upon joints and ligaments, than slim people. Moreover, fat people are predisposed to metabolic disorders. Statistics show that for men who are 10 per cent overweight life expectancy is reduced by 13 per cent, while for those who are 30 per cent overweight it is reduced by 42 per cent.

It is believed that at any one time one-third of people in the UK are following some sort of diet to control or reduce weight. Most people who try to slim do so by modifying their eating habits in some way and traditional methods of slimming mainly concern themselves with reducing energy intake by cutting down the amount of food eaten. This is because people become fat when the energy intake derived from food is greater than the total energy used by the body. The food which is surplus to the body's energy requirements is stored as fat in the fat depots of the body. In this connection it is important to appreciate that it is not only fatty foods which contribute to fat reserves; excess carbohydrate and protein also contribute.

It is evident from the above that fat reserves may be depleted by reducing the energy intake to below that used by the body. Alternatively, the energy intake can be maintained and the energy used increased by doing more physical work. Unfortunately a great deal of exercise is needed to have much effect—about 2 hours strenuous exercise is needed to dispose of a good meal—and as increased exercise leads to increased appetite, loss of weight achieved through exercise is likely to be counteracted by subsequent increase in weight through extra eating and drinking.

Much research has been, and is being, done into the causes of obesity. Many theories have been proposed but it seems increasingly certain that not one but several different factors are involved in causing obesity. Genetic factors, enzyme defects, environmental and social factors, psychological stress may all be involved. It has been known for a long time that people have different weight responses to a given food energy intake. In simple language some people get fat more easily than others. Although the factor that plays the central role in energy balance remains unknown one possibility put forward recently is that it involves increased heat production or *thermogenesis* caused by brown adipose tissue. The precise role of brown adipose tissue remains unclear but it is possible that lack of brown adipose tissue reduces heat loss in the body thereby contributing to obesity.

Slimming diets involve eating less food; also in selecting carefully which foods to eat. The object is to reduce the amount of food energy in the diet. One way of doing this is to 'count calories'; another is to reduce carbohydrate.

Carbohydrate serves no other function except the provision of energy and it is therefore preferable to limit consumption of carbohydrate rather than that of protein because the latter, in addition to providing energy, contributes to tissue maintenance and the control of body processes. Most people who slim by changing their eating habits adopt a low-carbohydrate diet; the great majority cut down on starchy foods and/or sugar. A relatively small proportion of slimmers reduce the amount of food they eat because any diet which leaves the slimmer feeling hungry is unlikely to be popular or last for long.

Special foods are available to help slimmers, the most drastic of which—known as formula diets—completely replace normal meals. They are calculated to contain sufficient of all nutrients to maintain health, but they contain less than the required amount of food energy. Formula diets are usually made from protein rich foods, such as soya flour and skim-milk powder to which calculated amounts of minerals and vitamins and some carbohydrate are added. An increasing range of low-energy foods is becoming available; in such foods sugar may be partly or wholly replaced by saccharin.

An alternative is to use a *bulking aid*, that is a substance which either contributes to the bulk of the food without contributing significantly to its available energy value or which produces bulk upon ingestion. One such bulking aid is *polydextrose* which is able to replace all or part of the water-soluble carbohydrates, such as sugars, which are normally used in foods. In effect polydextrose replaces sugar in food providing bulk and sweetness without contributing to energy value. The use of polydextrose makes it possible to produce foods with up to 50 per cent less energy value than equivalents made with traditional ingredients but with no loss of texture or organoleptic properties.

Alpha-cellulose is a second bulking aid allowed to be used as a 'filler'. It has a similar molecular weight to natural cellulose but is produced as a highly refined, pulverized form of cellulose being available in several forms from coarse fibres to fine powders. It provides bulk but has no nutritional value whatever; it is able to absorb about fifty times its own weight of water and once in the stomach it swells giving a feeling of fullness. Alpha-cellulose is normally added to foods at levels of 10–20 per cent on a dry weight basis. It is a convenient way of producing slimming foods with a high content of dietary fibre. Like certain other forms of fibre such as pectin (see p. 172) it is thought to lower blood cholesterol. Like natural cellulose alpha-cellulose is not broken down in the body.

Goals for a Healthy Diet

The emergence of *Social Nutrition*, mentioned at the beginning of the chapter, is an area of growing interest and demonstrates current concern about factors that govern food choice and how that choice may be influenced in the interests of achieving healthy diets. We have already seen in this chapter how in times of restricted food choice healthy diets based on a handful of carefully chosen foods can be achieved. In general however, with unlimited choice, healthy diets can most easily be devised by eating as wide a variety of foods as possible.

The generalization that we need to eat many different foods is an inadequate guide to a healthy diet. In affluent countries where choice is very wide there is a growing realization that many people choose diets that are unhealthy. The belief that diet is linked with a number of diseases has emphasized the need for clear guidance as to how to achieve a healthy diet. It needs to be emphasized, however, that diet is only one factor involved and that the nature of our lifestyle is extremely important. In addition there is a danger of isolating a particular dietary factor and casting it in the role of villain, when in all probability many factors, both dietary and non-dietary, are involved.

In affluent countries of the West certain 'diseases of affluence' have become common. These include coronary heart disease, certain diseases of the bowel such as appendicitis, cancer and diverticulitis, diabetes and dental caries. Such diseases are prevalent in countries which have a lifestyle that includes cigarette smoking, a significant alcohol intake, little exercise and a tendency to be overweight. The diet in affluent countries tends to include many fatty foods, foods rich in sugar, refined convenience foods and also alcohol. In addition intake of salt may be high.

In the light of the prevalence of certain diseases and of some unhelpful eating habits in affluent countries, there have been several attempts to produce dietary goals over recent years. Taking a consensus of such goals and guidelines, we can formulate the following simple set of objectives for improving diet in affluent countries:

1 Avoid being overweight by reducing energy intake.
2 Avoid eating too much fat, particularly saturated fat.
3 Avoid too much sugar.
4 Where necessary balance energy needs resulting from reduced fat and sugar intake by eating more 'complex' carbohydrates eg. bread, fruit and vegetables.
5 Avoid too much alcohol.
6 Avoid too much salt.
7 Eat cereals and vegetables for fibre.

The reasons for such recommendations will be found in the relevant chapter except for those concerning salt. Experiments with animals suggest that a salty diet may lead to high blood pressure which in turn is related to coronary heart disease. There is some confirmation of this link from human studies so that, although proof is lacking, it seems prudent to avoid too much salt in the diet.

SUGGESTIONS FOR FURTHER READING

BROWN, M. A. and CAMERON, A. G. *Experimental Cooking.* Arnold, 1977.

BURNETT, J. *Plenty and Want—A Social History of Diet in England from 1815 to the Present Day.* Nelson, 1966.

CRADDOCK, D. *Obesity and its Management.* Churchill Livingstone, 1973.

DEPARTMENT OF HEALTH AND SOCIAL SECURITY. *Eating for Health.* HMSO, 1978.

DEPARTMENT OF HEALTH AND SOCIAL SECURITY. *Nutrition Survey of the Elderly.* HMSO, 1972.

DEPARTMENT OF HEALTH AND SOCIAL SECURITY. *Present-day Practice in Infant Feeding.* HMSO, 1974.

DEPARTMENT OF HEALTH AND SOCIAL SECURITY. *Research on Obesity.* HMSO, 1976.

DEPARTMENT OF HEALTH AND SOCIAL SECURITY. *Recommended Daily Amounts of Food Energy and Nutrients for the UK.* HMSO, 1979.

DRUMMOND, Sir J. C. and WILBRAHAM, A. *The Englishman's Food: a History of Five Centuries of English Diet.* Cape, 1957.

FOOD AND NUTRITION BOARD, USA. *Towards Healthful Diets.* National Research Council, USA, 1980.

FOOD AND NUTRITION BOARD, USA. *Recommended Daily Allowances*, 9th edition. National Academy of Sciences, 1980.

LENNON, D. and FIELDHOUSE, P. *Community Dietetics*. Forbes Publications, 1979.

MCWILLIAMS, M. *Nutrition for the Growing Years*. 3rd edition, Wiley, USA, 1980.

MEDICAL RESEARCH COUNCIL. *National Food Survey Committee Report*. HMSO, annual.

ODDY, D. and MILLER, D. (Eds). *The Making of the Modern British Diet*. Croom Helm, 1976.

TURNER, M. (Ed). *Nutrition and Lifestyles*. Applied Science Publishers, 1980.

WEBB, J. *Microwave, the Cooking Revolution*. Forbes Publications, 1977.
An elementary but practical and readable review.

YUDKIN, J. (Ed). *Diet of Man: Needs and Wants* (Symposium Report). Applied Science Publishers, 1978.

Chapter Thirteen

Food spoilage, preservation and hygiene

Most unprocessed foods deteriorate when kept and as a result become inedible. Butter, cheese, bacon, dried fruit and several other traditional food products have their origin in a desire to make use of food surplus to immediate requirements. In spite of such conversions of perishable foods into more permanent forms, however, vast quantities of food are still lost annually as a consequence of various types of food spoilage. It has been estimated that between 10 and 20 per cent more food would be made available if such wastage could be completely prevented.

Drying, staling, contamination with dirt or chemicals and damage by animals or insect pests all play their parts in food spoilage. In many cases, spoilage of this sort can be avoided if care is taken in the transport and storage of food. The occurrence of undesirable chemical reactions, such as oxidation, also causes spoilage. The most important single cause of food spoilage, however, is attack by micro-organisms such as moulds, yeasts and bacteria.

Microbiological Food Spoilage

In appropriate circumstances foodstuffs are efficient growth media for micro-organisms and moist food kept in a warm place is likely to 'go-bad' or 'go-off' as a result of their rapid multiplication. Some micro-organisms, or the toxins they produce, are harmful to human beings and if food contaminated by them is eaten *food poisoning* may result. Food which has been attacked by micro-organisms may look offensive or have a peculiar smell. In many instances, however, it is not possible to tell by looking at a sample of food, or by tasting it, whether it has been attacked. In fact, food may be heavily infected and still appear to be wholesome and such foods are more likely to cause food poisoning than those which have obviously deteriorated. It must be emphasized, however, that the presence of micro-organisms is not always harmful. Indeed, many of the most highly prized food flavours are a consequence of microbial activity. For example, blue cheeses such as Roquefort, Stilton and Gorgonzola owe their characteristic flavour to the presence of the mould *Penicillium roqueforti*.

Micro-organisms vary in size from certain algae just large enough to be seen by the naked eye (about 100 μ) to viruses which are much too small (about 0·1 μ) to be seen by a normal microscope but can be discerned by an electron microscope. The micro-organisms principally responsible for food poisoning are moulds, bacteria and yeasts.

MOULDS. Moulds are microscopic forms of plants known as fungi which do not possess any chlorophyll. They grow as fine threads or filaments which extend in length and eventually form a complex branched network or mat called *mycelium*. At this stage mould growth on foods is easily visible as a 'fluff'. Moulds also produce *spores* or seeds and these can be carried considerable distances by air currents and in this way infect other foods.

Most moulds require oxygen for development and this is why they are usually found only on the surface of foods. Meat, cheese and sweet foods are especially likely to be attacked by moulds. In alkaline or very acid foods (pH below 2) mould growth is inhibited although some moulds will grow even under these conditions. Moulds grow best at a pH of 4 to 6 and a temperature of about 30° C; as the temperature decreases so does the rate of growth although slow growth can continue at the temperature of a domestic refrigerator. Mould growth does not occur above normal body temperature but it is very difficult to kill moulds and their spores by heat treatment. To ensure complete destruction of all moulds and their spores sterilization under pressure is necessary (i.e. at above 100° C). Alternatively the food may be heated to 70–80° C on two or more successive days so that any spores germinating between the heat treatments will be destroyed.

Mycotoxins. It is becoming better appreciated that some fungi produce toxic substances. For example, the fungus *Aspergillus flavus* which grows in groundnuts and other cereals produces a mycotoxin called *aflatoxin* which produces disease in a number of animals. There is growing evidence that mycotoxins can effect man also and *Aspergillus flavus* is known to have caused over 100 deaths in India in an outbreak of Hepatitis when contaminated maize flour was consumed.

There is a growing appreciation of the dangers of eating mouldy foods whether they are contaminated accidentally or intentionally for improving flavour and texture.

BACTERIA. Bacteria are the smallest form of plant life. They are minute living particles either spherical (cocci), rod-shaped (bacilli) or spiral (spirella). It is difficult to get any idea of the size of bacteria but 10^{13} of them would weigh only about a gram. Bacteria grow by absorbing simple substances from their environment and when they reach a certain size the parent organism splits to form two new ones. In favourable circumstances this fission may occur every 20 minutes or so and in 12 hours one bacterium can provide a colony of some 10^{10} bacteria.

When bacteria multiply in or on food their presence becomes obvious when they are present to the extent of 10^6–10^7 per gram of foodstuff. Bacteria grow most readily in neutral conditions and growth is usually inhibited by acids. Some bacteria, however, will tolerate fairly low pH. For example, *Lactobacilli* which cause souring of milk with the production of lactic acid and *Acetobacter* which convert ethyl alcohol to acetic acid flourish in acid conditions. Some bacteria will only grow in the presence of oxygen whereas others, known as *anaerobes*, will only grow in its absence.

Bacteria grow best within a given temperature range and in their vegetative state (i.e. when they are actually growing) all of them can be killed by exposure to a temperature near to $100°$ C and at this temperature they are destroyed instantly. The heat resistance of bacterial spores varies from species to species and with the pH of the surrounding medium. This is considered in more detail on page 310.

The commonest food spoilage organisms are *mesophilic bacteria* which originate in warm blooded animals but are also found in soil, water and sewage. Mesophilic bacteria grow best at about normal body temperature between 30–40° C. *Psychrophilic bacteria*, which have their origin in air, soil and water grow best at a somewhat lower temperature—about 20° C—although some of them are quite happy at considerably lower temperatures. Such psychrophilic bacteria can grow quite easily at the temperature of a domestic refrigerator. A small group of bacteria can grow at temperatures up to 60° C and these are known as *thermophilic bacteria*. The spores of thermophilic bacteria can be very heat resistant.

YEASTS. Yeasts are fungi but, unlike moulds, they reproduce themselves by budding, i.e. by the formation of a small offshoot or bud which becomes detached from the parent yeast cell when it reaches a certain size and assumes an independent existence. Yeasts can also form spores but these are far less heat-resistant than mould and bacterial spores. Yeasts occur in the soil and on the surface of fruits. For example, the presence of yeasts on the skin of grapes is the reason why grape juice ferments to become wine. Yeasts can grow in quite varied conditions; they can tolerate quite low pH, high salt or sugar concentration and the absence of oxygen. Yeasts and yeast spores are easily killed by heating to 100° C.

As well as being useful for converting sugars to alcohol in wine and beer manufacture, yeast and yeast extracts are also used as flavouring agents for a variety of foods such as meat pies, sausages and potato crisps. Marmite is a familiar form of yeast extract. Yeast extracts are rich in vitamins of the B group.

Food Preservation

Micro-organisms are present in the air, in dust, soil, sewage and on the hands; they are in fact so ubiquitous that their presence in or on food is inevitable unless special steps are taken to kill them. If food is to be kept in good condition for any length of time it is essential that the growth of micro-organisms be prevented. This can be done either by killing them and then storing the food in conditions where further infection is impossible or by creating an environment which is not suitable for their proliferation.

The principal methods of food preservation, which fall into one or both of the above categories, are listed below:

1 Treatment with chemicals
2 Dehydration
3 Sterilization by heat
4 Use of low temperatures
5 Irradiation.

As well as suppressing the growth of micro-organisms an effective method of food preservation must retain, as far as possible, the original characteristic of the food and impair its nutritive value as little as possible.

TREATMENT WITH CHEMICALS. Chemicals have been used in the preservation of foods for many centuries; sodium chloride, sodium and potassium nitrate, sugars, vinegar, alcohol, wood smoke and various spices have come to be regarded as traditional preservatives. Many of these compounds carry out their function as preservatives by dissolving in the water of the food to form a concentrated solution in which micro-organisms cannot live. When a micro-organism is surrounded by a concentrated aqueous solution water passes from its cells to the solution and the micro-organism becomes dehydrated and dies. This is the basis of the preservation of meat by curing, in which the meat is impregnated with a mixture of salt, saltpetre and sometimes a little sugar, all of which dissolve in the meat fluids. Meat can absorb up to 6 per cent of its weight of soluble solids in this way. Salting of meat and fish is a very ancient technique and is used even in the most primitive societies where salt is available.

An example of the preservative action of strong sugar solutions has already been encountered in Chapter 7 in connection with jams and other sugar preserves. These are not susceptible to mould growth because of the very high concentrations of sugar in the aqueous phase. If condensation of water on the surface of the jam should occur, however, the sugar concentration at that point may be reduced to such a level that moulds appear. Condensed sweetened milk, which contains large amounts of sugar, is another excellent example of this principle. It can be kept for several weeks after opening the can without growth of micro-organisms occurring. Micro-organisms cannot tolerate high concentrations of alcohol and this is why fortified wines, such as sherry and port wine, keep better than unfortified wines. Similarly, vinegar discourages the growth of many micro-organisms and it performs this function in pickles (see Chapter 5).

The preservation of meat by curing, dates from byegone days when the weaker animals were killed off in the autumn because insufficient feeding stuff was available to keep them alive through the winter. Whole bullocks were salted and little or no fresh meat was available during the winter months. The necessity to preserve meat by curing has now disappeared, but bacon and ham still form part of the normal diet and provide a link with the past. Smoking, which was usually carried out on meat or fish which had been heavily salted, is another ancient technique of chemical food preservation. When food is smoked the outer layers become coated with a gloss or patina consisting of condensed tars, phenols and aldehydes which has a powerful bactericidal action and this is why the process has a preservative effect. Spices were often used in former times and it is often supposed that they functioned as preservatives. In fact, however, their principal purpose was to disguise the smell and taste of food which was, by modern standards at least, far from fresh.

In Great Britain the use of chemicals to preserve food is controlled by the Preservatives in Food Regulations (1979). In these regulations the word preservative means any substance which is capable of inhibiting, retarding or arresting the growth of micro-organisms or any deterioration of food due to micro-organisms or of masking the evidence of any such deterioration.

The Preservatives in Food Regulations lists the foods in which preservatives may be used and specifies the maximum permissible amount of preservative which may be present; its main provisions are summarized in Tables 13.1 (a) and (b). For the purposes of the regulations the following substances are not regarded as preservatives:

(a) any permitted antioxidant
(b) any permitted artificial sweetener
(c) any permitted bleaching agent
(d) any permitted colouring matter
(e) any permitted emulsifier
(f) any permitted improving agent
(g) any permitted miscellaneous additive
(h) any permitted solvent
(i) any permitted stabiliser
(j) vinegar
(k) any soluble carbohydrate sweetening matter potable spirits or wines
(l) herbs, spices, hop extract or essential oils when used for flavouring purposes
(m) common salt
(n) any substance added to food by the process of curing known as smoking

It should be noted that most of the traditional preservatives are included in this list and hence, from a legal point of view, are not regarded as preservatives at all.

Certain other substances which exert a preservative action may be present in foods without being regarded as preservatives. For example, any food may contain not more than 5 ppm of formaldehyde derived from wrapping materials or containers.

In the past numerous other substances have also been used as preservatives. Borates, fluorides formaldehyde and various phenols have all been

Table 13.1a. Names of Permitted Preservatives

Code number	Name of preservative	Alternative forms
1	Sulphur dioxide	Sodium sulphite and metabisulphite Potassium metabisulphite Calcium sulphite and bisulphite
2	Benzoic acid	Sodium, potassium and calcium salt
3	Propionic acid	Sodium, potassium and calcium salt
4	Sorbic acid	Sodium potassium and calcium salt
5	Methyl, ethyl and propyl p-hydroxy benzoates	Corresponding sodium salts
6	Diphenyl	
7	Nisin	
8	Sodium nitrate	Potassium salt
9	Sodium nitrite	Potassium salt
10	o-phenyl phenol	Sodium salt
11	Thiabendazole	
12	Hexamine	

Table 13.1b. Use of Permitted Preservatives

Food	Code numbers of Perservatives	Max. permitted amount in mg per kg food
Beer	1, 2, 5	70
Bread	3	3000
Cheese	4	1000
Cheese, exc. Cheddar, Cheshire	8	100
or soft cheese	9	10
Provolone cheese	12	25
Cider	1, 4	200
Coffee extract, solid	1	150
Colouring matter	2, 5	2000
	4	1000
Flavourings (including syrups)	1	350
	2, 5	800
Flour confectionery	3, 4	1000
Fruit, dried exc. prunes	1	2000
Fruit, fresh		
Bananas	11	3
Citrus fruit	6	70
	10	12
	11	10
Fruit juices	1	350
	2, 5	800
Gelatin	1	1000
Glucose drinks	1	350
	2, 5	800
Jam, exc. diabetic	1	100
Meat, cured	8	500
	9	200
Pickles	1	100
	2, 5	250
	4	1000
Potatoes, raw, peeled	1	50
Sausages or sausage meat	1	450
Sugar	1	70
liquid glucose syrups	1	450
Vinegar, malt	1	70
Yoghourt, fruit	1	60
	2, 5	120

used but in the course of time it become apparent that their efficiency in killing micro-organisms was coupled with considerable toxicity to man. This did not deter unscrupulous individuals from using them, however, often in injurious amounts. Preservatives were often used to mitigate the effect of unhygienic practices in the production and distribution of food. Milk, for example, remains fresh for comparatively long periods if first treated with formalin and this practice was once prevalent. Formalin is an aqueous solution of formaldehyde; it is extremely toxic and is widely used for preserving zoological specimens. The addition of formalin, or any other preservative, to milk is now forbidden.

Preservatives which exert their antimicrobial effect by virtue of their acidity include sulphur dioxide—the commonest preservative at present in use—benzoic acid, propionic acid, sorbic acid and these have already been considered, together with methyl and propyl p-hydroxy benzoates, in Chapter 5.

Diphenyl   o-Phenylphenol

Diphenyl and *o—phenylphenol* are solids which suppress mould growth but because of their strong smells and tastes they are not suitable for general use as preservatives. The sodium salt of o-phenylphenol is used as a spray or dip for citrus fruits. Diphenyl is used to impregnate the wrapping papers used for fruit. Both compounds are of a low order of toxicity and if fruit is washed or peeled before it is eaten no danger of poisoning exists.

Sodium or *Potassium nitrite* and *nitrate* are used as preservatives for bacon, ham and some sausages and canned meats and certain cheeses. The preservative may be added as nitrite or a mixture of nitrate and nitrite, because nitrate is reduced to nitrite by the action of enzymes in bacteria. The nitrite so produced combines with the haemoglobin of the pig's blood and forms *nitrosomyoglobin*, a red compound which is responsible for the colour of uncooked cured pork. The colour develops more quickly if sodium nitrite is used instead of sodium nitrate and only about one-tenth as much nitrite is needed.

Thus the use of nitrite in food improves the colour of processed meats. However, it has a much more important function because nitrites have the remarkable property of inhibiting the growth of *Clostridium botulinum* which are responsible for a deadly form of food poisoning. Without the use of nitrite, foods such as salt beef and many canned meats—especially large cans where heat processing may have been less effective in killing the extremely heat-resistant *Cl. botulinum* spores— would become much more of a health hazard.

Unfortunately nitrites are extremely toxic, because in food they are party converted to form traces of *nitrosamines* which are powerful carcinogens. However, there is no evidence to suggest that the minute amounts of nitrite occurring in food as a result of its addition as a preservative causes cancer. The level of nitrite in food is at a level of 0·5 parts per billion or less.

The use of nitrites and nitrates in foods as preservatives is a subject of much debate and research. It highlights the dilemma of whether or not the use of such additives is justified. On balance—and considering their contribution in reducing health hazards by destroying *Cl. botulinum*—it would seem that their continued use is justified until the effects of the presence of minute amounts of nitrosomines in the body are known. In reviewing the use of nitrites and nitrates in food the Food Additives and Contaminants Committee (1978) recommend that the amount of nitrite permitted in a given food should be reduced to the *minimum* needed to inhibit the growth of *Cl. botulinum* in that food.

Even if nitrites and nitrates were no longer to be permitted as preservatives we should still consume small quantities. Nitrate is widely used as a fertiliser in agriculture and thus appears in water supplies and in vegetables. Thus if nitrates and nitrites in food are to be forbidden the use of nitrate fertilisers would also have to be restricted.

Current research indicates that the formation of nitrosomines in bacon can be inhibited by the presence of ascorbic acid. If this can be confirmed and extended to other meat products it may allow the nitrite problem to be resolved.

Antibiotics. Antibiotics are chemical substances produced by micro-organisms which are very efficient at destroying or inhibiting the growth of other micro-organisms. Penicillin and streptomycin are well-known examples of antibiotics which are used therapeutically. Several hundred other antibiotics are known but few of these have been used as food preservatives.

There are many objections to the use of antibiotics as preservatives for food. In the first place the common practice of feeding animals with food containing small amounts of antibiotics may lead to the development in the animal of strains of bacteria which are resistant to these antibiotics. Treatment of the carcasses of such animals with antibiotics may not be effective as a means of preservation. Again, infection of the carcasses by organisms from humans harbouring resistant strains is also possible. It is also conceivable that resistant strains of bacteria could develop in the consumers' intestines through prolonged consumption of small amounts of antibiotic. This could have unfortunate results if, at some later date, it became necessary to use the antibiotic therapeutically.

Nisin is the principal antibiotic permitted as a food preservative. It is produced by certain strains of the organism *Streptococcus lactis* and it occurs naturally in milk and Cheshire and Cheddar cheeses. Its presence makes these cheeses relatively immune to spoilage from gas-forming bacteria. These bacteria, which are mainly *Clostridia*, cause blow-holes and sometimes cracks to appear in the cheese. Nisin is effective against a very limited range of organisms. It is not effective against Gram-negative organisms, moulds or yeasts but only against certain species of Gram-positive organisms. For this reason it is not suitable as a general-purpose food preservative but is attractive a 'mopping-up' preservative for heat-processed foods such as canned foods, as heat-resistant spores are found only among the Gram-positive bacteria.

There are no 'medical' uses for nisin and there is no danger that if bacteria develop a resistance to it they will also be resistant to other antibiotics. Nisin is a polypeptide and when eaten it is digested and absorbed without ill-effect in the same way as other polypeptides.

Nisin is permitted as a preservative for cheese, clotted cream and canned foods. As it is harmless to man no maximum permitted quantity is specified. This would, in any case, be difficult because of the variable amounts which may be present through natural causes. The quantity of nisin required to prevent clostridial spoilage is about 2–3 ppm. Nisin prevents the development of bacterial spores; it does not kill them. Addition of nisin to canned foods will prevent spoilage such as flat sours and hydrogen swells (see p. 312) caused by bacterial spores which are not killed during heat-processing.

Apart from nisin, the only other antibiotic allowed for preserving food is *thiabendazole* which is used to control rot on the skins of bananas and citrus fruit.

Tetracyclines are antibiotics which have been used for preserving food. Very small amounts (5 ppm) have been added to the ice used to preserve fresh fish on trawlers though this is no longer permitted in the UK.

Tetracyclines have been used extensively in the USA and other countries for increasing the storage life of eviscerated poultry but this is not permitted in Great Britain. Such poultry is particularly prone to spoilage and it has been found that cooling the eviscerated carcasses in ice-water, containing about 10 ppm of oxytetracycline or chlortetracycline, inhibits bacterial growth. The amount of antibiotic in the treated poultry is of the order of 1–2 ppm. After cooking, however, the quantity remaining is too small to be detected in the flesh and reaches only about 0.4 ppm in the skin.

Antioxidants. The preservatives discussed above prevent or reduce attack by micro-organisms, but they do not prevent deterioration of food through atmospheric oxidation. Fatty foods and foods such as cakes and biscuits, which contain fat, are particularly prone to this type of spoilage and become rancid or 'tallowy' on keeping. The rancidity is caused by oxidation of the unsaturated fatty acid radicals in the triglycerides of which fat is composed. Oxidative changes are also responsible for loss of ascorbic acid and the development of brown colours in fruits and vegetables, especially those which have been cut, crushed or peeled. Loss of vitamin A, carotene, biotin and vitamin K is another consequence of oxidation.

Substances known as antioxidants which occur naturally in fats tend to prevent the oxidative changes which produce rancidity. Chief among these is vitamin E, which is found widely distributed in vegetable oil-bearing tissues and to a smaller extent in animal tissues. These natural antioxidants, however, are usually not present in sufficient amount completely to prevent oxidative changes which occur when food is stored.

In the Food Regulations an antioxidant is defined as any substance that is capable of delaying, retarding or preventing the development in food of rancidity or other flavour deterioration due to oxidation. For the purpose of the regulations certain substances are not regarded as antioxidants even though they exert an antioxidant effect. These include lecithin and permitted artificial sweeteners, bleaching agents, colouring matter, emulsifiers, stabilizers and preservatives.

The Antioxidant in Food Regulations, 1978, permit the use of the following in specified amounts in named foods; propyl, octyl or dodecyl gallate, butylated hydroxyanisole (BHA), butylated hydroxytoluence (BHT) ethoxyquin, diphenylamine, L-ascorbic acid (and its sodium and potassium salts), ascorbyl palmitate and various natural and synthetic tocopherols. The first three substances named are esters of gallic acid which is a phenolic acid. BHA and BHT are also derivatives of phenols and ethoxyquin is a dihydroquinoline derivative. Ethoxyquin and diphenylamine may only be used on apples and pears and it prevents the development of 'scald'. If such antioxidants were not allowed there would be considerable wastage of apples and pears due to mould growth during storage. Table 13.2 summarizes the main provisions of the Antioxidant in Food Regulations. In addition BHA and BHT may be used in permitted amounts in walnuts, vitamin A preparations and in chewing gum.

The small amounts of antioxidants permitted are sufficient to delay substantially the onset of rancidity. For example, the presence of 100 ppm of butylated hydroxyanisole in lard increases its storage life from a few months to two or three years.

Table 13.2. Antioxidants Permitted in Food

Specified food	Permitted antioxidants	Max. amount in mg per kg food
Edible oils and vitamin concentrates	Gallates, BHA, BHT or mixture	100 200
Emulsifiers or stabilisers	Gallates, BHA, BHT or mixture	100 200
Butter	Gallates, BHA, BHT or mixture	100 200
Essential oils	Gallates, BHA, BHT or mixture	1000 1000
Apples and pears	Ethoxyquin Diphenylamine	3 10
Potato, dried	BHA, BHT or mixture	20

DEHYDRATION. Micro-organisms require water in order to grow and reproduce; preservation by dehydration makes use of this fact. The water content of the food is reduced to below a certain critical value (which varies from food to food) and growth of micro-organisms becomes impossible.

Dehydration is a time-honoured method of preserving food; the sun-drying of fish and meat was practised as long ago as 2000 B.C. and dried vegetables have been sold for about a century and dried soups for much longer. A cake of 'portable soup' believed to have formed part of Captain Cook's provisions for his voyage round the world in 1772 is still in existence. It resembles a cake of glue and chemical analysis has shown that it has changed little in composition with the passage of years.

Dried fruits have been produced for many years by drying in the sun, but such unsophisticated techniques are not suitable for the dehydration of most other types of food. In modern practice many types of equipment are used for dehydrating food. Drying is usually accomplished by passing air of carefully regulated temperature and humidity over or through the food in tray driers, tunnel type driers or rotating drum driers. Heated vacuum driers are also used; the temperature necessary for dehydration under reduced pressure is much lower than would be required at ordinary pressures. In vacuum-drying the atmosphere above the food contains a much lower concentration of oxygen than in the normal methods of drying and this reduces the extent to which oxidative changes occur.

A modern development of vacuum-drying is *freeze-drying* in which *frozen* food is dried under high vacuum. It may seem surprising that frozen food can be dried at all but it is common knowledge that frozen puddles gradually 'dry-out' in winter time and that washing will dry slowly on a clothes line even though it is frozen stiff. This is an example of sublimation—the ice becomes converted to water vapour without passing through the liquid phase. Drying by this method is very slow at normal pressures but it can be speeded up tremendously by reducing the pressure at which the sublimation occurs and by supplying heat to provide the latent heat of sublimation of the ice. The rate of input of heat is carefully controlled so that the temperature of the food does not rise above the freezing point. Modern techniques, known as *Accelerated Freeze Drying* (AFD), which reduce the time required for drying are now used commercially.

Freeze-drying is particularly attractive for drying heat-sensitive foods. Dehydration occurs without discoloration and sensitive nutrients such as vitamins remain unharmed. In most methods of dehydration the food has to be sliced or minced to present the maximum possible surface area to the hot air current which carries away the moisture. Large pieces of food, such as complete steaks, can be freeze-dried, however, and this is a great advantage. As the ice at the surface of the food sublimes during freeze-drying the drying front recedes into the food until all the water has been abstracted. The highly porous product contains only a few per cent of water and it can be stored for long periods in moisture-proof packs at normal temperatures. Freeze-dried food can be rapidly re-hydrated, by adding cold water, and the product closely resembles the starting material.

Freeze-drying is a relatively slow process and one which requires expensive equipment; freeze-dried products are therefore more expensive than foods dried by more conventional means. Nevertheless their superior quality ensures that this technique will survive albeit on a fairly modest scale. A fairly wide range of freeze-dried foods is available commercially including coffee, vegetables and sea-foods such as prawns.

Before vegetables are dehydrated, whether by freeze-drying or other methods, they are scalded or 'blanched' by immersion in boiling water or by treatment with steam. This inactivates oxidative enzymes such as *catalase* and *ascorbic acid oxidase* and improves the stability of the dehydrated product. With coloured vegetables, blanching also improves the colour of the product. Some loss of water-soluble vitamins occurs during water-blanching but this can be minimized by allowing the concentration of water-soluble substances in the blanching water to build up. Sodium sulphite is usually added to the water used for blanching vegetables because this improves both the colour and ascorbic acid retention. In steam-blanching, vegetables may be treated with a sodium sulphite spray before steaming. Losses due to solution of water-soluble substances are much less with steam-blanching than with water-blanching. Blanching also destroys a large proportion of micro-organisms present. For example, the microbial count is reduced by a factor of 2000 for peas and over 40000 for potatoes.

It is not necessary to remove all the water from food in order to prevent the multiplication of micro-organisms. Bacteria will not multiply in food which is in equilibirum with (i.e. would neither lose water to, nor gain water from) air of less than 95 per cent relative humidity. Drier conditions are necessary to prevent the growth of yeasts and moulds but they will not grow on food which is in equilibrium with air of less than 75 per cent relative humidity. In practice, dehydrated food contains much less moisture than this. The actual moisture content varies from food to food but, except in the case of freeze-dried foods, is usually such that the food would be in equilibrium with an atmosphere of 30 per cent relative humidity. Freeze-dried foods contain practically no moisture.

Multiplication of micro-organisms should not occur in properly processed dehydrated food but they are not immune to other types of food-spoilage. Dehydrated foods containing fats are prone to develop rancidity after a period, particularly if the water content is reduced to too low a figure. This is true of potatoes but for non-fatty vegetables, such as cabbage, as much water as possible should be removed, because this helps to conserve ascorbic acid. The storage life of dehydrated food is much increased, and the loss of vitamin A and ascorbic acid much decreased, in the absence of oxygen. By completely filling the container with compressed dehydrated food the amount of oxygen can be reduced to a minimum. Replacement of the air in the container with nitrogen is far preferable: most dehydrated foods can be stored for two years or more in sealed tins in which the air has been replaced by nitrogen.

One of the great advantages of dehydrated foods is that they occupy very little space. Dehydrated potato in powder form, for example, has a volume only 10 per cent that of ordinary potatoes.

REFRIGERATION. Micro-organisms do not multiply nearly as rapidly at low temperatures as at normal temperatures. This is taken advantage of in the domestic refrigerator which is used for keeping foods for short periods. The temperature in such a refrigerator is usually about $5°C$, which is sufficient to chill the food and reduce the activity of micro-organisms but insufficient to give a long storage life. This is because micro-organisms are not killed and can still grow and reproduce but at a much slower rate. Moreover, enzyme action continues, albeit at a reduced rate, leading to chemical changes in the food and loss in quality.

Commercial refrigeration or chilling is applied to many foods including meat, eggs, fruit and vegetables. When meat is chilled the temperature is reduced to about $-1°C$ and depending upon its condition before chilling it will remain in good condition for up to a month.

For large-scale use, chilling can be advantageously combined with 'gas storage', that is, storage in an atmosphere which has been enriched in carbon dioxide. Microbes produce carbon dioxide by their own respiration and addition of this gas to the atmosphere surrounding them retards their growth. Chilled beef, for example, will keep for ten weeks in an atmosphere containing 10–15 per cent carbon dioxide. Higher concentrations of carbon dioxide would be even more effective, but they are not used because they cause the meat to become brown, owing to the conversion of the haemoglobin to *methaemoglobin.*

FREEZING. Although chilling to about $5°C$ enables food to be stored for short periods it must be frozen and stored at a low temperature if long term storage is required. Micro-organisms which are the main spoilage agents become inactive at about $-10°C$ while enzymes which cause chemical spoilage and consequent loss of quality are largely inactivated below $-18°C$. Domestic freezers store food at about $-18°C$ while commercially a temperature of $-29°C$ is employed to ensure high quality and a long storage life.

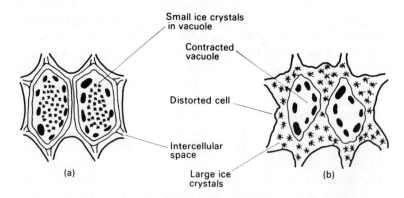

FIG. 13.1. Plant cells (*a*) after quick freezing (*b*) after slow freezing

Most fresh foods contain over 60 per cent water (see p. 219), some of which—known as *bound water*—is tightly attached to the constituent cells the rest—known as *available* or *freezable water*—being mobile. On average, plant cells contain 6 per cent bound water and animal cells 12 per cent. Available water does not freeze at $0°C$ because of the solids dissolved in it which lower the freezing point. For example, at $-5°C$ 64 per cent of the water in peas is frozen, at $-15°C$ 86 per cent is frozen while at $-30°C$ 92 per cent (virtually all the available water) is frozen.

The *rate* at which foods are frozen is important. Good quality is only obtained if freezing is quick, usually defined as meaning that the temperature at the thermal centre of the food pack should pass through the freezing zone $0°C$ to $-4°C$ within 30 minutes. It is within this temperature range that most of the available water is frozen and most heat (latent heat of freezing) must be removed.

The way that freezing rate affects quality can be appreciated from Fig. 13.1. Plant cells have relatively large vacuoles which contain most of the available water. During fast freezing tiny ice crystals are formed within the vacuoles and because they have little time to grow they do not distort the cellular structure. However if freezing is slow, crystals start to form in the inter-cellular spaces outside the cell walls and as they grow they draw water from within the cells leaving the cells dehydrated and distorted. Some ice crystals may also be formed within the vacuoles. The process in animal cells—which have smaller vacuoles and which contain less water—is broadly similar.

Commercial Freezing Methods. In *plate freezers*, which were the first to be developed, food is packed in trays which are inserted between plates cooled by a cold circulating liquid in a large cabinet. The food is in direct contact with the plate which cools by conduction. This method of freezing is particularly suited to flat products, such as fish fillets, fish fingers and beefburgers which are packed into shallow cartons before freezing. In *blast freezers* food is frozen by a blast of cold air either in a cabinet or in a tunnel. More recently fluidized bed freezers, in which the food to be frozen floats on a cushion of supercooled air as it travels through the freezer tunnel, have been developed. This latter method is used particularly for free flowing vegetables such as peas and gives very fast uniform freezing.

The most recent technique to be developed is *cryogenic freezing*. In this method a very cold liquid such as liquid nitrogen (boiling point $-196°C$) is used. If food is immersed in it, or sprayed with it, boiling occurs as the result of rapid heat transfer from the food to the nitrogen. Nearly instantaneous freezing occurs and the food retains its original shape and appearance. Although relatively expensive this technique is useful for high cost products where the highest quality is required. It has been used particularly for fruits such as strawberries and raspberries and frozen foods such as scampi, shrimps and salmon.

Nutritional Value. Although the total loss of nutritional value on freezing and subsequent storage is small, some losses do occur not so much during freezing as in the preliminary preparation of fruit and vegetables and during the storage of most food.

In good commercial practice there is little delay between harvesting vegetables and freezing—normally a matter of hours and for peas as little as 90 minutes—and consequently nutritional loss is insignificant. Vegetables, and some fruits such as apples, are blanched with boiling water or steam before freezing to destroy enzymes and some microorganisms. This causes some loss of water-soluble vitamins, mainly ascorbic acid and also, to a lesser extent, thiamine. In a series of experiments involving peas the loss of ascorbic acid in blanching was 25 per cent and the loss of the less soluble thiamine, 7 per cent. Loss of ascorbic acid in other vegetables varied from 5 per cent for asparagus to as much as 33 per cent for spinach. The actual loss will depend on the way blanching is carried out but, overall, blanching conserves ascorbic acid by reducing the final cooking time required and by inactivating ascorbic acid oxidase thus reducing loss of ascorbic acid on storage.

After freezing, foods are usually stored at $-18°$ C in home freezers or at $-29°$ C commercially. At these low temperatures there is a very slow and gradual loss of quality but little loss in nutritional value. Ascorbic acid is lost only very slowly on storage. For example, in one experiment the loss of ascorbic acid in peas stored for 3 months at $-18°$ C was found to be only 4 per cent. If the temperature rises above $-18°$ C food starts to deteriorate more rapidly. For example, although strawberries can be stored successfully at $-20°$ C for over a year, at $-10°$ C they show some flavour deterioration after a few months.

When many frozen foods are thawed there is some loss of liquid—known as *drip*—which causes loss of soluble nutrients from the food. The extent to which drip occurs depends on the rate at which freezing was carried out, the duration and temperature of storage and the cellular nature of the food. Plant material is more liable to drip than animal food because plant cells have larger vacuoles containing more available water (Fig. 13.1) and consequently suffer greater distortion on slow freezing. Fruit, particularly soft fruit such as strawberries, suffer extensive drip and consequent loss of vitamin C on thawing. (Thawing of vegetables also causes some loss of vitamin C and they are best cooked without thawing.) Soft fruits also suffer partial collapse of their cell structure on thawing, which makes them mushy. When meat is thawed there may be considerable loss of soluble nutrients, including protein and B vitamins. However, loss of nutrients in drip may be avoided if the drip from meat is incorporated in gravy and the liquid (often syrup) from fruit is consumed as is usually the case.

In conclusion it may be said that nutritional loss in food which has been properly frozen and stored is very small, and its nutritional value may well be superior to that of equivalent 'fresh' food which may well have suffered a delay of several days between harvesting and consumption.

Cook-freeze Catering. Not only has domestic consumption of frozen foods been increasing rapidly in recent years but the use of frozen foods in large-scale catering has also been developing rapidly. The principle of cook-freeze catering is that food is prepared and cooked on a large scale and immediately frozen so as to provide a large store of convenient packs. When required the food is rapidly reheated in convection ovens. Cook-freeze catering is being used in hospitals and schools and has proved that it can provide variety and good quality at relatively low cost

CANNING. Canning is by far the most important method of food preservation in terms of tonnage and variety of foods preserved. Canning developed from bottling and, in essence, both processes are the same. The principle of food preservation by canning is delightfully simple—the food is sealed in a can which is then heated to such a temperature that all harmful micro-organisms and sporing bacilli capable of growth during storage of the can at normal temperatures are killed. As no micro-organisms can gain access to the food while the can remains sealed decomposition does not occur.

Almost any type of food may be canned and its nature largely determines what pre-canning operations are carried out. It is first cleaned and inedible parts such as fruit stones, peel or bones are removed as far as possible. Fruit and vegetables may be subjected to a preliminary blanching before canning in order to soften them and enable a larger quantity to be pressed into the tin without damage. With vegetables, blanching also serves to remove air and causes a certain amount of shrinkage. The food is placed in the can and the can filled to within about half an inch of the top with liquor, which is usually sugar syrup in the case of fruits or brine in the case of vegetables. The lid is now placed loosely in position and the can and its contents are heated to about 95° C by hot water or steam. This process, known as 'exhausting', causes the air in the headspace of the can to expand and displaces air from the fruit or vegetable tissues. Exhausting also reduces strain on the can during subsequent heat-treatment. It also substantially reduces the amount of oxygen in the headspace and so minimizes internal corrosion of the can and oxidation of nutrients, particularly ascorbic acid, after sealing. The can is sealed when exhausting is complete and it is then ready for heat sterilization or 'processing' as it is called.

Most canned food is processed in batch-type cookers which are, to all intents and purposes, large-scale, steam heated versions of the domestic pressure cooker. The temperature of processing is controlled by adjusting the pressure at which the equipment operates.

A great deal of work has been carried out to determine the optimum conditions for processing canned foods. Over-processing has an adverse effect on quality and it is desirable to reduce the time and temperature of processing as much as possible. Processing conditions must be severe enough, however, to ensure that all harmful micro-organisms in the canned food are destroyed or inactivated. Bacterial spores are easily killed by heating in acid conditions, and the temperatures at which fruits are processed are not as high as those used for vegetables and meat.

Canned vegetables and meat are usually processed at $115°C$ whereas fruits may be processed in boiling water. The size of the can and the physical nature of the food it contains are other factors which influence the amount of heat processing needed because they both affect the rate of heat penetration. If a liquid is present heat is distributed to all parts of the can by convection currents. With solid foods, on the other hand, the rate of heat penetration is slower and the time of heating must be correspondingly greater. Processing times for non-solid foods can be reduced by up to two-thirds by agitating the contents of the can, as this assists heat penetration.

HTST Canning. By substantially increasing the temperature at which it is carried out it is possible to reduce considerably the duration of heat-processing, and in theory if very high temperatures could be used processing times could be very short indeed. In practice, however, the rate at which heat penetrates to the centre of the food in a can imposes a limitation on such high temperature short-time (HTST) processes and so they can only be used for processing food *before* canning. Sterilization is carried out at about $120°$ C in special equipment designed to achieve a high rate of heat transfer. The food is then cooled somewhat before sealing into cans which have been previously sterilized with superheated steam. This procedure, known as *aseptic canning*, can be used at present only for liquid or semi-solid foods where a high rate of heat-transfer to a thin film of the food is possible. The heating time varies from six seconds to about six minutes depending upon the type of food being canned.

An advantage of HTST processes is that as the food is cooked in thin layers there is less likelihood of some of it being *over*-processed to ensure that all of it is adequately processed. This, of course, is the situation with normal 'in-can' processing. Another advantage is that large cans, convenient for large-scale catering, can be used because there are no problems about heat penetration to the centre of the can.

Sterilizable Pouches. Another way of reducing processing time is to replace the rigid can by a flexible pouch. The food to be processed is packed in a thin laminated flexible container which can be heated in a modified canning retort. The container is a 3-ply pouch made up of a polyester outer film (to give resistance to puncturing and abrasion), aluminium foil in the middle (to give barrier protection) and a high density polythene inner film (to allow the container to be heat sealed). Such pouches have low volume and weight compared to cans because the container is wrapped round the product so eliminating the need to fill the container with liquid to aid heat penetration.

The time of heat processing for sterilizable pouches is only about one-third that required for cans and this improves the quality of the product which is good enough to compare with frozen and boil-in-the-bag products.

Pouches are normally protected by an outer carton and in this state have a shelf life of at least two years. At present such products are expensive compared with canned foods but a considerable variety—including vegetables, meat products and high quality sauces—are available.

Heat Resistance of Micro-organisms. The death of bacterial spores in heat-treated food follows a logarithmic course in which equal proportions of surviving cells die in each successive unit of time. Thus if 10 000 spores per unit volume were initially present and 9000 were killed by exposure to a particular temperature for one minute, 900 would be killed in the second minute, 90 in the third minute, 9 in the fourth minute and so on. One thousand times as many spores would be killed during the first minute's exposure as during the fourth.

The heat resistance of a particular micro-organism can be expressed in terms of its *thermal death time* (TDT) at a particular temperature. The TDT is the time required to achieve sterility in a culture or preparation of bacterial spores containing a known number of organisms in a specific medium. At a particular temperature the TDT of a given spore preparation depends upon the number of spores present. The relationship between TDT and temperature is logarithmic and when TDTs are plotted on a logarithmic scale against temperature on a linear scale a straight line results as shown in Fig. 13.2. A thermal death time curve is characterized by the TDT at some particular temperature, usually 121° C and the slope. The symbol F is used to designate the TDT at 121° C and z to designate the slope. The slope of the curve is defined as the temperature difference, in Fahrenheit degrees, required to produce a tenfold increase or decrease in TDT, i.e. for the TDT to traverse one log cycle. In Fig. 13.2, F is 2.78 minutes and z is 18.

Thermal death time curves can also be drawn for vegetative bacteria (as opposed to bacterial spores). The TDT of vegetative cells is almost zero at 121° C and so 65·5° C is used as the reference temperature for these organisms. To avoid confusion the TDT of vegetative cells is given the symbol F^1.

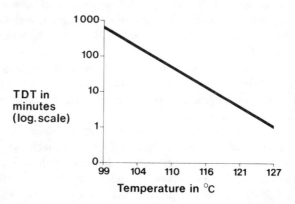

FIG. 13.2. Thermal death time curve for *Clostridium botulinum* spores

Thermal death times may be used to compare the heat resistance of organisms but it is also convenient to have some method of comparing the effectiveness of various heat processing *procedures*. This is done by adapting the concept of the TDT and using the symbol F to denote the *sterilizing value* or *lethality* of a process. The F value of a process is defined as the number of minutes at 121° C (assuming instantaneous heating and cooling at the beginning and end of the exposure) which will have a sterilizing effect equivalent to that of the process. If the sterilizing value is calculated on the basis of $z = 18$ the symbol F_0 is used. The symbol F^1 is used for the lethality of pasteurizing processes, the reference temperature in this case being 65·5° C.

Conditions drastic enough to kill the spores of the organism, *Clostridium botulinum*, which are heat-resistant above pH 4·5, and particularly dangerous (see p. 324) will also kill all other harmful organisms. The heat-resistance of these spores forms a standard of comparison against which the efficiency of a heat-treatment process can be judged. Fig. 13.2 is based upon the pioneer work of Esty and Meyer who showed that a preparation of *Clostridium botulinum* containing 6×10^{10} spores was killed by exposure to $121°$ C for 2.78 minutes. This figure has been approximated to 3 and used as the minimum sterilizing value acceptable for a safe process, i.e. an $F_0 = 3$ process. Such a process is referred to as a minimum safe process or, less formally, as a 'botulinum cook'. The spore preparation used by Esty and Meyer passed through twelve decimal reductions (i.e. reduced successively to one-tenth twelve times) before no spores were detected and hence a process with an F_0 value of 3 is sometimes referred to as a $12D$ process. The possibility of a spore of *Clostridium botulinum* surviving such process is less than 1 in 10^{12}. From this it is apparent that the risk of an outbreak of botulism occurring as a result of eating properly canned food is very small.

Although relatively small numbers of viable micro-organisms may remain in canned food they are unobjectionable and, in normal circumstances, will not cause spoilage. Spores are unable to develop in acid foods and the processing given to fruits is designed primarily to kill moulds, yeasts and non-sporing bacteria, the presence of bacterial spores being quite acceptable. In 'non-acid' foods only highly resistant thermophiles will survive the high processing temperatures and under normal storage conditions they will be unable to develop.

Addition of the antibiotic nisin to canned food prevents the development of bacterial spores and this is now a common practice. When nisin is used in canned food with a pH of more than 4·5 the heat processing given to the food must be sufficient to destroy the spores of *Clostridium botulinum* in the absence of nisin. This is a safeguard to prevent manufacturers of canned food cutting down the heat processing to such an extent that dangerous conditions could result if, for any reason, the nisin proved to be ineffective.

Canned food cannot really be said to be sterile but it is as sterile as it need be—a condition euphemistically described as 'commercial sterility'.

Nutritive Value of Canned Foods. Some nutrient loss occurs during heat processing and more thiamine may be lost from meat during processing than would be lost during normal cooking. Reduction in ascorbic acid content also occurs during processing but much more disappears during the first few weeks of storage as a result of oxidation by the small amount of oxygen remaining in the headspace of the can. Further destruction of thiamine may occur during storage but in normal conditions this should not exceed 10–15 per cent during two years' storage.

Apart from the losses of thiamine and ascorbic acid mentioned above canned foods are quite as good, from a nutritional point of view, as corresponding fresh foods. Indeed, canned fruits and vegetables may be better because they are often canned within a few hours of being picked and this reduces pre-canning losses of ascorbic acid to a minimum. The total loss of ascorbic acid in canned fruit and vegetables may be much less than in 'fresh' vegetables bought in a semi-fresh condition and cooked at home.

Spoilage of Canned Foods. Properly canned foods remain edible for very long periods if the cans are not corroded. In 1958 a number of cans which had been sealed for many years were examined. A tin of plum-pudding prepared in 1900 was opened and the contents were found to be in excellent condition. The meat in two cans sealed in 1823 and 1849 was found to be free from bacterial spoilage but the fat was partially hydrolysed into glycerol and fatty acids. The contents of a number of cans taken to the Antarctic by Shackleton in 1908 and Scott in 1910, and brought back to this country in 1958, were found, with some exceptions, to be in first-class condition.

When spoilage of canned foods occurs it is commonly caused by a defect in the can. Spoilage may also arise from inadequate heat treatment which is insufficient to kill all the micro-organisms present in the food. Certain heat-resisting bacterial spores produce acids when they germinate in foods and if this happens a *flat sour* results. No gas is produced and the spoilage is not evident until the can is opened and the unwholesome smell of the contents becomes evident. The organism particularly responsible for flat sours is *Bacillus stearothermophilus* the spores of which are able to survive exposure to 120° C for twenty minutes. Non-acid foods such as peas are most likely to be affected. The organism finds its way to the food via infected equipment or ingredients such as sugar or flour and spoilage of this type may be an indication of low standards of hygiene at the canning plant.

Another type of spoilage to which canned foods are prone is the *hydrogen swell* or *hard swell*. This is caused by heat-resisting bacteria such as *Clostridium thermosaccharolyticum* which produce hydrogen gas as they grow in the canned food. The ends of the can may bulge, as a result of increased pressure, to produce what is known as a blown can.

Sometimes improperly canned foods smell offensively of bad eggs and may be very dark in colour. This is an example of sulphide spoilage (or, in more descriptive American parlance, a sulphide stinker!) and is caused by the presence in the can of *Clostridium nigrificans*. This organism produces hydrogen sulphide gas which is responsible for the foul smell. Not enough gas is produced to cause distortion of the can. Spoilage of this type is not common in Great Britain.

The three types of spoilage organism mentioned above are not harmful but they make the canned food unfit to eat. The fact that these organisms have survived the heat-treatment process, however, indicates that the food has been inadequately heat-treated and there is the possibility that more harmful organisms such as *Clostridium botulinum* may also be present. Spoiled canned food should never be eaten. The antibiotic nisin, which has a powerful sporostatic effect, is particularly effective against heat-resistant spores and food treated with nisin before canning should not be subject to the three types of spoilage discussed above.

Canned foods should be stored in dry, fairly cool conditions because storage at higher temperature will encourage the growth of any thermophiles which may have survived heat processing. Cans stored in damp conditions may become rusty and, in time, the can may be penetrated and spoilage of the contents may occur.

HEAT TREATMENT OF MILK. Milk is such a rich source of nutrients that it is an ideal medium for the growth of micro-organisms. Although milk should be practically free of bacteria at the time it is obtained from a clean and healthy cow, it is almost impossible to maintain it in this condition. Bacteria from the milk container, from the milker or milking machine and from the air pass into the milk, where they find congenial conditions in which to flourish. In addition to this, unhealthy cows contribute disease-bearing bacteria to the milk, the most dangerous of which is the *tubercle bacillus*. In the past this micro-organism has caused thousands of deaths annually in both cattle and humans. In Britain in 1931 two thousand people died from tuberculosis contracted from milk. Other organisms such as *Brucella abortus*, which causes the disease referred to as undulant fever, and *Streptococcus pyogenes*, which causes sore throats and scarlet fever, may also pass from infected cows to man via untreated milk.

Most milk in Great Britain is now heat-treated to ensure that harmful organisms are destroyed before it is consumed. As well as preventing the spread of disease, heat-treatment of milk also considerably improves its keeping properties since lactic bacilli which cause milk to become sour are also killed.

Pasteurization of milk is carried out in Britain in one of two ways. In the *holder process* the milk is heated until the temperature reaches 65 to 68° C. This temperature is held for thirty minutes and the milk is then cooled rapidly. This method is now nearly obsolete, however, having been superseded in most dairies by the *high temperature, short time* (HTST) or *flash* method. In this method milk is heated to at least 72° C for not less than fifteen seconds, after which it is rapidly cooled. Both treatments are effective in killing at least 99 per cent of the bacteria and although the product is not completely sterile all harmful organisms are destroyed. The organisms which are not killed, together with any heat-resistant bacterial spores, are inactivated by the rapid cooling which follows pasteurization.

The temperatures used in pasteurization are not high enough to cause any significant physical or chemical changes in the milk, so that there is no noticeable change in palatability due to pasteurization. In some cases pasteurized milk has a flavour different from that of fresh milk but this is due to faulty pasteurization; either the milk has been heated to a temperature higher than normal or the process has been carried out in unsuitable equipment and the milk has thereby become tainted.

Pasteurization causes some slight decrease in nutritional value but unless the recommended temperature and time of pasteurization are exceeded only ascorbic acid and thiamine are appreciably affected, some 10–20 per cent of each being lost. Milk is not an important source of these vitamins, however, and even if this loss did not occur, it would only supply a small proportion of the body's needs. In addition, ascorbic acid is destroyed by storage in direct light, especially sun light, so that even non-pasteurized milk is a doubtful source of this vitamin.

Sterilized milk is milk that has been homogenized, filtered and subjected to heat treatment so that it will remain fit for human consumption for at least a week and usually much longer.

The object of homogenization is to break up the oil globules so that they will remain uniformly distributed through the milk and not form a layer at the surface. This is achieved by heating the milk to 65° C and forcing it through a small aperture under high pressure. This breaks up the oil droplets and the fine emulsion so formed is stabilized by protein which is adsorbed at the surface of the oil droplets. Although such milk is said to be homogenized it is not homogeneous in the scientific sense, for by definition an emulsion must contain two separate phases. After homogenization the milk is filtered, sealed into narrow-necked bottles and heated to at least 100° C and maintained at this temperature for up to an hour. In practice higher temperatures and shorter heating times are used, a typical example being 112° C for fifteen minutes.

Ultra-high temperature (UHT) sterilization of milk is carried out before the milk is bottled. The milk is first homogenized and it is then heated to 135–150° C for one to three seconds by flowing over a heated surface. A completely sterile product is thus obtained which after cooling is packed in sterile containers.

Sterilization by traditional methods causes a change in the flavour and physical composition of the milk and also causes a slight decrease in nutritional value owing to loss of vitamins. Lactalbumin and lacto-globulin are coagulated, some calcium phosphate is precipitated and about 30 per cent thiamine and 50 per cent ascorbic acid are destroyed. Milk sterilized by the UHT process resembles pasteurized milk much more closely, both in flavour and vitamin retention. The main virtues of sterilized milk are that its cream content is uniformly distributed, it is safe and it can be kept for considerable periods.

Preserved Forms of Milk. Milk is a valuable food but, as we have already seen, it is perishable and even after pasteurizing needs rapid distribution and careful handling. It is also bulky and expensive to transport. For these reasons, and also because seasonal surpluses of milk occur, effective methods of preserving milk in concentrated form are most desirable. Milk may be concentrated by removing a proportion of its water and it may be rendered safe by suitable heat treatment. The water is removed by evaporation, this being carried out in closed vacuum pans under reduced pressure. The temperature is kept below 70° C so that the proteins are not coagulated and the production of a cooked flavour is avoided. Evaporated milk, also called unsweetened condensed milk in Britain, is pasteurized milk which after evaporation is homogenized and then sterilized in sealed cans. Condensed sweetened milk is made in a similar way, except that sugar is added and homogenization omitted. After evaporation further heat treatment is not necessary, because of the preservative action of the sugar.

Evaporated milk still contains about 68 per cent water and a much greater proportion of the water in fresh milk may be removed by drying it. Whole milk may be dried by passing a film of it between heated rollers and scraping off the powder which results. The product has a distinct 'cooked' flavour, however, and is only about 80 per cent soluble in water. Roller dried milk is widely used for feeding babies but, strange as it may seem, is not acceptable for other purposes.

A superior form of dried milk may be produced by spray-drying. In this process the milk is first concentrated under vacuum at a low temperature and it is then dried by spraying it in the form of minute droplets into a current of hot air. The product is almost 100 per cent soluble in water and is nutritionally only slightly inferior to pasteurized milk. Dried full cream milk can be stored for fairly long periods but develops a tallowy taste after being stored for 9 to 24 months, owing to oxidative changes. Such changes can be prevented by packing the dried milk in sealed containers from which the air has been replaced by nitrogen. Properly stored spray-dried milk does not deteriorate as a result of the growth of micro-organisms. In fact, very few survive the spray-drying process and those that do gradually die.

Although spray-dried milk is completely soluble in water it is not easily wetted by water and this causes difficulty in reconstituting it in such a way that no lumps form. 'Instant' milk powders which can be reconstituted with ease are made from spray-dried skim milk by rewetting the particles in warm moist air and allowing them to clump together into porous spongy aggregates which are subsequently redried.

FOOD PRESERVATION BY IRRADIATION. It has been known for over sixty years that X-rays can kill micro-organisms but it is only comparatively recently that use has been made of ionizing radiations for the preservation of foods. Two types of radiation may be employed. The first is the high-energy electron beam produced by a linear accelerator or a cyclotron. Electrons, as we have already seen (Chapter 4) carry a negative charge and advantage can be taken of this in a cyclotron or linear accelerator which accelerates them to very high speeds. The other type of radiation used in preserving food processing are γ-rays which are electromagnetic radiation produced during the decay of certain radioactive isotopes, e.g. cobalt-60 or caesium-137. The cobalt isotope can be produced quite cheaply by irradiating cobalt metal in the type of reactor used in nuclear power stations. Caesium-137 is present as a fission product in the fuel elements used in nuclear reactors and hence is readily available.

Radiation of both types is effective in killing micro-organisms but there are certain important differences between them. An electron beam has limited penetrative powers, and electrons accelerated to an energy of 3 million electron volts will only penetrate about half an inch into a foodstuff. In this respect electrons are inferior to γ-rays which, being uncharged, can penetrate foodstuffs to a much greater depth. Radiation is obtainable from accelerators at a greater rate than from radioisotopes but accelerators are complex and highly expensive whereas γ-emitting radioisotopes are readily available. Indeed, caesium-137, an inevitable by-product of the nuclear power industry, has few other uses.

The unit of radiation dose is the *rad*, which is equivalent to the absorption of energy at the rate of 10^{-5} J per gram of the substance irradiated. Doses used in processing foods are of the order of thousands of rads (1000 rads = 1 kilorad or krad) or millions of rads (1 000 000 rad = 1 megarad or Mrad).

Three types of radiation treatment of food may be distinguished. If all (or practically all) the micro-organisms in a food are killed by irradiation the process is called *radappertization*. This rather bizarre term incorporates the name of the Frenchman, Appert, who unwittingly discovered that food could be sterilized by heat and invented the process of canning. The terms *radurization* and *radicidation* are used to describe a lower level of irradiation. Irradiation which destroys sufficient micro-organisms to extend substantially the storage life of a food—comparable in many ways to pasteurization—is called radurization. If radiation treatment is designed to eliminate a specific harmful organism—such as salmonellae—the term radicidation is employed.

As well as being effective in killing micro-organisms, ionizing radiations also disturb certain physiological processes and a fairly low dose is sufficient to inhibit sprouting in stored potatoes. Insects succumb easily to radiation and by irradiating cereal grains before storage it is possible to eliminate losses through consumption by insects almost completely. Parasites in meat, such as the larvae of *Trichina spiralis*, which causes the disease trichinosis in man, can also be killed by a fairly low radiation dose. Radappertization of food, in which micro-organisms are more-or-less completely destroyed and a degree of sterility equivalent to that of canned food is produced, requires large radiation doses. To achieve a 10^{12} reduction in *Clostridium botulinum* spores (i.e. a 12D process—see p. 311) a radiation dose of about 4·8 Mrad is required. Table 13.3 gives a rough idea of the radiation doses required for various process.

Ionizing radiations are harmful to man and radioactive isotopes emitting them have to be heavily shielded with lead. A lethal dose for man is about 0·7 krad—much less than the doses used for food perservation purposes listed in Table 13.3.

Table 13.3. Irradiation of Foods

Food	Purpose	Dose level (krad)
Potatoes	Inhibition of sprouting	5–10
Meat	Destruction of parasites	10
Wheat	Disinfestation	20
Oranges	Destruction of surface moulds and yeasts	75–200
Fish	Radurization	300
Meat	Destruction of *Salmonellae*	650
Meat	Radappertization	4800

Irradiation does not destroy the nutrients present in food to any extent except that the effect upon vitamins is comparable to that of cooking. Food does not become significantly radioactive when it is irradiated, providing that the energy of the radiation used is less than 5 million electron volts. The energy of the radiation from cobalt-60, which is the isotope most likely to be used, is only about one quarter of this and so no danger is likely to arise. At high dose rates food may acquire an unusual flavour because as well as killing micro-organisms radiation causes chemical reactions to occur in the food. The products of these reactions are not only objectionable from the point of view of flavour but it is also possible that they may be harmful, particularly if eaten consistently over a long period. There is no evidence to indicate that this is so, however, and in over twenty years of tests on irradiated foods no toxic effects have been observed. Nevertheless, irradiation of food intended for human consumption is not at present permitted in Great Britain. In the USA it may be used for sterilizing bacon, for disinfestation of wheat and wheat products, for inhibiting the sprouting of stored potatoes and for the inhibition of surface and subsurface organisms on oranges.

FOOD POISONING

Food poisoning occurs when foods containing poisons of chemical or biological origin are eaten. The characteristic symptoms are abdominal pain and diarrhoea, usually accompanied by vomiting, which follow some one to thirty-six hours after eating such food will be familiar to most readers from personal experience. The poisonous nature of some plants is well known—poisonous berries and certain species of mushrooms and toadstools spring immediately to mind—but poisonous fish and shellfish are also known and even the humble rhubarb plant has poisonous leaves. Foods may also be poisonous as a result of contamination from inappropriate packaging materials or equipment used during processing. For example, if acid foods are mixed in galvanized iron vessels zinc may be taken up by the food in harmful quantities. Similarly, low-quality vitreous enamel vessels may be a source of antimony in acid foods. By far the most common cause of food poisoning, however, is the presence in food of harmful bacteria or poisonous substances produced by them. This is what is generally meant by the term 'food poisoning' and in what follows the term will be used in this sense.

An outbreak of food poisoning may be caused by food which appears to be quite wholesome in spite of the fact that it is heavily infected by bacteria. In fact, food which has obviously 'gone off' or 'gone bad' is unlikely to be eaten and hence will not give rise to food poisoning. Most food poisoning incidents occur as a result of unhygienic practices and this means that they are preventable.

Harmful bacteria, or *pathogens* as they are called, find their way into food in a number of ways. Animal foods may be infected at source, i.e. they may come from animals which are themselves hosts to food poisoning bacteria. Man is another potent source of food poisoning organisms, which are transferred easily from the mouth, nose and bowel to food. Pathogens can be 'carried' and passed on to others by individuals who are themselves not ill. Such carriers may have recently suffered an attack of food poisoning and still be harbouring the organisms in their body. In some instances carriers of food poisoning organisms act as 'hosts' over a period of many years having themselves acquired an immunity to the organism concerned. More often than not they are unaware of their role as reservoirs of infection. Animals may also harbour food poisoning organisms and pass them on to human beings via food with which they come into contact. Rats, mice, cockroaches and domestic pets can all be instrumental in transmitting food poisoning in this way.

Types of Bacterial Food Poisoning

TOXIC FOOD POISONING. Some bacteria produce toxins or poison outside the bacterial cell when they are growing and multiplying in food; such toxins are known as *exotoxins*. The exotoxins are not living cells; they are poisonous chemicals. The incubation period—that is the period of time between the entry of the poison into the body and the appearance of the first symptoms—is normally short with toxic food poisoning. The toxins produce irritation of the stomach and vomiting occurs, often within two hours of eating the food. Abdominal pain and diarrhoea normally follow.

Toxins are less easily destroyed than the bacteria from which they come. Thus if food is only heated sufficiently to kill the bacteria the exotoxins may survive and would still cause food poisoning when the food was eaten. Food poisoning bacteria are killed in 1–2 minutes in boiling water, whereas exotoxins may take up to 30 minutes to be destroyed.

INFECTIVE FOOD POISONING. This type of food poisoning is caused by the bacteria themselves. As they grow and multiply in food they produce poisonous substances within the bacterial cell; such substances are known as *endotoxins* and they cannot be released from the cells in which they are formed until the bacteria die. When food containing this type of bacteria is eaten no ill effects, are experienced until sufficient bacteria have died to produce enough endotoxins to cause symptoms to appear. Thus the incubation period is normally longer— at least 12 hours—with infective food poisoning than with toxic food poisoning. The symptoms are fever, headache, diarrhoea and vomiting.

In order to prevent infective food poisoning it is enough to heat the food sufficiently to kill the pathogenic bacteria as this will also destroy the endotoxins which they contain.

INTESTINAL FOOD POISONING. Certain types of bacteria cause food poisoning in a particular way. The bacteria produce toxins only when they are multiplying in the intestinal tract; such bacteria do not produce toxins, therefore, in the food itself. The incubation period is 8–24 hours and the main symptoms are abdominal pain and diarrhoea.

Table 13.4. Types of Food Poisoning and their Cause

Type of food poisoning	Organisms involved
Toxic	Staphylococci *Clostridium botulinum* *Bacillus cereus*
Infective	Salmonellae
Toxin in intestine	*Clostridium perfringens*

Bacteria Causing Food Poisoning

The types of pathogenic bacteria which most commonly cause food poisoning in the UK are Salmonella, Staphylococcus and Clostridium perfringens. Food poisoning due to *Bacillus cereus* is fairly common, mainly in connection with rice, whereas food poisoning caused by *Clostridium botulinum,* though frequently fatal is fortunately extremely rare.

Certain other groups of bacteria are also known to cause food poisoning, though they are relatively unimportant in the UK *Esherichia coli,* for example, normally occurs in the intestines of both man and animals, but certain pathogenic strains ingested in food may cause food poisoning, the symptoms being similar to those of salmonella food poisoning. Such food poisoning, like that of Salmonella, is infective in nature with an incubation period of 4–36 hours.

Vibrio parahaemolyticus, though not an important source of food poisoning in the UK, causes at least half the food poisoning incidents in Japan. The organisms, which produce infective food poisoning, are found in fish, shell-fish and other sea-foods and also in coastal sea-water. The average incubation period is about 15 hours and the symptoms include diarrhoea, vomiting and fever.

Table 13.5. Bacterial Food Poisoning

Organisms involved	Foods commonly affected	Illness		
		Incubation period	Duration	Main symptoms
Salmonellae	Meat, especially sliced cooked meat and meat pies. Duck eggs. Synthetic cream. Ice-cream. Shellfish.	12–36 hours	1–8 days	Abdominal pain, diarrhoea, vomiting, fever
Clostridium perfringens	Gravy, stews, pre-cooked meat.	8–22 hours	12–24 hours	Abdominal pain and diarrhoea
Staphylococci	Pies, meat, especially sliced meats, pies and gravy. Synthetic cream. Ice-cream.	2–6 hours	6–24 hours	Vomiting, abdominal pain diarrhoea
Clostridium botulinum	Inadequately processed canned meat, vegetables and fish.	24–72 hours	Death within a week or slow recovery	Double vision, headache constipation paralysis
Bacillus cereus	Rice, cornflour, meat products	2–15 hours	6–24 hours	Vomiting, abdominal pains diarrhoea

The characteristics of the main types of food poisoning are summarized in Table 13.5.

SALMONELLA. Food poisoning caused by the salmonella group of organisms is infective food poisoning and is referred to as salmonellosis. There are approximately 700 different types of salmonellae many of which take their names from the places where they were first observed. Examples are *Salmonella typhimurium*, *Salmonella dublin*, *Salmonella saint-paul* and *Salmonella heidelberg*. Salmonellae can survive outside the body for long periods and in warm moist conditions multiply rapidly on foods. The source of infection is usually human or animal excreta. Illness only occurs if large numbers of salmonellae are ingested and it is therefore prudent to keep food in such conditions that salmonellae, if present, will not multiply. By keeping food below 4°C multiplication of salmonellae on foods can be prevented. Meat which has been cooked and is not to be eaten at once should be cooled quickly so that the temperature zone in which salmonellae multiply rapidly is passed through as quickly as possible.

The organism *Salmonella typhimurium* is the chief cause of food poisoning in Great Britain. The foods most often infected are meat (particularly processed meats such as pies and brawn), eggs and egg-products, custard cakes, trifles and artificial cream. Farmyard and domestic animals often act as carriers of *Salmonella typhimurium* and ducks' eggs are one of the classic sources of infection from this organism. Such eggs may be infected inside the duck before the egg is laid or a non-infected egg may be contaminated through contact with infected duck excreta. Ducks' eggs should always be thoroughly cooked to ensure that any salmonellae present are destroyed. Hens' eggs are less frequently infected with salmonellae but bulk liquid hens' eggs may become infected through the inclusion of one infected egg or by contamination from a dirty shell. For this reason no unpasteurized liquid or frozen whole egg may be used in the preparation of food in Great Britain (The Liquid Egg Regulations, 1963). Dried egg may be infected with salmonella (spray-drying does not kill it) and for this reason it should be used as soon as it is reconstituted and must be well cooked.

Rats and mice may be carriers of *Salmonella typhimurium* and are a common source of infection especially where it is possible for their excreta to come into contact with food. Domestic animals may also excrete salmonella without exihibiting symptoms of food poisoning. Horse meat or kangaroo meat imported into Great Britian for use as pet food is commonly heavily contaminated with salmonellae and if such uncooked infected meat is fed to cats or dogs the probability is that they, too, will become infected and act as a reservoir of food poisoning organisms. This is one good reason for excluding dogs from food shops.

Meat is often infected by salmonella and as a result meat products, particularly if they are made from meat 'trimmings' and scraps from the outside of meat carcasses, may be heavily contaminated. If manufactured meat products are thoroughly cooked, however, any salmonellae present will be destroyed and if precautions are taken to prevent re-infection such products should be safe to eat. Fish and poultry are often contaminated with salmonellae and there is a particular danger of food poisoning where frozen poultry are only partly thawed before cooking, especially if they are undercooked. Salmonellae are easily killed and provided that cooking is thorough so that the temperature at the centre of the food is high enough (i.e. at least 60°C) all such bacteria will be destroyed.

CLOSTRIDIUM PERFRINGENS. This organism is found in the soil, in human and animal intestines and in excreta. The spores of the organism are fairly heat-resistant and are not destroyed during cooking unless a temperature of 110°C is reached. After cooking, the spores may germinate and multiply rapidly in the food while it is cooling. *Clostridium perfringens* can grow at temperatures of up to 50°C and as it is an anaerobe it grows in the absence of oxygen—just the conditions likely to be found at the centre of a slowly cooling piece of meat or at the bottom of a stewpot! When the food is later eaten the organism multiplies in the intestine where the bacterial cells and the toxin they produce cause food poisoning. Food poisoning from *Clostridium perfringens* often occurs in canteens and other large-scale catering establishments where meat is cooked some time before it is required, is allowed to cool, and is then re-heated before serving. Large pieces of meat used in catering establishments are often tightly tied into rolls before cooking. As a result contaminated outer surfaces may be transferred to the interior of the piece of meat where the temperature is insufficient to kill the spores of *Clostridium perfringens*.

Clostridium perfringens does not grow below 10°C and if cooked meat cannot be eaten at once it should be quickly cooled and held below this temperature. Similarly, meat and meat dishes which have to be re-heated before consumption should be *heated* and not warmed. The Food Hygiene (General) Regulations, 1970, which lays down minimum standards of hygiene for food premises in Great Britain, requires that foods liable to transmit disease which are brought into a catering premises shall be brought to a temperature of at least 63°C or below 10°C without delay and held at this temperature until required for consumption.

STAPHYLOCOCCUS. Food poisoning produced by this type of organism is toxic in nature being caused by toxins produced by the bacteria in the food before it is eaten. The main organism responsible for staphylococcal food poisoning is known as *Staphylococcus aureus*. Staphylococci are found in the human nose and throat and on the skin and 50–60 per cent of normal people carry staphylococci in their noses or throats. They are also present in abundance in whitlows, infected burns and wounds and in nasal secretions following colds. Staphylococci find their way into foods via the hands of infected persons.

Staphylococci can be fairly easily killed by heating food but the toxin is more heat-resistant and is only completely destroyed by boiling for at least thirty minutes. Staphylococcal food poisoning is usually caused by eating cream-filled cakes, custard cakes or processed meats which have been cooked and then heated through before being eaten. This allows the food to become contaminated by the food handler after it is been cooked. Subsequent warming through is then insufficient to destroy the toxin. Staphylococci are able to grow in higher concentrations of salt than other food poisoning bacteria with the result that they are often responsible for food poisoning involving salty foods, (especially meat) such as ham and bacon.

CLOSTRIDIUM BOTULINUM. Food poisoning from *Clostridium botulinum*—known as botulism—is extremely serious. This organism produces a toxin which is the most virulent poison known, one gramme of which would be sufficient to kill 100 000 people. The mortality rate from botulism is about 65 per cent but fortunately poisoning of this type is rare in Great Britain. *Clostridium botulinum* occurs in the soil and on vegetables which have been in contact with contaminated soil. It is also found in fish and the intestines of pigs and certain other animals. Like *Clostridium perfringens* it is a sporeforming anaerobe.

The spores of *Clostridium botulinum* are extremely heat-resistant and may survive in canned or bottled foods which have been inadequately heat-treated. As the organism is anaerobic it may develop within the can if the pH is above 4·5 (see p. 311), with drastic consequences when the food is eaten. Indeed, the majority of cases of botulism are caused by improperly canned contaminated meats, vegetables or fish. Commercial canners are well aware of the dangers of botulism and ensure that canned foods with a pH above 4·5 are heat-processed sufficiently to destroy all *Clostridium botulinum* spores. If non-acid foods are bottled or canned at home, however, insufficient heat-processing may inadvertently be given and *Clostridium botulinum* spores may survive. For this reason bottling or canning of non-acid foods by amateurs is not advisable.

BACILLUS CEREUS. Like the Clostridia bacteria *Bacillus cereus* can form spores where conditions for growth are unfavourable but unlike them it is an aerobe and so requires air for growth. The spores of *Bacillus cereus* are often found in cereals, especially in rice, cornflour and spices. The spores of *Bacillus cereus* can survive light cooking and if the cooked food is cooled slowly or kept warm for a considerable time the spores germinate producing vegetative bacteria which multiply rapidly in the presence of air producing toxin in the food.

In order to prevent food poisoning from *Bacillus cereus* cooked food should be cooled rapidly and stored in a refrigerator. If the food is reheated, this should be done rapidly and thoroughly and the food eaten without delay. The incubation period and symptoms of food poisoning due to *Bacillus cereus* are given in Table 13.5.

Food Hygiene

Everyone engaged in the preparation and handling of food should have high standards of personal hygiene and a basic knowledge of the principles of food hygiene. Food should be handled in such a way that infection is unlikely to occur and stored in conditions unfavourable to the multiplication of food poisoning organisms. Persons habitually handling food should undergo regular medical inspections to confirm that they are free from infection. Meat and manufactured meat products are the greatest causes of food poisoning in Great Britain and particular care should be taken whenever meat is handled. Animals should be slaughtered under the most hygienic conditions practicable and the meat produced should be carefully prepared and stored so that when it is ready to be cooked the bacterial count is as low as possible.

Persons handling food in domestic kitchens are just as likely to infect it as workers in less homely surroundings and personal cleanliness is of great importance. It cannot be stressed too highly that hands should always be *thoroughly* washed after using the toilet and a *clean* towel should be used for drying them. Dirty towels can be sources of infection and can re-infect hands which have been carefully washed. The nose and mouth are other sources of infective organisms, and coughing or sneezing can infect food with staphylococci up to a distance of twenty feet. Soiled handkerchiefs and infected wounds are other potent sources of infection. Smoking is not permitted where food is handled because bacteria from the mouth may be conveyed to food via the hands in this way. For the same reason cleansing fingers of adherent food particles by licking them is most unhygienic. Food should not be kept in open vessels or plates but should be covered to prevent access of air-borne bacteria, or bacteria expelled by coughing or sneezing.

Cooking can destroy food-poisoning organisms or, as we have already seen, it can provide ideal conditions for their multiplication. If it is borne in mind that bacteria are destroyed by high temperatures and multiply only slowly at low temperatures it should be obvious that food should be either *hot* or *cold*. Food which is slightly infected by food poisoning organisms may be tolerated or, at most, may cause a mild stomach upset. If such food is warmed and kept warm for any length of time, however, or if it is allowed to cool slowly the consequences of eating it are likely to be far more serious.

The Incidence of Food Poisoning

Food poisoning bacteria were described as long ago as 1888 and during the next 60 years the main types of bacteria causing food poisoning were identified. Since the Second World War there has been a notable increase in recorded incidents of food poisoning and this has occurred in spite of an increased understanding and awareness of the causes of food poisoning and considerably improved standards of living and of hygiene.

During the 1960's between four and five thousand cases of food poisoning were notified yearly in English and Wales, though the actual numbers of cases were certainly considerably higher as milder cases are often not reported. During the 1970's there was a gradual rise in reported cases of food poisoning. For example, between 1972 and 1976 the number of cases *doubled* from six to twelve thousand.

There are many reasons for the increase in food poisoning in the UK over recent years, but some of the more important are as follows:

1 *A great increase in communal feeding.* Large scale catering whether in hospitals, schools, canteens, or restaurants means that a single infected food can produce many cases of food poisoning.

2 *Varied menus and rapid food service.* In order to have a wide menu and be able to produce dishes quickly food may be pre-cooked and kept warm until it is required or it may be reheated rapidly and perhaps inadequately in a microwave oven or under an infra-red grill when it is ordered.

3 *Increase in the use of convenience foods.* Although factory processes are carefully controlled and carried out under hygienic conditions, one source of infection can lead to the contamination of thousands of pre-packed items. In addition the use of convenience foods, especially meat products, which are eaten cold or only warmed through increases the risk of food poisoning.

4 *Increase in factory farming.* The intensive rearing of poultry and animals increases the possibility of large scale infection of such food supplies, especially of Salmonella.

5 *Rapid increase in consumption of take-away meals.* Such food may be kept warm for long periods or briefly reheated in the home thus

allowing rapid bacterial growth. For example, 'take-away' rice may be a source of *Bacillus cereus.*

6 *Changing patterns of shopping and food storage in the home.* A weekly rather than a daily shopping routine means that food has to be stored for greater periods of time. Incorrect storage can lead to increased growth of bacteria. Increasing use of freezers means that meat, especially poultry, needs to be thawed before it is cooked. Incomplete thawing followed by normal cooking may not kill all bacteria, especially Salmonellae, in the centre of the food.

7 *Increased use of packed meals.* The incidence of food poisoning is much higher in summer than in winter largely because of inadequate cold storage. The increasing tendency to have a packed meal, often including cooked meat in sandwiches, in the middle of the day increases the risk of food poisoning in summer.

8 *Use of staff untrained in hygiene in catering establishments.* Large scale handling of food by staff not trained or conscious of hygiene requirements is a major source of infection. In such circumstances *cross-contamination,* that is the transfer of bacteria from a contaminated source to an uncontaminated source, can easily occur and spread the risk of infection.

In the UK Salmonellae are responsible for most food poisoning, and account for 70–80 per cent of all cases. *Clostridium perfringens* is next in importance accounting for 15–25 per cent. Outbreaks of food poisoning due to this cause are often due to foods having been prepared in bulk and hence tend to be on a large scale.

The foods most commonly causing food poisoning in the UK are meat and poultry which together account for at least 80 per cent of all cases. *Clostridium perfringens* is mainly concerned with infected meat and poultry which is reheated while Salmonellae are mainly concerned with cold and fresh meat and poultry. Staphylococci on the other hand cause infection in salty meats such as ham and bacon.

Meat and poultry are examples of foods which have a high protein and moisture content. This combination is particularly conducive to bacterial growth and explains why other foods, such as eggs, milk and 'made-up' products containing them, are also causes of food poisoning.

SUGGESTIONS FOR FURTHER READING

ALCOCK, P. A. *Food Hygiene Manual.* H. K. Lewis, 1981

ATOMIC ENERGY COMMISSION. *Food Preservation by Irradiation.* US Atomic Energy Commission, 1968.

BRITISH ASSOCIATION. *Salmonella, the Food Poisoner* (A review). British Association, 1978.

COOK, D. J. and BINSTEAD. R. *Food Processing Hygiene.* Food Trade Press, 1975.

HERSOM, A. C. and HULLAND, E. D. *Canned Foods: Thermal Processing and Microbiology,* 7th edition. Churchill, 1980.

HOBBS, B. C. *Food Poisoning and Food Hygiene,* 7th edition. Edward Arnold, 1978.

LEACH. M. (Ed). *Freezer Facts.* Forbes Publications, 1975.

MINISTRY OF AGRICULTURE, FISHERIES AND FOOD. *Refrigerated Storage of Fruit and Vegetables.* HMSO, 1979.

MOORE, E. *Food Preservation.* Unilever Booklet, 1969.
An elementary but well-presented review.

NICKERSON, J. T. R. and SINSKEY, A. J. *Microbiology of Foods and Food Processing.* Elsevier, 1973.

REED, G. (Ed). *Enzymes in Food Processing.* 2nd edition. Academic Press, 1975.
A comprehensive text dealing with both properties and applications.

ROGERS, J. L. and BINSTED, R. *Quick-frozen foods.* Food Trade Press, 1972.
The commerce and technology of processing, packaging and distribution.

SALMON, J. *et al. Frozen Food in the Home.* Royal Society of Health, 1977.
A booklet containing 4 papers including 'Nutritional Aspects' and 'Microbiological Aspects'.

Chapter Fourteen

Chemicals in food

Food itself is composed of chemicals; this should be clear to all who have read the preceding chapters. What is usually meant by 'chemicals' in connection with food are those substances which do not normally form a part of the food in its natural or traditional state. Their presence may arise as a result of accidental contamination or they may be deliberately added to improve processing or keeping qualities or to supplement the nutrients already present. Deliberate adulteration practised with intent to deceive is fortunately not as common today as in former years. The addition of alum to flour and water to milk, and other crude methods of adulteration, though once commonplace occurrences no longer happen to-day.

Chemical Contaminants

Food can become contaminated with chemicals in a multitude of ways. There are, however, some sources of contamination which are of outstanding importance today, and it is with these that we shall be concerned here.

CONTAMINATION WITH AGRICULTURAL CHEMICALS. Many crops are treated with insecticides to prevent infestation by insects, fungicides to prevent growth of fungi, and weedkillers or growth regulators to kill weeds selectively. The treatment of growing crops with chemicals is by no means new. Insecticides containing sulphur have been used for well over a hundred years and the arsenical spray *Paris Green* and *Bordeaux Mixture*, which contains copper, were first used in 1870 and 1885 respectively.

Modern agricultural chemicals are for the most part complex organic compounds and are becoming increasingly complex as years go by. They are often toxic to animals and human beings, but they are usually applied to the plants before the part which is eaten has appeared or at least a sufficient length of time before harvesting to permit their removal by rain. Unfortunately, however, some of the compounds concerned are so stable that they may remain in the soil or in natural waters for a period of years. Two insecticides which have been used on a very large scale are DDT and dieldrin, both of which are chlorinated hydro-carbons. Their presence has been detected, albeit in very small quantities, in soil, water and vegetables and animal tissues in all parts of the world. The very air we breathe has been shown to contain traces of DDT and dieldrin and even the polar ice-caps are not free from contamination as has been demonstrated by the fact that fat from penguins contains traces of chlorinated insecticides.

In dietary studies carried out between 1966–75 in the UK it has been found that the daily intake of persistent chlorinated pesticides has declined and that, apart from dieldrin, intakes are extremely low compared with acceptable daily intakes (ADI) calculated by FAO/WHO. ADI are based on worldwide studies as to how much on average humans could safely consume over a lifetime, and a large safety factor of at least 100 is included.

Dietary studies also show that in the UK organochlorine residues are present in cereals, fruits and preserves in the form of BHC and in meat in the form of DDT. The only organophosphorus residues are found in cereals in the form of malathion.

The number of pesticides in use has increased dramatically in recent years. Whereas in 1926 there were a mere 12 pesticides in common use there are now over 600. In the UK over two-thirds of these substances are herbicides. The rapidly increasing use of pesticides has meant that their control has become more important and the FAO/WHO issue maximum permitted concentrations for many pesticides. In the UK the *Pesticides Safety Precautions Scheme* is a non-statutory scheme whereby new pesticides are evaluated first for safety then for efficiency so that no such substances come into use before they have been carefully assessed. In the future EEC regulations are intended to provide statutory control of all pesticides with maximum permitted levels for residues in food.

Antibiotics. As well as treating soil and crops with chemicals, farmers treat animals with chemicals in the form of antibiotics. Antibiotics are used to cure animal diseases such as mastitis, enteritis, pneumonia and infected wounds and feet. By using antibiotics many animal infections which formerly were a source of great trouble to farmers can now be easily controlled. Farmers are also increasingly encouraged to dose pigs and poultry with antibiotics when there is apparently nothing wrong with them. It is supposed that by so doing the animals will be given blanket protection against disease or will be better able to resist stress and hence will grow faster or give higher yields of eggs. The antibiotics may be added to the animals' food or to their drinking water.

Most people would agree to the use of antibiotics for treating infected animals. Indeed, the use of antibiotics in veterinary practice has been a great boon for farmers and, even more so, to the animals themselves. The use of antibiotics as animal food supplements is a different matter, however, and this practice is widely opposed.

Indiscriminate use of antibiotics by farmers is not approved by most veterinary workers and it is generally accepted that antibiotics should only be used to treat specific infections. The reason for this is that micro-organisms which are continually exposed to low concentrations of an antibiotic may become antibiotic-resistant and when this occurs the antibiotic is valueless when it is required to treat an illness caused by the organism concerned. An organism which has acquired resistance to an antibiotic can, in some circumstances, transmit this resistance, merely by contact, to a previously sensitive organism. This is known as *infective drug resistance*.

When organisms become resistant to antibiotics it is more difficult for veterinary surgeons to deal with infected animals. Also, because of the interchange of organisms which inevitably occurs between animals and man, similar difficulties may arise in treating infected humans. It would be most unfortunate, if, as a result of veterinary use, the organism *Salmonella typhi* became resistant to the antibiotic chloramphenicol (Chloromycetin) as this is by far the most effective drug available for treating typhoid fever in man. There are, however, no indications at present that this is likely to occur. Chloramphenicol has been extensively used for treating animals since 1956 and during this period there have been no cases of typhoid which did not respond to treatment with it.

A further objection to the widespread use of antibiotics by farmers is the danger that an individual who is allergic to a particular antibiotic may be made ill if he drinks milk in which the antibiotic is present. To prevent this happening farmers are not permitted to sell milk taken from cows within 48 hours of antibiotic treatment. Less than 1 per cent of samples of bulk milk examined in Great Britain are found to contain antibiotics but, even so, the danger of an allergic reaction still exists.

RADIOACTIVE CONTAMINATION. Contamination of food with radioactive materials which enter the atmosphere as a result of nuclear explosions is another serious modern problem. During the explosion of an atomic bomb, atoms of heavy metals such as uranium are split into smaller particles called fission products. The fission products are unstable isotopes of naturally occurring elements and over a period of time they change into more stable isotopes. This decay, as it is called, is accompanied by the emission of particles and radiation of various kinds and, as we noted earlier, the isotopes are called radioactive isotopes or radioisotopes. The particles and radiation emitted are damaging to living tissues and exposure to them can have severe consequences.

The fission products produced in a nuclear explosion enter the atmosphere and may attain high altitudes. They settle down slowly, and 'fall-out' from a single explosion may continue for several years. By this time the fission products have been widely distributed by atmospheric currents and may finally reach the ground thousands of miles away.

The fission products fall on soil and vegetation and may be absorbed by growing plants. When these are eaten by man and animals and the nutrients absorbed, the radioisotopes may become incorporated into the body tissues. Many radioisotopes are produced as fission products, but most of them decay fairly rapidly and remain radioactive for only a comparatively short time. The isotopes *strontium-90* and *caesium-137*, however, remain radioactive for long periods and if absorbed by the body can cause severe damage.

Strontium is chemically similar to calcium and, because of this, strontium-90 is found in greatest amounts in those foods which are sources of calcium. A further consequence of this similarity is the fact that strontium, whether strontium-90 or the natural non-radioactive variety, is treated by the body in the same way as calcium and ultimately finds its way into the bone structure. Cows and other grazing animals can ingest strontium-90 as a result of eating contaminated grass. The strontium-90 becomes concentrated in their bones and also finds its way into cow's milk and hence into the human diet. In humans it is deposited in the bones and because of its radioactivity can cause bone tumours and leukaemia. Some authorities consider that doses of strontium-90 below a certain critical value, or threshold as it is called, are not harmful. There is no convincing evidence in support of this theory and it would seem wisest to assume that all doses of strontium-90, however small, are harmful.

Caesium, one of the alkali metals, is chemically similar to sodium and potassium and its compounds are absorbed by the body in the same way as sodium compounds. Absorbed caesium-137 finds its way into the soft tissues of the body where it may cause genetic harm.

Carbon-14 is another radioisotope produced during the explosion of nuclear weapons and in the course of time it will be converted into carbon dioxide and may then be incorporated into plant tissues by photosynthesis. The carbon-14 may ultimately find its way into any organ of the human body when the plants are eaten by man, or when animals which have eaten the plants are in turn eaten by man. Carbon-14 decays very slowly and remains radioactive for thousands of years.

Modern nuclear bombs are said to release into the atmosphere a very much smaller amount of harmful radioactive isotopes than the original types. Nevertheless, contamination of the atmosphere still occurs when such bombs are exploded and this is why, apart from other more obvious reasons, the testing of nuclear weapons should be avoided.

The problems of safety in nuclear power stations have been the subject of much debate. The particular danger as far as diet is concerned is that an accident might result in the escape into the atmosphere of *iodine-131*. This radioisotope rapidly finds its way into the food chain through the contamination of milk. Fortunately alternative supplies of milk can be provided rapidly and furthermore the radioactivity of iodine-131 decays rapidly so that more intractable problems resulting from long-term contamination of plant materials do not arise.

CONTAMINATION FROM PACKAGING MATERIALS. There has been a great deal of concern in recent years about the possible contamination of foodstuffs by migration of chemicals from the materials in which they are packed. Plastics are increasingly used as packaging materials and while the polymers themselves are non-toxic, compounds which may have been added to them to improve their properties may not be equally innocuous. Catalysts such as organic peroxides or complex metal salts may have been used to initiate polymerization and these remain in the polymerized product. Plasticizers are incorporated in many plastic materials to increase their flexibility. They are usually viscous organic liquids such as the esters of phthalic, phosphoric or ricinoleic acid. Plastics may be adversely affected by atmospheric oxidation, especially when they are in the form of thin sheets which present a large surface to the air, and antioxidants are used to mitigate this. Unfortunately, however, the antioxidants used are not those approved for use in foods. Stabilizers, which may be organo-tin salts or calcium salts of fatty acid, may be used in some plastic materials and pigments, anti-static agents, bactericides and fungicides may also be present. When plastics are used as packaging materials for food any of these substances may find their way into the food. Only very small amounts will be present in the food, but even these minimal amounts may prove to be toxic if ingested over a period.

Paper-based packaging materials are widely used for foodstuffs and even these may be a source of contamination if, as often happens, the paper or board has been treated to increase its strength when wet. Such wet-strength paper is made by impregnating paper or pulp with urea-formaldehyde or melamine-formaldehyde resin and it is possible for formaldehyde to migrate from the treated paper to the foodstuff. The Preservatives in Food Regulations specifically permits the presence in foods of 5 ppm of formaldehyde arising from any resin used in the manufacture of wet strength papers or of plastic food containers or utensils.

FOOD ADDITIVES

The food processing industry in the UK is a product of the industrial revolution of the nineteenth century. As people moved from the country into industrial towns they could no longer grow their own food or buy it direct from the producer. Up to this time food had been preserved in small quantities in the home; now there was a need for preservation on a large scale in order to feed new industrial communities living far from agricultural areas. Thus the initial stimulus for the use of food additives arose from the need to preserve food commercially.

As the world population has grown the need to preserve food has increased. It has been estimated that 20–25 per cent of food grown is lost between the time the crop is planted and when it is consumed. This loss is due to many causes among which are attacks on plants by pathogens, pests and rodents; microbiological decay; physical and chemical deterioration and finally losses during processing, storage and distribution. Thus chemical additives came to be used to increase the shelf life of foods i.e. to make them keep longer, and to reduce food wastage due to the causes mentioned.

At first the manufactured foods produced by processing were relatively simple but with the passage of time they have become increasingly sophisticated and the final product may bear little if any resemblance to the raw materials from which it is made. Instant deserts and many breakfast cereals are fairly obvious examples. In recent years the food industry has been undergoing major changes in order to produce mass-produced convenience foods of uniform and high quality for selling through supermarkets. New or improved methods of preservation, processing and packaging have been introduced in order to do this. Such new convenience foods can only be produced with the help of an ever-increasing array of chemical additives.

The original use of additives to preserve food has been extended in many directions. Thus one of the main uses of additives is to make food more attractive. To do this additives are used to improve such qualities as flavour, colour and texture. Indeed, in terms of value, flavouring agents account for one-third of the total value of additives used in the UK, while thickeners and stabilising agents which contribute to texture come second and account for one-quarter of the total value.

The attractiveness of food is clearly a quality of importance to both the manufacturer and the consumer. There are some who decry the addition of chemicals to food to make it more attractive, but if consumer acceptability is to be taken into account there is little doubt as to their effectiveness, as is shown by the following example. Some years ago a leading UK food retailer decided to stop adding synthetic colours to a range of traditional food products. As a result the colour of canned garden peas became a greenish-grey, the colour of strawberry and raspberry jam became a brownish red and canned strawberries became straw coloured. The consequence in terms of consumer acceptability was unequivocal—sales fell by about 50 per cent!

Additives are also used to maintain the nutritional quality of food. During heat processing, for example, some heat-sensitive nutrients such as vitamin C may be lost. In the manufacture of dried potato, for instance, vitamin C present in the potatoes is destroyed and synthetic vitamin C may be added to replace it. Bread provides another and more significant example. During milling (see p. 162) vitamins and mineral elements are lost and to restore these losses iron, thiamine, nicotinic acid and chalk are added to all flour (except wholemeal). The amounts added are such as to replace all losses due to milling.

Food additives may be used not only to maintain nutritional value but also to improve it. This is known as food *fortification* or *enrichment* Such addition of nutrients may either be a legal requirement to safeguard public health or it may be done voluntarily by the manufacturer. In the first category comes the enrichment of margarine with vitamins A and D so as to make its vitamin content equivalent to that of summer butter. In the second category comes the fortification of some breakfast cereals with a range of vitamins, iron, calcium and sometimes protein; also the addition of vitamin C to soft drinks and fruit juices.

A final use of additives remains to be considered; namely as aids to processing. As already mentioned the continuing development of convenience foods suitable for selling in supermarkets has necessitated the use of additives for many additional purposes concerned both with methods of processing and also with the properties required of modern convenience foods.

The variety of additives listed in Table 14.1 indicates the many purposes for which additives are now required. For example, the development of an aerosol food product requires the use of a propellant gas, while some instant foods, such as instant potato, are best packed in an inert gas if oxidative changes are to be minimized. Humectants are substances that absorb moisture and so can reduce the effect of humidity

Table 14.1. Additives used as Processing Aids

Acids and bases	Firming agents	Packaging gas
Anti-caking agents	Glazing agents	Propellants
Anti-foaming agents	Humectants	Release agents
Buffers	Liquid freezants	Sequestrants

on a food such as baking powder. Anti-caking agents help prevent particles of food from adhering to each other to improve their flow properties during processing while firming agents keep the tissues of fruit and vegetable firm and crisp. Sequestrants are substances such as citrates, tartrates and phosphates that combine with metal ions to form complexes. They help to retain the colour, flavour and stability of a number of products. For example, citric acid added to wine combines with iron and copper and so helps to prevent cloudiness.

In all, 130 chemicals have been approved as miscellaneous additives the aim being to ensure that no new substances are introduced for the purposes mentioned without their safety and their need having been determined.

Food Laws and the Control of Food Additives

The adulteration of food has its origins in antiquity, and in England the earliest action to prevent adulteration was taken by the guilds. For example, in the reigns of Henry II and Henry III pepper was widely used to preserve meat and other foods but because it was expensive adulteration was common. To remedy this the guild of Pepperers was granted powers to sift spices so as to control quality. In the sixteenth and seventeenth centuries adulteration increased and practices such as the mixing of flour with mustard, the addition of leaves e.g. scorched oak leaves to tea, the addition of water and lard to coffee, the mixing of sand, ashes and sawdust to bread doughs and the addition of water to milk became commonplace. Some forms of adulteration, e.g. the addition of sulphuric acid to vinegar, were even more serious and made the food poisonous.

Adulteration of food continued unabated in the eighteenth and nineteenth centuries and following increasing expressions of public concern and the publishing of the findings of a Select Parliamentary Commission in 1855 the Adulteration of Food and Drink Act was passed in 1860 and further strengthened in 1872. As a result of these Acts of Parliament adulteration of all food was prohibited and public analysts were appointed to analyse food suspected of having been adulterated.

Modern food laws derive from the Food and Drugs Act of 1955 which laid down two important principles. First, food should be fit for human consumption and free from health hazards and second, it must be of the nature, substance and quality demanded. It is from these concepts, and the consequent powers given to Ministers to make regulations under the Act, that the whole of our protective system for food stems.

The 1955 Act was a milestone in legislative history in the UK. Whereas previous legislation had been negative in concept, concerned with preventing the adulteration and wrongful description of food, the new Act introduced a new principle into food law. It was primarily concerned with the positive aspect of maintaining the *quality* of food and laid down minimum standards of composition for a number of foods. It also prescribed labelling requirements for the listing of ingredients and the proper description of the product. The law as it now stands exists to ensure that the consumer is able to buy good wholesome food, unadulterated, uncontaminated, of the required quality and properly described.

Under powers given to them by the 1955 Act Government Ministers are advised by the Food Standards Committee (FSC) which is concerned with all matters relating to the composition, description, labelling and advertising of food. In 1964 an additional and independent committee—the Food Additives and Contaminants Committee (FACC)—was set up to advise on matters relating to additives and contaminants. These two bodies have published many reports, the more important of which are as follows;

Bread and Flour (1974), Colouring Matters (1979), Artificial and Synthetic Cream (1951), Cream (1967), Emulsifiers and Stabilizers (1972), Flavouring Agents (1976), Gelatine (1950), Ice-cream (1957), Jams and other Preserves (1968), Liquid Freezants (1974), Mineral Hydrocarbons (1975), Novel Protein Foods (1974), Soft Drinks (fruit juices) (1975), Solvents (1978), Yogurt (1975), Further Food Additives (1968), Meat Products (1980), Water in Food (1978), Flavour Modifiers (1979), Margarine and other Table Spreads (1981).

The advice and recommendations contained in reports of the FSC and the FACC are usually followed by legislation in the form of regulations known as *Statutory Instruments* (SI) which imposes legal obligations on food manufacturers and others. The more important regulations relating to additives are as follows:

Artificial Sweeteners (1969), Preservatives (1979), Emulsifiers and Stabilizers (1975), Mineral Hydrocarbons (1966), Antioxidants

(1978), Colouring Matter (1975), Solvents (1967), Miscellaneous
Additives (1974).

FOOD LAWS AND THE EEC. The fact that the UK is a part of the European
Economic Community (EEC) means that domestic legislation must be
harmonized with that of the Community. EEC food legislation takes
two forms; first there are legally binding *Regulations* and second
there are less obligatory *Directives*. The current process of harmoni-
zing UK food laws with those of the EEC is both lengthy and
complex.

The UK's membership of the EEC and the consequent need to
harmonize food legislation has emphasised the need to replace the 1955
Food and Drugs Act by a new Comprehensive Act. The 1955 Act is
based on the need to control food at the point of sale i.e. it assumes that
offences are mainly committed by retailers. The development of
supermarkets, however, and the consequent development of convenience foods, food substitutes and pre-packaging of nearly all food
makes this inappropriate. New legislation is required that takes into
account the fact that responsibility for maintaining quality rests not
with retailers but with manufacturers and importers. Moreover, new
legislation needs to be based on co-operation rather than relying on legal
enforcement.

Recent reports by the FSC foreshadow major changes in the concept of
food laws in the UK. For example, at present regulations concerning the
composition and labelling of meat products are contained in 6 different
Statutory Instruments and in addition a separate SI governs general
labelling of all food. It is recommended that in future a minimum meat
content should apply to a few important and easily identifiable meat
products and that all other meat products would simply have a
declaration of their content of lean meat. This would greatly simplify
existing legislation.

FAO, WHO AND FOOD LAWS. As mentioned on p. 330 the FAO and WHO
are concerned to estimate the accepted daily intake (ADI) of pesticides
in food and this concern extends to all additives in food (and indeed to
many other aspects of food, health and trade). The joint FAO/WHO
Expert Committee on Food Additives is concerned with the safety of
proposed food additives and in estimating ADI values. This evidence is
then submitted to the *Codex Alimentarius Commission* which is concerned to establish worldwide standards. Before the use of any additive
is permitted the technological need for its use and its safety has to be
established. Only approved additives at stipulated levels are included in

the international standards. Some 2000 food additives are included in Codex Standards.

Food Labelling

Over recent years there has been a remarkable growth in the number of food products available to the consumer. New products becoming available have tended to become increasingly sophisticated often containing a large number of ingredients, some of which are unfamiliar to most consumers. An ever increasing range of additives is available and all this coupled with the fact that most foods are pre-packed has increased both the need for and the possibility of more effective labelling. In addition the rise of consumerism has produced a strong lobby demanding that the public should be given more information about the food it buys.

So far legislation has concerned itself with the provision on a label of information about what the food is, what is in it and who made it. Since 1970 UK consumers have had a much better opportunity of knowing the nature of the food they purchase. Most products sold must have a name that indicates their true nature, and the label must also list the ingredients used (in descending order of quantity present) and indicate the name and address of the packer.

In reviews of food labelling (1980) and on claims and misleading descriptions of food (1980) the FSC has sought to produce recommendations that will meet the demand for more detailed and accurate descriptions of food on labels and also to harmonize UK laws with EEC food labelling directives.

One particular aspect of labelling has received much attention, namely that of *nutrition labelling*. Demand for such labelling has come particularly from doctors, scientists and nutritionists rather than from consumers' organizations, mainly because of the problems involved in how to provide nutritional information that will assist rather than confuse potential consumers. In general, all nutritional labelling schemes require the major nutrients (protein, fat and carbohydrate) plus total energy value to be declared in terms of amount per serving or per 100 g. Certain other nutrients, primarily mineral elements and vitamins, are declared in terms of their recommended daily allowance (RDA). Fig 14.1 shows what a label for cornflakes would look like as a result of current recommendations.

It is considered that there is a particular need for careful nutritional labelling in respect of foods for which particular claims are made eg. claims relating to protein, vitamins and minerals, and foods claiming to be suitable for slimmers and diabetics.

Cornflakes (with added vitamins and minerals)

Nutritional information – per 25 g serving (10 per pack)

Energy	392 kJ (92 k cal)
Protein	2·2 g
Fat	0·4 g
Carbohydrate (as monosaccharide) 21 g	

Minimum percentage of Recommended Daily Amount (RDA) per 25 gram serving

Thiamine	40%
Riboflavine	20%
Niacin	25%

Contains less than 5% of the RDA for vitamin A, Vitamin B_{12}, Vitamin C, Vitamin D, Folic acid, Calcium, Iodine and Iron.

Fig. 14.1. Nutritional Label for Cornflakes

It is clearly important that nutritional information on a label does not mislead the consumer; in the light of the level of nutritional knowledge of the average consumer it is difficult to find ways of conveying useful nutritional information on a label. In spite of this, certain food manufacturers are now providing nutritional information on their packs, often in a pictorial form. Indeed it may be argued that for many people, reading the back of their cereal packets may be the easiest way of improving their knowledge of nutrition!

One other aspect of labelling deserves a mention and that is date marking. The object of date marking is to make clear the shelf life of the food, that is the period from when it is packed to when it can no longer be expected to retain its specific properties. *Secret date coding,* i.e. the coding of food so that the manufacturers, and sometimes the retailer, can work out the packaging date, has been practised on packaged food for a number of years. However, there has been much pressure in recent years, particularly from consumer organizations, for manufacturers to carry out *open date marking.* This gives clear information about the shelf life of the food to the consumer.

The Food Labelling Regulations (1980) will ensure that by 1985 all UK foods (with certain exceptions such as fresh fruit and vegetables and frozen food) which can reasonably be expected to retain their specific properties—if properly stored—for only 18 months or less will be marked with a date indicating *minimum durability.* Minimum durability indicates the minimum time for which the food will be in prime condition; after this time some deterioration would be expected though the food would still be safe to eat. Minimum durability is most easily expressed by a 'best eaten before' date. Any necessary storage conditions must also be given alongside the date.

For a food with a short shelf life of six weeks or less the open date mark would be in one of the following forms;

Sell by....................   or   Best before........
Best eaten within 3 days of
purchase   Keep refrigerated.
Keep refrigerated

Classes of Food Additive

Several classes of food additive have already been considered. For example, the function of acids as preservatives was described in Chapter 5 while preservatives generally were dealt with in Chapter 13. Earlier in this chapter the use of nutrients as additives and additives used as aids to processing were discussed. Remaining classes of additive are described in the rest of this chapter.

EMULSIFIERS AND STABILIZERS. The function and uses of these additives have already been considered in Chapter 6 and reference need only be made here to the legal position. The basis of present regulations is that emulsifiers and stabilizers permitted in food must not only be safe in use but that the *need* for their use must be established.

Apart from natural foods, such as eggs and starches, which have some emulsifying or stabilizing power and which are excluded from the regulations, all emulsifiers and stabilizers permitted in food are listed. The list is extensive and includes edible gums, such as locust bean gum (carob gum), tragacanth and acacia (gum arabic); alginic acid and alginates; lecithins; cellulose derivatives; mono- and di-glycerides of fatty acids such as GMS; pectins; various sorbitan derivatives etc. The large number of emulsifiers and stabilizers which are permitted reflects their widespread use in a large variety of different types of manufactured food.

COLOURING MATTER. Although the nutritional value of food is one of the prime concerns of this book, it must be conceded that the appeal of food is determined by its taste, appearance and smell rather than its food value. Indeed, the appearance and smell of food stimulate the flow of digestive juices and thus aid digestion (p. 27). Since earliest times the importance of colour has been recognized—the attractiveness of fruit and vegetables, for example, is partly due to their colour which is caused by the presence of very small amounts of colouring matter. Such substances as *carotenoids* in carrots and tomatoes, *anthocyanins* in plums and strawberries, *anthoxanthins* in onions and potatoes and *chlorophyll* in green leafy vegetables are responsible for their characteristic colour.

It has also become accepted over many centuries that where the natural colour of food is unattractive colouring materials may be added. Natural colouring materials such as *cochineal, annatto* and *saffron* have achieved respectability through long usage. All of these are natural colouring matters, which are obtained from animals and plants. Cochineal, for example, which colours food red, is made by crushing the bodies of dried insects. Saffron and annatto, both of which impart a yellow colour, are obtained from the saffron plant and the fruit of the annatto tree respectively. Other plant materials primarily added to foods to improve their aromatic or savoury properties also improve their colour; such substances as *paprika, turmeric* and *sandal-wood* come into this category.

A few colouring materials usually classified as natural or traditional are produced by heat treatment of vegetable material. *Caramel*, produced by heating sucrose or other edible sugars, and *carbon* are the most familiar examples and are used to give brown and black colours to food respectively.

During the last hundred years or so purely synthetic coal tar dyes have been developed, mainly for use in dyeing fabrics and they have been used to a considerable extent in colouring goods. Many of these synthetic dyes are now known to be toxic. Even very small quantitites, if consumed over a sufficiently long period of time, may produce cancer. Such cancer-producing (carcinogenic) substances are called carcinogens. It is of the utmost importance to exclude all carcinogens from the diet. Many people consider that the addition of synthetic dyestuffs to food should not be permitted because the questionable benefits of colouring food are more than offset by the possible risks to the health of the consumer. It is still not possible to be certain that ingestion of small quantities of a particular dyestuff over a long period will be harmless.

Regulations governing the use of colouring matter in food have gradually reduced the number of coal tar dyes that are permitted in food. Until recently there was a chaotic situation in which different countries allowed the use of different coal tar dyes, no two countries having the same list of permitted substances. The earliest EEC directive concerned with food additives was that relating to food colours and this has caused new Regulations to be issued in Britain. The progressive reduction in the number of coal tar dyes permitted in food is being accelerated by EEC legislation. It seems likely that the use of all coal tar dyes in food will eventually be prohibited. In general legislation concerning colourings in food is moving in the direction of ever stricter controls.

The reduced number of coal tar dyes available is leading to renewed interest and research into natural colours, the latter being defined as colours found in edible raw materials or the same substances made synthetically. Such materials include anthocyanins, betalaines (derived from beetroot), carotenoids, chlorophyll and xanthophylls. There is also a trend, particularly in Continental Europe, towards not adding any colouring material to a wide variety of foods.

All colouring matters that may be added to food in the UK are listed in the regulations; no colour not on the permitted list may be used. Apart from the permitted coal tar dyes and natural vegetable and animal colours certain metallic compounds such as oxides of *iron* and *titanium* may be used in food and as surface colours, on, for example, sugar-coated confectionery.

In general permitted colouring matters may be added to any food, though certain foods may not contain any added colour. These include meat, fish, raw fruits and vegetables, tea, coffee and dried and condensed milk. It is recommended by the FAAC that in future colouring matter should not be permitted in baby foods.

FLAVOURING AGENTS. Flavour is one of the most important attributes of food and is detected by the senses of taste and smell. Taste itself is made up of the four primary tastes—sweet, sour, salt and bitter—which are detected by taste buds situated in the mouth mainly on the tongue, palate and cheeks. Smell is detected by extremely sensitive cells situated at the top of the nasal cavity.

Flavouring agents have been used from earliest times to increase the attractiveness of food, although it is only recently that their nature has become known. The FSC report on flavouring agents gives a useful classification of natural and synthetic flavours, the latter being classified according to their chemical nature as shown in Table 14.2. The table

Table 14.2. Classification of Flavouring Agents

Natural	Synthetic		
Herb, spices (152)	Acids (48)	Ethers (39)	Esters (514)
Essential oils, extracts,	Acetals (28)	Ketals (2)	Others (50)
distillates (229)	Alcohols (76)	Ketones (78)	
Foods (e.g. cocoa) (28)	Aldehydes (34)	Lactones (26)	

also shows (in brackets) the number of each type of flavour in use and the large total (1323) serves to emphasize the fact that flavours constitute the largest group of food additives.

Originally flavouring agents were the dried, and sometimes powdered, forms of spices, herbs, berries, roots and stems of plants. For example spices, such as pepper, cloves and ginger were prized for their ability to add interest and palatability to a monotonous diet. Condiments and spices were invaluable not only for their flavour but also because they were able to disguise the tainted flavour of meat which was past its best.

As the demand for flavouring agents increased the crude natural plant material was found to be inadequate and methods for extracting the active principles were devised. The most important types of natural flavouring agent are *essential oils* which are oily substances—though chemically unrelated to oils and fats—which are volatile (easily vaporized) and which have a flavouring power about 100 times that of the raw material from which they come. They are extracted from plant material either by fractional distillation or with a suitable solvent the resulting liquid being concentrated by evaporating under vacuum.

Having isolated the essential oil it became possible to synthesize the active principle, and so synthetic flavouring agents were developed until today—apart from herbs and spices and a few natural flavours such as vanilla, peppermint, orange and lemon—most flavouring agents are synthetic. Synthetic flavours, usually in the form of a solution in alcohol or other permitted solvent, are more concentrated, cheaper and far more convenient to use than the corresponding natural flavours. More recently synthetics have been produced in a powder form by spray drying the flavouring material in a gum arabic solution. Such powders are widely used in powdered convenience foods, such as instant dessert mixes.

In recent years it has become possible to analyse natural flavours by vapour-phase chromatography, which is a very sensitive technique for splitting up mixtures of volatile compounds into their components. The results of such experiments show that natural flavouring agents are usually extremely complex mixtures of many different substances, many of which are present in extremely small amounts. Occasionally, however, the flavour of a natural flavouring agent depends very largely on the presence of a single substance which may be the main ingredient—such as *eugenol* in oil of cloves which constitutes 85 per cent of the oil—or which may be a minor ingredient—such as *citral* in oil of lemon which constitutes only 5 per cent of the oil.

In the rare cases where a natural flavour is composed of one chemical, a synthetic flavour is easy to prepare as only one substance is required.

Usually, however a large number of substances need to be blended together to obtain a reasonable imitation of the natural flavour.

Many of the simpler artificial fruit flavours are *esters* (see p. 80) which are formed when carboxylic acids react with alcohols. Ethyl acetate, for example, which is a fruity-smelling liquid, is produced when acetic acid and ethyl alcohol are heated together:

$$CH_3COOH + C_2H_5OH \rightleftharpoons CH_3COOC_2H_5 + H_2O$$
ethyl acetate

The reaction also occurs at normal temperatures, but at a much slower rate, and esters, particularly ethyl acetate, are formed in this way during the maturing of wine and contribute to the much-prized bouquet. Other esters can be easily and cheaply made in the same way by heating together the appropriate acid and alcohol, usually in the presence of a catalyst.

Table 14.3 Esters used as Flavouring Agents

Name	Formula	Use
Ethyl formate	$HCOOC_2H_5$	Rum, raspberry and peach essences
Ethyl acetate	$CH_3COOC_2H_5$	Apple, pear, strawberry and peach essences
Pentyl acetate	$CH_3COOC_5H_{11}$	Pear, pineapple and raspberry essences
Pentyl butyrate	$C_4H_9COOC_5H_{11}$	Banana, pineapple and peach essences
Allyl caproate	$C_5H_{11}COOC_3H_5$	Pineapple essence

In the past synthetic fruit flavours have often been made up of a single ester and consequently rather poor imitations. Recently great improvements have been made because as the composition of natural flavours has become known it has become possible to blend together synthetic materials so as to imitate the natural flavour more closely. Esters are the most widely used of flavouring agent (Table 14.3).

Flavour Modifiers. A flavour modifier is officially defined as 'any substance which is capable of enhancing, reducing or otherwise modifying the taste or odour, or both, of a food but does not include water or enzymes or any substance primarily used to impart taste or odour, or both, to a food'. The 'miracle berry' (see p. 347) is a good example while *monosodium glutamate*, MSG, is the most widely used flavour enhancer (see p. 179).

Advances in biochemical techniques in recent years have made it possible to isolate *ribonucleotides* from micro-organisms and these are now produced on an industrial scale for use as food flavouring agents. Ribonucleotides are compounds formed from the sugar ribose, phosphoric acid and an organic base such as guanine. They occur in all animal tissues and are present in yeast extracts and contribute substantially to their characteristic meaty taste. As soon as an animal is killed, however, enzymes called *phosphatases* begin to break down the ribonucleotides and by the time the food reaches the table a great deal of the flavour-enhancing properties of the ribonucleotides may be lost. By adding ribonucleotides to foods of animal origin such loss of flavour may be made good.

Ribonucleotide flavour enhancers are used in soups, meat and fish pastes, all types of canned meat products, sausages, meat pies and other processed food products of which the main ingredient is meat or fish. As their flavour enhancing power is very great—ten times that of MSG—only very small quantities (as little as 20 ppm) are required.

Legislation. The very large number of flavouring agents available for use in food and the lack of evidence of possible toxicity makes it almost impossible to be certain that none of them is injurious to health. In Great Britain there is no list of permitted food flavouring agents, as there is in the United States and there are, in fact, no regulations governing the use of such materials in foods. However, in a recent review of flavourings (1976) the Food Additives and Contaminants Committee has recommended that in Great Britain the use of flavourings in food should in future be controlled by a permitted list system. A similar recommendation has also been made for flavour modifiers. It is also recommended that flavour modifiers should not be permitted in baby foods.

SWEETENING AGENTS. In many ways sugar is the ideal sweetener; it is fairly cheap, it easily and quickly dissolves in water and its sweet taste has no undesirable overtones of bitterness or saltiness. It also has major drawbacks—it is not sweet enough for an increasing range of sweet manufactured foods and its relatively high energy value makes it unsuitable for slimming products. Also, the rapid increase in sugar consumption which in Britain has risen from 2 kg per year in the early eighteenth century to about 41 kg now is a cause for concern on three counts: it contributes to obesity, it is a major cause of dental decay and it is possibly related to coronary heart disease (p. 121).

In this situation there has been a continuing search for sweetening agents that are sweeter than sugar. The main artificial sweetener in use—and the only one permitted in the UK—is *saccharin* (o-sulphobenzimide). It was discovered accidentally in 1879 and is a white

Table 14.4. The Relative Sweetness of Sugar and Sweetening Agents

Name	Sweetness	Name	Sweetness
Sucrose	1	d-6 chlorotryptophan	1000
Cyclamate	30	Miraculin	—
Saccharin	300–500	Monellin	3000
Aspartame	100–200	Thaumatin	750–1600

solid which is 300–500 times as sweet as sucrose. Saccharin has the disadvantage of an unpleasant bitter 'after taste', and although it is very sweet it does not have any nutritional or preservative value—neither can it contribute to the 'mouth feel' of soft drinks as sugar does. Also it is not very heat stable which produces problems in cooked, baked and canned goods.

Cyclamate was first used to sweeten food in the USA in 1950, though not in Britain for another 14 years. Although less than one tenth as sweet as saccharin it had the advantage that it gave no bitter after-taste. It was banned in the USA and UK and in a number of other countries in 1969 after feeding trials with prolonged high doses of a 10:1 cyclamate saccharin mixture produced bladder cancer in rats.

Continuing experiments indicate that both saccharin and cyclamate are safe when used in food in controlled amounts. It is possible that new evidence may allow cyclamate to be reinstated as a permitted sweetener.

The artificial sweetener *aspartame*, which is a dipeptide made from the amino-acids L-aspartic acid and L-phenylalanine, has been approved for restricted use in the USA and it may soon be permitted in the UK It is 100–200 times as sweet as sugar, and without the bitter after-taste of saccharin. Among other artificial sweeteners being developed is one derived from the amino-acid tryptophan which is 1000 times sweeter than sugar.

Apart from synthetic sweeteners three tropical berries containing protein material are being exploited. The 'miracle berry' contains the glycoprotein *miraculin*, which although not sweet itself is able to make sour-tasting food taste sweet, while the serendipity berry contains the protein *monellin*, which is 3000 times sweeter than sugar. The other berry contains the polypeptide *thaumatin* which is about three times as sweet as saccharin.

SOLVENTS. The flavouring agents considered above are often added to foods in the form of concentrated solutions in organic liquids. Solvents may also be used to facilitate the incorporation of other ingredients into food and their use is controlled by The Solvents in Food Regulations, 1967. For the purposes of the Regulations, water, acetic acid, lactic acid, any propellant or any permitted food additive (e.g. a preservative of emulsifying agent) is not regarded as a solvent. The nine solvents which may be used are shown in Table 14.5.

Table 14.5. Permitted Solvents

Ethyl alcohol	Glycerol	Glyceryl triacetate
Ethyl acetate	Glyceryl monoacetate	Isopropyl alcohol
Diethyl ether	Glyceryl diacetate	Propylene glycol

MINERAL OILS. Mineral oils and waxes are alkanes (see Chapter 3) of fairly high molecular weight. They are familiar in everyday life as lubricating oils, medicinal paraffin, petroleum jelly (e.g. Vaseline) and wax (e.g. candles). Hydrocarbons are not metabolized and hence they have no nutritive value. Their presence in food is undesirable because they may interfere with the absorption of the fat-soluble vitamins A and D and, if present in a highly emulsified form, they may become deposited in certain organs.

Mineral oils are not naturally present in foods but they may become incorporated into foods, in small amounts, as a result of food processing operations. Oils used for lubricating machinery may find their way into food and moving parts which actually come into contact with food should wherever possible be lubricated with vegetable oil. Unfortunately, although vegetable oils are effective as a lubricant when first applied, they tend to become 'gummy' and to have the reverse effect after a time.

Dried fruits such as prunes, currants, raisins and especially sultanas may be given a surface coating of mineral oil to prevent them sticking together in a tight mass during storage as a result of exudation of sugar syrup through surface cracks. The coating of mineral oil also improves the appearance of the fruit and is said to deter insect infestation. Dried fruits should always be washed before being used and this will remove most of the mineral oil. Citrus fruits may be given a coating of mineral oil to replace the natural protective oils which are lost during cleaning operations for removal of dirt and moulds. The mineral oil is said to prevent, or at any rate reduce, hardening and drying of the peel and softening of the fruit. The peel of citrus fruits is not normally eaten and hence the presence of mineral oil would not seem to be important.

Mineral oil is also used on the bandages in which some cheeses are wrapped. Some small cheeses such as Dutch Gouda and Edam cheeses are not bound in bandages and the rind of these cheeses may be coated directly with mineral oils. Whether the mineral oil is on a bandage or on the rind itself its effect is to minimize evaporation and hence loss of weight. If properly carried out it also eliminates mould growth and gives a cleaner and more attractive appearance. Mineral oil is also used for coating eggs which are to be preserved by chilling. The thin coating of oil tends to prevent diffusion of carbon dioxide and water vapour through the egg shell and to prevent mould growth. Egg shells are not eaten and hence there would seem to be little objection to this practice.

The use of mineral oils in or on foods in England and Wales is controlled by the Mineral Hydrocarbons in Food Regulations, 1966. The general basis of the regulations is that foods should not contain any mineral hydrocarbons. However, in certain circumstances very small quantities of mineral oil do confer particular advantages as indicated above, and so a small number of specified foods are permitted to contain mineral oil. These are as follows; dried fruit (up to $0 \cdot 5 \%$), citrus fruit (up to $0 \cdot 1 \%$), sugar confectionery, as a polishing or glazing agent (up to $0 \cdot 2 \%$), chewing gum (up to 60%), rinds of cheese and preserved eggs.

POLYPHOSPHATES. A range of phosphoric acids and their sodium, potassium, and calcium salts, are used as food additives. Twenty six such substances, from the simple acid orthophosphoric acid, H_3PO_4, to complex polyphosphates are permitted for use in food having been shown to be safe.

Phosphates, particularly polyphosphates, are added to flesh foods such as meat, fish and poultry in order to obtain increased retention of water and greater solubility of proteins. These effects are said to lead to improved texture. The use of any additives to food to increase water retention and therefore the weight of the food is questionable unless the presence of the additive is clearly stated. It is recommended, therefore, that where water is added to such products in this way the percentage water added should be declared as 'polyphosphate' solution on the label.

The Case for and against Food Additives

To what extent should the addition of chemicals to food be condoned? This is a question which arouses deep feelings. Individuals who swallow, without the slightest compunction, comparatively large amounts of chemicals in the form of patent medicines allow their imaginations to run riot where the subject of chemicals in food is concerned. Indeed, many people feel that the addition of chemicals of any sort, for whatever purpose, is a practice which deserves nothing but condemnation. Such people are apt to accuse food scientists of 'tampering' with man's food and hence in some way making it unwholesome. They do not often realize that many of the traditional foods we regard as 'natural foods' are often far removed from their original condition and have in many cases been treated with chemicals which, because of long standing usage, are not now regarded as additives. Traditional techniques for processing foods, such as cooking, smoking, pickling and curing bring about chemical and physical changes in foods and the idea that modern food processing techniques are in a different, and possibly harmful, category from these time honoured methods is quite without foundation.

It is undoubtedly true that were it not for the food scientist there would have been even less food available for the world's ever growing population than there is today. Against a background of rapid population growth and the knowledge that treatment of crops, farm animals and processed foods with chemicals makes available substantially greater quantities, most readers of this book will probably agree that the use of food additives is, in principle, justified.

A joint committee of the FAO and the WHO which considered this problem came to the conclusion that the use of additives was justified when they served one or more of the following functions:

1 Maintenance of nutritional quality of food.
2 Enhancement of keeping quality or stability with a reduction of food wastage.
3 Making food more attractive to the consumer in a manner which does not lead to deception.
4 Providing essential aids to food processing.

Situations in which the use of food additives would not be in the interests of the consumer, and should not be permitted, include the following:

1 When faulty processing and handling techniques are disguised.
2 When the consumer is deceived.
3 When the result is a substantial reduction in the nutritive value of a food

It is proper that there should be constant vigilance to ensure that the risks of ill-effects from the presence of chemicals in foods are negligible compared with the benefits which ensue. The food additives which may be used in Great Britain perform useful functions without producing any detectable harmful side effects. The same cannot be said of many 'additives' which were popular in former times as adulterants and which were undoubtedly harmful; their prohibition can only be supported.

Clearly, additives can neither be condemned nor condoned as a class, but each case must be considered and judged upon its merits. Some chemicals are so objectionable that their presence in food is indefensible. Formaldehyde, fluorides and similar toxic compounds which were formerly used as preservatives fall into this category; so do dyestuffs known to be carcinogenic. The use of such substances is prohibited by law and it is proper that this should be so.

Only slightly less objectionable than the above are those substances which may conceivably cause harm when eaten. Synthetic colouring materials are somewhat suspect because, as already pointed out, some of these may cause cancer. Many thousands of synthetic dyes are known and it would appear to be easy to draw up a list of a few dozen which would be adequate for colouring food and which could be guaranteed to be non-carcinogenic. It is not possible, however, in spite of the most rigorous tests, to be sure that a compound which is apparently harmless is in fact so. For example, the dye known as Butter Yellow was at one time on the list of colours permitted for use in foodstuffs in the USA. It was subsequently shown to be capable of producing liver-tumours in animals and was then withdrawn from the list of permitted colours.

Additives are widely used to confer on foods properties associated with the presence of traditional ingredients. The emulsifying agents used to decrease the amount of fat needed in the manufacture of cakes and bread come into this category. Although compounds of this type reduce the amount of fat required to produce familiar physical properties in cake, they do not, of course, fulfil its nutritional functions. The amount of fat lost in this way, when considered in terms of an individual is not large, but in the case of people already living on a diet inadequately supplied with fat it cannot be said to be insignificant.

Synthetic cream and meringues are today often made from cellulose derivatives which have absolutely no nutritional value. The use of colouring matter in cakes to give an impression of richness is also open to criticism. There are numerous other examples of this type, each contributing nothing to the nourishment of the consumer. The more luxurious classes of foodstuffs lend themselves particularly well to sophistication and it may be argued that these are not, in any case, eaten primarily for their nutritive value. This is a specious argument, however, and does not wholly remove the impression that the use of such substances is tantamount to a confidence trick.

The addition of nutrients to food has already been considered. The addition of calcium carbonate to bread, potassium iodide to salt, vitamin supplements to margarine and bread are examples which spring to mind. One might suppose that these would be above suspicion but this is not always so, and even here there is need for caution. The quantities of additives employed, however innocent they seem, should bear some relationship to the body's needs. The bad effect of an excessive intake of vitamin D, mentioned in Chapter 11, should be borne in mind when considering the addition of nutrients to food.

The trend towards caution in the addition of vitamins to food is reflected in the latest (1974) report of the FSC on Bread and Flour, in which it is stated that there is no advantage in continuing the present compulsory addition of nicotinic acid to flour. The emotive force of slogans proclaiming that a food is 'fortified with vitamins' needs to be balanced by the knowledge that in nutrition, as in so many other spheres, it is possible to have too much of a good thing.

THE RISK/BENEFIT BALANCE. The assessment of drugs in terms of balancing the risk of using them against the benefits they confer has long been an acceptable practice. A similar assessment is now being used for food additives. It is now becoming more generally accepted that no food additive can be proved to be absolutely safe. It is impossible to prove a negative i.e. it is impossible to prove that an additive causes *no* harm. In this situation it is helpful to balance possible risks against benefits conferred.

The assessment of a risk/benefit balance is well exemplified by the use of nitrites and nitrates to preserve meat products discussed in the last chapter. The benefit of using these additives is well established; they destroy *Clostridium botulinum* bacteria and so contribute to preventing food poisoning. There is the risk however that nitrites in food are partly converted into nitrosomines which are known to produce cancer in animals. At the low levels permitted in specified foods nitrites are not known to have caused any harm to any human being. Nevertheless the risk remains and it is a matter of judgement whether the risk is considered to be justified in the light of the known benefits.

With some types of food additive it is more difficult to assess the risk/benefit balance. Food colours provide a suitable example. The risk of using food colours is demonstrated by the discovery that some coal tar dyes are carcinogens. On the other hand the benefit of using food colours is harder to assess though it is true that they improve the attractiveness and appearance of food. It is clear that the risk in using known carcinogens is unacceptable; no such substance should be permitted in food. In these circumstances some people consider that the questionable benefits are more than offset by the possible risk to health.

Although the absolute safety of additives cannot be proved all additives allowed in food are evaluated to ensure that they are safe in use. In seeking to assess the risk/benefit balance it is important to appreciate that so far as is known no permitted food additive has ever caused detectable harm.

SUGGESTIONS FOR FURTHER READING

ACCUM, F. *Treatise on Adulterations of Food, 1820.* Reissued by Mallinckodt, USA, 1966.

BLAXTER, K. (Ed). *Food Chains and Human Nutrition.* Applied Science Publishers, 1980. Includes a discussion of pesticides and radioactivity.

BRITISH NUTRITION FOUNDATION. *Why Additives?* Forbes Publications, 1977. A short elementary review.

CONSUMERS' ASSOCIATION. *Pesticide Residues and Food.* Consumers' Association, 1980.

FAO/WHO. *Report on Pesticide Residues.* HMSO, 1973.

FURIA, T. E. (Ed). *Handbook of Food Additives,* 2nd edition. Chemical Rubber Co., USA, 1972.

HARVEY, B. (Ed). *Butterworth's Law of Food and Drugs* (2 vols). Butterworths. A complete, and regularly updated, account of all reports and legislation relating to food in the UK.

HEATH, H. B. *Flavour Technology.* Avi, USA, 1978.

HOUGH, C. A. M. *et al. Developments in Sweeteners* I. Applied Science Publishers, 1979.

LUCAS, J. *Our Polluted Food; a survey of the risks.* Charles Knight, 1975. A survey of agricultural chemicals, radioactivity and mineral elements.

MERORY, J. *Food Flavourings: Composition, Manufacture and Use,* 2nd edition. Avi, USA, vol. 1, 1973; vol. 2, 1980.

MINISTRY OF AGRICULTURE, FISHERIES AND FOOD. *Food Quality and Safety: A Century of Progress* (Symposium Report). HMSO, 1976.

WALFORD, J. *Developments in Food Colours*—I. Applied Science Publishers, 1980.

General Reading List

BANWART, G. J. *Basic Food Microbiology*. Avi, USA, 1979.

BENDER, A. E. *Dictionary of Nutrition and Food Technology*, 4th edition. Newnes Butterworths, 1975.

BENDER, A. E. *Food Processing and Nutrition*. Academic Press, 1978.

BIRCH, G. G. and PARKER, K. J. *Food and Health: Science and Technology*. Applied Science Publishers, 1980.

BIRCH, G. G., SPENCER, M. and CAMERON, A. G. *Food Science*, 2nd edition. Pergamon, 1977.

BORGSTROM, G. *Principles of Food Science;* Vol. 1, *Food Technology;* Vol. 2, *Food Microbiology and Biochemistry*. Macmillan, USA, 1968.

BERK, Z. *Braverman's Introduction to the Biochemistry of Foods*, 2nd edition. Elsevier, 1976. Contains some fairly advanced chemistry.

BRECKON, B. W. *You are What You Eat*. BBC Publications, 1976.

CALIENDO, M. A. *Nutrition and the World Food Crisis*. Macmillan, 1979.

CAMERON, A. G. *Food—Facts and Fallacies*. Faber Paperback, 1974. Complements the present work by giving a study in depth of the more important food topics of general interest.

CLYDESDALE, F. (Ed). *Food Science and Nutrition; Current Issues and Answers*. Prentice-Hall, 1979.

DAVIDSON, S., PASSMORE, R. *et al. Human Nutrition and Dietetics*, 7th edition. Churchill Livingstone, 1979. A comprehensive standard text.

EDELMAN, J. and CHAPMAN, J. M. *Basic Biochemistry; a visual approach*. Heinemann, 1978.

FORD, B. J. *Microbiology and Food*. Northwood, 1970. A useful elementary review.

FRAZIER, W. C. and WESTHOFF, A. *Food Microbiology*, 3rd edition. McGraw-Hill, USA, 1978.

GREEN, S. *Guide to English Language Publications in Food Science and Technology*. Food Trade Press, 1975.

HEINEMANN, W. *Fundamentals of Food Chemistry*. Wiley, USA, 1980.

GRISWOLD, R. M. *et al. The Experimental Study of Foods*, 2nd edition. Constable, 1980.

JAY, J. M. *Modern Food Microbiology*, 2nd edition. Van Nostrand, 1978.

MINISTRY OF AGRICULTURE, FISHERIES AND FOOD. *Manual of Nutrition*, 8th edition. HMSO, 1976.

MORTON, I. and RHODES, D. N. (Eds). *Contribution of Chemistry to Food Supplies* (Symposium Report) Butterworths, 1974.

NUFFIELD ADVANCED SCIENCE. *Food Science.* Penguin, 1971.
A useful short survey, including food processing aspects and experimental work.

PARRY, T. H. and PAWSEY, R. K. *Principles of Microbiology for Students of Food Technology.* Hutchinson, 1973.

PAUL, P. C. and PALMER, H. H. *Food Theory and Applications.* Wiley, USA, 1972.

PAUL, A. A. and SOUTHGATE, D. A. T. *McCance and Widdowson's 'The Composition of Foods',* 4th edition. HMSO, 1978.

PETERSON and JOHNSON. *Encyclopedia of Food Science.* Avi, USA, 1978.

POTTER, N. N. *Food Science.* Avi, 4th edition. USA, 1978.

PYKE, M. *Food Science and Technology,* 4th edition. Murray, 1981.

PYKE, M. *Technological Eating.* Murray, 1972.

ROBINS, G. V. *Food Science in Catering,* Heinemann, 1981.

ROYAL SOCIETY. *Food Technology in the 1980's* (Symposium Report). Royal Society, 1975.

SCIENTIFIC AMERICAN. *Human Nutrition.* Freeman, USA, 1978.

STEWART, G. F. and AMERINE, M. A. *Introduction to Food Science and Technology.* Academic Press, 1973.

TANNAHILL, R. *Food in History.* Eyre Methuen, 1973.
An interesting summary that includes a final section on 'The scientific revolution.'

TANNENBAUM S R (Ed) *Nutritional and Safety Aspects of Food Processing.* Marcel Dekker, USA, 1979.

Metric and imperial units

The following table shows the relation of non-metric units to metric equivalents.

	Non-metric	*Metric equivalent*
Energy	1 kilocalorie (Cal)	4200 joules (J). 4·2 kilojoules (kJ)
Temperature	32° Fahrenheit (F) 212° Fahrenheit (F) To convert °F into °C: −32° and then × $\frac{5}{9}$	0° Celsius (C) 100° Celsius (C)
Volume	1·8 pints 1 pint 1 gallon	1 litre (l) 1000 millilitres (ml) 568 millilitres (ml) 4·5 litres (l)
Weight	1 ounce (oz) 1 pound (lb) 2·2 pounds (lb)	28·4 grams (g) 454 grams (g) 1 kilogram (kg)
Length	1 inch (in) 1 foot (ft) 39·4 inches (in)	2·5 centimetres (cm) 30·5 centimetres (cm) 100 centimetres (cm) 1 metre (m)

Index

Page numbers in **bold** type indicate tables and charts